Multiculturalism, Postcoloniality, and Transnational Media

Rutgers Depth of Field Series

Charles Affron, Mirella Jona Affron, Robert Lyons, Series Editors

———————

Richard Abel, ed., Silent Film

John Belton, ed., Movies and Mass Culture

Matthew Bernstein, ed., Controlling Hollywood: Censorship and Regulation in the Studio Era

John Thornton Caldwell, ed., Electronic Media and Technoculture

Angela Dalle Vacche, ed., The Visual Turn: Classical Film Theory and Art History

Peter X Feng, ed., Screening Asian Americans

Marcia Landy, ed., The Historical Film: History and Memory in Media

Peter Lehman, ed., Defining Cinema

James Naremore, ed., Film Adaptation

Stephen Prince, ed., Screening Violence

Ella Shohat and Robert Stam, eds., Multiculturalism, Postcoloniality, and Transnational Media

Valerie Smith, ed., Representing Blackness: Issues in Film and Video

Janet Staiger, ed., The Studio System

Virginia Wright Wexman, ed., Film and Authorship

Alan Williams, ed., Film and Nationalism

Linda Williams, ed., Viewing Positions: Ways of Seeing Film

Barbie Zelizer, ed., Visual Culture and the Holocaust

Edited and with an Introduction by
Ella Shohat
Robert Stam

Multiculturalism, Postcoloniality, and Transnational Media

Rutgers
University
Press
New Brunswick,
New Jersey and
London

Library of Congress Cataloging-in-Publication Data

Multiculturalism, postcoloniality, and transnational media / edited and with an introduction by Ella Shohat and Robert Stam.
    p. cm.—(Rutgers depth of field series)
Includes bibliographical references and index.
    ISBN 0-8135-3234-5 (alk. paper)—ISBN 0-8135-3235-3 (pbk. : alk. paper)
  1. Minorities in motion pictures. 2. Aliens in motion pictures. 3. Exoticism in motion pictures. I. Shohat, Ella, 1959– II. Stam, Robert, 1941– III. Series.
    PN1995.9.M56 M855 2003
    791.43'655—dc21

2002012494

British Cataloging-in-Publication data for this book is available from the British Library

Manufactured in the United States of America

Contents

Acknowledgments

This book was first conceived when we were invited by Mirella Affron to edit a volume on film and multiculturalism. We are grateful for her suggestion to do the book, and more generally for her supportive and visionary engagement. We also thank her co-editors of the Depth of Field Series, Charles Affron and Robert Lyons, along with our Rutgers team, Leslie Mitchner and Melanie Halkias. We would also like to thank Jennifer Chan for her invaluable assistance with the book. Finally, we express our gratitude to George Custen, Cindy Wong, Shaista Husain, Michelle Zamora, Maja Horn, Cecilia Sayad, and Eser Selen. We especially thank Aydan Murtezaoğlu for the image on the cover.

Multiculturalism, Postcoloniality, and Transnational Media

Ella Shohat and Robert Stam

Introduction

The goal of this anthology is to multiculturalize and transnationalize media studies. The global nature of the colonizing process, and the global reach of the contemporary media, virtually oblige the cultural critic to move beyond the restrictive frameworks of monoculture and the individual nation-state. This volume strives to shape a conceptual space that challenges any single theory, engaging, rather, *theories*, seeing the activity of theorizing as itself grounded within multiply implicated historical and geographical contexts. In a transnational world typified by the global circulation of images and sounds, goods and peoples, the media impact complexly on national identity and communal belonging. By facilitating a mediated engagement with distant places, the media partially deterritorialize the process of imagining communities. And while the media can fashion spectators into atomized consumers or self-entertaining monads, they can also construct identity and alternative affiliations. Just as the media can exoticize and otherize cultures, they can also reflect and help catalyze multicultural affiliations and transnational identifications.

The past decade has witnessed a burgeoning academic interest in issues having to do with nation, race, gender, sexuality, and other axes of identity. The cornucopia of publications has evolved into subfields such as postcolonialism, multiculturalism, transnationalism, and diaspora studies, each commonly perceived as having its special emphasis. Our hope in this book is to bring all of these concerns under the same umbrella. *Multiculturalism, Postcoloniality, and Transnational Media* argues that these issues must be discussed in relation. Communities, societies, nations, and even entire continents exist not autonomously but in a densely woven web of connectedness, within a complex and multivalent relationality. Our aim, therefore, is to take a relational approach by crossing borders between geographies, communities, and disciplines. The book crosses borders first of all in spatial terms, in that it places the analysis of representation within a broader frame that embraces diverse geographies. But the book also crosses disciplinary borders and conceptual spaces, forging links between usually compartmentalized fields (especially media studies, literary theory, and critical anthropology) and areas of inquiry, particularly postcolonial studies, diasporic studies, the diverse ethnic studies, and area studies. By linking debates over colonialism, postcolonialism, and globalization, on the one hand, and race, ethnicity, and multiculturalism on the other, the book also attempts to place the ghettoized histories and discourses in productive relation. It challenges the linear temporality of historiographic periodization, and calls into question the inscription of neatly separate community narratives. Finally, the book crosses media borders by situating cinema in the classical sense in relation to changing audiovisual technologies and new media, thus transcending the hermetic sealing off of celluloid history from cyberculture. Our hope, in sum, is to multiply the perspectives and locations from which media studies speaks, and to rearticulate its own palimpsestic identity. The book offers a kind of methodological cubism, the deployment of multiple perspectives and grids.

Too much of cinema studies has been Hollywoodcentric, focusing on what is, in the end, only a tiny portion of world cinema, yet one that dominates the world's attention. Most of the films in the world are produced in Asia, Africa, and Latin America, yet precious little of this production makes its way into cineplexes, video stores, or cinema studies courses. We have called, therefore, for the transnationalization and the multiculturalization of the media studies curriculum. What has been most striking about "official" canonical film theory's relation to race is that theory and criticism have sustained for so long such a remarkable silence on these issues. European and North American film theory and criticism for most of the twentieth century seem to have had the illusion of being raceless. There are few references to racism in the film theory of the silent period, for example, even though that period coincided with the heights of European imperialism and scientific racism, and with myriad colonialist films. When European and North American critics of the silent period did refer to race, they tended to mean European nationalities. The commentary of theorists on films like *The Birth of a Nation*, similarly, tended not to focus on the film's racism but on its status as a "masterpiece." Eisenstein was an exception to the rule, since he spoke in "Dickens, Griffith, and the Film Today" of the "repellent" nature of Griffith's "celluloid monument to the Ku Klux Klan." Although there was a 1929 special issue of the journal *Close Up* dedicated to the treatment of the "Negro" in the cinema, most of the protesting and analyzing was left to the community newspapers of racialized communities and to organizations such as the NAACP. In retrospect, it seems quite astonishing that critics/theorists did not notice until 1996, when Michael Rogin pointed it out, that "the four transformative moments in the history of American film [Rogin is referring to *Uncle Tom's Cabin* in 1903, *Birth of a Nation* in 1915, *The Jazz Singer* in 1927, and *Gone with the Wind* in 1939]—moments that combine box-office success, critical recognition of revolutionary significance, formal innovations, and shifts in the cinematic mode of production—all organized themselves around the surplus symbolic value of blacks, the power to make African Americans represent something beside themselves" (Rogin, 1996).

Since the late 1980s and 1990s, we have witnessed a full-forth effort within media studies to take seriously the relevance of race and ethnicity. Certainly the establishment of the task force on race within the Society for Cinema

Studies suggested the beginning of an institutional recognition of scholarship that had been largely marginalized, often deemed pejoratively as "too sociological." One can safely say that a systematic effort to deal with images of racially marginalized communities, of imperial media ideologies, and of Third World and anticolonial cinema began in the 1970s, with examples from the work of Ariel Dorfman, Schiller/Mattalard, Ralph and Natacha Friar, and Donald Bogle. Since then a significant and important body of work has been produced within academe on this issue. Much of the work on race within the United States has tended to emphasize a discussion of particular ethnicities. There has not been much engagement with the interrelations among such communities, nor with how the multicultural debates cross various national borders.

The late 1990s also witnessed the emergence of whiteness studies. This movement responds to the call by intellectuals of color for an analysis of the impact of racism not only on its victims but also on its perpetrators. It was also a response to the multiculturalist questioning of the quiet yet overpowering normativity of whiteness, the process by which race and ethnicity were attributed to others while whites were tacitly positioned as invisible norm. In the wake of diverse multiculturalist critics, the whiteness scholars analyzed whiteness (like blackness) as merely a cultural fiction without any scientific basis. Others have suggested that whiteness was also a social fact with all-too-real consequences for the distribution of wealth, prestige, and opportunity (Lipsitz, 1998, p. vii). In the wake of historical studies by Theodor Allen and Noel Ignatiev of how diverse "ethnics" (e.g., the Irish and Jews) became "white," whiteness studies outed whiteness as just another ethnicity, although one historically granted inordinate privilege. This movement hopefully signals the end of the innocent white subject, and an end to the venerable practice of unilaterally racializing the Third World or minority others, while casting whites as somehow raceless. But in our view there are no others and no exotics; there are only processes of otherization and exoticization.

Whiteness studies at its best denaturalizes whiteness as unmarked norm, calling attention to the taken-for-granted privileges that go with whiteness. Within film studies, such approaches have raised questions about film technology and aesthetics. Even lighting technologies and the specific mode of movie lighting, Richard Dyer points out, have racial implications, and the assumption that the normal face is the white face runs through most of the manuals on cinematography. At its most radical, it calls for "race treason" in the John Brown tradition, for an opting out of white privilege. (An entire journal, *Race Traitor*, is dedicated to this proposition.) At the same time, whiteness studies runs the risk of once again narcissistically recentering whiteness, changing the subject back to the assumed center—a racial version of the show business dictum "speak ill of me but speak." Whiteness studies also needs to be seen in a global context, in which caste and religion—not black and white—are the operative categories. The important thing is to maintain a sense of the hybrid relationality and social co-implication of communities, to see the blackness of whiteness and the whiteness of blackness, without falling into a facile discourse of easy synthesis. (Robyn Wieg-man explores the advantages, and the limitations, of whiteness studies in her essay.) Whiteness studies, as we see it, can also reproduce the same isolationist approach to races, ethnicities, and nations. Even in more critical frameworks within U.S. academe, the production of knowledge tends to reproduce an implicit and even invisible U.S. nationalism. It undergirds certain versions of multicul-turalism as well as of feminism and queer studies. (In this volume, Inderpal Gre-wal and Caren Kaplan, as well as Robyn Wiegman challenge such intellectual scripts.) As a means of communication across borders, the media above all other fields require a study that is in the academic forefront of undoing disciplinary bor-ders and conceptual boundaries that continue to reproduce the discursive over-lapping quarantine of interconnected fields of inquiry.

This volume, then, hopes to transcend a certain tendency in critical dis-course to pit a rotating chain of marginalized communities against an unstated white norm, or to pit various Third World cultures against a Western norm. This discourse assumes a neat binarism of black versus white, Chicana versus Anglo, East versus West, or North versus South—a binarism that ironically repositions whiteness and Westernness as normative interlocutors. These conceptual bina-risms foreclose nonwhite interethnic relationships and put on hold those who do not fit easily into preexisting binarisms, forced to wait their turn to speak. This "on hold" analytical method ends up producing gaps and silences. The relation-ships among the diverse others remain obscure. Therefore, as we conceived this volume, our challenge was to produce knowledge within a kind of a kaleidoscope framework of communities in-relation without ever suggesting that their posi-tionings are identical. For this reason we were not interested in having clear and neat categorization of spaces allocated to specific regions, communities, and eth-nicities. We were more concerned with investigating what we term (after Bakhtin) multichronotopic links in the hopes of creating an intellectual dialogue that bypasses the institutional scenario of multiculturalism versus transnationalism and postcolonialism.

In a globalized world, it is perhaps time to think in terms of comparative and transnational multiculturalism, of relational studies that do not always pass through the putative center. What are the relationalities between Indian and Egyptian cinema, or between Chinese and Japanese cinema? How are issues of race and caste formulated in other national contexts? What discourses are deployed? Such studies would go a long way toward deprovincializing a discussion that has too often focused only on United Statesian issues and Hollywood representations. Multiculturalizing and transnationalizing the media studies curriculum opens up fascinating possibilities. Rather than focus exclusively on the Hollywood musi-cal comedy, for example, why not devise courses that feature Brazilian chan-chadas, Mexican cabaret films, Egyptian belly-dance films, and Bombay musicals? Too much of cultural studies, similarly, endlessly unpacks the progressive and regressive features of Madonna or Britney Spears in ways that ultimately reinforce

Americanocentric narcissism. But perhaps the practitioners of cultural studies should contemplate deploying their courses and writing to expand, rather than further constrict, the cultural horizons of readers and students.

Anyone teaching in the U.S. academy today has to be aware that contemporary students are vastly ignorant about the world they live in and their own positioning in that world. With a few remarkable exceptions, students tend to be provincial in temporal terms (they know little about world history) and in spatial/cultural terms (they know little about the world's cultures). (As teachers, we all have our horror stories on this account.) At the same time, students are intensely familiar with recent mass media products, with talk shows, music videos, sit coms, and commercials. Even as the world has become globalized in terms of political economy, the dominant U.S. media have continued their we-are-the-world provincialism. Unlike the more critical sectors of the academe, the media show little sensitivity to the politics of representation. Vast regions of the world are presumed to be unable to speak for themselves, while self-styled experts, who often do not even speak the language of the country in question, explain why the United States should intervene in their internal politics. It is therefore something of a relief to turn from U.S. network news, with its daily diet of human interest items and panda bear stories, and from the endless warmongering of the cable news programs, to BBC World News and Canada's News World International, which seem at least to acknowledge that there are many perspectives on the world, that other nations have an independent existence apart from U.S. or British interests. But in the United States we find a lethal combination, a kind of triple whammy that features U.S. governmental unilateralist arrogance, corporate-dominated and right-tilted media, and the general lack of knowledge displayed by too many Americans. Sine the 1980s, many cultural studies analysts have rightly criticized the Frankfurt-School style hypodermic needle and media imperialism models, which reduced TV viewers to "couch potatoes" and "cultural dopes," insisting instead on spectatorial agency, on resistant and subversive readings. At the same time, however, we would a posit an addendum: while it is true that disempowered communities can decode dominant programming through a resistant perspective, they can do so only to the extent that their collective life and historical memory have provided an alternative framework of understanding. In the current situation, U.S. power is global, yet the knowledge of too many of its citizens is local and monoperspectival. At this point in history, as a consequence, transnationalizing media studies has become a political and pedagogical responsibility.

❧

The Discourse of Multiculturalism

A serious discussion of our topic requires some preliminary conceptual groundwork vis-à-vis basic terms, most important, multiculturalism, postcoloniality, and transnationality. The concept of multiculturalism is polysemically open to various interpretations and subject to diverse political forcefields; it has become a contested and in some ways empty signifier onto which diverse groups project their hopes and fears. In its more co-opted version, it easily degenerates into the diversity of college catalogues or the state- or corporate-managed United-Colors-of-Benetton pluralism whereby established power promotes ethnic "flavors of the month" for commercial or ideological purposes. Multiculturalism, unfortunately, has not succeeded in defining itself. At this point in history it has been largely defined by its enemies, from both ends of the political spectrum. For the right, multiculturalism is a prolongation of 1960s revolutionism by other means, an assault on standards and canons and European and American culture. Multiculturalism for the Right is too radical, a social revolution that empowers Native Americans, African Americans, Latinos, and white radicals and thus balkanizes American society. For a certain Marxist Left, meanwhile, multiculturalism is not radical enough; it is a culturalist diversion from the real issues of class and political economy. Multiculturalism in this sense occupies a paradoxical space; for some it is too radical, while for others, it is too co-opted. Some Left intellectuals like Tod Gitlin worry less about multiculturalism dividing the nation than about its dividing the movement, through distracting ivory-tower debates about race. For Gitlin, identity politics and multiculturalism fracture the common dreams of real-world Left solidarity. Some feminists, meanwhile, see multiculturalism as splintering feminism and therefore as bad for women.

These debates are situated differently in other national, institutional, and discursive contexts. In countries like Canada and Australia, multiculturalism has come to refer to official government programs designed to placate and to some extent empower minorities by offering a modicum of representation within the existing political system, a form of multiculturalism challenged by some radicals as too co-optive and assimilationist. The concept of multiculturalism, then, is above all protean, plural, conjunctural, existing in shifting relation to various institutions, discourses, disciplines, communities, and nation-states. Multiculturalism is a situated utterance, inserted in the social and shaped by history. It can be top-down or bottom-up, hegemonic or resistant, or both at the same time. Its political valence depends on who is seeking multicultural representation, from what social position, in response to what hegemonies, in relation to which disciplines and institutions, as part of what political project, using what means, toward what end, deploying what discourses, and so forth.

Although we cannot discipline the anarchic dissemination of such a slippery concept as multiculturalism, we can at least schematize some of the diverse and even contradictory discourses that find shelter under its broad umbrella, while also clarifying what we ourselves mean by the term, at least in relation to the academic discussions.[1] In this essay, the term functions as convenient short-hand for a body of scholarly work—what might be called the multicultural corpus—that critically engages issues of power relations rooted in the practices and discourses of colonialism, imperialism, and racism. It designates a complex social and intellectual movement and debate produced at the intersection of critical knowledges. For us, the word *multiculturalism* above all points to a debate. While aware of its political ambiguities, we have tried to prod it in the direction of a radical critique of power relations, turning it into a rallying cry for a more substantive and reciprocal intercommunalism. What often gets ignored in the debate about multiculturalism is the concrete scholarly and analytic achievements of what might be called the multicultural corpus, the actual work that has been done within the general field or of a subfield that might be called multicultural media studies, a movement involving various subcurrents: the analysis of minority representation; the critique of racism and imperialism in the media; the work of colonial and postcolonial discourse and representation; the theorizing of third and diasporic and indigenous, and exilic cinema and media; the work on whiteness studies; the critical analysis of globalization, the project of antiracist and multicultural pedagogy—in short, precisely the kind of work featured in this volume.

To clarify some of the confusion surrounding the term *multiculturalism*, it is important to distinguish between the multicultural fact and the multicultural project. The fact references the obvious cultural heterogeneity of most of the world, to the multiple ethnicities, languages, and religions of countries like India or Nigeria, for example, and especially to the multination states (Kymlicha) of the Americas, with their intricately entangled multicultures—indigenous, Afro-diasoric, European, and extra-European. But what has triggered reactions of outrage on the part of the Right, the neo-conservatives, and even some centrist liberals[2] is not the indisputable fact of cultural heterogeneity, but the multiculturalist project. In our view, a radical version of this project calls for reinvisioning world history and contemporary social life from a decolonizing and antiracist perspective. The multiculturalist project, in this sense, entails a profound restructuring of the ways knowledge is produced through the distribution of cultural resources and power. In our view, multiculturalism should not be a purely celebratory form of national/ethnic narcissism. The multiculturalism project needs to be articulated in intellectual terms together with a critique of colonialism, racism, and imperialism, as well as of Eurocentric modes of thought as a substratal set of axioms undergirding conventional ways of mapping history and society. Furthermore, multiculturalism needs to be articulated in political terms in relation to other axes of social stratification having to do with race, class, gender, sexuality, and nation.

Although often derided as being anti-American and anti-Western, what we call "polycentric multiculturalism" is actually an assault not on Europe or Europeans or European-Americans but on Eurocentrism—the view that sees Europe as the world's center of gravity, as ontological reality to the rest of the world's shadow, as the originary fountain from which all good things flow. (We use "Europe" here not to refer to Europe as a political or geographical unit per se—e.g., the European Union—but to refer to both Europe and the neo-Europes, and more broadly, to European hegemony around much of the world.) Eurocentric thinking attributes to the West an almost providential sense of historical destiny. Like Renaissance perspective in painting, it envisions the world from a single privileged vantage point. It maps the world in a cartography that centralizes and augments Europe while literally "belittling" Africa.[3] It bifurcates the world into the "West and the Rest"[4] and organizes everyday language into binaristic hierarchies implicitly flattering to Europe: *our* nations, *their* tribes; *our* religions, *their* superstitions; *our* culture, *their* folklore; *our* defense, *their* terrorism. The residues of centuries of Eurocolonial domination have seeped into the everyday language and media discourses, engendering a fictitious sense of the axiomatic superiority and universality of Western culture. Eurocentric discourse projects a linear ("Plato-to-NATO") historical trajectory leading from classical Greece (constructed as pure, Western, and democratic) to imperial Rome and then to the metropolitan capitals of Europe and the United States. Eurocentric discourse embeds, takes for granted, and normalizes, in a kind of buried epistemology, the hierarchical power relations generated by colonialism and imperialism. Eurocentric discourse is diffusionist; it assumes that democracy, science, progress all emanate outward from the originary source which is Europe and Europeans.

The various attacks on multiculturalism, from both left and right, have made us forget that the term does have certain advantages. The *multi* in multiculturalism brings with it the idea of a constitutive heterogeneity, while *culture*—an integral part of the economy in the postmodern epoch—foregrounds an area of practice and analysis sometimes neglected by Marxist approaches. Putting the two words together enacts a coalitionary strategy that implicitly goes beyond the binarism of race relations or black studies or Asian studies or whiteness studies. Qualifiers like *critical, radical, counterhegemonic,* and *polycentric,* meanwhile, both warn against and provide an antidote to the eventual co-optability of the two constituent terms. The *ism* in multiculturalism, meanwhile, perhaps claims too much by placing itself in the same paradigm as other isms, such as those referring to explanatory grids (Marxism, feminism), discursive epochs (postmodernism), systems of production (capitalism), ideologies (Social Darwinism), or social systems (socialism). Many of the alternative terms are either too narrow or even more vague. *Revisionist history* focuses too narrowly on a single subfield of one discipline. *Oppression studies* is an overly inclusive, baggy monster. *Antiracist studies* is too negative, too locked into the same paradigm that is being combatted. *Postcolonial studies,* as we shall suggest later, is very much associated with one part of the world (Anglo-India and its diasporic offshoots), and has all the problems associated with a "post" that is really not completely "post." *Critical race theory* is too tied up with the legal discipline, and excludes other axes of oppression, like class and sexuality. *Whitness studies,* while having the advantage of exnominating or outing whiteness, runs the risk of recentering it as well. *Identity politics* is the preferred term for the enemies of multiculturalism, whether from the right (e.g., conservatives) or from the Marxist or deconstructionist left. Identity politics is easily rejected because the phrase carries with it a hint of personal and cultural narcissism, of a salami-slicing philosophy autocentered on constantly fissuring identities. *Transnational studies,* given its partial verbal congruency with transnational corporations, is potentially as co-optable and politically tainted as multiculturalism, and risks eliding forms of oppression which are national or infranational. But despite their limitations, each term does usefully cast some light on the subject. While the word *multiculturalism* might have become somewhat tainted by association with the attempts to co-opt it, that fact should not make us lose sight of the advantages just mentioned. And while the fashionability and correctness of the word *multiculturalism* might soon pass, the issues to which it points will not soon fade, for these contemporary quarrels are but the surface manifestations of a deeper seismological shift: the decolonization of Eurocentric power structures and epistemologies. Supporting that shift is more important, ultimately, than clinging to any word such as multiculturalism, which briefly crystallizes a movement of thought. The point, in any case, is to deploy all the conceptual categories in a differential, contingent and relational manner. It is not that one conceptual frame is wrong and the other right, but rather that each frame only partially illuminates the issues. We can use all the terms as part of a more mobile set of grids, a more flexible set of disciplinary and cross-cultural lenses adequate to the complex politics of contemporary location, while maintaining openings for agency and resistance.

Nation, Narration, and the Cinema

A constant concern in the background of the essays in this volume is the interrelated questions of nation, transnation, postcoloniality, and globalization. Contemporary theory sees nations as narrated, in the sense that beliefs about the origins and evolution of nations crystallize in the form of stories. The cinema, as the world's storyteller par excellence, was from the outset ideally suited to relay the projected narratives of nations and empires. National self-consciousness, that is, the shared belief of disparate individuals that they share common origins, status, location, and aspirations—generally seen as a precondition for nationhood—for Benedict Anderson was made possible by a common language and its expression in "print capitalism."[5] Prior to the cinema and television, the novel and the newspaper fostered imagined communities through their integrative relations to time and space. Newspapers—like TV news today—made people aware of the simultaneity and interconnectedness of events in different places, while novels provided a sense of the purposeful movement through time of fictional entities bound together in a narrative whole. Like novels, films proceed temporally, their durational scope reaching from a story time ranging from the few minutes depicted by the first Lumière shorts to the many hours (and symbolic millennia) of films like *Intolerance* (1916) and *2001: A Space Odyssey* (1968). Just as nationalist literary fictions inscribe onto a multitude of events the notion of a linear, comprehensible destiny, so films arrange events and actions in a temporal narrative that moves toward fulfillment, and thus shape thinking about historical time and national history. Narrative models in film are not simply reflective microcosms of historical processes; they are also experiential grids or templates through which history can be written and national identity created. Like novels, films can convey what Bakhtin calls "chronotopes," materializing time in space, mediating between the historical and the discursive, providing fictional environments where historically specific constellations of power are made visible. In both film and novel, "time thickens, takes on flesh" while "space becomes charged and responsive to the movements of time, plot and history."[6] There is nothing inherently sinister in this process, of course, except to the extent that it is deployed asymmetrically, to the advantage of some national and racial imaginaries and to the detriment of others.

As the products of national industries, produced in national languages, portraying national situations, and recycling national intertexts (literatures, folklores), all films are in a sense national. All films, whether Hindu mythologicals, Mexican melodramas, or Third Worldist epics, project national imaginaries. But if Hollywood filmmakers seem to float above petty nationalist concerns, it is because they take for granted the projection of a national power that facilitates the making and the dissemination of their films. Filmmakers from the "South," on the other hand, cannot assume a substratum of national power. Rather, relative powerlessness generates a constant struggle to create an elusive authentic representation to be constructed anew with every generation.

The concept of the national is contradictory, the site of competing discourses. Quite apart from the historical and ideological ambiguities of nationalism—the slippage between the original meaning of nation as racial group and its later meaning as politically organized entity, and the oscillation between nationalism's progressive and regressive poles—nationalism changes its valence in different historical and geographical contexts. An atomizing nationalism (such as that which fractured the former Yugloslavia) cannot be equated with the agglutinative nationalism of diasporic movements, which call both for local integrity and for larger interwoven collectivities. Some of the early Third World discussions of nationalism took it as axiomatic that the issue was simply one of expelling the foreign to recover the national, as if the nation were a kind of heart of the artichoke, to be found by peeling away the outer leaves, or as if, to change the metaphor, the nation were the ideal sculpted form lurking within the unworked stone. Roberto Schwarz calls this view the "national by subtraction," that is, the assumption that the simple elimination of foreign influences will automatically allow the national culture to emerge in its native glory.[7]

The topos of a unitary nation often camouflages the possible contradictions among different sectors of a society. The nation-states of the Americas, of Africa and Asia, for example, "cover" the existence of indigenous nations within them. But if this multipleness of nations is especially obvious in the Americas, with their complex orchestration of many constellations of cultures—indigenous, Afro-diasporic, European and non-European immigrants—it is also true that all countries are heterogenous, at once urban and rural, male and female, religious and secular, and so forth. The view of the nation as unitary muffles the polyphony of social and ethnic voices within heteroglot cultures. Third World feminists, for example, especially have highlighted the ways in which the subject of the Third Worldist nationalist revolution has been covertly posited as masculine. The precise nature of the national essence to be recuperated, in any case, is often elusive and chimerical. Some locate it in the precolonial past, or in the country's rural interior (e.g., the African village), or in a prior stage of development (the preindustrial), or in a non-European ethnicity (e.g., the indigenous or African strata in the nation-states of the Americas). But often even the most prized national symbols are indelibly marked by the foreign. Recently, scholars have emphasized the ways in which national identity is mediated, textualized, constructed, "imagined," just as the traditions valorized by nationalism are "invented."[8] Any definition of nationality, then, must see nationality as partly discursive in nature, must take class and gender into account, must allow for racial difference and cultural heterogeneity, and must be dynamic, seeing the nation as an evolving, imaginary construct rather than an originary essence.

Some recent work in media studies has begun to explore in greater depth the issue of the national in the cinema, opening up a new set of questions about national identity and representation. What are the assumptions undergirding the conventional periodization of national cinemas? In countries that have undergone radical changes or traumas and coup d'etats (e.g., Brazil in 1964 or Chile in 1973) the periodization often reflects these violent changes. What are the standard periodizations, then, and on what are they based—political history? technological developments? generic shifts? Does a subliminal ideology or teleology operate within this periodization? How is history emplotted in the official (and unofficial) versions of French or American history? How is the past imagined, narrated, constructed in conflicted sites such as Irish or Serbian or Bosnian cinema? What is the relation between the cinematic tradition and the literary tradition in a country like India or Mexico? How might one characterize the representation of the nation's colonized (or colonizing) past and history? To what extent has this representation been chauvinistic, critical, subversive? What is the relevance of anticolonial, neo-colonial, and postcolonial discourse? What is the relevance of what literary and film theorists such as Fredric Jameson and Ismail Xavier call "national allegory," keeping in mind that the category, pace Jameson, is relevant not only to the Third World but to all cinemas—to *Birth of a Nation* and *Forrest Gump* (as Robyn Wiegman suggests in this volume) as well as to to *Xala* and *Land in Anguish*. How are nations defined diacritically in relation to other nations? What alliances or oppositions are imagined? French nationalism, for example, tends to articulate itself vis-à-vis the Germans and the "Anglo-Saxons" (and now against the Islamic world). Other relevant questions include: What is the representation of religion within a nation's cinema? To what extent is Egyptian cinema Islamic? Indian cinema Hindu? Israeli cinema Jewish? Are there iconographic traces of religious motifs and artistic/literary traditions? If the nation, like most nations, is multifaith, how is the relation among these religions articulated? How are religious minorities represented (e.g., Copts or Jews in Egyptian cinema)? What are the anomalies of nationhood? Are any nations not anomalous? How is the image of the nation gendered and sexed? Is the nation implicitly represented as a woman, as in "Mother India"? or as a man, as in words like *patria* and *fatherland?* Is it at all seen as androgynous or bisexual?

To what extent is the concept of multiculturalism extrapolable to other national contexts? Issues of race and multiculturalism have been explored in relation to American, French, British, and Brazilian cinema, but what about Mexican cinema, Indian cinema, and Filipino cinema (Talitha Espiritu's project here)? Does one ethnic, religious, or racial group dominate film production? Are some communities stereotyped by a dominant group? How are Turks portrayed in German cinema, or Germans in Turkish cinema? Are representations of the Dalit ("untouchables") in India analogous to representations of blacks by Hollywood? What are the advantages (and limitations) of U.S.–style multicultural analysis in relation to other national cinema? What ethnicities are submerged? We have argued elsewhere that although issues of race and ethnicity are culturally omnipresent, they are often submerged in dominant cultural production. Therefore, the analyst of U.S. media, for example, needs to detect those moments of repression—whether through narrative structure (e.g., the racialized constitution of legitimate couples in "Good Neighbor" films about Latin America, where Carmen Miranda is not allowed to marry the white lead) or through generic bifurcations whereby the classical musical projects all-white utopias, while interracial romance is confined to the "tragic mulatto" melodrama, or through the co-optation of forms of music and dance (the omnipresence of African American and Latino rhythms and body movements in the all-white musical). The analyst must also ask about the relevance of such concepts as exile (as in Hamid Nafciy's essay here), diaspora (as in Faye Ginsburg's, Manthia Diawara's, and Brian Larkin's essays), and immigration (as in Binita Mehta's essay). What is the role of cultural narcissism, paranoia, fetishism? Many national cinemas are in fact international in terms of personnel (Germans in Hollywood film noir, Italians in Egypt and Brazil) or financing (co-productions between Spain and Brazil, Cuba and Mexico). How does this international mode of production impact representation? What is there about the specificity of cinema as a medium that enables or facilitates certain projections of the national imaginary? How does the cinematic articulation of national identity differ from that produced by literature or music or historiography? What is the relation between specifically cinematic techniques and the issue of the national? How might techniques like superimposition, sound-image contradiction, or syntagmatic displacements render the displacements of diaspora and exile? Could a dissonant, multilayered, contradictory, palimpsestic aesthetic render the dissonant nation in ways that go beyond plot and content? The essays in this volume, if they do not answer all these questions, at least point to the ways they might be answered.

Film, the Postcolonial, and Beyond

Other key terms in this volume are *postcoloniality* and *postcolonial discourse.* Postcolonial discourse theory refers to an interdisciplinary field (including history, economics, literature, the cinema) that explores issues of the colonial archive and postcolonial identity, often in work inflected by the poststructuralism of Lacan, Foucault, and Derrida. Postcolonial theory is a complex amalgam fed by diverse and contradictory currents: studies of nationalism (e.g., Benedict Anderson's *Imagined Communities*), the literature of Third World allegory (Xavier, Jameson, Ahmad), the work of the subaltern studies group (Guha, Chatterjee), and the work of the postcolonials per se (Edward Said, Homi Bhabha, and Gayatri Spivak). Postcolonial theory built on and assumed earlier anticolonial theory (Cesaire, Fanon, Memmi, Cabral, Dorfman/Mattelart) and dependency theory (Andre Gunder-Frank, Samir Amin, Emmanuel Wallerstein). Postcolonial theory recombined Fanon's insights with Derridean poststructuralism. Within academe, the foundational text for postcolonial theory was Edward Said's *Orientalism* (1978), where Said used Foucaldian notions of discourse and the power/knowledge nexus to examine the ways that Western imperial power and discourse constructed a stereotypical Orient. Representations of East and West were mutually constitutive, Said argued, locked together within asymmetrical power relations. The ideological production of European rationality went hand in hand with the production of Oriental irrationality. (Subsequent analysts criticized Said for homogenizing both West and East, and for ignoring the various forms of resistance to Western domination, a criticism answered in Said's subsequent book, *Culture and Imperialism.*)

Foucault, and not only through Said, was a major influence on postcolonial theory. Foucault replaced the concept of ideology with discourse, seen as more pervasive, more variegated, less tethered to Marxist concepts of class and production. More than a set of statements, discourse for Foucault has social materiality and efficacy and is always imbricated with power. For Foucault, power is, like God, everywhere and nowhere. Rather than emanating outward from a hierarchical center, power is everywhere; not because it dominates everything but because it emerges from everywhere. Stuart Hall has criticized the vagueness of Foucault's conception of power, arguing that Foucault saves himself for the "political" through his insistence on power, but denies himself a politics by having no idea of "relations of force" (Hall in Morley and Kuan-Hsing, 1996, p. 136). Other critics have pointed out the relentless Eurocentrism of Foucault's work not only in terms of his focus of study—European modernity —but also in his failure to discern the relations between modernity as lived in Europe and as lived in the colonized world. The "individuation of subjects that took place in Europe," as Ania Loomba puts it, "was denied colonized people." In the colonies, Europeans relied on brutally coercive power rather than the euphemistic, "productive" exercise of power more typical of the metropole (see Loomba, 1998, p. 52).

Within postcolonial studies, terms like *ambivalence, hybridity,* and *third space of negotiation,* often associated with Homi Bhabha, have become widely disseminated in cinema studies. In a series of essays, Bhabha drew on semiotic theories of language, deconstructionist theories of antiessentialism, and Lacanian theories of subjectivity to call productive attention to the equivocal, hybrid, and unstable nature of colonial exchange. What at first glance looks like colonial servility (mimicry), on closer inspection is revealed to be a sly form of resistance. (Bhabha's own mimicry of Derridean and Lacanian, within this perspective, could itself be seen as a sly form of subversion, although one no longer required in a postcolonial era.) Appealing to a lexicon of "slippage" and "fluidity," Bhabha usefully destabilized theory by focusing on the failure of colonialism to produce fixed identities. Yet critics were quick to note that Bhabha, in his fondness for the slippings and slidings of "sly civility," had in some ways depoliticized the anticolonial insights of Cesaire and Fanon, for whom the Manichean nature of colonialism was decreed not by nature but by the binaristic colonial power structure (see Robert Stam's essay here). It can also be pointed out that hybridity had long been given a positive valence by the literary modernisms of the 1920s and 1930s in Latin America and the Caribbean, and that the trope was given new energies by the Tropicalia movement of the 1960s and 1970s.

The wide adoption of the term *postcolonial* to designate work thematizing issues emerging from colonial relations and their aftermath, in the late 1980s, clearly coincided with the eclipse of the older Third World paradigm. The *post* in *postcolonial* suggests a stage after the demise of colonialism, and it is therefore imbued with an ambiguous spatiotemporality. "Postcolonial" tends to be associated with Third World countries that gained independence after World War II, yet it also refers to the Third World diasporic presence within First World metropolises. The term *postcolonial* blurs the assignment of perspectives. Given that the colonial experience is shared, albeit asymmetrically, by (ex)colonizer and (ex)colonized, does the *post* indicate the perspective of the ex-colonized (Algerian, for example), the ex-colonizer (in this case French), the ex-colonial-settler (pied noir), or the displaced hybrid in the metropole (Algerian in France)? Since most of the world is now living "after" colonialism, the *post* neutralizes significant differences between France and Algeria, Britain and Iraq, the United States and Brazil. By implying that colonialism is over, furthermore, "postcolonial" risks obscuring the deformative-traces of the colonial hangover in the present, while at the same time delegitimizing research into the precolonial past.

Postcolonial theory has highlighted the cultural contradictions and syncretisms generated by the global circulation of peoples and cultural goods in a mass-mediated and interconnected world, resulting in a kind of commodified or mass-mediated syncretism. (The culinary metaphors typical of both multicultural and postcolonial discourse often imply a fondness for this kind of mélange.) But postcolonial theory has been critiqued for (1) its elision of class; (2) its psychologism (the tendency to reduce large-scale political struggles to intrapsychic tensions); (3) its elision of questions of political economy in an age where economic neo-liberalism is the driving force behind the globalized cultural changes registered by postcolonial theory; (4) its ahistoricity (its tendency to speak in the abstract without specifying historical period or geographical location); (5) its denial of the precolonial past of non-European societies; (6) its ambiguous relation, in academe, to ethnic studies, where postcolonial theory is projected as sophisticated (and unthreatening) while ethnic studies is seen as militant and crude; and (7) its ambiguous relation to indigenous or "first" peoples. While postcolonial thought stresses deterritorialization, the artificial, constructed nature of nationalism and national borders, and the obsolescence of anticolonialist discourse, Fourth World indigenous peoples emphasize a discourse of territorial claims, symbiotic links to nature, and active resistance to colonial incursions.

Transnational Media: A Relational Approach

In an increasingly transnational world, the media reflect, refract, and transform cultural identity. The ethnically hybrid character of most world metropolises, meanwhile, turns cinemagoing into a revealing multicultural experience: screenings of "foreign" films for mixed audiences in New York or London or Paris, for example, can create a gap between cultural insiders, who laugh at the jokes and recognize the references, and the outsiders, who experience an abrupt dislocation. Not conversant with the culture or language in question, they are reminded of the limits of their own knowledge and indirectly of their own potential status as foreigners. Audiences in Nigeria, meanwhile, as Brian Larkin explains in his essay here, make Indian films their own through a cultural indigenization or appropriation, seeing them through the in some ways similar grids of local Nigerian culture. Contemporary spectatorship must also be considered in the light of the changing audiovisual technologies. These technologies make it possible to bypass the search for a pro-filmic model in the world; one can give visible form to abstract ideas and improbable dreams. The image is no longer a copy, but acquires its own life and dynamism within an interactive circuit. Computer graphics, interactive technologies, and virtual reality carry the bracketing of social positions to unprecedented lengths. Within cybernetic paraspace, the flesh-and-blood body lingers in the real world while computer technology projects the cybersubject into a terminal world of simulations. Such technologies expand the reality effect exponentially by switching the viewer from a passive to a more interactive position, so that the raced, gendered, and sexed sensorial body could be implanted, theoretically, with a constructed virtual gaze, becoming a launching site for identity travel. Yet the historical inertia of race, class, and gender stratification is not so easily erased, as Jennifer Gonzáles suggests in her essay in this volume.

The essays included in this book in some sense offer a relational approach to media spectatorship, whether the spectator is simply implied by the text, constructed historically, or grounded in actual places. In this sense, the essays cross borders and make connections between diverse geographies and disciplines and media. Their approaches are variously comparative, cross-cultural, diasporic, and transnational. At times the essays examine relationalities within single films. Julianne Burton-Carvajal in her essay analyzes the complex relationality between the Anglo-American, the Latino-American, and the African American communities in John Sayles's *Lone Star*. Edward D. Castillo examines the relationalities between native Americans and Euro-Americans, and between past and present, in his meticulous analysis of *Dances With Wolves*. Peter Bloom explores the intersection of North African and French culture in the films produced by Maghrebians in France—variously called *beur* or *banlieu* cinema. At other times, the essays explore the relationalities of disciplines and methodologies, as in Robyn Wiegman's exploration of the mutual invagination of blackness and whiteness not only in the film *Forrest Gump* but also in whiteness studies as a disciplinary field. Jennifer Gonzáles invokes another kind of relationality in her essay on race and identity as digital assemblage, where she explores the kinds of self-fashioning allowed, or not allowed, in the cyberworld.

Other essays make connections across diverse geographies. Robert Stam calls attention to the diasporic resonances, echoing from Martinique to France to Algeria, of Fanon's work and Isaac Julien's representation of that work in *Black Skin, White Mask*. Binita Mehta makes connections between India, Uganda, and the United States, and the relationalities of African American and Indian American in Mira Nair's *Mississippi Masala*. Brian Larkin analyzes the transnational reception of Indian films in diverse regions of Nigeria. Manthia Diawara explores a narrational technique—first-person narration—in a series of Afro-diasporic documentaries. Hamid Naficy takes a transnational approach to exilic cinema. Ana M. López develops a comparative framework to explore the complex global interactions that marked the diffusion of cinema in Latin America. Inderpal Grewal and Caren Kaplan disentangle the complex transnational ramifications of the debate on clitorodectomy in their analysis of *Warrior Marks*. Faye Ginsburg delineates the emergence of indigenous "first people's" media across continents, in such diverse sites as Australia, Alaska, Brazil and the United States. And Talitha Espiritu bypasses Hollywood and the center by comparing ethnic relationality and multiculturalism in two Third World cinemas—those of Brazil and of the Philippines.

Polycentric media studies, as this volume hopefully demonstrates, recon-figures media studies in temporal, spatial, and disciplinary terms. The point is not simply to amplify technically the quantity of information in an already infor-mation-saturated world, but to inculcate the habit of thinking multiculturally and transnationally and contrapuntally, of deploying multiple historical and cul-tural knowledges, of envisioning the media in relation to mutually co-implicated communities.

NOTES

1. Although multiculturalism operates within very diverse arenas of struggle, we will limit our discussion to the academic/scholarly incarnations of multiculturalism, which form the tar-get of these polemical essays.

2. At least on the part of neo-conservatives.

3. The world map designed by German historian Arno Peters corrects the distortions of tra-ditional maps. The text on the map, distributed by the UN Development Programme, Friend-ship Press, New York, points out that traditional maps privilege the Northern Hemisphere (which occupies two-thirds of the map), and that they make Alaska look larger than Mexico (when in fact Mexico is larger), Greenland larger than China (although China is four times larger), Scandinavia larger than India (which is in fact three times larger than Scandinavia).

4. The phrase "the West and the Rest," to the best of our knowledge, goes back to Chin-weizu's *The West and the Rest of Us: White Predators, Black Slaves and the African Elite* (New York: Random House, 1975). It is also used in Stuart Hall and Bram Gieben, eds., *Formations of Modernity* (Cambridge, Mass.: Polity Press, 1992).

5. Benedict Anderson, *Imagined Communities* (New York: Verso, 1983), pp. 41–46.

6. For more on the extrapolation of Bakhtin's notion of the chronotope, see Robert Stam, *Subversive Pleasures: Bakhtin, Cultural Criticism, and Film* (Baltimore: Johns Hopkins Uni-versity Press, 1989); Kobena Mercer, "Diaspora Culture and the Dialogic Imagination," in *Black Frames*, ed. Mbye Cham and Claire Andrade-Watkins (Cambridge, Mass.: MIT, 1988); and Paul Willemen, "The Third Cinema Question: Notes and Reflections," in *Questions of Third Cin-ema*, ed. Jim Pines and Paul Willeman (London: BFI, 1989).

7. See Roberto Schwarz, "Nacional por Subtracao," in *Que Horas Sao* (São Paulo: Compan-hia das Letras, 1987).

8. See Anderson, *Imagined Communities*; and E. J. Hobsbawm and Terence Ranger, eds., *The Invention of Tradition* (Cambridge: Cambridge University Press, 1983).

REFERENCES

Lipsitz, George. *The Possessive Investment in Whiteness: How White People Profit from Iden-tity Politics.* Philadelphia: Temple University Press, 1998.

Loomba, Ania. *Colonialism/Postcolonialism.* London: Routledge, 1998.

Morley, David and Kuan-Hsing Chen. eds. *Stuart Hall: Critical Dialogues in Cultural Studies.* New York: Routledge, 1996.

Rogin, Michael. *Blackface, White Noise: Jewish Immigrants in the Hollywood Melting Pot.* Berkeley: University of California Press, 1996.

Said, Edward. *Culture and Imperialism.* New York: Knopf/Random House, 1993.

Shohat, Ella and Robert Stam. *Unthinking Eurocentrism: Multiculturalism and the Media.* London: Routledge, 1994.

Robert Stam

Fanon, Algeria, and the Cinema:
The Politics of Identification

Frantz Fanon, the West-Indian-born, French-educated writer who practiced psychotherapy and revolution in North Africa, is best known as the eloquent critic of colonial oppression and as the astute diagnostician of the twinned pathologies of whiteness and blackness. Recent years have seen a resurgence of interest in his work, with important writing by Edward Said, Homi Bhabha, Benita Parry, Diana Fuss, Anne McClintock, Henry Louis Gates, Neil Lazarus, Kristin Ross, Ella Shohat, and Christopher Miller. A kind of posthumous wrestling over Fanon's legacy has generated lively debates about the gendered politics of the veil, the validity of Fanon's "therapeutic" theory of violence, and the relative merits of the psychoanalytically oriented *Black Skin, White Mask* versus the revolutionary socialism of *Wretched of the Earth*. In a postnationalist moment, queer and feminist readings have focused on Fanon's blind spots concerning forms of oppression rooted not in nation and empire but in gender and sexuality. What, contemporary analysts are asking, now seems archaic and retrograde in Fanon, and what anticipatory and prescient? After pointing to the broad contemporary relevance of Fanon's theories, I would like to explore the multifaceted relationship between Fanon and the cinema, as a prelude to the analysis of a film based directly on his life and work: Isaac Julien's *Black Skin, White Mask*.

In a postnationalist era, we have become more aware that Fanon was hardly infallible: he sometimes romanticized violence, idealized the peasantry, knew little about Arabic or Islamic culture, and had severe blind spots concerning gender and sexuality. Yet a contemporary rereading of Fanon also reveals his extraordinary prescience as an important precursor for a number of subsequent intellectual movements; in his lapidary phrases we find the germ of many subsequent theoretical developments. His anticolonialist decentering of Europe in *Wretched of the Earth* (1961) can now be seen to have both provoked and foreshadowed Derrida's claim (in "Structure, Sign and Play in the Discourse of the Human Sciences," 1966) that European culture has been "dislocated," forced to stop casting itself as the "exclusive culture of reference." Fanon, along with allied figures like Cesaire and Cabral, reversed the currents of intellectual exchange: the Third World was generating that auratic phenomenon called "theory." What Fanon called "socialtherapy," similarly, can now be seen to have anticipated the "antipsychiatry" of such figures as David Cooper, R. D. Laing, and Felix Guattari. How can Freud's "talking cure" facilitate a transition to "ordinary unhappiness," Fanon asks, when social oppression itself generates *extra*ordinary unhappiness"? How can psychoanalysis help the analysand adjust when colonialism provokes unending maladjustment? How can patients feel at home in their environment when colonialism turns the colonized into strangers in their own land? How can psychoanalysis cure mental distress when colonialism itself triggers veritable epidemics of mental distress? Isn't psychoanalysis, in such a context, a matter (to recycle Brecht's analogy) of rescuing the drowning rather than repairing the broken dam?

Although Fanon never spoke of Orientalist discourse, similarly, his critiques of colonialist imagery provide proleptic examples of anti-Orientalist critique à la Edward Said. When Fanon argued that the colonizer "cannot speak of the colonized without having recourse to the bestiary," he called attention to the "animalizing trope," the discursive figure by which the colonizing imaginary rendered the colonized as beastlike and animalic. Within colonial binarism, Fanon writes in *Wretched of the Earth*, "the settler makes history; his life is an epoch, an Odyssey," while against him "torpid creatures, wasted by fevers, obsessed by ancestral customs, form an almost inorganic background for the innovating dynamism of colonial mercantilism" (Fanon, 1963, p. 51). Here Fanon anticipates Johannes Fabian's critique of classical anthropology's projection of the colonized as "allochronic," as living in another time, mired in an incapacitating "tradition" seen as modernity's antithesis. For Fanon, in contrast, the colonizer and the colonized are contemporaneous and coeval. Rejecting the "progressive," Eurocentric paradigm of linear progress, he insists in *Wretched of the Earth* that "we do not want to catch up with anyone." It was in this same spirit that Fanon criticized psychoanalyst Octave Mannoni, who argued in his *Prospero and Caliban: The Psychology of Colonization* that colonized peoples suffered from a "dependency complex" that induced them to identify with the fatherlike colonizer. For Fanon, in contrast, the colonized did not necessarily identify with the colonizing Prospero, but rather with the rebellious Caliban. (Fanon's fellow Martinican and mentor Aime Cesaire pursued this same identificatory logic in his version of Shakespeare's *Tempest*, where Caliban becomes Caliban X, the militant who denounces Prospero for teaching him to jabber his language well enough to follow orders but not enough to study science.)

Fanon can also be seen as an advance practitioner of cultural studies. Although he was clearly never part of an explicit cultural studies project, Fanon already in the 1950s took all of cultural life as legitimate objects of study, analyzing a wide array of phenomena—the veil, dance, trance, language, radio, film—as sites of social and cultural contestation. Although he didn't use the talismanic phrase *cultural studies*, he certainly practiced what now goes by that name. Indeed, his practice casts suspicion on the conventional Anglo-diffusionist genealogical narrative that cultural studies began in England and then spread elsewhere. In a different perspective, when James Baldwin spoke of film reception, when Roland Barthes spoke of the mythologies of toys and detergents, when Leslie Fiedler anatomized popular cultural myths, when Henri Lefebvre analyzed the politics of everyday life, when C.R.L. James analyzed cricket, and when Fanon spoke of the differentiated spectatorship of Tarzan, all in the 1950s and 1960s, they were doing cultural studies *avant la lettre.*

Although Fanon has often been caricatured as a racial hard-liner, he in fact anticipated the antiessentialist critique of race. "Lumping all Negroes together under the designation of 'Negro people,'" Fanon writes in *Toward the African Revolution,* "is to deprive them of any possibility of individual expression." In 1939, he asserts, no West Indian "proclaimed himself to be a Negro," it was only the white man who "obliged him to assert his color" (Fanon, 1969, pp. 20–21). In Fanon's relational view in *Black Skin, White Mask,* the black man is obliged not only to be black, but "he must be black *in relation to* the white man" (Fanon, 1967a, p. 110). The black man, as Fanon put it, is "comparison." Nor was colonialism essentially a racial matter; colonialism, he argued, was only *accidentally* white. (In confirmation of Fanon's point, we can cite the case of Ireland, the first British colony, which was subjected to the same processes of otherization that other, later, epidermically darker, colonies also suffered.) For Fanon, racialized perception was inflected even by language; "the black," he wrote in *Black Skin, White Mask,* "will be the proportionately whiter in direct relation to his mastery of the French language" (Fanon, 1967a, p. 18). Fanon thus saw race as languaged, situated, constructed. "When the West Indian goes to France," he wrote, "his phenotype undergoes a mutation" (Fanon, 1967a, p. 19). As someone who became aware of his own blackness only in France, and who was regarded by some Algerians as culturally European (i.e., white), Fanon could not *but* have a lively sense of the conjunctural, constructed nature not only of racial categorizations but also of communitarian self-definition. Yet for Fanon the fact that race was on some level "constructed" did not mean that antiracism was not worth fighting for. In the era of the "posts," we know that social identity is constructed, but the more relevant question is by whom and by what social forces are they constructed, and to what ends. Fanon's was a mobilizing, rather than a quiescent, sense of construction, one they embraced fluidity but without abandoning the struggle for such constructs as black solidarity, the Algerian nation, and Third World unity.

Fanon can also be seen as the precursor of what is variously called dependency theory and systems theory. Fanon's claim in *The Wretched of the Earth* that "european opulence is "literally scandolous" becuse it "comes directly from the soil and the subsoil of the underdeveloped world," anticipated in stereographic, almost aphoristic, form the arguments of later theorists such as Andre Gunder Frank, James Petras, and Fernando Henrique Cardoso (for Latin America), Walter Rodney (for Africa), and Manning Marable (for Afro-America) (Fanon, 1963, p. 96). Fanon's remark that "objectivity always works against the native," similarly, provides a historically precocious example of the media critique that became so pervasive during the 1960s and 1970s. Speaking more generally, Fanon's key anticolonial concepts reverberated outward in many directions, impacting on feminism (which "gendered" and reinvoiced Fanon's three-stage theory of disalienation), situationism (which denounced the metaphorical colonization of everyday life), and sociological radicalism (which saw French peasants as "the wretched of the earth").

It is sometimes thought that the revolutionary Fanon of *Wretched of the Earth* has become passé, and that only the psychoanalytic Fanon of *Black Skin, White Mask* merits contemporary attention. But the more important point is the complementarity of the two projects, the inherent relationality between the sociology of the former and the psychology of the latter. And although Fanon argued in *Black Skin, White Mask* that only a psychoanalytic interpretation could reveal the "affective anomalies" that generate black pathologies Fanon in fact was a practicing *psychiatrist* with little practical experience of psychoanalysis. And although Fanon occasionally cited Lacan, he was not a Lacanian. As David Macey points out in his biography, Fanon departs from the basic tenets of Lacanian psychoanlysis by stressing the need to strengthen the ego, whereas Lacan saw such an emphasis as the capital sin of American "ego-psychology"(Macey, 2001, p. 323). Fanon also doubted the universality of the Oedipus complex, claiming that it was not to be found in the French West Indies. (Stuart Hall, in the Isaac Julien film, casts doubt on Fanon's doubt.) At the same time, Fanon himself did anticipate a discourse very much inflected by psychoanalysis, to wit, postcolonial discourse. Yet, here too he was more postcolonial in a political than in a theoretical sense, especially in his trenchant critique of nationalism in the chapter entitled "Pitfalls of National Consciousness" in *The Wretched of the Earth*.

The juxtaposition of the two words *Fanon* and *cinema* triggers a veritable torrent of associations. We might think of Fanon's prose—visceral, kinesthetic, sharply imaged, hard hitting, vulcanic, incendiary, with impact on the very nerves of the reader—as *itself* cinematic. Or we might explore the cinematic "afterlife" of Fanon's work, the myriad films that were influenced by or quote Fanon, including even Mario van Peebles's *Panther*, which features a full-screen shot of the cover of *The Wretched of the Earth*. Long before *Panther*, however, the Argentinian film *La Hora de Los Hornos* (Hour of the Furnaces, 1968) not only quoted Fanon's adage that "Every Spectator is a Coward or a Traitor," but also orchestrated a constellation of Fanonian themes—the psychic stigmata of colonialism, the therapeutic value of anticolonial violence, and the urgent necessity of a new culture and a new human being. One iconoclastic sequence entitled "Models" invokes Fanon's final exhortation in *The Wretched of the Earth*: "So, comrades, let us not pay tribute to Europe by creating states, institutions and societies in which draw their inspiration from her. Humanity is waiting for something other than such an invitation which would be almost an obscure caricature" (Fanon, 1963, p. 315). As the commentary derides Europe's "racist humanism," the image track parades the most highly prized artifacts of European high culture: the Parthenon, "Dejeuner sur l'Herbe," Roman frescoes, portraits of Byron and Voltaire. In an attack on the cultural hierarchies of the spectator, the most cherished monuments of Western culture are equated through lap-dissolves with the commercialized fetishes of consumer society. Classical portraiture, abstract painting, and Crest toothpaste are leveled as merely diverse brands of imperial export.

The couplet "Fanon" and "cinema" also elicits the memory of some very influential Third Worldist cinema manifestos, most notably Solanas-Getino's "Towards a Third Cinema" and Glauber Rocha's "Aesthetic of Hunger," both of which resonate with Fanonian overtones. Both stress anticolonial violence, literal/political in the case of Solanas-Getino and metaphoric/aesthetic in the case of Rocha. "Only through the dialectic of violence," Rocha wrote, "will we reach lyricism" (quoted in Avelar, 1995, p. 101). Indeed, Fanon's aura hovers over the entire initial phase of Third Worldist cinema, over films like Rocha's *Barravento* (1962), Carlos Diegues's *Ganga Zumba* (1963), and many other films of the 1960s and 1970s.

Here I will examine just two films deeply indebted to Fanon: Pontecorvo's *Battle of Algiers* and Sembene's *Xala*—before moving on to Julien's *Black Skin, White Mask*.

The Pontecorvo film, one of the many Third Worldist films portraying independence struggles, although directed by an Italian (in collaboration with the Algerians), is thoroughly imbued with a Fanonian spirit. An early European commercial feature treating anticolonial wars of liberation, the film reenacts the Algerian war for independence from France, a war that raged from 1954 to 1962, costing France 20,000 lives and Algeria infinitely more (with estimates ranging from 300,000 to a million and a half). Indeed, in an age when Arab, Muslim, and Algerian have become virtual synonyms for terrorist violence, it is important to recall that the violence in the Algerian situation had for at least a century been overwhelmingly perpetrated by the French. The French writer Victor Hugo, in *Choses Vues*, reports on an October 16, 1852 conversation with a French general in Algeria who told him that "it was not rare, during the French attacks, to see soldiers throwing Algerian children out of the window onto the waiting bayonets of their fellow soldiers. They would rip off the earrings of the women, along with the ears, and cut off their hands and fingers to get their rings."[1] A century later, during the Algerian war of Independence, violence continued to be disproportionately French; their actions included airstrikes on civilians, terror bombs in the casbah, collective punishments, and *ratonnades* (rat hunts) in which racist Europeans took revenge on any Arab they happened to meet. At times, the killing of a single French soldier would lead to destruction of an entire village. Indeed, the French "pacification" campaign resulted in the destruction of 8,000 villages. It is this disproportionate and asymmetrical violence that is forgotten when critics speak as if Fanon were the partisan of violence for its own sake. By focusing only on the reactive terrrorism of the colonized, the violence of other forms of terrorism—colonialist terrorism, state terrorism, the vigilante terrorism of the *ratonnades*—is rendered innocent and invisible.[2] As Ben M'Hidi puts it in the film: "Give us your planes and tanks, and we will no longer plant bombs in cafés." French intervention in Algeria was marked by horrendous massacres, such as that of May 8, 1945, which resulted in 103 French dead and at least 15,000 Algerian dead (according to French official accounts) or 45,000 dead (according to Algerian accounts). Nor was French violence compensated for by civilizational benefits for the Algerians. Already in 1847, not very long after the French takeover of Algeria, Alexis de Tocqueville complained, in his *Rapport sur l'Algerie*, that "we French have rendered Muslim society much more miserable, more chaotic, more ignorant and barbarous than it was when we first encountered it."[3] Despite myths of "integration," colonialism was inherently racist. For the 1948 election, each European vote was equal to eight Algerian votes under the double electoral college, a measure designed to thwart a nationalist electoral victory. And at the moment of independence, despite the French claims of a *mission civilisatrice*, Algerians were overwhelmingly nonliterate.

A number of recent incidents and a spate of publications have brought these issues now published in English as *The Battle of the Casbah*, to the fore. In his recently published memoir, a French "Special Services" agent who served in Algeria, General Paul Aussaresses, speaks proudly of having "committed, clandestinely and in the interest of his country, actions condemned by ordinary morality, which were often illegal and therefore kept secret, such as stealing, assassinating, vandalizing, and terrorizing. I learned to break locks, kill without leaving a trace, to lie, to be indifferent to my own suffering and to that of others. . . . And all that for France" (Ausaresses, 2001, p. 15). In his chillingly nonchalant account, Aussaresses defends summary executions and torture in all its forms, including electric shock and near-drowning, shown in *Battle of Algiers*. He speaks of being personally involved in the planning of a bomb plant in the casbah (much along the lines of the bombing portrayed in the Pontecorvo film), but which would have involved burning down most of the casbah by setting spilled fuel on fire. The projected death toll was 70,000 dead. Aussaresses speaks as well of personally hanging the prototype of the film's Ben M'Hidi "in a manner which would suggest suicide" (Aussaresses, 2001, p. 16). (At the end of the book, he speaks with pride of having worked at Fort Benning and Fort Bragg for the American special services to be engaged in Vietnam) (Aussaresses, 2001, p. 196). Some French intellectuals compared the impact of Aussaresses' revelations to that of Marcel Ophuls 1971 documentary *The Sorrow and the Pity*, which prompted the French to confront the similarly sordid history of Vichy collaboration.

Nor was French violence against Algerians limited to Algeria; it is also took place within France itself. On October 17, 1961, the same year that *The Wretched of the Earth* was first published in French, another battle took place, known as the "battle of Paris." On that day, after a peaceful Algerian protest march, the Parisian police fired machine guns into the crowd, literally clubbed Algerians to death, and threw many Algerian bodies into the Seine. A document published soon after the massacre by a tiny group of progressive policemen spoke of the bodies of the victims floating to the surface daily and bearing "traces of blows and strangulation." Six thousand Algerians were taken to a sports stadium, where many died in police custody. The official police-led coverup had it that Algerians had opened fire, that the police had to restore "law and order," and that only two people had died. Careful reconstructions of the events have established that the death toll was actually over 200 people, with hundreds missing. The presiding police chief was none other than Maurice Papon who, according to some reports, had several dozen Algerians clubbed to death in front of his eyes in the courtyard of the police prefecture.[4] Maurice Papon was the same man accused of organizing deportations of Jews under Vichy, when he was police chief in Bourdeaux, and who had also served in the French colonial administration in the 1950s. The events have received renewed attention of late, and on October 17, 2000, a commemorative plaque was installed in Paris. Yet Papon has recently been released from prison, and his crimes against Algerians are rarely mentioned in press accounts. But the French election of May 2002, with Jean-Marie le Pen becoming a serious candidate for President of the Republic, was also "haunted" by the war in Algeria, provoking a veritable "return of the repressed." Although its long-term origins trace back to Vichy and beyond, the movement led by Le Pen emerged in the early 1960s in the wake of what was seen as a humiliating defeat of France by Algeria. For Le Penism, the figure of the Maghrebian Aral simultaneously embodies the former colonized, the victor over France, and the immigrant "enemy." With Le Pen, the link to Algeria is very direct and personal. Le Pen was in Algeria from January to March, 1957—the period portrayed in *Battle of Algiers*—as a lieutenant in a regiment of parachutists linked to the Massu Division. In fact, Le Pen arrived on January 7, 1957, at the height of the "battle of Algiers," just when General Massu was given full police powers by the General Governor Robert Lacoste. As part of the "anti-terrorist" campaign, Le Pen was accused of various crimes. Although he admitted (in an interview in *Combat* in 1962, that he "tortured because [he] had to," Le Pen later fought off charges that he tortured and killed the Algerian Ahmed Moulay, in front of his wife, her 4-month old daughter, and their 12-year old son, on March 2, 1957. Moulay was submitted to water torture (forced to drink liters of soapy water) and to electric shock. Moulay's wife, who had witnessed everything, was subsequently informed by French police that her husband had been the victim of a "settling of accounts" among Algerians. But Moulay's son, Mohammed Cherif Moulay, kept a bitter souvenir of the episode, the sheaf of a knife on which was written: JM Le Pen, 1er Rep, which he subsequently donated to the Museum of the Revolution in Algiers. (See *Le Monde*, May 3, 2000)

Banned in France and threatened by the partisans of Algerie Francaise, *Battle of Algiers* offers a marked contrast with the timidity of 1960s French cinema in treating the war in Algeria. Apart from Godard's *Le Petit Soldat* (1962), which took a decidedly ambivalent stance toward the question of torture in Algeria, and apart from the brief, usually coded references to Algeria in films such as *Cleo de 5 a 7* (1962), *Adieu Phillipine* (1962), and *Muriel* (1965), most French fiction films simply ignored the Algerian war.[5] (Only a few documentaries like *Chronique d'un Ete* and *Le Joli Mai* managed to briefly bring the war center stage.) *Battle of Algiers* also offers a marked contrast to the French and American films set in North Africa, where Arab culture and topography form a passive backdrop for the heroic exploits of European heroes and heroines. Whether French (*Pépé le Moko*, 1936) or American (*Morocco*, 1930; *Casablanca*, 1942), the films exploit North Africa mainly as an exotic setting for Western love dramas, a tropical decor dotted with palm trees and lazily traversed by camels. The linguistic politics of most European features set in North Africa featured Arabic only as a dull background murmur, while the "real" language was the English of Gary Cooper or the French of Jean Gabin. In *Battle of Algiers*, in contrast, the Algerian characters, although bilingual, generally speak in Arabic with English subtitles; they are granted linguistic dignity. Instead of being shadowy background figures, picturesquely backward at best and hostile and menacing at worst, they are foregrounded. Neither exotic enigmas nor imitation Frenchmen, they exist as people with agency.

Recent publications have revealed the astonishing extent to which *Battle of Algiers* adheres to the actual historical events. In many cases, the names of the characters and their prototypes are the same: Ben M'Hidi and Ali-la-Pointe actually existed. Elsewhere the prototypes existed but their names are changed. Yacef Saadi, the Algerian leader of the "battle of Algiers" and author of a book of memoirs about the independence struggle (*Souvenir de la Bataille d'Alger*), plays himself in the film, but under the name "Djafar." Indeed, it was Yacef Saadi who first sought out Pontecorvo about the possibility of doing the film. The French police actually did place their bombs in the Rue de Thebes, the only street in the casbah wide enough for their getaway car. The terrorist bombs were actually placed in the sites depicted: a milk bar, a cafeteria, and an Air France office. The prototype of Coronel Mathieu, the head of the *parachutists,* was actually named General Jacques *Massu.* The *parachutists* formed an elite unit, with their own rituals and songs and their "romantic aura" was reinforced during the war by photo spreads in *Paris Match* and *France Soir.* Kristin Ross links the first appearance of Colonel Mathieu, in *Battle of Algiers,* to this publicity image of Massu and the *parachutists,* represented as "the mythical figure of the warrior, possessed of a cold, steely, faraway gaze, a distinctively rugged camouflage uniform, sunglasses, sunburn, and a special manner of walking" (Ross, 2002, p. 36). It was Massu who presided over the strike depicted in *Battle of Algiers,* and who ran a powerful death and torture apparatus that "disappeared" 3,000 suspects. In June, 2000, a former Algerian independence fighter, Louisette Ighilahrin, accused Massu of visiting the scene where she was tortured and raped by Massu's 10th division. (See *Le Monde,* October 28, 2002)

But the crucial innovation of *Battle of Algiers* did not have to do with factual accuracy: rather, it was to deploy the identificatory mechanisms of the cinema on behalf of the colonized, presenting the Algerian struggle as an inspirational exemplum for other colonized peoples. Interestingly, the issue of identification is at the heart of the work both of Fanon and of the cinema itself. For Fanon, the struggle between competing identifications and projections exists at the very core of the colonial encounter. The revolution, for Fanon, mobilizes popular identification; it exorcises the colonizing power that has occupied and settled even the intimate spaces of the colonized mind. Nation and psyche exist in a relation of homology. National revolution promotes a massive transfer of allegiance away from the metropole as introjected ideal ego. Even Fanon's celebrated "three phases" turn on the issue of identification. In the first phase (colonized assimilation), the colonized identify with the paternalistic colonizing power; in the second phase (nativist authenticity), they identify with an idealized myth of origin as a kind of Ur-mother or Ur-father; and in the third phase (revolutionary syncretism), they identify with a collective future shaped by popular desire.

As Diana Fuss points out in an essay on Fanon included in *Identification Papers*, Fanon worked at the point of convergence of anti-imperial politics and psychoanalytic theory, finding a link between the two in the concept of identification. The notion of identification, which "names not only the history of the subject but the subject in history," provided Fanon with a "vocabulary and an intellectual framework in which to treat not only the psychological disorders produced in individuals by the violence of colonial domination but also the neurotic structure of colonialism itself." For Fanon, identification was at once a psychological, cultural, historical, and political issue. The issue of identification also has a cinematic dimension, however, one closely linked to debates in film theory, which also speaks of identification and projection, of spectatorial positioning and suture and point-of-view and alignment as basic mechanisms constituting the cinematic subject. Fanon himself, interestingly, also delved into the issue of cinematic spectatorship. He saw racist films, for example, as a "release for collective aggressions." In *Black Skin, White Mask*, Fanon uses the example of Tarzan to point to a certain instability within cinematic identification:

> Attend showings of a Tarzan film in the Antilles and in Europe. In the Antilles, the young negro identifies himself de facto with Tarzan against the Negroes. This is much more difficult for him in a European theatre, for the rest of the audience, which is white, automatically identifies him with the savages on the screen. (Fanon, 1967a, pp. 152–53)

Fanon's example points to the shifting, situational nature of colonized spectatorship: the colonial context of reception alters the processes of identification. The awareness of the possible negative projections of other spectators triggers an anxious withdrawal from the film's programmed pleasures. The conventional self-denying identification with the white hero's gaze, the vicarious acting out of a European selfhood, is short-circuited through the awareness of a "screened" or "allegorized" colonial gaze within the movie theater itself. While feminist film theory has spoken of the to-be-looked-at-ness (Laura Mulvey) of female screen performance, Fanon calls attention to the to-be-looked-at-ness of spectators themselves, who become slaves, as Fanon puts it, of their own appearance: "Look, a Negro! . . . I am being dissected under white eyes, the only real eyes. I am fixed" (Fanon, 1967a, p. 116).

Identification formed part of the very process of production of *Battle of Algiers*. Production accounts tell us that the Algerian extras identified so much with the struggle, staged for the cameras just a few years after the events themselves, that they actually wept as they performed their grief over the destruction of the casbah.[6] More important, the film sees the events through a Fanonian anticolonialist prism, a result not only of Algerian collaboration in the filming but also of Pontecorvo's and Solinas's passionate reading of Fanon. Indeed, sequence after sequence provides audiovisual glosses on key passages from *The Wretched of the Earth*, beginning with the film's dualistic conceptualization of a socially riven urban space. The iterative pans linking the native medina and the French city contrast the settlers' brightly lit town, in Fanon's words, "a well-fed town, an easygoing town; its belly . . . full of good things," with the native town as a "place of ill fame, peopled by men of evil repute" (Fanon, 1963, p. 89). The dividing line between these two worlds, for the film as for Fanon, is formed by barbed wire and barracks and police stations, where "it is the policeman and the soldier who are the official, instituted go-betweens, the spokesman of the settler and his rule of oppression." The contrasting treatments provoke sympathy for the Algerians. While the French are in uniform, the Algerians wear everyday civilian dress. For the Algerians, the casbah is home; for the French it is a frontier outpost. The iconography of barbed wire and checkpoints reminds us of other occupations, eliciting our sympathy for a struggle against a foreign occupier. While never caricaturing the French, the film exposes the crushing logic of colonialism and fosters our complicity with the Algerians. It practices, in other words, a cinematic politics of identification. It is through Algerian eyes, for example, that we witness a condemned rebel's walk to his execution. It is from within the casbah that we see and hear the French troops and helicopters. Counter to the paradigm of the frontier Western, this time it is the colonized who are encircled and menaced and with whom we are made to empathize. It is with them that we are made to feel at home.

The circular flashback structure of *Battle of Algiers* begins and ends with scenes involving the tortured Algerian who shows the way to Ali-la-Pointe's hideout. Indeed, the film is punctuated by excruciatingly painful scenes of torture. Here too Pontecorvo adheres to the historical record by calling attention to a French practice that was denounced at the time not only by Algerians but also by French leftists like Francis Jeanson, Henri Alleg, and Jean-Paul Sartre. French anticolonialist Henri Alleg spoke in *La Question* (Interrogation, 1958) of being tortured by the French paratroopers.[7] The French generals themselves, meanwhile, did not deny that they tortured; they simply argued that it was necessary. Thus the prototype for "Colonel Mathieu," General Massu, published in 1971 his self-exculpatory memoir *La Vraie Bataille d'Alger* (The Real Battle of Algiers), where he explicitly challenged the contestatory tone of the Pontecorvo film. A recently published book by the anticolonialist Jules Roy, with the Zolaesque title *J'Accuse le General Massu* (I Accuse General Massu, 2001), answers Massu's defense of torture. Roy mocks Massu's euphemisms—which render torture as "forceful interrogation"—by saying:

"Torture for you is so sweet: just a tightening of the sexual organs in a vice, or an electric current along the throat with bare wires, or on the breasts . . . no big deal, nothing serious."[8] Yet the issue of torture came up again recently in May 2001 when a group of French intellectuals called for an official inquiry into torture during the Algerian War.

The Pontecorvo film, following along the lines of Fanon, sees torture as an integral part of colonialism. As Fanon wrote in "Algeria Face to Face with the French Torturers": "Torture is inherent in the whole colonialist configuration . . . the colonialist system, in order to be logical, must be prepared to claim torture as one of its important elements" (Fanon, 1969, pp. 65, 69). Colonel Mathieu, in the film, tells the journalists more or less the same thing: "If you believe in a French Algeria, you must accept the means of defending French Algeria."

At times, it is as if Fanon had written the script for *Battle of Algiers*. One sequence, in which three Algerian women masquerade as Europeans in order to pass the French checkpoints and plant bombs in the European sector, seems to illustrate a passage from "Algeria Unveiled" (in *A Dying Colonialism*), where Fanon, in one of the few passages where he actively empathizes with women of color (although still seeing them through a masculinist grid), speaks of the challenges facing the Algerian woman who crosses into the European city:

> The Algerian woman . . . must overcome a multiplicity of inner resistances, of subjectively organized fears, of emotions. She must at the same time confront the essentially hostile world of the occupied and the mobilized, vigilant, and efficient police forces. Each time she ventures into the European city, the Algerian woman must achieve a victory over herself, over her childish fears. She must consider the image of the occupier lodged somewhere in her mind and in her body, remodel it, initiate the essential work of eroding it, make it inessential, remove something of the shame that is attached to it, devalidate it. (Fanon, 1967b, p. 52)

The sequence from *Battle of Algiers* shows three Algerian women preparing their masquerade before a mirror. The mood is tentative, almost trembling. The lighting highlights the women's faces as they remove their veils, cut and dye their hair, and apply makeup to look more European. They look at themselves as they put on an enemy identity, ready to perform their national task. Whereas in other sequences Algerian women use the veil to mask acts of violence, here they use European dress for the same purpose. One woman, Hassiba, first seen in traditional Arab dress, her face covered by a veil, might in a Western context be received initially as a sign of the exotic, yet soon she becomes an agent in a national transformation where masquerading as the colonizer plays a crucial role. As the sequence progresses, we become increasingly close to the three women, although we become close to them, paradoxically, as they perform "Europeanness." At the same time, we are made aware of the absurdity of a system in which people warrant respect only if they look and act like Europeans. The film thus demystifies the French colonialist myth of assimilation, the idea that a select coterie of well-behaved subalterns could be "integrated" into French society in a gesture of progress and emancipation. Algerians can assimilate, the film suggests, but only at the price of shedding everything characteristically Algerian about them—their hair, their clothes, their religion, their language.

A number of Algerian women have written about their experiences as urban guerrillas. Malika Ighhilhariz, a twenty-year-old lycéene during the historical battle of Algiers, has written about how she would get broad smiles from the French guards at the checkpoints:

> People would see me getting out of the car just like a Frenchwoman. I would go into a block of flats and put on my veil and my face veil, come out veiled and go down into the Casbah. I would leave what I had to leave and pick up whatever—messages, weapons—had to be got out of the Casbah, and then I would pull off the samee trick. In the entrance to a block of flats, I took off the veil, put on my lipstick and my sunglasses, came out and got back into my beautiful car.[9]

In a related passage from *A Dying Colonialism*, Fanon writes:

> It must be borne in mind that the committed Algerian woman learns both her role as a "woman in the street" and her revolutionary mission instinctively. It is without apprenticeship, without briefing, without fuss, that she goes out into the street with three grenades in her handbag or the activity report of an area in her bodice. (Fanon, 1967b, p. 50)

While we can lament the masculinist overtones of Fanon's instinctiveness, the *Battle of Algiers* sequence (which leaves moot the question of instinct) is particularly subversive in controverting traditional patterns of cinematic identification. Many critics, impressed with the filmmaker's "honesty" in showing FLN terrorist acts against civilians, lauded this sequence for its "objectivity." But that the film shows such acts is ultimately less significant than *how* it shows them; the signified of the diegesis (terrorist actions) is less important than the mode of address and the positioning of the spectator. The film makes us want the women to complete their task, if not out of conscious political sympathy then through the specific protocols of cinematic identification: scale (close-up shots individualize the women); off-screen sound (the sexist comments of the French soldiers are heard as if from the women's aural perspective); and especially point-of-view editing. By the time the women plant the bombs, spectatorial identification is so complete that it is not derailed even by close shots of the bombers' potential victims. At the same time, the film does not hide the terrible injustice of terrorism; it is encapsulated in the absolute innocence of a child eating ice cream. The eyeline matches between close shots of the bomber and of her intended victims both engender and disturb identification; for although the patrons of the café she attacks are humanized by close-ups, the film has already prepared the spectator to feel at home within the bomber's perspective, to sense the reasons for such a mission. Historical contextualization and formal mechanisms have short-circuited, or at least made us reflect on, our often simplistic attitudes toward anticolonial violence, an issue very much linked to the events of September 11.[10]

Pontecorvo thus hijacks the apparatus of objectivity and the formulaic techniques of mass media reportage (hand-held cameras, zooms, long lenses) to express political views usually anathema to the dominant media. For the First World mass media, terrorism means only freelance or infrastate violence, violence without army uniforms, never state terrorism or government-sanctioned aerial bombardments. But *Battle of Algiers* presents anticolonialist terror as a response to colonialist violence: in Fanon's words, "the violence of the colonial regime and the counterviolence of the native balance each other and respond to each other in an extraordinary reciprocal homogeneity" (Fanon, 1963, p. 88). For Fanon, the term *violence* refers to both forms of violence. The colonialist, who is accustomed to a monopoly on the means of violence and who never tires of saying that "they" only understand the "language of force," is surprised when force is answered with force, fire with fire. At the same time, *Battle of Algiers*, in its portrayal of neatly sequenced tit-for-tat violence, is on one level overly generous to the French, since the French were the practitioners not only of high-tech violence (planes, helicopters, tanks) but also the administrators of systematic, quasi-industrialized torture. An oppressed people, Fanon tells us in *A Dying Colonialism*, "is obliged to practice fair play, even while its adversary ventures, with a clear conscience, into the uninhibited exploration of new means of terror" (Fanon, 1967b, p. 24).

At the checkpoints, the French soldiers treat the Algerians with discriminatory scorn and suspicion, while they greet the Europeans, including the Algerian women masquerading as Europeans, with amiable "bonjours." The soldiers' sexism, meanwhile, leads them to misperceive the three women bombers as French and flirtatious when in fact they are Algerian and revolutionary. The sequence almost literally stages the passage from "Algeria Unveiled," in which Fanon describes the Algerian woman's confrontation with the colonial police: "The soldiers, the French patrols, smile to her as she passes, compliments on her looks are heard here and there, but no one suspects that her suitcases contain the automatic pistol which will presently mow down four or five members of one of the patrols" (Fanon, 1967b, p. 52).

The *Battle of Algiers* thus underlines the racial and sexual taboos of desire within colonial segregation. As Algerians, the women are the objects of an overt military as well as a covert sexual gaze; they openly become objects of desire for the soldiers only when they masquerade as French. They use their knowledge of European codes to trick the Europeans, putting their own "looks" and the soldiers' "lookings" (and failure to see) to revolutionary purpose. (Masquerade also serves the Algerian male fighters who dress as Algerian women to better hide their weapons.) Within the psychodynamics of oppression the oppressed (the slave, the black, the woman) know the mind of the oppressors better than the oppressors know the mind of the oppressed. In *Battle of Algiers*, they deploy this cognitive

Figure 1. Passing at the checkpoint in Battle of Algiers. New Yorker Film.

asymmetry to their own advantage, consciously manipulating ethnic, national, and gender stereotypes to support their struggle.

At the same time, it would be a mistake to idealize the sexual politics of *Battle of Algiers* or of Fanon himself. Historically, Algerian women performed heroic service: they worked as nurses and combatants with the NLF in the *maquis*, they hid terrorists from paratroopers in their homes, they suffered torture at the hands of French soldiers (Djamila being the most famous case), and they shouted "Free Algeria" during de Gaulle's visit in 1958. The film shows some of these activities, but the women largely carry out the orders of the male revolutionaries. They certainly appear heroic, but only insofar as they perform their service for the Nation. In his writing, Fanon seems to confound a conjunctural situation—the revolution's need for women guerrillas—with a permanent condition of liberation. The film does not ultimately address the two-fronted nature of women's struggle within a nationalist but still patriarchal revolution; it elides the gender, class, and religious tensions that fractured the revolutionary process, failing to realize that nationalism revolutions are from the outset constituted in gender. (Mohammed Horbi, an Algerian interviewee in Isaac Julien's *Black Skin, White Mask*, a participant in the independence movement, points out that the more progressive Algerian revolutionaries saw Fanon's essay on the veil as a "rationalization for Islamic patriarchal conservatism.")

For Fanon, the liberation of the Algerian nation and the liberation of women went hand in hand: "The destruction of colonization is the birth of the new woman."[11] The final shots of *Battle of Algiers* encapsulate precisely the same idea. They feature a dancing Algerian woman waving the Algerian flag and taunting the

French troops, superimposed on the title "July 2, 1962: the Algerian Nation is born"; a woman "carries" the allegory of the "birth" of the nation. Yet the film does not bring up the annoying contradictions that plagued the revolution both before and after victory. The nationalist representation of courage and unity relies on the image of the revolutionary woman, precisely because her figure might otherwise evoke a weak link, the fact of a fissured revolution in which unity vis-à-vis the colonizer does not preclude contradictions among the colonized. In 1991 Pontecorvo returned to Algeria to examine some of these contradictions in *Gillo Pontecorvo Returns to Algiers*, a film about the evolution of Algeria in the twenty-five years elapsed since the release of the film, focusing on topics such as Islamic fundamentalism, the subordinate status of women, the veil, and so forth (the documentary was made before the civil war in Algeria had taken a toll of over 50,000 dead). And in the mid-1990s, an Algerian feminist film, Djamila Sahraowi's *La Moitie du Ciel d'Allah* (Half of God's Sky), interviews many of the actual women militants who hid weapons under their Islamic garb. They relate their youthful enthusiasm for the revolution, along with their subsequent disenchantment as the revolution became ever more patriarchal and oppressive, asking for endless sacrifice with precious few rewards.

The revolutionary leader Ben M'Hidi, in *Battle of Algiers*, at one point tells Ali-la-Pointe that "beginning the revolution is difficult, carrying it out is *more* difficut, and then the *real* problems begin." If *Battle of Algiers* portrays the independence struggle, another film throroughly informed by Fanonian ideas, Sembene's satirical film *Xala*, focuses on the struggles that come *after* independence. The Sembene film draws on a very different strain within Fanon's writing: his mordant critique of the indigenous postindependence bourgeoisie. The film revolves around a fable of impotence, in which the protagonist's *xala*, a divinely sanctioned curse of impotence, comes to symbolize the neo-colonial servitude of the black African elite. The protagonist, El Hadji, is a polygamous Senegalese businessman who becomes afflicted with the *xala* on the occasion of taking his third wife. In search of a cure, he visits various medicine men, who fail to cure him. At the same time, he suffers reverses in business, is accused of embezzlement, and is ejected from the Chamber of Commerce. In the end, he discovers that his *xala* resulted from a curse sent by a Dakar beggar whose land El Hadji had expropriated. He finally recovers from his malady by submitting to the beggars' demands that he strip and be spat upon; the film ends with a freeze-frame of his spittle-covered body.

In the world of *Xala*, the patriarchal structures of colonialism have given way to indigenous African class and gender oppression, precluding the utopia of liberation promised by nationalist rhetoric. Impotence thus betokens postindependence patriarchy as failed revolution. Like *Battle of Algiers*, *Xala* can be seen as an audiovisual gloss on Fanonian concepts. It is interesting, in this context, that at various points Fanon himself showed interest in the subject of impotence, for example, in the discussion in *Wretched of the Earth* of the case of the Algerian man rendered impotent by the rape of his wife by a Frenchman. (Fanon's masculinist stress is on the husband as victim of impotence and humiliation rather than on the wife as the victim of rape.) Furthermore, the draft of an unpublished paper by Jacques Azoulay, François Sanchez, and Fanon was to be a study of male impotence in the Maghrebian cultural context, within the native "knowledge system." The authors point out that North African men beset by impotence, like El Hadj in *Xala*, tended to bypass Western-trained doctors in favor of *marabouts* and *talebs* like those in the Sembene film, since they attributed the impotence to magical causes.[12]

Fanon's portrait of the national middle class as "underdeveloped" and "greedy," with "practically no economic power . . . not engaged in production, nor in invention, nor building, nor labor," perfectly suits El Hadji and his commercial activities. For Fanon, the energies of the national bourgeoisie are completely "canalized into activities of the intermediary type" (Fanon, 1963, pp. 148, 149), again a perfect description of El Hadji's merchandizing of secondary products such as Evian water and yogurt. The businessmen of the Chamber of Commerce, with their briefcases full of French bribe money, fit Fanon's description of "a greedy little caste . . . a get-rich-quick middle class . . . not the replica of Europe but its caricature." Completely identified with racist European values, this black elite avoids tourism in Spain because "there are too many blacks." Nationalism, for this new elite, means, as Fanon puts it, "quite simply the transfer into native hands of those unfair advantages which are a legacy of the colonial period." It is no accident that El Hadji finances his third polygamous marriage with money expropriated from peasants, precisely the class that Fanon lauded (with only partial accuracy) as the truly revolutionary class. As "the people stagnate in unbearable poverty"—emblematized by the beggars waiting on the sidewalk outside El Hadji's place of business—they "slowly awaken to the unutterable treason of their leaders." While the elite constantly calls to mind its heroic sacrifices in the name of the people, the people "show themselves incapable of appreciating the long way they have come . . . [they] do not manage, in spite of public holidays and flags . . . to convince themselves that anything has really changed in their lives."

Fanon's critique of the pitfalls of nationalism anticipated, and concretely influenced, subsequent Algerian (and North African) cinema. While accepting the basic anticolonialist thrust of Third Worldist discourse, postindependence films have interrogated the limits and tensions within the Third World nation, especially in terms of the fissures having to do with race, gender, sexuality, and even religion. Within this evolution from Third Worldist to post–Third Worldist discourse, Algerian cinema increasingly pays attention to the fissures in the nation, fissures that have recently turned into veritable chasms, and to a civil war that has taken over 50,000 lives. After the first "heroic" phase of independent Algerian cinema, which stressed the glories of the revolutionary struggle, for example, in *Wind from the Aures* (1965) and *Chronicle of the Years of Embers* (1975), Algerian cinema turned its attention toward social problems internal to Algeria, whether the status of women (*Wind from the South*, 1975; *Leila and the Others*, 1978), male sexuality (*Omar Gatlato*, 1977), or agrarian reform (*Noua*, 1977).

But some 1990s films offer an even more pronounced critique of the Algerian national revolution. Youcef, the protagonist in Mohamed Chouikh's *Youcef, Or the Legend of the Seventh Sleeper* (1994), escapes from an asylum—one is reminded again of Fanon's psychiatric ward—into what he believes to be Algeria in 1960, a world where the FLN is heroically battling French armies. A surreal time gap between Youcef's subjective perception and present-day Algeria becomes a satirical trampoline for exposing the minimal progress in the life of Algerian people since independence. Yesterday's heroes, Youcef soon learns, are today's oppressors, ready to sacrifice anyone who opposes their regime, including their old FLN comrades. Insanity no longer resides in an individual but in a social system. Other films call attention to gender-based oppressions. Tunisian director Moufida Tlatli's *Silences of the Palace* offers a gendered and class critique of Tunisia, where the hope for social transformation after independence has yet to be completely realized. The protagonist, the lower-class singer Alya, whose revolutionary lover had assured her, back during the climactic moment of anti-French struggle, that not knowing her father's identity would not matter in the new Tunisian society, is disappointed when he refuses, years later, to marry her. The film that began with her singing the famous Um Koulthum song "Amal Hayati" (The Hope of My Life) ends with her decision to keep her baby. Instead of the symbolic birth of a nation that concludes the *Battle of Algiers*—"The Algerian nation is born"— *Silences of the Palace* narrativizes literal birth, thereby giving voice to women's struggle against colonialism from within as well as from without.

To my knowledge, the film *Frantz Fanon: Black Skin, White Mask*, directed by Isaac Julien and produced by Mark Nash, is the only film dedicated exclusively to the subject of Frantz Fanon. The Julien film is a product of the age of the "posts": poststructuralism, postmodernism, and, most relevant to Fanon, postcolonialism.[13] With postcolonialism, the Manichean opposition of oppressor and oppressed, and the binaristic dualism of First World/Third World give way to a more nuanced spectrum of subtle differentiations, in a new global regime where First World and Third World (the latter now redubbed the "South"). Over time, the "three worlds" theory of the 1960s has given way to more subtly differentiated analyses of the global political topography. The nation-state, once the primary unit of analysis, has given way to analytical categories both smaller and larger than the nation. A paranoid and gendered discourse of penetration and violation has given way to a sense of resistance within intimacy. With globalization, models of Manichean oppression have given way to images of interdependency. Notions of ontologically referential identity have made way for identity seen as an endlessly recombinant play of constructed differences. Once rigid boundaries now are presented as more porous; imagery of barbed-wire frontiers à la *Battle of Algiers* have given way to metaphors of fluidity and crossing. The segregated space of the Algerie Francaise of the Pontecorvo film has become the miscegenated space of contemporary France and the miscegenated aesthetics—at once North African, French, and Afro-American, of *beur* cinema, the films made by Maghrebians in France. (See Peter Bloom's essay in this volume.) The brutal borderlines of colonial Algeria have been replaced by the more subtle borderlines separating the urban metropolises of France from the *banlieu*. Colonial metaphors of irreconcilable dualism give way to tropes drawing on the diverse modalities of mixedness: religious (syncretism), linguistic (creolization), botanical (hybridity), racial (*metissage*). Totalizing narratives of colonial domination have mutated slowly into an awareness of a modicum of reciprocity. Instead of binary oppositions, we find mutual shaping and indigenization within a Bakhtinian "in-between."

In this new epoch, both "Fanon" and "Algeria," historically shaped utterances, also mutate, changed by the new context. And just as we now know more about the savagery of French repression during the War in Algeria, we are also less likely to idealize the Algerian revolution in the wake of a civil war that has taken the lives of over 150,000 Algerians, a war rooted, in some ways, in fractures already present during the war for independence. In his *Une Vie Debout: Memoires Politiques*, Mohammed Harbi, one of the Algerians interviewed in the Julien film, has called attention to the deadly internicene battles between various factions in the independence movement, to the ethnic tensions between Arabs and Berbers, and to the murder of tens of thousands of harkis, Algerian collaborators with the French. Far from being a universally popular uprising, the independence movement was dominated by a small cadre of middle-class urban leaders. Thus we find a symmetrical repression of history; on the French side, of torture and colonial massacres, and on the Algerian side, of violent factional splits and the massacres of the harkis. As David Macey puts it, "the post-colonial Fanon is in many ways an inverted image of the revolutionary Fanon of the 1960s." The Third Worldist Fanon, for Macey, "was an apocalyptic creature; the postcolonial Fanon worries about identity politics, and often about his own sexual identity, but he is no longer angry" (Macey, 2001, p. 28). In this moment of the eclipse of revolutionary nationalist metanarratives, Julien obviouly has an altered conception of Fanon's emancipatory project. Which is not to say that Julien does not understand and appreciate Fanon's project. Indeed, Fanon and Julien can be seen as sharing certain features: (1) both are writers/artists: one with pen, the other with a camera (and also, occasionally, a pen); (2) both deal with taboo topics; they probe deep wounds, if only to suture them better; (3) both work against the grain of inherited genres and discourses: psychoanalysis/the art film; and (4) both meld theory with activism. Indeed, just as Fanon perceived the Eurocentric limits both of psychoanalysis and of Marxism, we might say that Isaac Julien interrogated the Eurocentrism of a certain avant-garde.

Just as Fanon's work emerges from the charged situation of colonialism, Julien's work comes out of the wave of black uprisings against police brutality in the 1970s and 1980s. If Fanon embodied the theory and practice of Third Worldism, Isaac Julien's film embodies the theory and practice of postcolonial post–Third Worldism. It acknowledges, in other words, that we are living in a very different historical/theoretical moment from that of the *Battle of Algiers*. Indeed, the frequent clips from the Pontecorvo film are meant to remind us of the passions of that other moment. But given the altered discursive context, the Isaac

Julien film offers a fairly "cool" and "post" take on Fanon's incendiary prose. The film conveys both identification with and distance from Fanon, while deploying a carefully calibrated self-reflexive and ironic distance from Third Worldist rhetoric. The film lacks the nationalist passion characteristic of Fanon's historical moment, when tricontinental revolution was assumed to be lying in wait just around the next bend of the dialectic, when the Third World Left and the First World Left were thought to be walking arm in arm toward a preordained victory celebration. It is this discursive shift that makes a 1960s militant film like *Hour of the Furnaces*, despite its versatility and brilliance, now seem somewhat dogmatic, puritanical, masculinist, and Manichean.

A founder of Sankofa, one of the black British film collectives of the 1980s, Isaac Julien has directed a number of politically and aesthetically interventionist films. It is not easy to sum up the semantic riches of his films. Even the generic label of "documentary" is misleading, since Julien's "documentaries" often include highly staged sequences set within stylized decors rooted in his background in the visual arts. At the same time, it is possible to posit some salient traits shared by the films. First, Julien's films constitute an ongoing and multileveled reflection on the role of Afro-diasporic artists/ intellectuals and of black cultural forms: Langston Hughes and the Harlem Renaissance in *Looking for Langston*, pirate radio in *Young Soul Rebels*, Fanon in *Black Skin, White Mask*. Apart from providing an hospitable filmic environment for intellectuals such as Paul Gilroy, Stuart Hall, Patricia Williams, Tricia Rose, and Robyn Kelly, the films unembarrassedly engage with film theoretical discourse and with cultural studies. A film like *Territories*, for example, superimposes a theoretical analysis over visual depictions of the Notting Hill Carnival; slow motion renders the process of thought as it plays over and around the arrested media image.

Julien's films also show constant concern with the critique of racism, homophobia, sexism. But that is to put the issue negatively. To put it positively, his films promote an open-ended reflection on multiple axes of difference having to do with nation/race/gender/sexuality/ and even generation and ideology (as in *Passion for Remembrance*), axes that mutually inflect and complicate each other within an overdetermined intersectionality, which are not reducible to each other, which confound any simplistic notions of essential identity. His films promote what might be called an audio-visual-textual dance of positionalities, within which race is gendered, class is sexualized, and so forth. A corollary of this openended dance is a pushing-the-envelope audacity, a constant flirtation with "incorrect" images, for example, the choice of a gay Langston Hughes to "represent" the African American community, or the disturbing sadomasochistic image of a black man being erotically whipped by a white man in *The Attendant*.

Third, Julien's films display a strong and variegated diasporic consciousness of blacks as cosmopolitan, international people. The films promote a kind of chronotopic superimposition. They rarely have single geographical locations, and even when they do, other locations are made to impinge on them through "alien" images and sound. Here we might think of the presence of Martinique, France, Algeria, and Tunisia in *Black Skin, White Mask*, or of the link between black British and African American musical culture in *Young Soul Rebels*. Related to this diasporic consciousness is a search for utopian spaces—the clubs in *Looking for Langston*, the disco scene in *Young Soul Rebels*—spaces typified by gender blurring, transracial intimacy, artistic freedom, and "gay relativity," spaces where black and gay culture do not have to be checked in at the door like winter over-coats. Often the diasporic consciousness is realized through the creative deploy-ment of Afro-diasporic music: jazz and blues in *Looking for Langston*, disco in *Young Soul Rebels*, rap in *Darker Side of Black*. Even *Black Skin, White Mask's* portrayal of Fanon's attempt to turn the psychiatric ward at Blida into a normal, humanized, hopeful space pays tribute to this utopian desire to transmogrify and redeem from alienation the negativities of everyday existence.

All of Julien's films display a clear option for stylization and reflexivity—in formal terms, a refusal of illusionism, a preference for reflexivity and flamboy-ant (and low-budget) theatricality. Julien's is a challenging cinema, characterized by a high multitrack density of information. Both image and sound are haunted by other texts. His films feature innovative ways of weaving archival footage with fiction films with staged scenes and interviews in a kind of audiovisual layering. The films also demonstrate a highly creative attitude toward the audiovisual archive, seen in the ways that archival footage is used to re-create, in a telescoped, almost minimalist fashion, the Harlem Renaissance (in *Looking for Langston*) or Algerie Francaise (in *Black Skin, White Mask*). In the latter film, Julien turns the very lack of moving image materials depicting the historical Fanon into a tram-poline for extraordinary creativity. Julien's films offer a palimpsestic aesthetic, one that goes against the grain of conventional expectations not only for the fic-tion feature but also for the documentary film. In Julien's work, interviews are never merely interviews; too much is happening in the shot or on the sound track. Think, for example, of the ways that Patricia Williams's commentaries are super-imposed on footage of the "Rush Limbaugh Show" in *Oh That Rush!* in such a way as to highlight the contradictions between the two. She is mobilized, made to move around, hover over, and surround Limbaugh in the manner of an intel-lectual guerrilla sniper. The frame itself seems unable to contain such explosively agonistic figures. Patricia Williams's subtle brilliance makes Rush Limbaugh look tawdry, defensive, mean-spirited; her intellectually vibrant persona gives the lie to Limbaugh's racist diatribes.

In sum, Julien's films challenge thematic as well as formal taboos; they fairly revel in unorthodoxy. They rub against the grain of at least two traditions: first, that of a "high modernist" avant-garde interested only in a festival of nega-tions of dominant cinema, that is, the negation of narrative, of fetishism, of iden-tification, of pleasure. This tradition betrays a certain Anglo-puritanism, an ingrained suspicion of fiction, beauty, and pleasure. Julien's films, in contrast, dis-play an unabashed fondness for beauty, pleasure, rhythm, expressed in antipuritanical films that avoid the dead-end anhedonia of a certain avant-garde. But Julien's films also go against the grain of another tradition, that of a certain strand of politically radical film. In *Black Skin, White Mask* we sense a committed film-maker but not a preachy one. The films do not deliver predigested a priori truths; the approach is dialogic rather than authoritarian. The films are multivoiced. Identification operates, but not in the conventional manner. It does not take place through idealized figures, through positive images, or through point-of-view editing or the usual protocols of subjectification. The identification is not with heroes or heroines, but with a conflictual community of aspiration, a polyvocal community that shares issues and questions rather than fixed or definitive answers.

Black Skin, White Mask does not cultivate the "aura" of its protagonist. It avoids the hackneyed, sycophantic formulas of "great man" documentaries: the ritual visit to the ancestral home, the shots of the actual desk where the artist worked; the reverential homages; the lachrymose reminiscences of prestigious friends; the knowing voice-over asserting irrefragable truths. More precisely, the film avoids three pitfalls typical of its genre of intellectual biography: (1) hagiography, that is, a blind adoration that would make Fanon a perfectly admirable man and an infallible prophet; (2) facile critique, that is, a patronizing censure of Fanon's "mistakes" as seen from the supercilious standpoint of an unforgiving present; (3) ventriloquism, that is, an approach that would turn Fanon into another version of Isaac Julien, which would present a contingent and personal reading of Fanon as if it represented a real ontological essence. Instead, the film dialogues with Fanon. It sees and critiques his blind spots, but it also sees Fanon's questions as burningly relevant to the present. It finds Fanon's contradictions themselves interesting and productive.

Just as Fanon mixed genres and discourses in his book, mingling psycho-analysis, sociology, poetry, literary criticism, and so forth, Julien mixes genres in his film, including archival footage; interviews with Fanon's family (brother, son), fellow psychiatrists (Azoulay), and scholars (Françoise Verges, Stuart Hall); quoted fiction films; stylized fantasy sequences; and soliloquies by the actor (Colin Salmon) playing Fanon. The film also places Fanon within a long historical context, moving from Martinique as one of the "old colonies" that predated the French Revolution, through references to Victor Schoelcher and the abolition of slavery in 1848, through to the turn-of-the-century heights of French imperialism. Despite the title, the film does not limit itself to Fanon's 1952 text. It speaks of Fanon's democratizing practices in the asylum at Blida, of his relation to the Algerian revolution, while drawing on materials from *The Wretched of the Earth* such as the case studies of colonial neurosis and psychosis related to the torture of Algerians. We learn about the sweeping changes and reforms Fanon made in a hospital where degradation, humiliation, and forced drugging had been the norm. Forced to retrofit psychoanalysis in light of the needs of the colonized, Fanon saw the psychiatric hospital itself as pathogenic, since it sealed off patients from the emotional sustenance of their ordinary relational life-worlds. Fanon hoped, consequently, to transform the ward under his jurisdiction into a relatively nonhierarchical space of interactive conviviality. In this sense a kind of isomorphism links Fanon's attempt (together with his Algerian Jewish confrere Azoulay) to create a microrevolution in the psychiatric ward in Blida-Joinville, on the one hand, with the macrostruggle of the NLF to revolutionize the Third World nation, on the other.

Within this task, Isaac Julien cites his own intertext, specifically, *Battle of Algiers*. He especially privileges the torture sequences, scenes perfectly relevant to Fanon as the psychoanalyst who had to deal with both the torturers (the French) and the tortured (the Algerians). The film also cites *Battle of Algiers* in ways that are almost subliminal. A trilled flute, taken from the sound track but detached from the image track, is deployed as a kind of minimalist leitmotif, a form of punctuation, an acoustic synechdoche for the situated, vibrating tension of the colonial agon.

Here, I will focus on three specific aspects of *Black Skin, White Mask*: its deployment of the gaze, of space/time, and of voice. The Fanonian analysis of the gaze, as is well known, inserts itself within an intertextual tradition that goes back at least as far as Hegel's anatomy of the master/slave dialectic, through Alexandra Kojeve's reexamination of that dialectic in his *Introduction a la Lecture de Hegel* (1947), through Sartre's existential unpacking of *le regard* (especially in *Anti-Semite and Jew*) and Lacan's neo-Freudian analysis of the gaze and the "mirror stage." In *Wretched of the Earth*, Fanon casts colonialism itself as a clash of gazes: "I have to meet the white man's eyes." The colonist trains on the colonized a look of desire, of appropriation, of surveillance. He overlooks, surveys, and oversees, without being looked at, surveyed, or overseen. "The look that the native turns on the settler town," meanwhile, "is a look of lust . . . to sleep in the settler's bed, with his wife if possible" (Fanon, 1963, p. 159). And the colonialist's greatest crime was to make the colonized look at themselves through colonizing eyes; the very act of self-regard was mediated by superimposed alien looks and discourses. It is consequently no accident that the Isaac Julien film proliferates in images of disturbed specularity, in Magritte-like images of mirrored shards, images reminiscent of other films, such as Hitchcock's *The Wrong Man*, where the fragmented mirror image literalizes psychic splitting to evoke a crisis in identity.

In his influential "Orphee Noir" essay that introduced Senghor's *Anthologie de la Nouvelle Poesie Negre et Malgache de Langue Francaise* (1948), Sartre described the project of "negritude" as a turning back of the gaze, by which the French, who had objectified Africans, were now obliged to see themselves as others saw them. In "ocularphobic" language that recalls the returned glance by which the camera/character turns its gaze on the surprised spectator, Sartre tries to make his French readers feel the historic, poetic justice of this process by which the distanced, sheltered colonial voyeur is abruptly *vu*:

> I want you to feel, as I, the sensation of being seen. For the white man has enjoyed for three thousand years the privilege of seeing without being seen. . . . Today, these black men have fixed their gaze upon us and our gaze

is thrown back into our eyes . . . by this steady and corrosive gaze, we are picked to the bone.[14]

In the wake of both Sartre and Fanon, Julien's film thematizes the racialized, sexualized look. It provides audiovisual object lessons illustrating Fanon's analysis, but it also expands and interrogates that analysis. Like that other filmic allegory of voyeurism, Hitchcock's *Rear Window*, the Julien film proliferates in words having to do with looking: "see," "regard," "the desiring gaze," "field of vision," "scopophilia," "voyeurism," the "look that fractures," the "sexualized nature of the look." Indeed, one can see the film as a theorized orchestration of looks and glances, captured and analyzed in all their permutations: the actor Fanon's direct look at the camera/spectator; de Gaulle's paternal look at Algeria as he parades through Maghrebian streets (edited in such a way that veiled women shield themselves from his regard, thus evoking the theme of "Algeria Unveiled"); the dumb, uncomprehending look of French soldiers on Algerian women, their misinterpretation of the hermeneutics of the veil; the arrogant, imperial look of French helicopters surveying Algerian crowds; the look of the sympathetic woman observer (cited from *Battle of Algiers*) who cries as she witnesses torture and empathizes with the victim.

A particularly complex sequence features "Fanon" as psychoanalyst listening (*j'ecoute*) both to the tortured and to the torturers, who tell their mutually implicating stories about fathers, mothers, children, and soldiers. Historically, Fanon would in the daytime treat French soldiers suffering the traumatic effects of having tortured Algerians, while at night he treated the victims of torture, often in a revolving door situation, where the victims were returned to health only to be delivered up once again into the maws of the French interrogation system. The sequence offers a suggestive combinatory of looks: the French soldier looks at Fanon, while Fanon looks elsewhere; Fanon looks at the soldier, while the soldier looks away. A rare reciprocal and homosocial look, interestingly, passes between Fanon and the Algerian fighter, in a mutual homosocial gaze of shared militancy that evokes Fanon's call in *Black Skin, White Mask* for a utopian world of mutual recognitions. The most disturbed look is Fanon's look at two men kissing; the gaze is returned when one of the men (played by Kobena Mercer, another theorist of the racialized, sexualized gaze) looks back at Fanon, after which Fanon looks away as if unable to sustain a homosexual gaze. We sense a kind of homoerotic panic, the anxiety provoked by a willed *dis*identification. Fanon denied, the film reminds us, the existence of homosexuality in Martinique; his claim that "there is no homosexuality here" ironically echoes the racist's "there is no racism here." Here the look is disrupted, named, disturbed, critiqued.

The film also points out the limitations of Fanon's view of heterosexuality. As Fanon scholar Françoise Verges points out in the film, Fanon practices a double standard. For him as a man, the choice of a white French wife is an expression of his own inalienable freedom; it in no way compromises his integrity. But in the case of Jacqueline Manicon, the black woman author of the novel *Je Suis Martiniquaise*, her choice of a white man as love object is a betrayal, a symptom of Europhile alien-ation, a desperate grasping for the magic "touch of whiteness." In short, Fanon prac-tices asymmetrical pathologization; he scapegoats black women for doing exactly what he has done, that is, choosing a lighter-skinned partner. The shallow analysis confirms Fanon's own admission, an echo perhaps of Freud's befuddled "What do women want!" of lack of knowledge about the black woman. "As for the black woman," Fanon tells us, "I know nothing about her." Here we find again a kind of willed cognitive blocking, a gendered *dis*identification.

Black Skin, White Mask also stages the kind of diasporic space/time lived by the biographical Fanon. The very scene of the film constitutes a dispersed anachronistic chronotope. The film's "home" location is the psychiatric ward in Blida-Joinville, where Fanon went in 1953, even though the film is largely based on a book published earlier, in 1952. The film's story evokes Martinique, France, Algeria, Tunisia. Yet other spaces enter the film through radio broadcasts allud-ing to the black struggle in the United States as a way of generalizing meanings beyond the originary space in which they were articulated. We find this palimpses-tic space/time in the sequence in which Fanon encounters the French mother and her frightened child: "Look a negro! I'm frightened!" The sequence alternates the image of Fanon confronting the woman and child, all three dressed in period cloth-ing, with images of present-day European metropolises and their immigrants: Arabs, West Indians, South Asians, and other manifestations of postcolonial karma. The sequence thus shuttles between past and present in such a way as to underline the scene's *contemporary* relevance and overtones.

Julien's film brings out a salient feature of Fanonian *ecriture:* its subtle orchestrations of voice, its ironic pseudoidentification with the alien voice. In his essays, Fanon sometimes impersonates the voice of his oppressor. Fanon's writing is thus double-voiced in the Bakhtinian sense; it mimics the voice of oppression while investing it with a contrary ideological orientation. In the film, the actor impersonating Fanon says, "there's no racism here; you're just as civilized as we are"—racist statements that pretend to be the opposite. Here racist discourse is projected or ventriloquized in a kind of discursive masquerade. It is this sly vocal mimicry that makes it possible for a dishonest polemicist like Denesh d'Souza to misquote Fanon—even when he quotes him verbatim in *The End of Racism.* Although the words are the same, the double-voiced signifying is lost. But in the film we sense the attitude behind the words; the double-voicedness is restored through performance, through the grain of the voice and the barely suppressed anger with which the actor articulates the phrases, as well as through facial expression, intonation, and mise-en-scène. "Fanon" cites the racist, but against the dialogizing backdrop of another ideological orientation.

Black Skin, White Mask is framed, interestingly, by statements that imply a critique of all dogmatism. The film begins with untranslated Arabic (the man obsessively asserts, "I didn't kill anyone), a usage which brings up the debate about Fanon's knowledge of Arabic and the implications of this knowledge (or lack of it) for Fanon's right to speak for the Algerians. But then Julien has his "Fanon" say: "I do not come with timeless truths." And the film ends with final words that refuse any "final word." Fanon looks directly at the camera and says: "Oh my body, make of me one who asks questions." (The corporeal genesis of the interrogation itself implies a transcendence of the mind/body binarism.) That Fanon makes the body the asker of questions is especially appropriate to the work of a filmmaker who has taught us new ways to look at and conceptualize the black body.

And like any open work, *Black Skin, White Mask* leaves us with our own questions. What is gained, and what lost, by choosing to read Fanon back to front, as it were, by privileging the psychoanalytic critique of early Fanon over the revolutionary socialist of *Wretched of the Earth?* Is there a danger of psychologizing Fanon? Of turning him into a posty pomo-poco academic? And what is lost in the hypersexualization of the issues? What, one wonders, about forms of colonialism or racism that have little to do with the sexualized gaze, for example, the colonial appropriation of native land, or the devastating electronic machinations of international financial agencies like the IMF? What about forms of oppression that operate by *refusing* to look, by refusing to take notice? What about the look that ignores, that renders invisible? Isn't there a danger of reducing complex historical and cultural issues to a racialized psychodrama, whose mysteries are penetrable only by a psychoanalytic master-discourse? Could it be that the goal of the colonized is not to win a reciprocal gaze, but to put the colonialist out of the picture altogether? Or does achieving the reciprocal gaze depend on first achieving independence? Might aural metaphors of voice be more productive than visual metaphors of gaze? And what else is lost in this privileging of the category of the gaze? Is there a danger that in emphasizing Fanon's blind spots we forget how much he helped us *see?* Or that we lose sight, as it were, of our *own* blind spots? Has the film missed an opportunity by not at least hinting at Fanon's relevance for contemporary *activism* in the age of the "posts," against globalization, for example? But that one ends up asking such questions is very much in the dialogical spirit of the film itself; the film makes us as spectators, alongside Fanon and Julien, the "askers of questions."

NOTES

1. Cited by Ignacio Ramonet in "Cinq Siecles de Colonialisme," *Maniere de Voir* 58 (July–August 2001): 7.

2. Robert Young in his book *Postcolonialism: An Historical Introduction,* misses this fundamental distinction in his emphasis on Fanon's "espousal of the virtues and necessities of violence" and of the "hyperventilating violence [which] always formed part of the original policy of the FLN campaign and equally of the French response," an out-of-sequence formulation that has the FLN initiating the violence and the French "responding."

3. Quoted in Benjamin Stora, *Histoire de l'Algerie Coloniale (1830–1954)* (Paris: La Decouverte, 1991), p. 28.

4. Pierre Vidal-Nacquet, *Memoire, tome II, La Trouble et la Memoire 1955–1998* (Paris: Seuil, 1998), p. 150, cited in Kristin Ross, *May 68 and its Afterlives* (Chicago: University of Chicago Press, 2002), p. 44. The fullest account of Oct 17, 1961 is to be found in Jean-Luc Einaudi. (see References)

5. For a comparison between French cinema's treatment of the Algerian war and American cinema's treatment of the war in Vietnam, see Benjamin Stora, *Imaginaires du Guerres: Algerie-Vietnam, e France et aux Etats-Unis* (Paris: La Decouverte, 1997).

6. For a detailed account of the production of *Battle of Algiers*, see Irene Bignardi's biography of Pontecorvo, *Memorie Estorte a uno Smemorato* [Memories Extorted from an Amnesiac] (Milan: Feltrinelli, 1999). The material on *Battle of Algiers* is summed up in Bignardi, "The Making of *The Battle of Algiers*," *Cineaste* 25, no. 2 (2000).

7. See also Alexis Berchadsky, *Relire "La Question"* (Paris: Larousse, 1994).

8. See Jules Roy, *J'Accuse le General Massu* (Paris: Seuil, 2001), p. 54.

9. Interview, cited from Djamila Smrane, *Les Femmes Algeriennes dans la Guerre*, in Macey, *Frantz Fanon: A Biography*, p. 404. These revolutionary women also appear and recount their experiences in the Algerian feminist film *Women Hold up Half the Sky of Allah*.

10. The relationality of these issues in both space and time became vividly clear to me the week of September 11, a week that I happened to be teaching Fanon's *Wretched of the Earth* in conjunction with *Battle of Algiers*. One student explained that he didn't have his copy of *Wretched of the Earth* because he had left it a few days before in the World Trade Center. I asked my students to compare the horrendous violence done at the World Trade Center to the violence done by the three women with the bombs in the *Battle of Algiers*. Was it the same kind of violence? Together, we made the following points. While both incidents constituted terrorism which took innocent lives, there were also clear distinctions. In the case of Algeria, a violent means was used for a worthy end—the independence of Algeria and the end of colonialism. In the case of Bin Laden, both the means (mass murder) and the ends (punishing the "infidel" according to codes that are arguably not even part of the religion being invoked) were completely reprehensible. In the Algerian case, the terrorism was clearly in reprisal for specific acts of French state terror (colonial domination, the bombing of the casbah) within the same national space; in the World Trade Center case, the terrorism could only be seen as a "reprisal" in a much more circuitous and inferential sense, and in any case the violence was not exercised against those responsible for what was claimed to be the initial offense. And while the WTC terrorists made no demands—for example, release of prisoners—the Algerian demands were quite clear: national independence.

11. See Frantz Fanon, *Sociologie d'une Revolution* (Paris: Maspero, 196), p. 83. Tr. Haakon Chevalier, *Studies in a Dying Colonialism* (Harmondsworth: Penguin, 1970).

12. See Macey, *Frantz Fanon*, pp. 237–238.

13. For more on the notion of post–Third Worldism, see Ella Shohat and Robert Stam, *Unthinking Eurocentrism: Multiculturalism and the Media* (London: Routledge, 1994).

14. Jean-Paul Sartre, *Black Orpheus*, trans. S. W. Allen, quoted in Martin Jay, *Downcast Eyes* (Berkeley: University of California Press, 1993), p. 294.

REFERENCES

Aussaresses, General Paul. *Services Spéciaux Algérie 1955–1957*. Paris: Perrin, 2001.

Avelar, Jose Carlos. *A Ponte Clandestina: Teorias de Cinema na America Latin*. São Paulo: Edusp/Edotora 34, 1995.

Einaudi, Jean-Luc. *La Bataille de Paris: 17 Octobre 1961*. Paris: Seuil, 1991.

Fanon, Frantz. *The Wretched of the Earth*. Trans. Constance Farrington. New York: Grove Press, 1963.

———. *Black Skin, White Mask*. Trans. Charles Lam Markmann. New York: Grove Press, 1967a.

———. *A Dying Colonialism*. Trans. Haakon Chevalier. New York: Grove Press, 1967b.

———. *Toward the African Revolution*. Trans. Haakon Chevalier. New York: Grove Press, 1969.

Harbi, Mohammed. *Une Vie Debout: Memoires Politiques Tome 1: 1945–1962* Paris: La Découverte, 1990).

Macey, David. *Frantz Fanon: A Biography*. New York: Picador, 2001.

Ross, Kristin. *May '68 and its Afterlives*. Chicago: University of Chicago Press, 2002.

Roy, Jules. *J'accuse le General Massu*. Paris: Seuil, 2001.

Young, Robert. *Postcolonialism: An Historical Introduction*. Oxford: Blackwell, 2001.

Peter Bloom

Beur Cinema and
the Politics of Location:
French Immigration Politics
and the Naming of a Film Movement

A 1991 compact disc entitled . . . *de la Planète Mars*, released by the French rap group IAM, features the city of Mars eilles as the planet Mars, and in a short glossary of terms in the liner notes calls the northern suburbs of Marseilles "le côté obscur de Mars"—"the dark side of Mars" that the French state refuses to see. Correspondingly, *beur* cinema stands as a significant metropolitan cultural referent for a resolutely fractured French identity. *Beur* cinema emerges out of the intersection between contemporary French immigration politics and popular culture, giving expression to the effects of an uneasy integration into metropolitan culture. As a loosely codified transnational film movement primarily based in France, *beur* cinema has explored the identity of a second generation of North African immigrants who have grown up in France. While related subjects have been depicted in feature-length films since the mid-1970s (Yves Boisset's *Dupont-la-Joie* [1974], for example), the term *beur* and its association with a generational consciousness in France is linked to recent political movements and uprisings in the housing projects throughout the 1980s and early 1990s.

The word *beur* is a back-slang derivation of *Arabe*, taken up by a second generation of North African immigrants, who, for the most part, grew up in housing projects on the peripheries of Paris, Marseilles, Grenoble, and Lyons. Terms such as *rhorhs* (verlan for *frères*, meaning brothers), *cousins*, and *reub* (in yet another back-slang derivation of *beur*) were also used around the same time in different regions of France (Horvilleur, 1985). The popularization of *beur* as an immediately comprehensible term for an outsider group also contained the more immediate connotation of Berber, the dominant ethnic group among the Algerian migrant population in France. *Beur*, the syllabic reversal of *Arabe*, also plays on the misunderstanding among French people concerning the diverse ethnic origins of North Africans in France. The Algerian village of Tlemcen, a still-remaining

From *Social Identities*, Vol. 5, No. 4, 1999. This version appears in a slightly edited form. Reprinted by permission of Taylor and Francis Ltd. For further information about *Social Identities*, please refer to the journal's web site: http://www.tandf.co.uk.

relic of the Roman Empire that was rebuilt by the French in 1842, was considered a rightful part of the early French medieval legacy during the colonial period. Tlemcen and the non-Muslim Berber and Kabyle population served as important territorial and spiritual justifications for the domination and assimilation of Algeria as part of the French colonial empire.

It is my intention here to trace the trajectory of the *beur* as a transitory sign of identification and protest during the 1980s and early 1990s. The resonance of the term *beur* as a transnational, hybrid identity can also be seen as the last hope for a French republican model of secular integration, and yet symptomatic of its breakdown, reviving age-old polarizing battles between secular and clerical values. In the nineteenth century, the secular values of the state represented a renewed French republican ethos in opposition to the clerical values of the Catholic Church and the monarchy. In the late twentieth century, the fear of Islam in France, as associated with "Islamic fundamentalism," has contributed to the reconsideration of the conditions for acquiring French citizenship rights for a second generation of Franco-Maghrebi citizens culminating in the 1993 Pasqua Laws. This has occurred in spite of the fact that less than half of Franco-Maghrebis in France are practicing Muslims (Hargreaves, 1995, p. 119).

Emerging out of social conflicts throughout the late 1970s and 1980s, *beur* identity is also tied to the postwar history of reconstruction, in which successive waves of North African immigrants were encouraged to come to France as part of a contractual manual labor force, transformed, as it were, from imperial subjects to immigrant workers. Overlapping histories of decolonization and successive waves of economic migration adapted a surplus of decolonized subjects to the contingencies of the metropolitan workplace. Born into the breakup of a colonial order, the second generation found themselves slotted between a working-class French identity and an emerging multiform immigrant population.

The national identity of the emerging *beur* youth population, who were born in France and largely of Algerian origin, has been continually contested by the state and resonates with the extensive media coverage of the 1989 Islamic headscarf controversy as well as rioting in Sartrouville (northwest of Paris), Vaulx-en-Velin (northeast of Lyon), and the northern suburbs of Marseilles. The Islamic headscarf controversy involved the suspension of three Muslim high-school girls, of Tunisian and Moroccan origin, from their school in Creil (thirty miles north of Paris) for wearing Islamic headscarves to class. The school headmaster, Ernest Chenière, claimed that the young women wearing the Islamic headscarves in school were engaged in a form of proselytism, which violated the secular nature of a state educational institution. Lest we forget, the French public educational system served as a bulwark for a secular social contract of *laïcité* dating from the beginning of the Third Republic, in the 1880s, under Jules Ferry.

On the grounds that Chenière's action discriminated against Muslim students and under pressure from antiracist organizations such as, the Movement against Racism and for Interracial Friendship (MRAP),[1] which had previously filed a complaint with the educational authorities in Creil, the then minister of education, Lionel Jospin, overturned Chenière's suspension order. The controversy in Creil stemmed, at least in part, from resentment among long-standing residents concerning the concentration of non-European immigrants in their communities, transformed from rural housing tracts in the late 1970s to state-financed middle- and low-income housing projects. In the aftermath of the controversy, Jean-Marie Le Pen's anti-immigrant National Front Party won the majority of seats in the December 1989 by-election held in Dreux (thirty miles west of Paris). The political fallout of the events in Creil were also linked to the ongoing confrontations between *beur* youths and police in the Parisian suburbs of Sartrouville and Mantes-La-Jolie.

Habitations à Loyer Modéré (HLMs), which I have referred to as housing projects, are housing developments built primarily to accommodate tenants of limited means. Les Minguettes in Vénissieux (east of Lyon), with 28,000 residents, was the largest of the HLMs, before being torn down in 1992. HLMs of various kinds exist throughout France and were primarily built as dormitory-like lodging for low-income families to replace the inner-city *bidonvilles*. The association between HLMs and North African immigrants has largely evolved from the legacy of SONACOTRAL[2] contractual labor dormitories, which were initially established in the 1950s as housing for Algerian workers in France (Diop and Michalak, 1996). The legacy of North Africans in France as a captive labor market and French soldiering force has contributed to a politics of separation and exclusion in the organization of HLMs and the adjacent suburban *cités*. The large, deteriorating HLMs have served as a symbol of regional and national disinterest in the emerging multiethnic working classes. Alec G. Hargreaves explains that as the facilities began to deteriorate during the 1970s, a hierarchy of HLMs emerged— the less well-maintained properties were allocated to immigrant families and the better-maintained properties, financed by a payroll tax, to French families (Hargreaves, 1995, p. 72). Consequently, the cyclical eruption of violence between Franco-Maghrebi youths and police in the deteriorating HLMs became tied to continued citizenship controversies. This very logic of containment and regulation has carried over to shifts in French immigration practices.

The pairing of claustrophobic HLM apartments with the accompanying tundralike wide-open empty spaces underscores a state of emotional and geographical dislocation prevalent in some of the best-known *beur* films, such as Medhi Charef's *Le Thé au harem d'Archimède* (Tea in the Harem, 1985). This film came to represent an early sketch of community belonging, petty thievery, and social rejection in the housing projects. This very dynamic of claustrophobic interior space and the high-rise expanse of anonymity is highlighted in a scene of attempted suicide. Joséphine, a single mother, has lost her job as a factory worker and resorts to prostituting herself for a group of manual laborers at a nearby construction site in order to provide for her young son, Stéphane. In a state of profound desperation, Joséphine is on the verge of jumping from her high-rise HLM apartment window. Her desperation is demonstrated through a contrast of phobic spaces; the claustrophobic interior of her apartment is opposed to the wide-open concrete desolate space before her. It is only the arrival of her young son that gives her the final will to live. Significantly, the presence of a human element in this instrumental world of inadaptable spaces and concrete expanse serves as the backdrop for a number of *beur* films, where the development of friendships and humane social interaction is the only means of surviving in a hostile social and spatial environment.

Produced by Michelle Ray-Gavras, this film received significant press coverage highlighting its themes of exclusion, life in the housing projects, and the problems facing the *beur* community. Charef was also portrayed as a representative *beur* in the press, which detailed his story of arrival in France at the age of ten accompanied by his parents, his difficulty with the French educational system, his "real" education as a mechanic at a Renault factory for eleven years, and finally his success as a novelist and filmmaker. Overcoming the obstacles of an immigrant working-class environment resonates with a long-standing narrative of militancy, internationalist solidarity, and education associated with the French Communist Party.

Le Thé au harem d'Archimède was released within the context of a number of short films, and associated with several other feature-length films depicting the social context of the second generation of North African immigrants. Such feature-length films as Roger Le Péron's *Laisse béton* (Forget About It, 1983), Abdelkrim Bahloul's *Le Thé à la menthe* (Mint Tea, 1984), and Rachid Bouchareb's *Baton Rouge* (Baton Rouge, 1985) established a fertile terrain for the reception of Charef's film. Furthermore, the swell of social movements throughout the early 1980s, climaxing with the 100,000-strong Marche pour l'Egalité (March for Equality) in 1983, created a broad base for the reception of films about the second generation.

As a film movement, *beur* cinema has been defined as a cinema of community identification. That is, images and scenes of life relating to this minority group are the central setting for a corpus of *beur* films. Since 1985, a substantial number of *beur* films have also received some form of state-sanctioned support through the Social Action Foundation (FAS) for immigrant workers and their families.[3] As a francophone film movement and as a representation of community, *beur* cinema addresses problems of national identity in addition to more specific issues related to integration in French society. Thematizations of imposed exile, family tradition, life in the housing projects, and various forms of delinquency overlaid with the lingering history of French colonial involvement link a number of these films. Urban decay and the coming of age of the invariably young *beur*, with an incapacitated or simply absent father figure, mark the process of socialization as a search for belonging beyond the suffering and indignities of the previous generation.

Farida Belghoul, political activist, organizer of the "1984 Convergences" rally, novelist, and independent filmmaker, describes *beur* cinema by connecting the nationality of the filmmaker to representations of *beur* identity in their films (Horvilleur, 1985). She distinguishes among those second-generation *beur* film-makers who were born or grew up in France (such as Medhi Charef and Rachid Bouchareb), others who grew up and were educated in Algeria but express a con-flictual vision of national belonging (such as Mahmoud Zemmouri), and French filmmakers whose films render an outsider's perspective on the *beur* community (such as Gérard Blain or Serge LePéron).

Belghoul's overly schematic divisions are a useful starting point, espe-cially considering that she was etching the contours of a film movement in the process of materializing in 1985. In the same interview, she acknowledged that the *beur* fad that followed the riots and the marches also established a quota sys-tem of *beur* filmmaking, a form of "reverse" discrimination, which pigeonholed the kinds of subjects to be treated by *beur* filmmakers themselves. It is not sur-prising, then, that there was a proliferation of short films made by *beur* filmmak-ers throughout the mid-1980s.

This flurry of short activist films about the second generation began with a series of Super-8 films produced by a group of youths from Vitry-sur-Seine (known as the Mohammed Collective) and distributed by Audiopradif from 1979 to 1983. Excerpts from their films were shown on French national television (Antenne 2) and four of their Super-8 films were shown at the documentary film festival known as "Cinéma du réel," held annually at the Centre Georges Pompi-dou (Dazat, 1985; Mohammed, 1981). The Super-8 short film *Zone Immigré* (Immigrant Zone, 1981), produced by the Mohammed Collective, addresses the numerous government policies for the development of low-income communities which all begin with the word *Zone*. A mere sampling of these acronyms, which include Zones d'Aménagement Concerté (ZACs) (Concerted Development Zones), Zones d'Education Prioritaires (ZEPs) (Educational Priority Zones), and Zones à Urbaniser en Priorité (ZUPs) (Priority Urban Development Zones), all point to their commonality as immigrant zones. In the name of state-sanctioned development initiatives, these housing and educational zones serve as regulated geographic quarantine zones.

The expanding reservoir of short films, which followed in the tradition of immigrant documentary filmmaking of the 1970s, established a variety of themes related to the *beur* experience, such as mixed coupling, violence between French and immigrant youths, images of the American dream, visions of suc-cessful integration, victimization by the police, and the double exclusion of immigrant young women (Dhoukar, 1990a). The rapid increase in the number of short films about the *beur* experience was linked to the new accessibility of video technology, as well as an already well-developed short-film circuit of financing and festivals.

The notion of a *beur* filmmaking aesthetic draws on short-subject films that foreground the cultural divide between immigrant parents and their assimi-lated children in the inhospitable, claustrophobic world of the housing projects

(Fahdel, 1990). In the short film entitled *Le Vago* (The Drifters) (dir. Aïssa Djabri, 1983), the filmmaker follows two unemployed *beurs* from a housing project who buy a secondhand car to return to Algeria, their imagined homeland. Their dream of return dissolves into despairing violence in the concrete world of the French housing projects, decrepit mall-like commercial centers, and poverty. As Abbas Fahdel suggests, the *beur* filmmaking aesthetic is the stylistic representation of a compressed spatial economy of HLM apartment living and a nostalgia for return, manifested as potentially violent confrontations.

In several films about the second generation, the *banlieue* (low-income suburbs), as well as certain areas of Paris, such as Pigalle, La Goutte d'Or (a.k.a. Barbès), and Belleville, become coterminous with the protagonists in the film. Abdelkrim Bahloul's *Thé à la menthe* was filmed almost exclusively in La Goutte d'Or, the daytime Arab and African capital of Paris (Vuddamalay, White, and Sparton 1991), and depicts varying degrees of assimilation into French society through the protagonist Hamou, a young hustler, and his mother, from a traditional village in Algeria on her first trip to Paris. Bahloul's second feature film, *Le vampire au paradis* (The Vampire in Paradise, 1991), inverts this geography of Paris in which Nathalie, the daughter of a family that lives in the exclusive sixteenth *arrondisement*, is bitten by a *beur* vampire. The sixteen-year-old Nathalie becomes prone to outbursts in Arabic that terrorize her family and tutors, compelling her father to enter the Arab cafés of Clichy in order to find the vampire and a cure for his daughter.

Nathalie's transformation from the obedient bourgeois daughter to a natty-haired Berber woman renders her nearly unrecognizable to passport officials upon her departure from Paris to Algeria. Her arrival at a hotel for the cure is finally complemented by an amorous encounter with another teenager, an Algerian who only speaks French and listens to classical music. The final scene of a shared psychotic political and cultural harmony between the two young lovers optimistically predicts the dawning of a new geopolitical psychology of return, where the vampire's bite establishes a psychological and cultural reversal—the cure can no longer be found in the metropolitan center.

The marking and demarcation of a Parisian geography, long depicted as the jewel of emotional and sexual centralization in a number of French poetic realist films from the 1930s, such as Julien Duvivier's *Pépé Le Moko* (1937) or in the numerous depictions of Pigalle as the tolerant locus of social and sexual transgression, is used as an essential mise-en-scène for many *beur* films. In Medhi Charef's *Miss Mona* (1987), for example, Pigalle stands as the transgressive atmosphere in which friendship is established between an aging transvestite and a young unemployed *beur* pickpocketer. The first feature film by young *beur* filmmaker Karim Dridi bears the title *Pigalle* (1995). It depicts the intrusion of a sadistic gangster figure who threatens to disrupt the workings of a sedate sex shop in Pigalle. Interestingly, the only *beur* figure in this film is a young orphan who befriends the leading male protagonist.

Other sections of Paris also serve as contested geographic spaces in which cultural and class-based differences are played out through the politics of assimilation. In Gérard Blain's *Pierre et Djemila* (1986), a housing project in the nineteenth *arrondisement* near La Villette serves as the backdrop for a tragic love affair between a young mixed couple. Djemila, from a traditional Algerian family, and Pierre, from an upwardly mobile French family on their way out of the housing complex, encounter one another at school and see each other secretly. Polarizations within the French Catholic community concerning the acceptability of Muslims and their religious practices provide a social context for the film and position Pierre's father as a voice of moderation. The film correlates assorted incidents of religious desecration, tire slashing, and physical confrontations, culminating with the stabbing of Pierre. The murder of Pierre by Djemila's brother, Djaffar, goes beyond the manifest conflict within the housing complex and is tied to a broader confrontation over historical, cultural, and familial values.

The individuated behavior of Pierre and Djemila is opposed to that of Djaffar, who represents "traditional" values, but acts alone. Djaffar kills Pierre in order to destroy the very individuating forces of assimilation that threaten to take Djemila away from the family. While Blain's depiction of community difference lacks cultural precision by stereotyping Djemila as the well-adapted *beurette* in opposition to her brother Djaffar as righteous reborn Muslim, these terms correspond to a continued geographic and emotional breach. In spite of the particularly clichéd romantic denouement that features the stabbing of Pierre followed by Djemila's final act of suicide, the polarization of community within the housing project suggests a site of incubation for the emergence of an avenging violence.

Transgressive acts of passion serve as a recurrent mediating force of geographic and cultural boundaries in several *beur* films. Cheikh Djemaï's short film, *La nuit du doute* (The Night of Doubt, 1989), features Monia, a second-generation Moroccan woman. The conflict between Monia's immigrant parents and her French boyfriend Frank demonstrates the gap that exists between both poles of belonging. Negotiating the normalizing standards of assimilation and a willed space of difference creates the conditions for a series of individual, family, and community-based conflicts. An interrelated set of marginal living conditions, sensibilities, and tactics of negotiation with the forces of order in *beur* cinema is developed within a transnational context—where notions of cultural belonging conflict with French national symbols.

Despite its history of activism, *beur* cinema is thoroughly dependent on French filmmaking institutions, existing between a politicized Third World filmmaking ethic and variations on a post–New Wave French filmmaking aesthetic. Teshome H. Gabriel's early articulation of three phases in Third World filmmaking politics and aesthetics is a useful starting point in elucidating this *in between* position of transnationalism (Gabriel, 1989a). Gabriel begins by describing the iterative practices of unqualified cinematic assimilation, in which Hollywood narratives are adapted. This phase is followed by a remembrance phase, or the return of the Third World exile. In the remembrance phase, the cinematic frame is a site of reflection, punctuated by thoughtful long takes and wide shots in which characters are dwarfed by the timeless expanse of the natural landscape. The third phase is combative, representing an aesthetic of political rupture and a search for ideological alternatives.

While Gabriel addresses a dynamic associated with a dialectic of decolonization in the cinema, the appearance and codification of *beur* cinema represents another kind of dynamic—where the terms of debate have permanently shifted. As a post–New Wave phenomenon, *beur* cinema in France does not pretend to offer a coherent array of stylistic innovations, as it is primarily unified through its treatment of social exclusion in France and appeal for social change; although contiguous with a combative decolonized cinema of the 1960s and 1970s, *beur* cinema addresses multicultural metropolitan situations.

Even the title of Mahmoud Zemmouri's *Les folles années du twist* (The Crazy Years of the Twist, 1983) subversively names the closing era of the Algerian war, deflating the militant black and white neo-realism of Gillo Pontecorvo's *Battle of Algiers* (1966). Zemmouri's comedy shows how the twist, introduced by the French army, symbolized a fraternization campaign prior to the signing of the Evian accords in 1962. The twist was a way to make young people forget—and in the film, we see how two brothers from a Muslim family, not particularly interested in listening to Ben Bella or de Gaulle, expressed the quotidian desire of simply trying to gratify themselves "by doing the twist" in the face of a crumbling political consensus (Dhoukar, 1990b; Dazat, 1985).

Zemmouri's film opens up a shared history between France and Algeria that cannot be reduced to nationalist rhetoric or paternal humanism. The creation of comic situations through dramatic historical events has become a frequently deployed device in a number of other *beur* films. The blurred boundaries of sovereignty between Algeria and France are also apparent in the work of Merzak Allouache, better known perhaps as an Algerian filmmaker, whose film *Bab el-Oued City* (1994) also invokes political parody as a form of social action within the seriousness of the dramatic contemporary situation. Gabriel's thematization of third cinema (Gabriel, 1989b) and Hamid Naficy's notion of exilic cinema (Naficy, 1993, 1999) explore the ways in which transnational experiences translate as cinema, reaching beyond a monolithic conception of national identities, that is, a passage into a new political landscape that can no longer define itself in opposition to Hollywood or a colonial dominant. Although the term *beur* might be understood as a combative position heralding a rupture or break with a dominant institutional order that advocates restrictive notions of French citizenship and identity, *beur* cinema locates itself firmly within the cracks of French institutional structures that are no longer considered a force to be vanquished, but to be negotiated. While both positions make a claim for French citizenship and cultural specificity, their difference resides in the tactics and potential outcomes of a "battle of position," to invoke Antonio Gramsci's well-worn turn-of-phrase.

Whereas a cinema of decolonization called for the creation of a national independent identity, unified in opposition, the postindependence period is the dawning and acknowledgment of fractured institutional and social identities. French national institutional structures cannot simply be addressed as monolithic forms of domination, regardless of a patronizing colonial humanist vocabulary of *francophonie* (Hargreaves and McKinney, 1997) and the *immigré*. French institutions, such as the now-defunct Agence de Cooperation Culturelle et Technique (ACCT) (Agency of Cultural and Technical Cooperation) or the FAS, provide financial support for filmmaking, publishing, and cultural events in former French colonies and for "immigrant" community initiatives in France. French colonial humanism in postcolonial France implies a willingness to fund educational, social, artistic, and cultural endeavors as a function of the state, which serves as the arbiter of often contradictory social and cultural values.

The term *beur* became part of a firmly established public lexicon following the massive antiracist demonstration, "La Marche pour l'Egalité," which numbered 100,000 upon its arrival in Paris from Marseilles on December 3, 1983. This march was precipitated by a series of riots in the housing projects at Les Minguettes in Vénissieux (east of Lyons), Gutenberg in Nanterre (northwest of Paris), and Val-Fourré in Mantes-La-Jolie (fifty miles west of Paris). Cars were burned and intermittent clashes ensued between police and the young people living in the projects. As these events began to appear on the news, a grassroots political effort was organized by a group of researchers at the Université de Bron in Lyon. These researchers invited twenty young people who were implicated in clashes from the HLMs to participate in a two-month internship to study the ways in which immigration was represented in the media, and to garner support for enhanced state initiatives in the projects.

The efforts of this research group were associated with Father Christian Delorme, who led a hunger strike in order to end the war of attrition between police and the youths in the projects (Abdallah, 1993). The hunger strikers called for direct negotiations with François Mitterand at the Elysée Palace; their request went unheard and led to a further escalation of violence between the police and youth activists. The near fatal shooting of Toumi Djaïdja, the spokesman for SOS Minguettes (the association that represented the youth activists at Les Minguettes), and the deaths of other youths at the hands of police culminated in the 1983 march.

The success of the march as a national event was secured when Mitterand received a delegation of marchers at the Elysée Palace. The march was subsequently commemorated the following year with a rally, during which thousands of participants on mopeds and bicycles converged on Paris in what was known as "Convergences 1984." These demonstrations underscored problems of exclusion, social integration, and hostile policing combined with gratuitous xenophobic attacks. The image of the obedient immigrant worker came to be displaced by a second generation coming of age, born, educated, and assimilated in France.

The second generation of Algerians in France, so often opposed to the "good" hardworking Portuguese immigrants under Valéry Giscard d'Estaing's term in office during the late 1970s, or the Italians from an earlier generation, remain at the center of citizenship controversies in France. With the unresolved legacy of the Algerian war, which is primarily understood as a war of independence, French, Algerian, and a panoply of formerly colonized peoples were pitted against one another—with alternating allegiances. As a profoundly significant political rupture within France, the Algerian war marked the decline and fracture of an imperial order, whose ruinous fragments still remain lethally present in both France and Algeria. In Algeria, a protracted civil war has claimed as many as 100,000 lives since 1992, in which the style of violence and terror tactics, involving throat-slitting or testicular torture methods, are reminiscent of the violence practiced during the Algerian war. In France, questions of national belonging are still under consideration. In particular, the sons and daughters of *harkis*, Algerians who served as volunteers in the French Army between 1954 and 1962, remain politically and socially marked in both France and Algeria. In fact, the incapacitated *harki* father, who is either mentally unstable or simply unable to work due to injuries incurred during the war, is a common feature in a number of *beur* films, such as Malik Chibane's film, *La douce France* (Gentle France, 1995).

The naming of the film movement—the appellation *beur*, between Arab, Berber, and butter (*beurre*)—contains difference and assimilation while facilitating a reversal. Serge Meynard's comedy, *L'oeil au beur(re) noir* (The Black Buttered Eye, 1987), featuring the well-known comedy team Les Inconnus (The Unknowns), focuses on one of its members' encounters, as a *beur* (Smaïn), searching for a moderately priced Parisian apartment. The *beur* as hybrid, which activates a comedy of refusals and repartees in *L'oeil au beur(re) noir*, is inserted into an ever-present ambivalence concerning racial, sexual, and class-based difference. Smaïn plays the successful *beur*, Rachid, with all the necessary documents for an apartment, overshadowing his two unemployed delinquent French cohorts, played by Didier Bourdon and Bernard Campan. Mireille Rosello has provocatively described *L'oeil au beur(re) noir* within the terms of the Rachid system of double and triple meanings, in which the redeployment of racial stereotypes by Rachid, as the *beur* and yet not like other *beurs*, serves as an ultimately humorous and yet unstable foil (Rosello, 1998).

The *beur* as connected with a social movement, however, takes on a significantly different configuration when associated with a visual coding. *Beur* cinema suggests an identity politics of visible difference which highlights the second generation, who do not fit into a universalist paradigm of difference. This particular tendency developed with great force in the early 1990s, following the decline of the associative social movements so vocal during the mid-1980s. The cover of the conservative *Le Figaro Magazine* from September 1991 depicts the indecision as to whether the *beur* (transformed into a Muslim) is capable of being integrated into French society. The cover photograph foregrounds the fully exposed face and open neck of Marianne (symbol of the French Republic) in opposition to an unknown woman in the Islamic headscarf, both of which are cast in white alabaster and titled, *"Immigration ou Invasion?"*

The magazine cover (Figure 1) served as a lead-in to a polemic launched by Valéry Giscard d'Estaing, who called for a move toward citizenship based on family tradition and blood (*droit du sang*) in opposition to citizenship based on territorial rights (*droit du sol*). A polemic grounded in a fear of invasion, it came to symbolize immigration as a threat to an essential French identity. Although Giscard favored a notion of "affirming and developing our French identity," rather than "defending our [French] identity" (Giscard D'Estaing, 1991, p. 57), these two concepts seem remarkably similar rhetorically. Nonetheless, "defending French identity" is a slogan and symbol frequently associated with Vichy, which remains dear to Jean-Marie Le Pen and the extreme-right National Front. "Affirming and developing our French identity" is more related to the universalism of Marianne and the French Revolution (as depicted in the cover photo)—a vision that keeps open the possibility for successful integration. In the cover photo, the unknown, veiled woman suggests the dark shadow of Marianne's universalism. With the caption "Immigration or Invasion?" the unseen face of the female subject, as pupil and childbearer, represents the refusal of French republican social and educational values. The transformation of the headscarf into a fear of unassimilated immigration, or "invasion," hails a defensive strategy in the name of protecting Marianne's universalism for all.

The negative sign of the headscarf, which obscures and potentially engulfs Marianne, is directly relevant to the representation of *beurs* in the media, as opposed to *beur* cinema. News magazine programs often addressed the question of *beur* integration as a means of capitalizing on the violent flare-ups in the housing projects, in which cars were set aflame and schoolteachers were assaulted. Within weeks of Giscard d'Estaing's September 1991 polemic, the prime-time news magazine show "Le droit de Savoir" (The Right to Know) featured Charles Pasqua, the well-known minister of interior, in a program entitled "Immigrés: l'integration en perdition" (Immigrants: Integration in Crisis). It posed the provocative question: Why do they (the *beurs* as Muslims) reject the French state? This depiction of ungrateful Franco-Maghrebi youth was tied to the return of the center-right, under pressure to accommodate Le Pen's anti-immigrant populism.

The exclusionary 1993 Pasqua Laws, which created a new framework of immigration restrictions for Franco-Maghrebis residing in France, were part of a longer history of immigration legislation that focused on regulating a foreign workforce—a workforce historically tied to the rescue of French industry from a shortage of labor during the First World War (Mauco, 1933). The idea of zero immigration, however, dates from the mid-1970s, and is tied to a moratorium on immigration that Giscard d'Estaing enacted while serving as head of state during the late 1970s. As a response to an anticipated labor surplus precipitated by the 1973 oil price shocks, Giscard d'Estaing's government introduced repatriation

Figure 1. Cover photograph from Le Figaro Magazine. *(September 21, 1991, Nß 1464321). Image of Marianne, symbol of the French Republic, overlaid with a woman wearing the Islamic headscarf. The text reads, "Immigration or Invasion? Valéry Giscard d'Estaing analyses our polling event."* Photo by François Gonin. ©Le Figaro Magazine.

assistance for Portuguese, Spanish, and North African contractual laborers. Algerian immigrants in particular were targeted for repatriation due to remaining animosity left by the Algerian war (Weil, 1988, pp. 56–57). Nonetheless, the economic repatriation of immigrant families only had a limited impact on foreign immigration. The immigration reforms proposed by Giscard d'Estaing were rejected by the French legislative assembly on the grounds that they were in conflict with the long-standing French policy that protected political asylum seekers.

With the beginning of François Mitterand's term as head of state, more than 130,000 illegal foreign workers, who had entered the country before January 1, 1981, were legalized. More than 110 propositions regarding immigration were passed in the early years of French socialism under Mitterand, leading to a subsequent backlash in 1986, under the terms of the first of several cohabitations with conservative prime ministers. As prime minister, Jacques Chirac enacted the beginnings of legislation to restrict the automatic acquisition of French nationality by people of foreign origin in 1986, putting in motion the first legislation associated with the Pasqua Laws. These laws addressed the entry and residence of foreigners and attempted (unsuccessfully) to modify the law on the acquisition of French citizenship—rejecting the principle that citizenship is dependent upon one's place of birth. Although the short-lived Pasqua Laws of 1986 were abolished once Mitterand was reelected in 1988, and Chirac was replaced by the socialist prime minister Michel Rocard, a series of subsequent events, such as the Islamic headscarf controversy in 1989 and the Gulf War in 1991, raised new questions about the legitimacy and place of the Franco-Maghrebi population in France.

The Pasqua Laws of 1993 (June and July) limited French nationality for Franco-Maghrebis to: (1) children born in France after January 1, 1963, to parents born in Algeria before that date (i.e., previous to the dissolution of French Algeria), only if their parents had been living in France five years prior to their birth; (2) children of *harkis* and other Muslims repatriated to France since 1962 whose parents were French or had the right to apply for French citizenship until 1967; and (3) other foreigners (such as Tunisians and Moroccans), only if they were born in France and resided there from thirteen to eighteen years of age. As of June 1993, Franco-Maghrebis can only become French citizens if they willingly apply for French nationality before a magistrate between the ages of sixteen and twenty-one; however, citizenship may be denied if they have received prison sentences for more than six months (Wihtol de Wenden, 1994).

A partial representation of the consequences of 1993 Pasqua Laws is depicted in the film *Cheb* (dir. Malik Chibane, 1993). The film begins with documentary footage of police confrontations at Les Minguettes housing project and an assortment of clips from protest rallies pertaining to immigration in France from the 1980s and early 1990s. Following this black-and-white actuality footage, the harsh, windswept yellow dunes of the Algerian desert appear. The protagonist, Merwan, appears amid the dunes, running toward a truck filled with passengers; once he climbs on board, the driver asks him if he has any identity papers. To this question, Merwan says no and the flashback of Merwan's story of deportation from France begins. Merwan grew up in the French working-class suburb of Roubaix (northwest of Lille) and is cast as a disaffected *beur* youth of Algerian parents with limited means. After being arrested and detained for eight months on charges of vandalism in France, Merwan is expelled from France under the 1993 Pasqua Laws, and sent to Algeria, in spite of the fact that he speaks no Arabic and has no family there.

Upon his arrival in Algeria without any identity papers, he is unable to register at a hotel room for lack of identification, his luggage is stolen, and he arrives late for his prearranged interview at the Algiers recruiting office. Unable to obtain an assignment in a major city, Merwan is sent on his first assignment to the Algerian desert, as part of a foot-soldier patrol squadron. From the desert command post, Merwan writes to his *beurette* girlfriend, Malika, who decides to join him in Algeria. Upon Malika's arrival in Algeria, she is met by her uncle, who holds her captive in his village and forbids her to see Merwan. Meanwhile, Merwan deserts his army commission when Malika does not arrive at the appointed local airport near Merwan's command post. Merwan finds Malika locked up in her uncle's village and they run away together in search of a new life. A Malian cab driver, who drives a nonregistered taxi, offers to help them escape from Algeria. As they make their way toward the border region with Morocco, they are finally stopped at an army checkpoint. After being questioned by the police, Malika is sent back to her uncle's village and Merwan is released. Merwan is taken in by an Algerian family and has a chance encounter with a French deserter on the run in Algeria from the French Army. Finally, Merwan exchanges his identity papers with the French deserter and serves the remainder of his counterpart's military service in France. In the final scene of the film, Merwan appears in a French army uniform, marching in formation—putting an ironic twist on the French Foreign Legion film genre.

In the summer of 1993, Jean-Marie Cavanna's popular prime time show "La Marche du Siècle" (The Marching Century) presented a program entitled "Les beurs," which contextualized the restrictive immigration framework implied by the 1993 Pasqua Laws in terms of Islamic fundamentalism, rather than *beur* integration. In the imagery of Giscard d'Estaing's Marianne, this show presented integration as a dark shadow looming over the republic. The occasional presence of filmmakers on other news magazine shows, such as Sylvain Auger's "Rencontres" (Encounters), was among the few challenges to the representation of *beur* integration as synonymous with Islamic fundamentalism. The more politically charged debates staged by associative structures, such as France Plus (led by Areski Dahmani) or SOS Racism (led by Harlem Désir), had lost their privileged relationships of political patronage, ceding their position to film auteurs and multiethnic rap groups by the late 1980s and early 1990s. It is in this sense that the dynamics of the media marketplace have overshadowed a political climate once favorable to issues of immigration and racial difference during the early years of Mitterand socialism.

Immediately preceding the French presidential elections in 1995, the release of Matthieu Kassovitz's film *La haine* (Hate) demonstrated how a seemingly social activist film was neutralized by presidential sloganeering. Upon being elected to office, Jacques Chirac publicly ordered his cabinet to see *La haine*, in a dubious gesture reinforcing his successful campaign theme of mending the "social rupture" in French society. In a recent article about *La haine* (Elstob, 1997–1998) it has been noted that the minister of interior and the prime minister had watched the film three times in order to better understand the underlying causes for the July 1995 riots in the Parisian suburbs of Chanteloup-les-Vignes, in the Noé Concerted Development Zone (ZAC de la Noé)—where the film was shot. The visual immediacy of this film as part of a new New Wave of in-your-face, Tarrantino-influenced French filmmaking rather than an in-depth depiction of a long-standing history of social unrest puts into question the role and function of cinema as a voice of social activism. Clearly, watching *La haine* three times, while it might be gripping cinematically, does not substitute for sustained political engagement with immigration policy and the geographic exclusion of the HLMs located in low-income suburbs.

La haine is a uniquely stylized social activist film, featuring a slick steadycam music-video look with box office appeal. The no-exit depiction of the friendship between three young men of Arab, West African, and Jewish backgrounds is staged in the concrete expanses of the ZAC de la Noé in the aftermath of an all-night battle between youths and the French riot police, unleashed by the police beating of a local teenager. The inexorable clock, which appears intermittently, is counterpointed by the youths' discovery of a gun, lost by one of the French riot policemen, and leads to the final violent denouement of the film. The gun and the clock contribute to the action-packed, black-and-white, fast-paced violence of *La haine*, in which the carceral violence of the housing projects dips into the oblivious Parisian center. Although this film resonates stylistically with a number of black American gangster films and Reebok sneaker commercials featuring black American athletes, the aesthetics of violence and a coded slang overcomes any possibility for negotiation with the forces of order. To its credit, the film did call popular attention to the psychological underpinnings of the deadly standoff between police and youths in the HLMs. However, the promotion and reception of *La haine* was subject to the fickle sensationalism of the French domestic media marketplace that trivialized the historical roots and activism associated with this ongoing social crisis.

Finally, the term *beur* can no longer accurately characterize this second generation of naturalized immigrants. The ubiquity of the term, which was picked up by the media and even incorporated into the French dictionary by the Académie Française as early as 1984, has blunted its initially resistant edge. A four-page spread in the April 1984 issue of the woman's magazine *Marie Claire* even proclaimed the *Look Beur*, which is *beau et beur à la fois*—drawing in part on the 1970s American slogan, "black is beautiful" (Battegay and Boubeker, 1993).

Thus, the republican *beur* as a stylish ethnic look, an acculturated *métissage*, came to contain a new chain of oppositions.

Since the Islamic headscarf controversy in 1989 and the Gulf War in 1991, the term *beur* has become almost a misnomer. The blurring of the term *Muslim* with the fear of Islamic fundamentalism has led to the wide-scale abandonment of the HLMs by the regional authorities. Islamic youth associations like the Young Arabs from the Greater Lyons area, known as the Jeune Arabes de Lyon et sa Banlieue (JALB), have taken on the crucial community functions previously fulfilled by the publicly elected city councils, such as soup kitchens, basic health care, after-school recreation, and child care in several of the impoverished HLMs. The building of mosques and the proliferation of Muslim organizations have been tied to a resurgence in conversion to Islam among the second generation.

Islam is the second largest religion in France after Catholicism. In fact, a significant number of low-income French citizens of French ancestry who were born Catholic have also converted. Since Islam has become integral to the social fabric of the low-income *banlieues*, the term *beur* has also become more closely associated with a *beur-geoisie*, broken off from its former activist past. That is, a *beur-geoisie* who live in the urban centers and do not experience the same cultural exclusion associated with the HLMs, a lower standard of education, and high levels of unemployment. The label *beur*, as Battegay and Boubeker describe in their sociological study on media representations of immigrants in France, has also become a means of marking the success of a republican notion of integration, and thus the end of this "immigrant" community as such (Battegay and Boubeker, 1993). This analysis of the successful *beur* as a fully integrated French citizen also implies that the remaining second- and third-generation Franco-Maghrebi citizens still residing in low-income, poorly maintained HLMs with other multiethnic and French working-class people, exist on an exclusionary vanishing point of limited social, educational, and economic expectations.

To return to *beur* cinema, however, we are still confronted with the question of how these social movements are linked to the cinema. I have tried to illustrate that the social movements related to the second generation created a context for the reception of *beur* cinema. The eruption of violence in the housing projects still remains a powerful point of reference, but the activism has lost its center. More than ten years later, a series of riots in Vaulx-en-Velin (triggered by the death of youth activist Claudio Thomas) in 1990, and others in Sartrouville, Mantes-la-Jolie, Val-Fourré in 1991, and Chanteloup-la-Vigne in 1995, have underscored the persistence and intensification of the very same issues related to exclusion and integration that were brought to light in the early 1980s, which have expanded beyond the particularism of *beur* identity.

As Battegay and Boubeker report, the terms used by the media to represent this population have shifted from "immigrant workers" in the 1980s to a more recent set of terms in the 1990s: *beurs, illegals,* and *Muslims.* In this sense, a film movement might be initiated through a series of events reported in the media, but then establishes its own autonomy as a series of loosely amalgamated films that are produced, distributed, and promoted as popular spectacle in the theaters. In effect, a series of violent events and images of social contestation in the news creates a reservoir of social meaning which can be dipped into and presented as a relevant story, congruent with the naming and organization of current events.

Classifying these events as *immigration*, *integration*, *beurs*, *marches*, and *banlieues* is closely tied to a process of staging and saturating public opinion. These terms come to act as vectors of a flow that serves a repetitive and hypnotic machine of media representations—a maligned media dreamwork of social reality. In fact, the accumulation of indexical imagery fails to distinguish between the building of a mosque in Lyon, rioting on the outskirts of Marseilles, and Islamic fundamentalism in Algeria. It is in this sense that the reception of *beur* cinema can be understood through a series of political and social conjunctures in the accretion of current events. These media representations in turn, are transformed into handles that exist on a continuum with the making and distribution of films. These terms act as indexical sites that facilitate the social interpenetration of cinema and establish it as a form of visual currency.

Media imagery establishes relationships of equivalence, creating an index in which related events are staged, interpreted, and continually repeated. The concrete phobic expanse of the housing projects, as well as an aesthetics of violence so well portrayed in so many *beur* films such as *Le Thé au harem d'Archimède*, *Cheb*, and *La haine* will continue to appear as part of a French political mediascape. Although subject to the tides of political patronage and uneasy racial and ethnic integration, these peripheral housing communities, on the outskirts of Paris, Marseilles, Lyons, and Grenoble, serve as advance guard experimental communities for an emerging multiethnic France.

NOTES

1. MRAP is an acronym for Le Mouvement contre le Racisme et pour l'Amitié entre les Peuples, which translates as the Movement against Racism and for Interracial Friendship.

2. SONACOTRAL is an acronym for La Société nationale de construction de logements pour les travailleurs algériens, which translates as the National Construction Company for the Construction of Housing for Algerian Workers. Since 1963, Algerian was dropped from the acronym and it is now called SONACOTRA. It remains one of the largest organizations for hotels and housing in France.

3. FAS is an acronym for Fonds d'Action Social pour les travailleurs immigrés et leurs familles, the Social Action Foundation for Immigrant Workers and Their Families. The FAS was initially established in the late 1950s as a means of transferring the income of migrant workers back to their families in the country of origin; the FAS mandate was substantially expanded, however, as they were charged with the housing and reintegration of the *pieds noir* community in France following the Algerian war. A recent retrospective of films that were financed, at least in part, by the FAS, was screened at the World Arab Institute in Paris in 1995. As Fernanda Da Silva, head of the cinema and audiovisual program, remarks, "the FAS also supports community centers as well as dance and music programs. These programs have been the most successful in encouraging teenage involvement; some of the best known French rappers, such as Jimmy Jay and MC Solaar, got their start through these FAS-supported associative structures" (personal communication, October 1995).

REFERENCES

Abdallah, M. H. "Dix ans d'enquête en pays beur." *M Scope: Revue Média* 4 (April 1993): 93–98.

Battegay, A., and A. Boubeker. *Les images publiques de l'immigration*. Paris: CIEMI L'Harmattan, 1993.

Bosséno, C. "Du Collectif Mohammed: *Le Garage, Zone immigré, La mort de Kader*: des films provocateurs." *CinémAction-Cinémas de l'émigration* 3, no. 24 (January 1982): 128–131.

———. "Immigrant Cinema: National Cinema, The Case of Beur Film." In *Popular European Cinemas*, ed. R. Dyer and G. Vincendeau, pp. 47–57. London and New York: Routledge, 1992.

Dazat, O. "Entretien avec Mahmoud Zemmouri." *Cinématographe* (July 1985): 13–15.

Deleuze, G. "Postscript on the Societies of Control." *October* 59 (Winter 1992): 3–7.

Dhoukar, H. "Les thèmes du cinéma beur." *CinémAction* 56 (July 1990a): 152–160.

———. "Mahmoud Zemmouri: Le mythe de l'Algérie, c'est fini." *CinémAction* 56 (July 1990b): 182–185.

Diop, M., and L. Michalak. "*Refuge* and *Prison*: Islam, Ethnicity, and the Adaptation of Space in Workers's Housing in France." In *Making Muslim Space*, ed. B. D. Metcalf, pp. 74–91. Berkeley: University of California Press, 1996.

Elstob, Kevin. "Reviews: *Hate (La Haine)*." *Film Quarterly* 51, no. 2 (Winter 1997–1998): 44–49.

Fahdel, A. "Une esthétique beur?" *CinémAction* 56 (July 1990): 140–151.

Gabriel, T. H. "Towards a Critical Theory of Third World Films." In *Questions of Third Cinema*, ed. J. Pines and P. Willeman, pp. 30–52. London: British Film Institute. 1989a.

———. "Third Cinema as a Guardian of Popular Memory: Towards a Third Aesthetics." In *Questions of Third Cinema*, ed. J. Pines and P. Willeman, pp. 53–64. London: British Film Institute, 1989b.

Giscard D'Estaing, V. "Immigration ou Immigration." *Le Figaro Magazine* 14643 (September 21, 1991): 48–57.

Hargreaves, A. G. *Immigration, 'Race' and Ethnicity in Contemporary France*. London and New York: Routledge, 1995.

Hargreaves, A. G., and M. McKinney. "Introduction." In *Post-Colonial Cultures in France*, ed. A. G. Hargreaves and M. McKinney, pp. 3–25. New York and London: Routledge, 1997.

Horvilleur, G. "[Interview with] Farida Belghoul." *Cinématographe* 112 (July 1985): 18–19.

Lopate, Phillip. "Grim, Shocking, Didactic, a New New Wave Rolls In." *New York Times*, (November 22, 1998), pp. 15, 26.

Mauco, G. "Immigration in France." *International Labour Review* 27, no. 6 (June 1933): 781–782.

Mohammed [Collectif]. "Un outil d'enquête." *CinémAction-Tumulte* 7 (1981): 86–88.

Naficy, H. "Exile Discourse and Televisual Fetishization." In *Otherness and the Media*, ed. T. H. Gabriel and H. Naficy, pp. 85–116. Langhorne, Pa.: Harwood Academic Press, 1993.

———. "Phobic Spaces and Liminal Panics: Independent Transnational Film Genre." *East-West Film Journal* 8, no. 2 (1994): 1–30.

———. "Between Rocks and Hard Places: The Interstitial Mode of Production in Exilic Cinema." In *Home, Exile, Homeland: Film, Media, and the Politics of Place*, ed. H. Naficy, pp. 125–147. New York and London: Routledge, 1999.

Ricoeur, P. "Événement et Sens." *Raisons Pratiques : L'événement en perspective* 2 (1991): 41–56.

Rosello, M. "Third Cinema or Third Degree: The 'Rachid System' in Serge Meynard's *L'Oeil au beur(re) noire*." In *Cinema, Colonialism, Postcolonialism*, ed. D. Sherzer, pp. 147–172. Austin: University of Texas Press, 1996.

———. *Declining the Stereotype*. Hanover and London: University Press of New England, 1998.

Tarr, C. "Questions of Identity in Beur Cinema: From *Tea in the Harem* to *Cheb*." *Screen* 34, no. 4 (Winter 1993): 321–342.

———. "Beurz N the Hood: The articulation of Beur and French Identities in *Le Thé au harem d'Archimède* and *Hexagone*." *Modern and Contemporary France* NS 3, no. 40 (1995): 415–425.

———. "French Cinema and Post-Colonial Minorities." In *Post-Colonial Cultures in France*, ed. A. G. Hargreaves and M. McKinney, pp. 59–83. London: Routledge, 1947.

Vieillard-Baron, H. "Deux Z. A. C. de banlieue en situation extrême: du grand ensemble stig-
matisé de Chanteloup au 'village' de Chevry." *Annales de Géographie* 564 (March–April
1992): 188–213.

Vuddamalay, V., P. White, and D. Sporton. "The Evolution of the Goutte d'Or as an Ethnic Minority District of Paris." *New Community* 17, no. 2 (1991): 245–258.

Weil, P. "La politique française d'immigration." *Pouvoirs* 47 (November 1988): 45–60.

White, P. "Images of Race in Social Housing Estates in France." *Immigrants and Minorities* 16,
no. 3 (November 1997): 19–35.

Wihtol de Wenden, C. "The French Debate: Legal and Political Instruments to Promote Integration." In *European Migration in the Late Twentieth Century*, ed. H. Fassmann and R.
Münz, pp. 67–80, Laxenburg, Austria: IIASA, 1994.

MUSIC CITATIONS

... *de la Planète Mars*. I AM. Labelle Noir. (1991) Virgin CD 30834. (I AM is an acronoym for
the Imperial Asiatic Men's League).

FILM TITLES
(unless noted, all films are French productions)

Bab el-Oued City (Algeria-France, dir. Merzak Allouache, 1994)

Baton Rouge (Baton Rouge) (dir. Rachid Bouchareb, 1985)

Battle of Algiers (Italy, dir. Gilles Pontecorvo, 1966)

[La] douce France (Gentle France) (dir. Malik Chibane, 1995)

Cheb (dir. Malik Chibane, 1993)

Dupont-la-Joie (dir. Yves Boisset, 1974)

[Les] folles années du twist (The Crazy Years of the Twist) (dir. Mahmoud Zemmouri, 1983)

[La] haine (Hate) (dir. Matthieu Kassovitz, 1995)

Laisse béton (Forget About It) (dir. Roger Le Péron, 1983)

Miss Mona (dir. Medhi Charef, 1987)

[La] nuit du doute (The Night of Doubt) (dir. Cheikh Djemaï, 1989)

[L'] oeil au beur(re) noir (The Black Buttered Eye) (Serge Meynard, 1987)

Pépé Le Moko (dir. Julien Duvivier, 1937)

Pierre et Djemila (dir. Gérard Blain, 1986)

Pigalle (dir. Karim Dridi, 1995).

Thé à la menthe (dir. Abdelkrim Bahloul, 1984)

[Le] Thé au harem d'Archimède [Tea in the Harem] (dir. Medhi Charef, 1985)

[Le] Vago (The Drifters) (dir. Aïssa Djabri, 1983),

[Le] vampire au paradis (The Vampire in Paradise) (dir. Abdelkrim Bahloul, 1991)

Zone Immigré (The Immigrant Zone) (dir. Audiopradif/ Collectif Mohammed, 1981)

Edward D. Castillo

Dances With Wolves

Dances With Wolves is not only a well-crafted film by a first-time director, it also touches on a number of important spiritual, social, and environmental issues vital to all Americans at the beginning of a new millennium. American Indian historians have long been well aware of many important stories that resulted from the encounters between native peoples and Euro-Americans in the past century. Hope, fear, hatred, dread, humor, guilt, and loathing can be found in nearly every such encounter. From a native point of view, we have long been mystified as to why this rich mine of human experience has been studiously avoided by Hollywood filmmakers. Within the Indian world, Costner's powerful directing debut is for certain the most talked about mainstream Hollywood Indian film in two decades. Despite some negative reviews by jaded Eurocentric urbanites, Costner's vision of an alternate Lakota encounter with Americans has captured the imagination of Americans from a variety of social, economic, and racial backgrounds.

From a native viewpoint, the film's primary virtue is its sensitive exploration of a native culture. The screenplay, without preaching, engenders understanding and sympathy for Lakota culture. I am thinking especially here of small scenes, as when Kicking Bird and his wife get into bed and we sense concern and confusion in his face; then he pulls out one of his children's dolls that he has lain upon. This vignette tells us in purely cinematic terms of the humanity of this family, and rings warmly familiar to all parents in the audience. With such small touches the director achieved his goal of demonstrating that the most important aspect of the picture was "the sentiment, the humanity, not the politcs."[1]

As non-Indian archaeologists, ethnographers, and historians have been painfully reminded over the past twenty years, all contemporary endeavors to interpret Indian history and culture have the dual potential of possibly hurting or helping contemporary Indians. In this respect, most native peoples seem pleased with Costner in this most recent portrayal of our people in the past century. However, those expecting immediate reform in the social, economic, and political fortunes of the Sioux or any other tribe are sure to be disappointed. This film may help bring about much-needed reform in our nation and our tribes, but true reform will always require more than Hollywood can offer. Nevertheless, to minimize the power of the mass media to generate sympathy, concerns, and demands for reform is to ignore reality. For that reason alone it seems worthwhile to devote

From *Film Quarterly*, Vol. 44, No. 4; Summer, 1991: pp. 14–23. Copyright © 1991 by The Regents of the University of California.

some thoughtful reflection to the shadows of the Indians whom Costner and screenwriter Michael Blake have lyrically dance upon the screen, thrusting us backward in time for a fleeting moment.

The characters portrayed are both engaging and varied. Kicking Bird is of course the most sympathetic of the Lakotas, the father figure who rescues and raises the small white girl (Christine/Stands With Fists) who had escaped a Pawnee raiding party, and who eventually opens communication between Dunbar and the Lakota. He is a shaman/warrior whose poised and convincing portrayal by Canadian-born Oneida Indian Graham Green rivals Costner's, and gained him an Academy Award nomination. The archetype Lakota warrior in the story is Wind In His Hair, played by Omaha Indian Rodney Grant. His commanding presence is sexually charged, with an aura of danger just beneath his angry bluster. Early on in the film his character is dramatically revealed in a confrontation with Dunbar: he charges on horseback directly toward Dunbar, stopping only feet from the soldier, shouts his defiance and lack of fear of this strange white man, and disdainfully turns his back on a cocked pistol to demonstrate his contempt for Dunbar—who promptly faints.

The most familiar Native American actor is folksinger/activist Floyd Red Crow Westerman, a Lakota Indian. He plays Ten Bears, chief of the film's Lakota band. His understated performance is in sharp contrast to his real character: for those who know him, he is nearly always smiling and a performer with an easygoing demeanor. Perhaps reflecting the growing dominance of warriors in Lakota society as the crisis of the frontier enveloped the Plains Indian societies, the film offers few prominent parts for Indian women. The most important Indian female part is Canadian Cree/Chippewa Tantoo Cardinal as Black Shawl, wife of Kicking Bird. It is a small part which she performs skillfully. She delivers one of the best one-liners in the film: when Kicking Bird declares that his crying stepdaughter, Stands With Fists, is being difficult, Black Shawl observes sardonically that it is perhaps Kicking Bird who is being difficult, since Stands With Fists is the one who is crying. While women in the audience will find this an appropriate rejoinder, it offers little comfort for the curious lack of strong females or, for that matter, any young Indian women/children roles in the remainder of the screenplay. On the other hand, young viewers will be especially pleased with the trio of prepubescent Lakota boys led by Lakota Indian Nathan Lee Chasing His Horse (Smiles A Lot), who appropriately displays the independence, foolishness, and self-sacrificing courage typical of Indian youth both then and today. The other Lakota characters inhabiting Ten Bears's village, while undeniably likable, are rather conventional and lack the delightfully quirky characters found in *Little Big Man*'s Cheyenne camp—a saucy berdache (homosexual) and the frustrated contrary warrior.

The "enemy" Pawnee portrayal has generated a good deal of discussion among Indians. Some viewers have decried the one-dimensional and negative portrayal of Pawnee so badly maligned earlier in *Little Big Man* (1970). Despite a largely negative image, careful viewers will note the Pawnee war party that attacks the mule skinner Timmons is led by the unidentified actor and character I call "Violent Leader," who seeks to both humiliate and drive his hesitant followers into attacking the yet unseen whites. Later we see the Pawnee scouts helping the soldiers track down Ten Bears's people. One recalls Jack Crabbe's acerbic declaration, "Pawnees always were sucking up to whites" from *Little Big Man*. In reality much of Indian frontier history is characterized by a native survival response that varied between fight, flight, and accommodation. Earlier, the Pawnee offered considerable armed resistance to white encroachment upon their territory; later they assisted the U.S. government in pursuing their traditional enemies, the Sioux. These unfortunate people were subjected to the purposeful introduction of smallpox by traders along the Santa Fe trail in 1831.[2] The film makes it too easy to dismiss these much maligned Indians as stereotypical "bad Indians." Their kind of imprudent judgment is today often chided by those living comfortably with full bellies and not faced with the horrible leadership decisions that could spell violent death or starvation for their men, women, and children. In the last quarter of the nineteenth century various bands of Sioux faced these terrible choices too and ultimately cooperated with federal authorities, riding with the blue coats as scouts, auxiliaries, and even as U.S. soldiers.[3] Thoughtful viewers wishing to know more about the tortuous history of the Pawnee can find the works of Pawnee authors James Murie and Gene Weltfish in a recently published Pawnee bibliography.[4]

The non-Indian characters present some striking contrasts as well. I've discussed this film with some colleagues who claim the whites in it were negatively portrayed throughout its three-hour running time. That type of generalization does not do justice to Michael Blake's subtly textured screenplay. In fact, the film is really about the transformation of the white soldier Lieutenant John Dunbar into the Lakota warrior Dances With Wolves. Kevin Costner's sensitive and convincing character transformation earned him an Oscar. What Blake has done with Dunbar's character is to assume that, as in the race- and class-conscious nineteenth-century James Fenimore Cooper leatherstocking tales, largely white American audiences will not endure a story centered around Indians only. Therefore, a white central character is mandatory to capture audience sympathy. However, unlike Cooper's protagonist Natty Bumppo, a white frontiersman of common social origin, Blake at first sight provides us with another type of frontier hero, the "military aristocrat"—a hero who combines high status and potential leadership in Eastern society with the ability to both survive and triumph in the wilderness. This traditional type of frontier hero has a future in a postfrontier America beginning to evolve into a rather rigid system divided by class and race, based on land ownership and wealth. He has the resourcefulness and skills to fight and conquer Indians as well as the wilderness. He is supposed to be able to do this without developing savage traits or forgetting that he is the agent of progress and order in the wild. But that is precisely what Costner's character ultimately rejects. Dunbar does the unthinkable: he breaks out of the rigid confines of the frontier aristocrat prototype. The widespread abhorrence of Indians and their wilderness empire shared by all classes of frontier whites is slyly demonstrated by Blake's screenplay that has the illiterate and sadistic Private Spivey (Tony Pierce) stealing Dances With Wolves/Dunbar's journal of his gradual evolution into a Lakota warrior and using it for toilet paper![5]

Stands With Fists is of course the other major non-Indian character in the story. However, it could be argued that she is in fact "Lakota"—her family was killed by marauding Pawnee (again!) and she was rather completely assimilated into Ten Bears's band as a mourning widow of a recently killed Lakota warrior. It is to the filmmaker's credit that such a skilled and mature actress as Mary McDonald was cast in this pivotal role. Costner recently revealed his reasoning in selecting McDonald: "the key word in characterizing Stands With Fists was woman not girl. I wanted someone with lines on her face. That's not an easy thing to explain to a studio."[6] While the character is inherently likable, McDonald's skillful performance adds immeasurably to her appeal—strong yet vulnerable, possessing beauty without vanity. Especially noteworthy is the actress's authentic Lakota cadence and accent throughout the film. Her scenes where she relearns English are skillfully executed with pathos and conviction. For all of the above reasons she has gained the respect and acknowledgment of her peers, who nominated her for the Academy's Best Supporting Actress category.

Other white characters in the film also show a great deal of variety. The flatulent mule skinner Timmons (Robert Pastorelli), despite limited screen time, manages to steal scenes from Costner. His role evokes humor, disgust, and ultimately pathos. One can only suppose it was someone of Timmons's character that prompted Thomas Jefferson to observe that when the Indians encountered the typical frontiersman in the wilderness it was hardly an elevating experience for the Indians. Screenwriter Blake juxtaposes Timmons's painfully detailed violent death with his unexpected plea that his killers not hurt his mules. Just when the audience is ready to see the dirty, disgusting, crude, and racist Timmons killed, Blake introduces us to an unexpectedly compassionate side of the character and leaves the audience the disquieting reflection on our eagerness to see this low-lifer killed. That scene also clearly shows us that in the Pawnee "Violent Leader" scalping of Timmons, there is no honor.

Even among the soldiers we find all types—good, bad, insane, and brutal. The enlisted men at the beginning of the film are shown to be tired, disgusted, and demoralized by the indecisiveness of their leaders. While we are witness to General Tide's personal pledge to save the "hero" of St. David's Field, the majority of the military leaders are shown to be cruel, brutal, or alcoholic. The suicidal Major Fambrough is quickly shown to be an isolated and insane alcoholic; he perhaps serves as a warning to Dunbar that the same fate awaits him at Fort Sedgewick. Blake perhaps went over the top with having this pathetic individual announce he had wet his pants! However, we can be reasonably sure that the audience clearly recognizes Fambrough's alcoholic insanity. Unquestionably the most brutal soldiers were to be found near the end of the film at the regarrisoned Fort Sedgewick. The filmmakers leave no question in our minds that this is a particularly unsavory and dangerous bunch. This group kills Dances With Wolves's magnificent buckskin Cisco. They repeatedly brutalize Dances With Wolves, and threaten to hang him if he does not lead them to the "hostiles." Finally, they kill the partly domesticated wolf Two Sox. The filmmakers show us by this senseless act the all too familiar fear and hatred in the American psyche of the natural world. Yet even among this motley crew, careful observers will find Lieutenant Elgin (Charles Rocket). Perhaps out of military respect for a fellow officer of equal rank, or sense of common decency, he repeatedly acts to curb the excesses of enlisted men as well as the indifferent major in command.

While the characters in Blake's screenplay are satisfactorily varied, some violence has been done to the historical realities in which this story is set. Blake's original novel centered on the Comanche of the Southern Plains, not the Lakota. According to producer Jim Wilson, the change of tribes occurred because the production company gained access to a 3,500-strong herd of buffalo available on the private ranch of former Lieutenant Governor Roy Houck of South Dakota. Yet we are still presented with a Lakota chief called Ten Bears. In fact, the real Ten Bears (Par-Roowah Sermehno) was a Southern Plains Yapparika Comanche chief and signer of the Medicine Lodge Treaty of 1867.[7] One rather obvious overlooked transitional casualty of the relocation of the story to the Northern Plains is revealed when Ten Bears shows Dances With Wolves and Kicking Bird an aged Spanish morion and explains, "The men who wore this came in the time of my grandfather's grandfather. Eventually we drove them out. Then came the Mexicans. They do not come here anymore. In my own time, the Texans . . ." The Lakota could never have encountered this assemblage of Southern colonists on the Northern Plains. The real Kicking Bird was a principal chief (not shaman) of the Kiowas, yet another Southern Plains tribe. Blake is said to have fashioned the film's Kicking Bird after the Kiowa chief because he favored peace with whites. Ironically the real Kicking Bird was believed to have been poisoned by a rival Kiowa shaman/warrior called Ma Man-ti (Skywalker) for his role in imprisoning resisting tribesmen in 1875.[8] Perhaps the film's most glaring factual inaccuracy is the depiction of a winter military campaign by soliders hunting for Dances With Wolves and Ten Bears's band in the winter of 1864. In fact no U.S. Army winter campaign was undertaken on the Plains until November 1868. Interestingly enough, this was Lieutenant Colonel George A. Custer's 7th Cavalry massacre of Cheyenne at Washita Creek on Thanksgiving Day. That massacre, which killed thirty-eight warriors and sixty-seven women and children of the luckless Chief Black Kettle's people (earlier subjected to yet another massacre at Sand Creek, 1864), was portrayed with chilling authenticity in *Little Big Man*.[9]

In addition to factual errors, the film contains a number of unlikely absurdities. Audiences are asked to believe that the Confederate infantry at the St. David's battlefield in 1863 could not hit a lone Union officer at a slow gallop within fifty feet of its picket lines. Viewers literate in Civil War battlefield history will have difficulty reconciling the known Confederate accuracy in small arms fire with the film's myopic troopers. We are also asked to believe that an Eastern neophyte would need to inform a highly skilled, hungry, and presumably alert band of Indians that a thunderously noisy herd of buffalo was in their neighborhood. However, there is an intriguing alternative interpretation of these events (see box).

The costumes have received wide praise and were beautifully executed by Kathy Smith and Larry Belitz. Costume designer Elso Zamparelli received a much deserved Academy Award nomination as well. Indeed, they appear to have sprung to life from the works of nineteenth-century painters Karl Bodmer and George Catlin. And that may be precisely the problem: all of the Indian characters appear to be wearing their finest ceremonial regalia all the time, every day! While it makes for colorful and picturesque village life, it certainly would have been impractical. In a similar vein, we witness the marriage of Stands With Fists to Dances With Wolves taking place in the middle of the day, and in a white buckskin dress. The latter is certainly outside of acknowledged Lakota culture norms. Finally, we are asked to believe that Army rifles buried in the ground for weeks and soaked from a fierce storm could be used functionally by Lakota who, within hours of an impending attack, had only used war clubs, bows and arrows, and lances. It makes for great drama but presses the limits of our willing suspension of disbelief.

A little acknowledged aspect of the appeal this film has for both Indian and non-Indian audiences is its sly sense of humor. A good part of that humor is at the expense of non-Indians. Nervous chuckles are heard among audiences as the mad Major Fambrough scavenges through his bottle-laden "files" and disjointedly converses with a bewildered and shocked Lieutenant Dunbar. We are disgustingly amused by the ill-mannered ignorance of the mule skinner Timmons and his bizarre behavior. Costner himself provides a good many laughs. Audiences are delighted with Dunbar's buffalo pantomime and coffee-grinding antics as he desperately attempts to communicate with an incredulous Lakota visiting party. Indians in the audience are especially amused by Dunbar's perplexed reaction to the Lakota ritual of eating the raw buffalo liver following Dunbar's kill.

Perhaps director Costner's best remembered amusing visuals are a series of delightful sight jokes centered around the many Lakota attempts to steal Dunbar's magnificent buckskin mare Cisco. Much of the humor here is in fact at the expense of the Indians. A naked Lieutenant Dunbar confronts a startled Kicking Bird and causes him to flee. A trio of Lakota youth led by Smiles A Lot gallop away leading Cisco and boasting of their soon-to-be-acknowledged warrior status when abruptly their dreams of glory are literally yanked out of their hands and instead of acclaim, they consequently face a whipping. Even Wind In His Hair has Cisco's persistent loyalty to Lieutenant Dunbar thwart his best efforts to capture the prized mount. Yet the best belly laugh of this running gag is the delayed realization that during one of the attempts to steal Cisco, Dunbar has knocked himself unconscious on the low doorjamb of his Fort Sedgewick sod house.

Perhaps in the same vein, although in this instance made ironically poignant, is Wind In His Hair's boastful soliloquy, "When I heard that more whites are coming, more than can be counted, I wanted to laugh. We took 100 horses from those people, there was no honor in it. They don't ride well, they don't shoot well, they're dirty. They have no women, no children. They could not even make it through one winter in our country. And these people are said to flourish? I think they will be dead in ten years." These moments of humor relieve the tension of early contact and eventual hunted lives that the Indians, we all know, were inevitably subjected to.

The film's phenomenal popularity can be attributed to a number of factors. Thoughtful viewers are conscious of the film's powerfully evocative images of our country in the mid-nineteenth century, struggling with the persistent issue of slavery and the ubiquitous "Indian Problem." Those problems have unrelentingly dogged the American psyche for over 100 years and remain largely unresolved to this day. But perhaps more to the point, the character of Lieutenant Dunbar is very appealing to today's audience precisely because he is a 1990s man, not an 1860s white man. Dunbar is for the Baby Boomer generation the disillusioned soldier seeking personal redemption in a wilderness experience. In the process he is literally transformed before our eyes from an officer into a Lakota warrior. He tells the quietly deranged Major Fambrough that he wants to be stationed in the west to "see the frontier . . . before it's gone." That simple, childlike desire touches an unspoken yearning in many Americans, young and old. Who can blame Dunbar for wanting to escape the mass killing of the Civil War battlefields?

Confronting the solitude of Fort Sedgewick we are only provided with a presumption that the military post had been abandoned, not plundered by Indians. Actually the filmmakers reportedly filmed a segment showing the nearly starving and desertion-ridden garrison abandoning the fort. Nevertheless, as Dunbar surveys his post we are treated to an elevated back panning shot revealing a disturbing foreground scene of the former soldiers' hovels burrowed in the hill, a fouled water source littered with trash and partially devoured animal carcasses. It is clear the white men from the East have been reduced to a condition that is truly barbaric by their attempt to conquer the Indians and their natural world. We witness Lieutenant Dunbar cleaning up the animal carcasses and the trash and filling in the burrow holes, just as sensible Americans everywhere work to heal the ecological mess the first wave of Euro-Americans have left in their frenzy to possess the American landscape. Still, Lieutenant Dunbar's growth in ecological consciousness and personal transformation into a "native" is gradual and incremental. First his beard, then his jacket, his hat, and then his moustache is exchanged for Lakota breastplate armor, knife, and long hair with feathers. His journal entries speak of his awe and love of this new territory, although he habitually longs for company. Done entirely on location, Dean Semler's stunning cinematography effectively captures the unspoiled plains biosphere. It becomes apparent to Dunbar and the audience that he can find an unexpected satisfaction in relationships with animals (Two Sox and Cisco) as well as the natural world around him. His first instinct upon seeing the wolf later called Two Sox is to raise his rifle and kill it. Only as he pauses do we begin to realize he is truly changing, perhaps driven by loneliness to allow the magnificent predator to live.

The pivotal event in Dunbar's transformation is just prior to the magnificently photographed buffalo hunt. As Ten Bears's band approach the herd they come upon two dozen buffalo carcasses, shot for their hides with the bodies left to rot upon the plains. Although the mass slaughter of buffalo became rampant a few years later, the scene evokes strong emotions—we know this is only the beginning. Dunbar notes in his journal, "Who would do such a thing? The field was proof enough that it was a people without value and without soul, with no regard for Sioux rights. The wagon tracks leading away left little doubt, and my heart sank as I knew it could only be white hunters." Not seen in the theatrical release is a scene of Dunbar coming upon Ten Bears's hunting camp as a scalp dance is in progress. Fresh white scalps are seen and the suggestion is that the white buffalo hunters have been discovered and killed.

In the buffalo hunt audiences are treated to a sight not witnessed for over 120 years. To be sure it was for Native Americans the high point of the movie. Bareback Lakota hunters are shown charging among a thunderous avalanche of large and dangerous bison. Non-Indians are shown that this too is a part of the natural order, a world of predator and game animals. In the feasting and celebrations that follow, we see Dunbar begin to exchange his uniform for native attire. When Dunbar returns to Fort Sedgewick, he builds a fire and dances around it alone. Powerful drumbeats rhythmically signal a deeper transformation of Dunbar as he joins in the rhythm of the earth and perhaps harks back to a race memory of his own neolithic ancestors.

It is the next day that Kicking Bird gives Dunbar his Indian name, Dances With Wolves, after the Indians witness his extraordinary relationship with the wolf Two Sox. Interestingly enough, it is the white captive Stands With Fists who mentors and entices Dances With Wolves deeper into Lakota culture, teaching him the language and thus opening up communication between the Indians and this newcomer to their land. The significance of this should not be underestimated. Those who wish to embrace the land physically and spiritually must first learn how from its native people. When Dances With Wolves and Stands With Fists first embrace near a stream we cannot ignore the cattail pollen that fills the air around them—symbolizing germination of their new love for one another and also a new ecological consciousness among the Euro-Americans who have embraced the Indians. Their marriage follows and represents not only the union of the white woman who had preceded Dunbar in her own transformation into an "Indian woman," but also a final rite of passage of Dances With Wolves into a tribal citizen.

Yet another scene missing from the theatrical release occurred after the marriage. In this instance, Kicking Bird and Dances With Wolves encounter a sacred forested area that whites had recently despoiled. The bloated bodies of dozens of small animals killed for target practice swarming with flies, half-consumed deer, and empty whisky bottles littered the landscape. It was this senseless carnage that ultimately prompts Dances With Wolves to tell Kicking Bird that whites will be coming, "more than can be counted, . . . like the stars." When this frightening specter is revealed to Ten Bears he seems unable to grasp the terrible physical and ecological carnage that we know will eventually envelop the Lakota and all other Indians.

Perhaps because that scene was excised from the print of the film the public saw, the shock value of the capture of Dances With Wolves by the regarrisoned Fort soldiers is more powerful. As if to underscore the ominous hints of the impending campaigns to ruthlessly exploit or destroy the winged creatures, those that crawled, the two-legged, and the four-legged, we witness the recently metamorphized Dances With Wolves/Dunbar captured after the soldiers heartlessly kill his beloved buckskin Cisco. In the brutal interrogation that follows, despite kicks, punches, and clubbing with a rifle, Dances With Wolves refuses to cooperate in "hunting hostiles and returning white captives." We know Dances With Wolves has completely assumed his Lakota persona when he refuses to speak English to his captors. As he is being transported back to Fort Hays, his brutal escorts stop long enough to kill his companion Two Sox. In a shot that cinematically tells us all we need to know, as this scene progresses the camera reveals that just behind the ridge on which Two Sox is killed a Lakota rescue party is tracking the soldiers. Naturally the brutal despoilers of Lakota territory are summarily dispatched in stylish Hollywood fashion. This is a very satisfying scene for 1990s audiences. The Indians on an ecologically moral high ground become a kind of environmental SWAT team for the future Americans.

If there is any lingering question about the meaning of all this personal transformation and evolution of ecological ethos for this new white man and woman who have internalized Lakota culture, it is confirmed in the film's final scene. Deciding his presence will only further endanger his Lakota brothers, Dances With Wolves and Stands With Fists sadly leave their mentors to their inevitable fate and strike off on their own, perhaps to search for an America where they can live in peace and flourish with a new ecological ethos. While exchanging parting gifts, Dances With Wolves tells Kicking Bird, "You were the first man I ever wanted to be like. I will not forget you." Indians know that no white man or woman can become Indian, but many of us hope those who have learned of our cultures and appreciate their unique humanity will be our friends and allies in protecting the earth and all of her children. An interesting postscript to this tale of personal transformation and rebirth of an ecologically sound ethos for the Plains has a parallel in real life. Currently efforts are under way to create a "buffalo commons" amid the failed federal-subsidized farming that replaced the great Plains buffalo range. Imagine, a huge area where buffalo could again roam free! Perhaps the Ghost Dance prophets were right: the buffalo may be returning after all.

While Hollywood has a dismal record of employing Indian actors and technical staff, *Dances With Wolves* has clearly demonstrated that an American Indian presence in a film can make it work. The Native American actors naturally lent an air of authenticity to the work. This viewer, like thousands of other Native Americans, remains mystified as to why Hollywood still continues to employ non-Indian actors in red-face to play speaking parts (e.g., Trevor Howard in *Windwalker*). Many of us had hoped that Dan George's endearing performance of "Old Lodgeskins" in Arthur Penn's *Little Big Man* would throw open the doors of opportunity for Indian actors. It didn't happen then, but happily today we again have a major film with a number of important and significant roles for Native Americans. Certainly Tantoo Cardinal, Nathan Lee Chasing His Horse, Graham Green, Rodney Grant, and Floyd Red Crow Westerman created memorable performances and demonstrated there is a significant pool of talented Native American actors out there.

Responsible for a good deal of the authenticity of the Indian roles was South Dakota's Sinte Gleska Indian College Linguist Doris Leader Charge. She is the Lakota linguist who translated Michael Blake's screenplay into Lakota, coached the actors in the language, and played a small role in the film. This was no small feat, since none of the actors spoke Lakota confidently. However, the Indian grapevine reports that among the Plains Indians it was the twenty-four Native American bareback stunt riders who charged in among a 3,500-strong herd of buffalo (a feat that had not been accomplished in more than a century) who were the true heroes of the film. My Cheyenne and Comanche friends tell me the buffalo hunt alone was worth the price of admission. No doubt about it, Costner counted coup (gained honor by taking risks) on all Hollywood Indian movies and touched something deeply significant in the Plains Indian cultures with that magnificent buffalo hunt.

Some audiences and critics have commented on the violence in the film and called it excessive. Especially disturbing and painful to watch is the Pawnee killing of the muleskinner Timmons. In Stands With Fists's childhood flashback, we witness a hatchet murder of a white farmer. When Pretty Shield (Doris Leader Charge) crushes a Pawnee skull with a burning log and Stands With Fists shoots another Pawnee during an attack, we clearly see these women are not to be messed with. The soldiers at the end of the film are particularly sadistic and themselves meet a brutal end. Even youth get in the act: after being pistol whipped Smiles A Lot kills the sadistic Sergeant Bauer by burying a hatchet into his chest to the hilt. As awful as these and other violent acts are, they hardly compare to the violence of the real American frontier. Despite a highly romantic and mythologized popular view of the American past, the American Indian frontier was an incredibly heartless, sordid, violent, and chaotic scramble by Euro-Americans to get something (Indian land and resources) for nothing. For viewers upset over this cinematic tip of an iceberg of violence that Costner reveals for the popcorn-eating masses, I suggest they stick to Roy Rogers Westerns or similar pablum. Costner has reminded all popular culture consumers of the violent underpinnings of the American Indian policy.

I suppose it is inevitable and perhaps de rigueur that comparisons will be made between Costner's epic and other recent films that prominently feature Indian culture and actors or themes. Thematically, perhaps *Windwalker* (1973) makes the best comparison. That film also featured a mythological death and rebirth. Furthermore, it also took pains to show Indian society in a positive light, where grandparents, children, and families dominate the portrait of Cheyenne society just prior to sustained colonial contact. While *Windwalker* does feature a touching love story, it is somewhat troublesome to Indians that its most important leads are played by non-Indians. Many writers have commented on the extensive use of the Lakota language in Costner's film, but it was not the first such use in Indian films; in fact, *Windwalker* holds that distinction. (*Little Big Man* began using Cheyenne but soon switched over to English.) However, it is probably the brooding and melancholy American Playhouse epic *Roanoak* (1986) that best utilized an Indian language effectively to demonstrate communication problems between whites and America's native people.

A film that may not be considered by critics as an Indian film but nevertheless shows some important links to mainstream Indian films is Clint Eastwood's *The Outlaw Josey Wales* (1975). This last great American Western was adapted from Cherokee writer Forrest Carter's novel *Gone to Texas.* On the surface it is about an embittered and extremely violent Civil War guerrilla's attempt to escape the madness of the Reconstruction South. It could be interpreted as another attempt to retell the familiar story of a lone white man on the Indian frontier who ultimately attracts an ethnically diverse following, ultimately makes peace with local Indians, and finds physical and spiritual refuge in that diverse milieu. Especially memorable in the Phillip Kaufman–Sonia Chernuss adaptation of Carter's story is the charming performance of Dan George as Confederate Cherokee Lone Watie and Will Sampsom in a powerful and menacing role as the Comanche chief Ten Bears.

One can almost feel sorry for the "creative talents" that recently completed the four-hour mini-series adaptation of Evan S. Connell's *Son of Morning Star* (1991). This utterly boring, dramaless, flat, one-dimensional, and totally humorless attempt to tell the story of Lieutenant Colonel George Armstrong Custer's career and his fateful encounter at Little Big Horn is a lesson for filmmakers everywhere. While it was laudable for its conscientious attempt to give an even-handed account of the clash of Americans and Plains Indians, its Indians were not allowed to speak. All native reactions and motivations are relegated to a voice-over narration (Buffy St. Marie) that instead of providing insights further isolates the Indians by denying them a voice in history. It is perhaps symptomatic of the contempt network moguls hold for their audiences. In contrast, PBS programmers offered the haunting *Roanoak*, in which more than two-thirds of the film is in the Chippewa dialect.

Unquestionably the film that invites most comparison is Arthur Penn's 1970 classic *Little Big Man*. Again we find the theme of a white man encountering the Indians and discovering their humanity. Yet that bawdy parody of the American frontier only focused on Indians for less than one-third of its screen time. The real similarities of the two films lay in their unusual juxtaposition of humor and drama. Jack Crabbe's humorous sexual encounter with his wife's three sisters is immediately followed by Custer's murderous attack upon the Cheyenne camp at Washita River, where his wife and newborn child are massacred along with many others. In a similar vein, *Dances With Wolves* invites us to laugh both with and at the ignorant mule skinner Timmons only to shortly witness his frightening murder by Pawnee. Both films featured an elaborate and memorable set piece; for Costner it was the buffalo hunt, in Penn's film it was the reenactment of the battle of Greasy Grass (Custer's Last Stand). However, significant differences exist. Penn's film was made at the height of the Vietnam War and emphasized the military assault on America's native peoples. Costner's film, on the other hand, is concerned with the reestablishment of a spiritual and ecologically sound American ethic with which Euro-Americans can enter the twenty-first century. Costner has been widely quoted as calling his film his personal love letter to the past. It also seems to offer one artist's optimistic blueprint for a new America, where a spiritually based and ecologically sound future awaits those willing to learn from this land's first children.

There is an alternative interpretation of *Dances With Wolves* that cannot be ignored by those knowledgeable about Native American shamanistic traditions. Costner's film can be interpreted as a shamanistic allegory of symbolic death and rebirth. From this perspective, Dunbar in fact "dies" in his suicidal ride before Confederate pickets at St. David's field but not in the same manner as the spy in Robert Enrico's brilliant adaptation of Ambrose Bierce's *An Occurrence at Owl Creek Bridge* (1961). All of the film's events immediately following this "death" are part of his journey to the Land of the Dead. As this is understood in most tribal societies, there are a number of dangerous trials along the way. But perhaps more important, it is a similar symbolic death (coma) which precedes the acquisition of spiritual knowledge by individuals who are to become shamans. There are a number of intriguing clues that this could be a subtext to the surface story. In many Indian cultures the Land of the Dead is in this world, but at a distance in one of the cardinal directions. For instance, when Dunbar journeys to the West he stops in a field of wild wheat and carefully caresses the ripe stocks. Similarly, when we first encounter the Lakota shaman, Kicking Bird, he also stands among the wild wheat caressing it in exactly the same manner as Dunbar. Did he sense a new spiritual presence in his midst?

When the Lakota in council are discussing the appearance of a lone white man in their territory, the impatient Wind In His Hair argues in favor of going to

Fort Sedgewick and shooting him with arrows and adds that if he has "power" (spiritual power) he will not be harmed. Did Wind In His Hair and others suspect this was no normal man? A neophyte shaman trains under the tutelage of a more experienced shaman, and we note the special relationship that Kicking Bird develops with Dunbar. In fact, Kicking Bird is anxious to communicate with Dunbar to acquire knowledge that Dunbar may possess. Later Kicking Bird declares, "I see one white man alone, without fear in our country. I do not think he is lost, I think he might have medicine [spiritual knowledge/power]."

Later, as Ten Bears's band is becoming alarmed by their failure to find the buffalo, it is Dunbar who discovers the herd in a decidedly surrealistic scene. He fearlessly walks toward a thundering herd of buffalo charging at night in a blue, dreamlike mist. Dunbar shares his sighting (vision?) with Ten Bears's band and it proves to be accurate.

The acquisition of native shamanistic power is commonly derived from developing a compact with an earth or animal spirit that appears in one's ecstatic journeys to the Land of the Dead or spirit world. Could the wolf, Two Sox, have been Dunbar's spiritual ally and assisted in his transformation from a normal man into a man of power? Sometimes Indian doctors emerge from trances and assume new names. Viewers will recall Kicking Bird's observation of Dunbar's highly unusual relationship with the (spiritually) powerful wolf and the coining of his (Dunbar's) new name.

The buffalo hunt seems to be the pivotal point of the film from many perspectives. One way of explaining Dunbar's unexpected hunting prowess is the "power" he may have received from his powerful predator ally wolf.

Especially interesting in this respect is Wind In His Hair's revelation that Stands With Fists's first husband was his best friend. He then goes on to say, "It has been hard for me to like you. But now I think he went away because you were coming."

Did not Dunbar's secret power (hidden rifles) help the Lakotas defeat their Pawnee enemies? When native societies were on the verge of collapse because of deadly introduced diseases and the destruction of native land and resources, new religious leaders arose who recombined old religious elements with new moral teachings. The Pueblo shaman Pope, the Shawnee prophet Tenskawatawa, and the Paiute Wovoka led messianic religious movements to revitalize their suffering people morally. The Ghost Dance is for many Americans the most familiar of these movements. When Dances With Wolves decides to leave Ten Bears's people he declared, "I must go . . . I must try and talk to those who would listen."

Could Dances With Wolves be the messiah the New Agers are seeking to lead the white man back to a balanced physical and spiritual embrace with he earth, our mother?

NOTES

Dances With Wolves

Director: Kevin Costner
Script: Michael Blake
Producer: Jim Wilson

Cinematography: Dean Semler
Music: John Barry
Editing: Neil Trans. Orion Pictures

1. Kevin Costner, et al., *Dances With Wolves, The Illustrated Story of the Epic Film* (New York: New Market Press, 1990).

2. William Miles, "Enamored with Civilization: Isaac McCoy's Plan for Indian Reform," *Kansas Historian* 38 (1972): 268–286.

3. Thomas W. Dunlay, *Wolves for the Blue Soldiers, Indian Scouts and Auxiliaries with the United States Army, 1860–90* (Lincoln: University of Nebraska Press, 1987).

4. Martha Royce Blaine, *The Pawnees: A Critical Bibliography* (Bloomington: Indiana University Press, 1979).

5. Richard Drinnon, *Facing West: The Metaphysics of Indian Hating and Empire Building* (New York: New American Library, 1980).

6. Costner et al., *Dances With Wolves*, p. 44.

7. Robert M. Utley, *Frontier Regulars, The United States Army and the Indian, 1866–1891* (New York: Macmillan, 1973).

8. Wilber S. Nye, *Bad Medicine and Good, Tales of the Kiowas* (Norman: University of Oklahoma Press, 1962).

9. Utley, *Frontier Regulars*, pp. 150–156.

Faye Ginsburg

Screen Memories and Entangled Technologies: Resignifying Indigenous Lives

In the summer of 1998, I found myself in the midst of paparazzi, limousines, and Native Americans, for the opening of *Smoke Signals* at the New York City branch of the National Museum of the American Indian. The film, directed by Chris Eyre, the only Cheyenne descendant to attend NYU film school, is the first independent narrative fiction feature created and acted by Native Americans. It tells a latter-day coming of age saga of two young Coeur d'Alene men tied by the loss of their fathers and their dilemmas of cultural identity, a story adapted by screenwriter Sherman Alexie (Spokane) from his book, *The Lone Ranger and Tonto Fistfight in Heaven* (1994). *Smoke Signals* opened to critical acclaim, got picked up by Miramax, a major American film distributor, and played in major theaters throughout the United States, an unqualified cross-cultural success on any culture's terms.

When I arrived on a balmy June night for the opening at the museum, I was stunned and amused to have to make my way through a line of slickly dressed handlers and pushy journalists who were there as part of the entourage of the two movie stars in attendance, Matt Damon and Winona Ryder (who had recently come out as a strong supporter of Native American causes). While the patina of glamour was exciting, the event's great appeal was the convergence of that glitter with the more grounded spirit of community celebration. In an evening filled with both cultural pride and irreverence, people who had worked on the film joked with, thanked, and praised one another in an auditorium filled with Native American performers and artists and many other fellow travelers and supporters. Author and co-producer Sherman Alexie looked around him at the posh auditorium and offered an impeccably gauged moment of sardonic "Indian humor" that spoke volumes about the distance between the "here" of the evening and the "there" of the film (and his youth) set on an economically marginal "res" (reservation). Gesturing to the elegant stage and screen of the museum, Alexie suggested that an "authentic" viewing of the film would require an old black-and-white television on the stage, topped by rabbit ears covered with tin foil to help capture the signal. After the

This is an expanded version of "Screen Memories: Resignifying the Traditional in Indigenous Media," published in *Media Worlds: Anthropology on New Terrain*, edited by Faye Ginsburg, Lila Abu-Lughod, and Brian Larkin (University of California Press, 2002).

screening, the Native American a capella women's singing group Ulali performed, followed by a traditional men's drum group.

The sense of community accomplishment that accompanied the opening of *Smoke Signals* was heightened by the unspoken recognition that American Indians are finally able to produce their own images and narratives that can effectively speak back to a U.S. cinema industry that has flourished on the marketing of stereotyped depictions of their lives, cultures, and histories. In a poignantly reflexive moment in the film, the philosophical character Thomas, one of the movie's two young protagonists, comments wryly on the costs of that circumstance to Native American subjectivity: "The only thing more pathetic than seeing Indians on TV is seeing Indians sitting around watching Indians on TV." Nonetheless, Thomas admits, reluctantly, to having watched *Dances With Wolves* multiple times. The film also provides a way to speak to audiences from the dominant culture for whom the lives and sensibilities of native peoples are a cipher; and finally, to speak for and about Native American communities, through the compelling voices of a generation of cultural activists who are finally "wiping the warpaint off the lens," the apt phrase that is the title of a forthcoming book on native media by Santa Clara Pueblo scholar and filmmaker Beverly Singer (2002). This anecdote indicates how crucial it is to understand these media not just as texts but also as embedded in a world of cultural production, tracking how they acquire meaning and value over time through multiple circuits of social circulation.

Cultural Activism and the Activist Imaginary

The opening of *Smoke Signals* is one particularly public event in a much more long-standing process in which indigenous and minority peoples have begun to take up a range of media in order to "talk back" to structures of power that have erased or distorted their interests and realities. The work they have been producing might be considered cultural activism, a term that underscores the sense of both political agency and cultural intervention that people bring to these efforts, part of a spectrum of practices of self-conscious mediation and mobilization of culture that took particular shape beginning in the late twentieth century. Indigenous media[1] developed in response to the entry of mass media into the lives of First Nations people, primarily through the imposition of satellites and commercial television. In almost every instance, they have struggled to turn that circumstance to their advantage, a point effectively made by activist researcher Eric Michaels in the central desert of Australia where, in the 1980s, he worked with Warlpiri people to develop their own low-power television—what he called *The Aboriginal Invention of Television in Central Australia* (1986)—as an alternative to the onslaught of commercial television.[2] Such formations are typically small in scale and offer an alternative to the mass media industries that dominate late capitalist societies; they occupy a comfortable position of difference from dominant cultural assumptions about media aesthetics and practices.

The range of the work is wide, moving from small-scale community-based videos, to broadcast quality television, to major independent art and feature films. Indigenous people who live in or closer to metropoles, such as the urban Australian Aboriginal filmmakers discussed in this essay, participate in a wider world of media imagery production and circulation (e.g., national film and television industries), and feel their claim to an indigenous identity within a more cosmopolitan framework is sometimes regarded as inauthentic. Debates about such work reflect the changing status of "culture," which is increasingly objectified and mediated as it becomes a source of claims for political and human rights both nationally and on the world stage. As Terry Turner has shown regarding the work of Kayapo mediamakers living in the Brazilian Amazon, cultural claims "can be converted into political assets, both internally as bases of group solidarity and mobilization, and externally as claims on the support of other social groups, governments and public opinion all over the globe" (1993, p. 424). Appadurai (1996) suggests the word *culturalism* to denote the mobilization of identities in which mass media and the imagination play an increasingly significant role. This activist objectification of culture encompasses not only indigenous work but media being produced by other colonized and minority subjects who have become involved in creating their own representations as a counter to dominant systems, a framework that includes work being done by people with AIDS (Juhasz, 1995), Palestinians in Israel's occcupied territories (Kuttab 1993); the transnational Hmong refugee community (Schein, 2002), and African American musicians (Mahon, 2000).

The broader questions this work raises—whether minority or dominated subjects can assimilate media to their own cultural and political concerns or are inevitably compromised by its presence—still haunts much of the research and debate on the topic of the cross-cultural spread of media. In the context of indigenous peoples, some anthropologists have expressed alarm at these developments (Faris, 1992); they see these new practices as destructive of cultural difference and the study of such work as "ersatz anthropology" (Weiner, 1997), echoing the concerns over the destructive effects of mass culture first articulated by intellectuals of the Frankfurt School.[3] Other scholars actively support indigenous media production while recognizing the dilemmas that it presents. Roth, for example, queries whether a state supported Aboriginal Peoples Television Network in Canada is a breakthrough or a "media reservation" (Roth, 2002), presenting a kind of Faustian contract with the technologies of modernity, enabling some degree of agency to control representation under less than ideal conditions (Ginsburg, 1991). However, the capacity to narrate stories and retell histories from an indigenous point of view—"screen memories"—through media forms that can circulate beyond the local has been an important force for constituting claims for land and cultural rights, and for developing alliances with other communities. The anthropologist and filmmaker Harald Prins, who has catalyzed indigenous filmmaking for Native American claims to land and cultural rights, nonetheless points out "the paradox of primitivism" in which traditional imagery of indigenous people in documentaries about native rights, while effective and perhaps even essential as a form of political agency, may distort the cultural processes that indigenous peoples are committed to preserving (Prins, 1997). Others, on the other hand, make a compelling argument that despite the colonial origins of film and photography, it is now so firmly inserted into everyday practice that it is best seen at the confluence of overlapping visual regimes rather than the province of one (Pinney, 1998, p. 112).

Meanwhile, as anthropologists and media scholars debate the impact that media technologies might have on the communities with which they work, indigenous mediamakers are busy using the technologies for their own purposes. Activists are documenting traditional activities with elders; creating works to teach young people literacy in their own languages; engaging with dominant circuits of mass media to project political struggles through mainstream as well as alternative arenas; communicating among dispersed kin and communities on a range of issues; using video as legal documents in negotiations with states; presenting videos on state television to assert their presence televisually within national imaginaries; or creating award-winning feature films.

Rather than casting judgment on these efforts to use media as forms of expressive culture and political engagement, a number of us see in the growing use of film and other mass media an increasing awareness and strategic objectification of culture. As Daniel Miller has argued regarding the growing use of media more generally,

> These new technologies of objectification [such as film, video, and television] . . .create new possibilities of understanding at the same moment that they pose new threats of alienation and rupture. Yet our first concern is not to resolve these contradictions in theory but to observe how people sometimes resolve or more commonly live out these contradictions in local practice. (1995, p. 18)

Whatever the contradictions, as new technologies have been embraced as powerful forms of collective self-production, they have enabled cultural activists to assert their presence in the polities that encompass them, and to enter more easily into much larger movements for social transformation for the recognition and redress of human and cultural rights, processes in which media play an increasingly important role (Castels, 1997). Yet, it is important to recognize that these processes are deeply rooted in some of the earliest cinematic cross-cultural encounters.

Entangled Technologies

In a familiar moment in the history of ethnographic film,[4] a well-known scene in Robert Flaherty's 1922 classic *Nanook of the North*, the character identified on the intertitle as "Nanook, Chief of the Ikivimuits" (played by Flaherty's friend and guide Allakariallak) is shown being amazed by a gramophone. He laughs and tests the record three times with his mouth. We now recognize the scene as a performance rather than documentation of first contact, an image that contradicts Flaherty's journals describing the Inuit's sophisticated response to these new recording technologies, as well as their technical expertise with them by the time the scene was filmed (Rotha, 1980). Like the gramophone scene, the film itself obscures the engagement with the cinematic process by Allakariallak and others who worked on the production of Flaherty's film in various ways as, in today's parlance, we might call technicians, camera operators, film developers, and production consultants. Not long after the character of Nanook had achieved fame in the United States and Europe, the person Allakariallak died of starvation in the Arctic. While he never passed on his knowledge of the camera and filmmaking directly to other Inuit, the unacknowledged help he gave Flaherty haunts Inuit producers today as a paradigmatic moment in a history of unequal-looking relations (Gaines, 1988). Their legendary facility with the camera—from imagining and setting up scenes, to helping develop rushes, to fixing the Aggie, as they called the camera— foreshadows their later entanglement with mediamaking on their own terms.

Figure 1. Photogravure of Allakariallak, who played the character Nanook, ca. 1920. Photo courtesy International Film Seminars.

The Nanook case reminds us that the current impact of media's rapidly increasing presence and circulation in the lives of people everywhere and the globalization of media that it is part of—whether one excoriates or embraces it—is not simply a phenomenon of the past two decades.[5] The sense of its contemporary novelty is in part the product of the deliberate erasure of indigenous ethnographic subjects as actual or potential participants in their own screen representations in the past century. These tensions between the past erasure and the current visibility of indigenous participation in film and video is central to the work of the Aboriginal mediamakers who are engaged in making what I call *screen memories*. Here I invert the sense in which Freud used this term to describe how people protect themselves from their traumatic past through layers of obfuscating memory (Freud, 1975, p. 247).[6] By contrast, indigenous people are using screen media not to mask but to recuperate their own collective stories and histories—some of them traumatic—that have been erased in the national narratives of the dominant culture, and are in danger of being forgotten within local worlds as well. Of course, retelling stories for the media of film, video, and television often requires reshaping them, not only within new aesthetic structures but in negotiation with the political economy of state-controlled as well as commercial media, as the following case makes clear.

The Development of Inuit Television

Half a century after *Nanook* was made, in the 1970s, the Inuit Tapirisat, a pan-Inuit activist organization, began agitating for a license from the Canadian government to establish their own Arctic satellite television service, the Inuit Broadcast Corporation (IBC), which was eventually licensed in 1981 (Marks, 1994). The Tapirisat's actions were a response to the launching over their remote lands of the world's first geostationary satellite to broadcast to northern Canada, *Anik B* (David, 1998). Unlike the small-scale encounter with Flaherty's film apparatus, Canadian Broadcast Corporation (CBC) television programming was dumped suddenly into Inuit lives and homes, as the government placed Telsat receiving dishes in nearly every northern community, with no thought to or provision for aboriginal content or local broadcast (Lucas, 1987, p. 15). The Inuit Tapirisat fought this imposition and eventually succeeded in gaining a part of the spectrum for their own use. The creation of the IBC—a production center for Inuit programming of all sorts—became an important development in the lives of contemporary Canadian Arctic people, as well as a model for the possibilities of the repurposing of communications technologies for indigenous peoples worldwide.

By 1983, it became apparent that while IBC programming was remarkably successful, distribution was still problematic, as Inuit work was slotted into the temporal margins of the CBC late-night schedules. In 1991, after considerable effort,[7] a satellite-delivered northern aboriginal distribution system, TV Northern Canada (TVNC), went to air, the first unified effort to serve almost 100 northern communities in English, French, and twelve aboriginal languages (Meadows, 1996; Roth, 1994). By 1997, TVNC, seeking ways to hook up with aboriginal producers in southern Canada, responded to a government call for proposals for a third national cable-based network that would expand beyond northern communities to reach all of Canada. The group was awarded the license and formed the Aboriginal Peoples Television Network (APTN). This publicly supported and indigenously controlled national aboriginal television network, the first of its kind in the world, officially went to air in September 1999 (David, 1998, p. 39).[8]

Rather than destroying Inuit cultures as some predicted would happen,[9] these technologies of representation—beginning with the satellite television transmission to Inuit communities of their own small-scale video productions—have played a dynamic and even revitalizing role for Inuit and other First Nations people, as a self-conscious means of cultural preservation and production, as well as a form of political mobilization. Repurposing satellite signals for teleconferencing also provides a practical vehicle for a range of community needs served by the acceleration of long-distance communication across vast Arctic spaces for everything from staying in touch with children attending regional high schools to the delivery of health care information (Brisebois, 1991; Marks, 1994).

Prominent among those producing work for these new aboriginal television networks is Inuit director and producer Sak Kunuk, a carver and former Inuit Broadcast Corporation producer. Kunuk has developed a community-based production group in Igloolik, the remote Arctic settlement where he lives, through a process that, ironically, evokes the method used by Robert Flaherty in *Nanook*. Kunuk works collaboratively with people of Igloolik, in particular elders, to create dramatic stories about life in the area around Igloolik in the 1930s, prior to settlement. Along with his partners, cultural director and lead actor Paloussie Quilitalik (a monolingual community elder) and technical director Norman Cohen, a Brooklynite relocated to Nunavut, who together make up the production group Igloolik Isuma, Sak has produced tapes such as *Qaggiq* (Gathering Place) (1989, 58 min.), which depicts a gathering of four families in a late winter Inuit camp in the 1930s; or *Nunavut* (Our Land) (1993–1995), a thirteen-part series of half-hour dramas that re-create the lives of five fictional families (played by Igloolik residents) through a year of traditional life in 1945, when the outside world is at war and a decade before government settlements changed that way of life forever.[10]

These screen memories of Inuit life are beloved locally and in other Inuit communities. They also have been admired in art and independent film circles in metropolitan centers for their beauty, ethnographic sensibility, humor, intimacy, and innovative improvisational method.[11] While reinforcing Inuktitut language and skills for younger members of the community, at a more practical and quotidian level, the project provides interest and employment for people in Igloolik

Figure 2. Igloolik Isuma Productions Executive Committee, 1990 Baffin Island. Photo courtesy Igloolik Isuma, www.isuma.ca.

(Berger, 1995a, b; Fleming, 1991, 1996; Marks, 1994). For Inuit participants and viewers, Igloolik Isuma serves as a dynamic effort to resignify cultural memory on their own terms. Not only is their work providing a record of a heretofore undocumented legacy at a time when the generation still versed in traditional knowledge is rapidly passing, but by involving young people in the process, the production of these historical dramas requires that they learn Inuktitut and a range of other skills tied to their cultural legacies, thus helping to mitigate a crisis in the social and cultural reproduction of Inuit life. In the words of an Igloolik elder posted on their web site, "We strongly believe this film has helped in keeping our traditional way of life alive and to our future generations it will make them see how our ancestors used to live."[12] In December 2000, they premiered *Atanarjuat* (The Fast Runner), the world's first feature-length dramatic film written, produced, and acted by Inuit, based on a traditional Igloolik legend, set in sixteenthth-century Igloolik. Since then, *Atanarjuat* went on to take the Camera D'Or prize at the 2001 Cannes Film Festival (awarded to the best first film), picking up more prizes as it circulated around the globe; it finally opened in March 2002 in New York City as part of the prestigious New Directors/New Films series.

There are those who argue that television of any sort is inherently destructive to Inuit (and other indigenous) lives and cultural practices. This is despite the

Figure 3. Atanarjuat, the legendary Inuit hero played by Natar Ungalaaq, escapes his enemies. Production still from Atanarjuat, The Fast Runner, *2002, directed by Zacharias Kunuk.* Photo courtesy Lot 47 Films.

fact that many of those participating in it had themselves been critical of the potential deleterious effects of media, and sought ways to engage with media that would have a positive effect on local life. They are also acutely aware of the necessity of such work in a wider context in which native minorities in Canada are struggling for self-determination. For them, these media practices are part of a broader project of constituting a cultural future in which their traditions and contemporary technologies are combined in ways that can give new vitality to Inuit life. This is apparent not only in the narrative constructions of Inuit history on their own terms, but in the social practice of making the work, and in seeing it integrated with Canadian modernity, embodied in the flow of television. One outside observer, after spending time in the Arctic in the 1980s in a number of settlements where Inuit were making community-based videos about their lives for the IBC, concluded that

> The most significant aspect of the IBC's progammes is that they are conceived and produced by the Inuit themselves . . . and it brings a new authority to the old oral culture. . . . When IBC producers first approached elders in order to record songs and stories from their childhood, they took a lot of persuading because many believed that these activities had been officially banned by missionaries. But now, as old crafts and skills have appeared on the IBC screens, so they have proliferated in the settlements. Watching the fabric of their everyday lives, organized into adequate if not glossy TV packages introduced by titles set in Inuktitut syllabics, has helped to weaken for the Inuit the idea that only the whites, with the unrelenting authority of the literate

and educated south, can make the final decisions on the value of the Inuit lifestyle. (Lucas, 1987, p. 17)

This effort to turn the tables on the historical trajectory of the power relations embedded in research monographs, photography, and ethnographic practice is intentional, a deeply felt response to the impact of such representational practices on Inuit society and culture. Thus, it is not only that the *activity* of media-making has helped to revive relations between generations and skills that had nearly been abandoned. The *fact* of their appearance on television on *Inuit* terms, inverts the usual hierarchy of values attached to the dominant culture's technology, conferring new prestige to Inuit "culture-making."

Claims to the Nation: Aboriginal Media in Australia

A decade after the Inuit postwar encounter with televisual media, indigenous Australians faced a similar crossroads. In part due to their early consultation with Inuit producers and activists, they too decided to "invent Aboriginal television" (Micheals, 1986), initially by making video images and narratives about and for themselves, shown locally via illegal low-power outback television similar to the Inuit projects described above. By the late 1990s, Aboriginal media production had expanded from very local television in remote settlements to feature films made by urban filmmakers that have premiered at the Cannes Film Festival. Today, the people who are engaged in media work across many divisions within Aboriginal life are themselves influenced by the shifting structures of the Australian polity that have provided resources and ideological frameworks for the development of indigenous media.[13]

The embrace of media—film, video, television—as a form of indigenous expression coincided with an increasing sense of empowerment for Aboriginal people that has accelerated since the 1960s. Until the 1996 elections, which brought in the conservative government headed by John Howard, Australian social policy under Labor Party leadership had made a commitment to social justice for indigenous Australians, establishing in 1990 an indigenous body, the Aboriginal and Torres Straits Islanders Commission (ATSIC)—a complex and sometimes controversial Aboriginal bureaucracy—to govern the affairs of Aboriginal people.[14] In these kinds of formations, media played an increasingly important role in dramatizing Aboriginal claims on the nation. By the 1980s, as part of their demands, both remote living and urban activists increasingly insisted on Aboriginal control over media representation of their lives and communities, which quickly escalated into explicit interest in gaining access to production. At the same time, Aboriginal culture was becoming critical to a distinctive Australian national imaginary linked to its land and oriented away from its European origins. The evident and often conflicting interests of both

Aboriginal Australians and the Australian state in media as a site for the production of local identity and sociality as well as claims to a presence in the national imaginary is apparent in the extraordinary development of indigenous media over the past two decades.[15]

Questions about the impact of mass media on Aboriginal lives first received widespread public attention in the mid-1980s with plans for the launching of Australia's first communications satellite over central Australia. As in the Inuit case, its launch generated considerable debate among Aboriginal people, policy makers, and academics about the impact of "dumping" mainstream television signals into traditional indigenous communities in this remote desert area (Ginsburg, 1991, 1993; Michaels, 1986). To preempt the impact of the satellite, the Warlpiri-speaking Aboriginal community of Yuendumu, with the help of American adviser and researcher Eric Michaels, developed its own video production and low-power television station, enabling it to make and show its own productions, in place of the imposition of mainstream Australian television via satellite. It became a model for government efforts to duplicate its success through some not very effective schemes to bureaucratize efforts to bring indigenously governed small media to other Aboriginal outback settlements.[16] Through Michaels' writing, scholars alarmed at the wasteland of television took Warlpiri low-power television as exemplary of the possibilities of alternative TV production, distribution, and reception, although few seem concerned with what has actually happened either to WMA or with Aboriginal media more generally since the late 1980s, despite considerable changes that have occurred.

Since its inception in 1983, WMA has had an unpredictable life based on the presence or absence of certain key players in the community such as Michaels, as well as the variable reliability of white advisers whose crucial impact on these operations—both negative and positive—has been neglected in the analysis of these projects. Frances Jupurrurla Kelly, the Warlpiri man with whom Eric Michaels worked very closely (1994), carried on the work of WMA for a number of years after Michael's death in 1988, but increasingly acquired other responsibilities in his community that made it difficult for him to sustain the same level of activity and interest. It was only in the late 1990s that WMA was reactivated with the presence for a few years of an energetic and entrepreneurial young white adviser and the renewed interest of community members, especially women, in using video to record their efforts to solve some of their community problems. Most recently, radio has become a focus of community interest.

Since the late 1990s, with the growth of the indigenous media sector across Australia, WMA has been involved intermittently with co-productions. In 1997, WMA worked with two other groups—a regional as well as a national indigenous media association—to produce a piece for a new initiative, the National Indigenous Documentary Series,[17] meant to reflect media being produced in Aboriginal communities throughout Australia and broadcast in late 1997 on the American Broadcasting Corporation (ABC), Australia's prestigious state-sponsored channel. Such efforts are much applauded for supporting cooperation between remote and urban Aboriginal people. However, attention to the production process reveals some of the tensions inherent in trying to bring remote Aboriginal media, produced at its own pace for members of the Warlpiri community, into the domain of broadcast television's relentless, industrially driven programming schedules and the imperative to attract mass audiences.

In this case, WMA decided to create a piece about the activities of some of the senior women at Yuendumu who had organized what they had called Munga Wardingki Partu (Night Patrol) to control drinking, abuse, and petrol sniffing at Yuendumu.[18] For a community used to producing video on its own terms and time frame, outside the industrial logics of dominant television practice, the need to have a work on schedule for the anticipated national air date on the ABC and one that could be understood by diverse television audiences created considerable tension during the production process. Indeed, during the delay from the time the proposal had to be submitted to the ATSIC bureaucracy until the project was approved and funding was available, the night patrol had become relatively inactive (in part due to its success) although it managed to reconstitute itself for the documentary. Still, WMA was having difficulty meeting the broadcast deadlines.

Eventually, Rachel Perkins, a Sydney-based Aboriginal filmmaker (whose work I discuss in detail below) and executive producer of the series, called in Pat Fiske, an experienced and sympathetic white documentary filmmaker, to help WMA complete the piece on schedule, with a time frame of only three weeks and a small budget. The working style required by such constraints was a source of friction; what in the dominant culture is regarded as a normal production schedule under such circumstances—twelve hours a day—was not appropriate to the pace of life at Yuendumu. To complicate things further, every senior woman who had served on the night patrol insisted on being interviewed (and paid) although it wasn't possible to include them all in the half hour of time they were allotted for the show. Decisions had to be made as well as to how to show some of the scenes where violence occurs, finally agreeing to stylize them in a way that obscured the identity of the people involved. In the end, it is one of the few works of indigenous media that address these kinds of community-based problems positively by focusing on efforts to solve them internally. Despite the difficulties in making it, people at Yuendumu now proudly claim *Munga Wardingki Partu* as their own.[19] It was considered one of the more innovative pieces in the national series and has translated successfully to non-Aboriginal audiences abroad as well.[20]

Aboriginality and National Narratives

Aboriginal participation and visibility in the Australian mediascape has developed not only for local access to video in remote areas, but also for more Aboriginal representation on national television and, most recently in Australia's lively independent film culture, which is one of the nation's most visible exports. The concern to be included in that dimension of Australia's culture industries is not simply about equal access to the professional opportunities but a recognition that distortion or invisibility of Aboriginal realities for the wider Australian public and even international audiences can have potentially powerful effects on political culture. Aboriginal activists from urban areas were particularly vocal in demanding a positive and creative presence on state-run national television such as Australia's ABC and its alternative multicultural channel, the SBS. The indigenous units that were established out of that moment became an important base for a small and talented group of young urban Aboriginal cultural activists—many of them children of the leaders of the Aboriginal civil rights movement—to forge a cohort and gain the professional experience and entree that is placing them and their work onto national and international stages.

The twenty or so urban Aboriginal people who have entered filmmaking recognize the potential their work has to change the way that Aboriginal realities are understood for the wider Australian public and even international audiences. As a case in point, I want briefly to track the career of Rachel Perkins. The daughter of the late Charlie Perkins, a well-known Aboriginal activist/politician and former sports hero, she exemplifies those most active on the indigenous media scene today, a generation of cultural activists who came of age when the struggle for Aboriginal civil rights was already a social fact, due in large measure to the efforts of their parents. She grew up with new political possibilities in place, but a recognition that the world of representations and the cultural spaces available for them were not so easily changed. For example, when she was born in 1970, just after citizenship was granted to Aboriginal Australians in 1967, blacks and whites were still segregated in cinemas in some parts of Australia.

In 1988, at the age of eighteen, hoping to gain some skills in media and make some contact with Arrernte people, from which her family was descended, Rachel trained originally at a regional Aboriginal media association[21] that serves both remote communities and the small towns and cities that dot Australia's Northern Territory. Once there, she worked her way up to produce and direct language and current affairs programs. In 1991, Rachel came to Sydney to head the indigenous unit of the Special Broadcast Service (SBS), Australia's state-run multicultural television station.[22] While there, she commissioned and produced *Blood Brothers* (1992), a series of four one-hour documentaries focused on different aspects of Aboriginal history and culture told through the personal lives of four prominent Aboriginal men. Her agenda was, in a sense, to find a way to create "screen memories" for the majority of Australians—black and white—who knew virtually nothing of the role of Aboriginal people in the formation of modern Australia. The first was about her father Charles Perkins, a national soccer champion who became the first Aboriginal student at Sydney University. In 1965, he worked with other student activists to organize "freedom rides" to challenge the racist conditions under which Aboriginal people lived in rural towns at the time. The documentary retraces the history of this initial stage of the Aboriginal civil rights movement through the retrospective accounts by Perkins and his fellow protesters, both black and white, as they revisit the places where they had carried out civil disobedience over twenty-five years ago.

Rachel and other indigenous producers who have worked for Australian state television carry a specific burden of representation: they must create an Aboriginal presence on national mass media in settings where they are subject to large Euro-Australian television bureaucracies. For them, questions of cultural accountability are worked out quite differently than in remote areas where the primary audience is from the producer's own community. Rachel, for instance, had to make compromises with SBS editors because of what they felt would draw non-Aboriginal audiences. As she explained to me,

> I scripted to include the massacres which happened in the area in the early 1800s right up to 1985 where a guy was gunned down in the street, But the script editor was just saying, "Look, you're not making an epic film here, . . .you've got to concentrate on the guts of the story which is the freedom ride." So all of those sort of really bloody relations couldn't be part of the film . . . I wanted to make it entertaining and personal and humorous so that people would watch it, you know and become more involved in it. There was a lot of violence that happened within that period though that I didn't show, and that's also because people didn't necessarily want to talk about it. . . . But you don't have to measure racial inequality by the amount of people that are killed. In Australia, it's more of a psychological warfare with people, growing up under that regime, that was the thrust of what I was trying to get across.

In reaching out to a mixed but still predominantly non-Aboriginal national audience, *Freedom Ride* spoke directly and deliberately to their relationship to the struggle for Aboriginal civil rights, serving as a reminder of the possibility of white activism on behalf of that cause nearly thirty years before, at a contemporary moment when political separatism too often serves as an excuse for apathy. Using archival footage, re-creations of historical scenes, oral histories, and contemporary vérité footage, the documentary is powerful testimony to how political consciousness was created in everyday experiences of discrimination, and transformed through direct action, much of it inspired by knowledge of the American civil rights movement gained in part through the mass media. In a particularly poignant moment that also reveals the key role of such mediations in creating transnational links among activists, Charles Perkins recollects a solidarity visit from an African American delegation and how unexpectedly moved the Australians were when the visitors sang "We Shall Overcome," a song they had heard many times on records, radio, and television. This example of the role that such media played historically in creating contact between social movements in different parts of the world points to a broader frame: the documentary itself is embedded in a context of social action in which its presence on national television is yet another level of assertion and insertion of a rarely visible Aboriginal presence and perspective on Australian history.

Rachel's father, in the 1960s, was inspired to become an activist in part by his knowledge of African American civil rights leaders. Now, thirty years and a generation later, Rachel names as models a new generation of African American cultural activists such as Spike Lee, whose feature films, based on his own cultural experience, still speak to many audiences. As she explained to me,

> We don't see making only Aboriginal stuff, as being ghettoized; we see it as leading to a really dynamic area of the industry which is black film-making. . . . There's a huge perception that Aboriginal stuff is only interesting to Aboriginal people, and that it's boring. Yet *Blood Brothers* was one of the highest rating doco [documentary] series that has ever been on SBS. Until *Once Were Warriors* [the 1994 feature film made by Maori director Lee Tamahori], all I'd heard was that indigenous films will never get an audience, people aren't interested in indigenous characters, that audiences are racist.

In 1993, frustrated by lack of funds and compromises she had to make, Rachel left the SBS.[23] Eventually, she formed her own production company, Blackfella Films, in order to complete her first feature film, *Radiance* (1997). Adapted from a work by Euro-Australian playwright Louis Nowra, the story unfolds as unspoken complex secrets are revealed about the relationships among three Aboriginal sisters, each of whom embodies a different relationship to her cultural identity, and who reunite after the death of their mother. The film was a major success in Australia, and in the summer of 1997, it screened at the Cannes Film Festival in France.

Rachel Perkin's work as filmmaker, producer, and activist is exemplary of a young Aboriginal cultural elite engaged in constituting a vital Aboriginal modernity through a variety of media, including music, visual arts, film, and drama. These forms provide vehicles for new narrations of the place of Aboriginality in the nation—*Freedom Ride*, *Night Patrol*, and *Radiance* are but three examples—that are not tied to traditional practices. This work has helped to establish and enlarge a counter public sphere in which Aboriginality is central and emergent, especially in the context of the changed circumstances signified by the 1993 Australian High Court Mabo decision recognizing Native Title. In an article written in 1994, in the post-Mabo euphoria, cultural critic Stephen Muecke argued that these transformations would mobilize

> new ways of positioning Aboriginal history identity and culture . . . in which Aboriginal Australians occupy a very different and very crucial site from which new post national subjectivities can be constituted, in which new stories enable new "structures of feeling" and of agency that in turn translate into a new politics of nation. (1994, p. 254)

Muecke's optimistic claims clearly were written before the 1996 elections of the politically conservative government of John Howard. Nonetheless, if one looks at the indigenous media sector, these concerns—to broaden the representation of national narratives to include Aboriginal life-worlds past and present—are still the issues engaging the cohort of mediamakers of which Rachel is a part. The notion of nationhood that helped establish Aboriginal media's emergence in the 1980s embraced Australia's own regional and cultural diversity, underscoring a sense of national identity that is decentered, flexible, and inclusive of indigenous cultures. The work has continued under the Howard regime, which has mobilized right-wing and racist backlash among some white Australians against what are seen as undue cultural and political gains by Aboriginal people and other claims to multiculturalism as a legitimate frame for the Australian nation. Thus, at the beginning of the twenty-first century, Aboriginal mediamakers are engaged in a broader war of position over the question of Australian national identity in which the visibility of Aboriginal lives and histories plays a key role.

Central to that process are efforts to reverse and resignify the history of colonial looking relations in which film and photography became the visible evidence of an indigenous world that was expected to disappear but instead persists. The paradigmatic instance of this process occurred in the landmark Murray Island Land Case (1992), commonly known as the Mabo land rights, after one of the plaintiffs, the late Eddie Mabo, a Torres Straits Islander Man, whose case eventually became the basis for the historic legislation that granted native title to Australia's indigenous people, overturning 200 years of *terra nullius*, recognizing prior indigenous ownership of so-called Crown Land. Part of the evidence for rights to land on Mer Island (north of Australia), was footage of the one of the first films ever made of indigenous people: English anthropologist Alfred Court Haddon's documentary of Mer (Murray) Islanders performing dances in 1898 that are still in use today, proving continuity of tradition. There is some irony in this resignification, since Haddon, in the tradition of his day, was interested in capturing images of these people before they disappeared from the face of the earth (Holgate, 1994). Instead, the Haddon footage provided the visible evidence—the screen memories—that proved the very opposite: that they are still very much alive and continue to occupy the land that has been part of their cultural legacy. The use of this ethnographic footage for the purpose of a land claim reversed its status as a late-nineteenth-century sign of the imagined extinction of Aboriginal culture. It turned the footage instead into an index of their cultural persistence and a basis for indigenous claims to their land and cultural rights in the present. This reversal stands, metaphorically, for the ways in which indigenous people have been using the inscription of their screen memories in media to "talk back" to structures of power and state that have denied their rights, subjectivity, and citizenship for over 200 years.

Alternative Accountings

Film, video, and television—as technologies of objectification as well as reflection—contain within them a doubled set of possibilities. They can be seductive conduits for imposing the values and language of the dominant culture on minoritized people, what some indigenous activists have called a potential cultural "neutron bomb," the kind that kills people and leaves inanimate structures intact (Kuptana cited in David, 1998, p. 36). On the other hand, these technologies—unlike most others—also offer possibilities for "talking back" to and through the categories that have been created to contain indigenous people. It is not the technologies themselves, of course, that produce the latter possibility, but the timing and social location of their arrival. Despite his facility with the camera, Allakaraialak's participation in Flaherty's film was not acknowledged, nor were the structures in place that would have enabled him to really make use of the "Aggie." For Inuit fifty years later, politically mobilized and subject to the regimes of the state in their lives, access to a satellite has been crucial, linking communities across the Arctic (and Canada) in ways that are culturally and politically powerful.

Similarly, after a long history as objects of photographic representation, media was first embraced by Aboriginal people at a particular historical conjuncture in Australia. In the 1980s, progressive state policy, indigenous activists, an independent and alternative film culture, and remote and urban Aboriginal people all became interested—sometimes for different reasons—in how these media could be indigenized formally and substantively to give objective form to efforts for the expression of cultural identity, the preservation of language and ritual, and the telling of indigenous histories. Socially, they are creating new arenas for meaningful cultural production for people living in both remote and urban-based communities. In cosmopolitan centers like Sydney, groups such as the Indigenous Programs Unit at the ABC serve as a critical node in a mixed race network of filmmakers, musicians, activists, artists, and writers who make up an elite strata of Australia's equivalent of a post–civil rights generation. And increasingly, new bureaucratic structures of state-mediated Aboriginal modernity are emerging, such as the National Indigenous Media Association of Australia and the Indigenous Branch of the Australian Film Commission. In 1997, the Branch launched a new initiative to train Aboriginal people in drama and feature film production, marking a significant shift from the usual consignment of indigenous media to either the extreme localism of outback television that marked its emergence in the mid-1980s or the genre-defined limits of documentary that shaped its presence on national television after 1988.

Tracking these emergent media practices, one can see how they have developed in relation to Aboriginal concerns and national policies. The experimental efforts of the 1980s by people in remote communities who began to document their lives, cultures, and histories were spurred by an initial protectionist desire to block the penetration of Western television while also working out the formal, social, and cultural protocols for indigenizing media—what media scholar and activist Eric Michaels called *The Aboriginal Invention of Television in Central Australia* (1986). By the late 1980s, spurred by the moment of national redefinition constituted around Australia's bicentenary, Aboriginal interest in media expanded to the urban sector and the creation of an indigenous presence on state television. In that context, producers focused initially on the presentation to national audiences— indigenous and otherwise—of what they called positive imagery of their lives and of Australian history from an Aboriginal point of view. This was intended to counter both the absence and the unremitting negativity of their representation in the media more generally, from the celebratory history of *Freedom Ride* to the efforts to combat problems such as alcoholism and violence against women through local forms of self-determination exemplified in *Night Patrol.*

By the mid-1990s, when a new cohort started to leave the confines of doc- umentary and work in dramatic genres, they found yet another mode of expres- sive possibility. These more recent fictional works offer self-conscious, alternative, and multiple accountings of indigenous life-worlds, as in the complex gendered, cultural landscape given almost surreal shape in feature films such as Rachel Perkin's *Radiance* (1997), or in the stark, supernatural Inuit universe invoked in the retelling of the ancient Inuit legend *Atanarjuat* (The Fast Runner, 2001). These works are, increasingly, circulating on a world stage. In June 2001, *Message Sticks: Blak Screens/Blak Sounds*, a three-day festival of indigenous film and music from Australia, opened to a packed and mixed audience at the presti- gious Sydney Opera House with the premiere of Rachel Perkin's latest dramatic film, *One Night the Moon* (2001), which opened at the Sundance Film Festival six months later. Two months earlier, at the 13th Nordic Film Festival in Guovdageaidnu, Norway, festival organizer Anne Lajla Utsi, announced to atten- dees that "filmmaking is a Sami tradition," one that began in 1987 with Nils Gaup's award-winning dramatic feature *The Pathfinder.* These works, and their circulation, are testimony to the range of experience and practice contained within the category "indigenous media"; their vitality speaks to the importance of the recuperation of "screen memories" for contemporary generations of indige- nous activists worldwide. Positioned somewhere between the phenomenological life-worlds of their everyday lives, the colonial categories through which they have been constituted, and a globalizing image economy that is increasingly receptive to their work, the making of these media are part of a broader set of prac- tices through they are reflecting on and transforming the conditions of their lives.

NOTES

This essay is expanded from an earlier one, "Screen Memories: Resignifying the Traditional in Indigenous Media," published in *Media Worlds: Anthropology on New Terrain*, ed. Faye Gins- burg, Lila Abu-Lughod, and Brian Larkin (Berkeley, Calif., 2002). Thanks to Bob Stam and Ella Shohat for their comments for this version, and Lila Abu-Lughod, Brian Larkin, Fred Myers, Bar- bara Abrash, and Jay Ruby for their helpful readings of earlier versions of this draft; and to the many people engaged in indigenous media in Australia and Canada who have generously shared their time and insights with me while I was there, including Brian Arley, Philip Batty, Norman Cohen, Brenda Croft, Graham Dash, Jennifer Deger, Francoise Dussart, Pat Fiske, Melinda Hink- son, David Jowsey, Tom Kantor, Zack Kunuk, Frances Jupurrurla Kelley, Brett Leavy, Marcia Langton, Mary Laughren, Michael Leigh, Rachel Perkins, Frances Peters, Catriona McKenzie,

Michael Meadows, Helen Molnar, Nicki McCoy, Michael Riley, Sally Riley, Lorna Roth, Walter Saunders, and many others. Support for travel for this research has come in part from Guggenheim and MacArthur Fellowships.

1. While *indigenous* can index a social formation "native" to a particular area (e.g., "I Love Lucy" is indigenous to America), we use it here in the strict sense of the term, as interchangeable with the neologism *First Peoples* to indicate the original inhabitants of areas later colonized by settler states (Australia, the United States, New Zealand, Canada, most of Latin America). These people, an estimated 5 percent of the world's population, are struggling to sustain their own identities and claims to culture and land, surviving as internal colonies within encompassing nation-states.

2. *Bad Aboriginal Art: Tradition, Media, and Technological Horizons*, a posthumous collection of Eric Michaels's writings based on his activist research in Australia, was published in 1994.

3. For this debate in the context of indigenous media, see the spring 1997 issue of *Current Anthropology* (Weiner et al.) and the spring 1998 issue of *Lingua Franca* (Palatella).

4. *Nanook* is discussed in nearly every book written on documentary, as well as in much of the revisionist scholarship on the genre. For other discussions of the gramophone scene, see Rony (1996), Ruby (2000), Taussig (1995).

5. In the case of *Nanook*, for example, in terms of the broader political economy, the film bears traces of the end of the global fur trade that fueled much of the settlement of North America. *Nanook* was sponsored by Revillon Freres, the French fur company that owned the trading post in the film, and was completed in 1922 at a historical moment when the fur of Arctic foxes, which Nanook hunts in the film and brings to the post, graced many a Parisian shoulder. These global trading processes underwrote and set the stage for the initial engagement of Allakarialik and others with the technologies of cinematic objectification (Ray, 2000).

6. Through processes of displacement and condensation, Freud writes: "what is important is replaced in memory by something else which appears unimportant" (1975, p. 248). For a fuller discussion of his concept of screen memory, see Chapter V in *The Psychopathology of Everyday Life* (1901/1975).

7. A 1986 report by the Federal Task Force on Broadcasting Policy, in its support of aboriginal broadcasting as an integral part of the Canadian broadcasting system, called for a separate satellite distribution system to carry aboriginal language programming (David, 1998).

8. The APTN is a unique TV experiment in many ways. The Canadian government has ordered cable systems to carry it as part of their basic package, a mandate that has met with some opposition from the Canadian Cable Television Association; "guilt tax," although others have been more enthusiastic. For further information, see their web site at www.aptn.ca.

9. Jerry Mander (1991), for example, argues that video and television technologies are irredeemably destructive to native life. His argument, as Laura Marks pointed out in her overview of Inuit media, "equates tradition with rigidity, rather than understand adaptability itself as a longstanding value" (1994, p. 6) and also fails to account for what kind of media are actually being made. A more recent example is anthropologist James Weiner's 1997 polemic, "Televisualist Anthropology," directed against indigenous media, which he calls "ersatz culture," and those who study it, including myself. We argue that far from being subsumed by contact with mass cultural forms, as these critics have argued, indigenous mediamakers have taken on Western media technologies to defend themselves against what they see as the culturally destructive effects of mass media, producing work about their own lives, a strategy some have called "innovative traditionalism." A more poetic phrasing, "Starting Fire With Gunpowder," used for the title of a film made about the IBC (Poisey and Hansen, 1991), captures the sense of turning a potentially destructive Western form into something useful to the lives of indigenous people.

10. Their works are produced in the Inuktitut language and syllabics (for titling) and are subtitled in English and French. For those interested in finding out more about the work of this extraordinary group, I recommend their web site, www.isuma.ca.

11. Produced with the support of Canada Council, National Film Board, and Government of the Northwest Territories, the work of Igloolik Isuma has been seen on TVNC and in screenings at many institutions, including the National Gallery of Canada, the Museum of Modern Art in New York, the American Film Institute, Museé d'art moderne, Paris, and the Museum of Northern Peoples, Hokkaido, Japan. Reviews from mainstream papers have been appreciative to laudatory.

12. See comments by T. Nasook on www.isuma.ca.

13. Elsewhere, I situate the work within more global developments, from the marketing of satellites and small media technologies, to the growth of transnational political networks supporting the rights of indigenous peoples, to more specialized cultural arenas such as international indigenous film festivals, which have become important sites for constituting linkages among indigenous mediamakers worldwide (Ginsburg, 1993).

14. These state policies and bureaucracies must be understood in part as an outgrowth of modern movements for Aboriginal rights. The expansion of indigenous political and cultural activism—inspired in part by the civil rights and Black Power movements in the United States—helped catalyze constitutional changes that granted Aboriginal Australian voting rights in 1962 and Australian citizenship in 1967, and set the stage for the developing recognition of Aboriginal claims for land rights and cultural autonomy beginning in the 1970s.

15. In 1980, only a few radio shows existed. In a 1994 survey of indigenous involvement in media (not including the growth in radio), remote communities had 150 local media associations, eighty small-scale television stations, and two satellite television services with indigenous programming. By 1993, a representative body, the National Indigenous Media Association of Australia (NIMAA), was formed to advocate for and help to link the hundreds of indigenous broadcasters working in radio, video, and television throughout Australia. Additionally, the creation of Indigenous Program Units at the state-sponsored television stations, ABC and SBS in 1989, helped create a base for a strong urban cohort of mediamakers that came into their own a decade later.

16. For scholars alarmed at the "wasteland" of TV, the Yuendumu experiment acquired the aura of a plucky outback David whose tiny satellite dishes and culturally distinctive video productions served as a kind of well-targeted epistemological slingshot against globalizing satellites and mass media programming (e.g., Hebdige, 1994). This valorization of circumstances in which indigenous people are represented as existing comfortably with both their own traditions and Western technologies is embodied not only in state policy, but also in popular media, a particular embrace of Aboriginal modernity that elsewhere I have called hi-tech primitivism (Ginsburg, 1993, p. 562).

17. WMA has worked with the regional group the Central Australian Aboriginal Media Association (CAAMA), based in Alice Springs, as well as the national indigenous advocacy organization, the National Indigenous Media Association of Australia (NIMAA), which sponsored the series with support from the Aboriginal bureaucracy ATSIC, as well as the ABC and the Olympic Arts Festival.

18. The video project about the night patrol was directed by a Warlpiri woman, Valerie Martin, who worked with the help of WMA's white adviser, the late Tom Kantor.

19. While some of this was going on while I was in Central Australia in 1997, I am also grateful to Pat Fiske and Tom Kantor for providing me with their views of the situation.

20. For example, it was one of two works from the series selected for the Margaret Mead Film Festival in New York City and was warmly received at the screenings I attended there.

21. The station she trained at was CAAMA, located in Alice Springs. For an account of the formation of this station, see Ginsburg (1991). Rachel's knowledge of work from remote communities and regional media associations was influential in bringing that work into urban Aboriginal settings; she has continued to play a key role in programming work from both remote and urban Aboriginal communities on national television.

22. Faced with a small budget and few resources, she created work at SBS but also brought in material from regional and local Aboriginal media associations through her links to CAAMA and more remote groups in its orbit, such as the Warlipri Media Association (WMA) at Yuendumu.

23. The next year, she was recruited to head up the Indigenous Programs Unit at the ABC where, in addition to continuing their Aboriginal cultural affairs show, "Blackout," she produced a series on Aboriginal music, "Songlines," and negotiated the agreement with NIMAA to act as executive producer for the eight works for the National Indigenous Documentary Series—*Night Patrol* was one—made in 1997 and screened on the ABC later that year. During that period, Rachel took a temporary leave from the ABC in order to complete *Radiance* with her partner, Euro-Australian filmmaker Ned Lander.

REFERENCES

Alexie, Sherman. *The Lone Ranger and Tonto Fistfight in Heaven.* New York: Harper Perennial, 1994.

Appadurai, Arjun. *Modernity at Large: Cultural Dimensions of Globalization.* Minneapolis: University of Minnesota Press, 1996.

Berger, Sally. "Move Over Nanook." *Wide Angle* 17, nos. 1–4 (1995a): 177–192.

———. "Time Travellers." *Felix: A Journal of Media Arts and Communication* 2 no. 1 (1995).

Brisebois, Deborah. *Whiteout Warning: Courtesy of the Federal Government.* Inuit Broadcasting Corporation, 1991.

Castels, Manuel. *The Rise of the Network Society.* Oxford: Blackwell, 1997.

David, Jennifer. "Seeing Ourselves, Being Ourselves: Broadcasting Aboriginal Television in Canada." *Cultural Survival Quarterly* 22, no. 2 (summer 1998): 36–39.

Faris, James. "Anthropological Transparency, Film, Representation and Politics." In *Film as Ethnography*, ed. P. Crawford and D. Turton, pp. 171–182. Manchester: University of Manchester Press, 1992.

Fleming, Kathleen. "Igloolik Video: An Organic Response from a Culturally Sound Community." *Inuit Art* 11, no. 2 (1996): 30–38.

Freud, Sigmund. *Abstracts of The Standard Edition of the Complete Psychological Works of Sigmund Freud*, ed. Carrie Lee Rothgeb. Rockville, Md: NIMH, 1975.

Gaines, Jane. "White Privilege and Looking Relations: Race and Gender in Feminist Film Theory." *Screen* 29, no. 4 (1998): 12–27.

Ginsburg, Faye. "Indigenous Media: Faustian Contract or Global Village?" *Cultural Anthropology* 6 no. 1 (1991): 92–12.

———. "Aboriginal Media and the Australian Imaginary." *Public Culture* 5, no. 3 (1993). Special Issue, Screening Politics in a World of Nations, ed. Lila Abu-Lughod, 557–578.

———. "Culture/Media: A (Mild) Polemic." *Anthropology Today* (1994).

Hebdige, Dick. Foreword. In *Bad Aboriginal Art: Tradition, Media, and Technological Horizons.* Minneapolis: University of Minnesota Press, 1994.

Hendrick, Stephen, and Kathleen Fleming. "Zacharias Kunuk: Video Maker and Inuit Historian." *Inuit Art* 6, no. 3 (1991): 24–28.

Holgate, Ben. "Now For a Celluloid Dreaming." *Sydney Morning Herald*, November 23, 1994.

Juhasz, Alexandra. *Aids TV: Identity, Community, and Alternative Video.* Durham, N.C.: Duke University Press, 1995.

Kuttab, Daoud. "Grass Roots TV Production in the Occupied Territories." In *Channels of Resistance: Global Television and Local Empowerment*, ed. Tony Downmunt. London: British Film Institute, 1993.

Lucas, Martin. "TV on Ice." *New Society* 9 (1987): 15–17.

Mahon, Maureen. "Black Like This: Race, Generation, and Rock in the Post-Civil Rights Era." *American Ethnologist* 27, no. 2 (2000): 283–311.

Mander, Jerry. *In the Absence of the Sacred: The Failure of Technology and the Survival of the Indian Nations.* San Francisco: Sierra Club Books, 1991.

Marks, Laura. "Reconfigured Nationhood: A Partisan History of the Inuit Broadcasting Corporation." *Afterimage* (March): 4–8

Meadows, Michael. "Indigenous Cultural Diversity: Television Northern Canada." *Culture and Policy* 7, no. 1 (1996): 25–44.

Michaels, Eric. *The Aboriginal Invention of Television in Central Australia: 1982–1986.* Canberra: Australian Institute of Aboriginal Studies.

———. *Bad Aboriginal Art: Tradition, Media, and Technological Horizons.* Minneapolis: University of Minnesota Press, 1994.

Miller, Daniel. Introduction: Anthropology, Modernity, Consumption. In *Worlds Apart: Modernity Through The Prism of the Local*, ed. Daniel Miller, pp. 1–23, London: Routledge, 1995.

Miller, Toby. "Exporting Truth from Aboriginal Australia: Portions of Our Past Become Present Again, Where Only the Melancholy Light of Origin Shines." *Media Information Australia* 76 (1995): 7–17.

Muecke, Stephen. "Narrative and Intervention: Aboriginal Filmmaking and Policy." *Continuum* 8, no. 2 (1994): 248–57.

Pinney, Chris. *Camera Indica: The Social Life of Photographs*. London: Blackwell, 1998.

Poisey, David, and William Hansen. 1991. *Starting Fire with Gunpowder*. Video by Tamarack Productions, Edmonton, Canada.

Prins, Harald. "The Paradox of Primitivism: Native Rights and the Problem of Imagery in Cultural Survival Films." *Visual Anthropology* 9, no. 3–4 (1997): 243–266.

Rony, Fatima. *The Third Eye: Race, Cinema, and Ethnographic Spectacle*. Durham, N.C.: Duke University Press, 1996.

Roth, Lorna. *Northern Voices and Mediating Structures: The Emergence and Development of First Peoples' Television Broadcasting in the Canadian North*. Unpublished dissertation, Concordia University, Montreal, Canada, 1994.

———. *Something New in the Air: Indigenous Television in Canada*. Montreal: McGill Queens University Press, 2002.

Roth, Lorna, and Gail Valaskakis. "Aboriginal Broadcasting in Canada: A Case Study in Democratization." In *Communication for and Against Democracy*, ed. Marc Raboy and Peter Bruck, pp. 221–234. Montreal: Black Rose Books, 1989.

Rotha, Paul, with Basil Wright. "Nanook and the North." *Studies in Visual Communication* 6, no. 2 (summer 1980): 33–60.

Ruby, Jay. "Introduction: Nanook and the North." *Studies in Visual Communication* 6, no. 2 (summer 1980).

———. *Picturing Culture: Explorations of Film and Anthropology*. Chicago: University of Chicago Press, 2000.

Schein, Louisa. "Mapping Among Media in Diasporic Space." In *Media Worlds: Anthropology on New Terrain*, ed. Faye Ginsburg, Lila Abu-Lughod, and Brian Larkin. Berkeley: University of California Press, 2002.

Singer, Beverly. *Wiping the Warpaint off the Lens: Native American Film and Video*. Minneapolis: University of Minnesota Press, 2001.

Taussig, Michael. *Mimesis and Alterity* New York: Routledge, 1994.

Turner, Terence. "Anthropology and Multiculturalism: What is Anthropology That Multiculturalists Should Be Mindful of It?" *Cultural Anthropology* 8, no. 4 (1993): 411–429.

Weiner, James. "Televisualist Anthropology: Representation, Aesthetics, Politics." *Current Anthropology* 38, no. 2 (1997): 197–236.

Ana M. López

"Train of Shadows": Early Cinema and Modernity in Latin America

The early years of the silent cinema in Latin America, roughly 1896–1920, are the least discussed and most difficult to document in Latin American media history. This period was overshadowed by wars and other cataclysmic political and social events and, subsequently, its significance was eclipsed by the introduction and development of other media—the "Golden Ages" of sound cinema and radio in the 1940s and 1950s, television in the 1960s and 1970s. These developments seem to fit better with the narratives of Latin American modernity some scholars want to tell, be they tales of foreign technological and ideological domination and inadequate imitation (à la Armand Mattelart and Herbert Schiller) or contemporary chronicles of global mediations (à la Martín Barbero).[1] Nonetheless, in this early period, we find not only complex global interactions but also extensive evidence of the contradictory and ambivalent transformative processes that would mark the later reception and development of the sound cinema and other media. These early forms of mediated modernities already complexly refracted and inflected the production of self and other imagined communities, and, I argue, lay bare the central characteristics of the processes through which subsequent media engaged with and contributed to the specificity of Latin American modernity.

The Arrival

According to Paulo Antonio Paranaguá, "The cinema appear[ed] in Latin America as another foreign import."[2] This is perhaps the most salient characteristic of the experience of early Latin American cinema: rather than developed in proto-organic synchronicity with the changes, technological inventions, and "revolutions" that produced modernity in Western Europe and the United States, the appearance and diffusion of the cinema in Latin America followed the patterns of neo-colonial dependency typical of the region's position in the global capitalist system at the turn of the century. As Ella Shohat and Robert Stam point out, "The beginnings of cinema coincided with the giddy heights of the imperial project,"

From *Cinema Journal*, 40:1, pp. 48–78. Copyright © 2000 by the University of Texas Press. All rights reserved.

and "the most prolific film-producing countries . . . also 'happened' to be among the leading imperialists."[3]

The cinematic apparatus—a manufactured product—appeared, fully formed, on Latin American soil a few months after its commercial introduction abroad. Subsequently, on the very same ships and railroads that carried raw materials and agricultural products to Europe and the United States, Lumière and Edison cameramen returned with fascinating views of exotic lands, peoples, and their customs. Thus, in reference to Latin America, it is difficult to speak of the cinema and modernity as "points of reflection and convergence,"[4] as is the presumption in U.S. and European early cinema scholarship. Rather, the development of early cinema in Latin America was not directly linked to previous large-scale transformations of daily experience resulting from industrialization, rationality, and the technological transformation of modern life, because those processes were only just beginning to occur across the continent. In turn-of-the-century Latin America, modernity was, above all, still a fantasy and a profound desire.

In Latin America, modernization has been a decentered, fragmentary, and uneven process.[5] As José Joaquín Brunner has argued, modernity (and, simultaneously, postmodernity) in Latin America is characterized by cultural heterogeneity, by the multiple rationalities and impulses of private and public life. Unequal development led not only to "segmentation and segmented participation in the world market of messages and symbols" but also to "differential participation according to *local codes of reception*" that produced a decentering of "Western culture as it [was] represented by the manuals."[6] In other words, Latin American modernity has been a global, intertextual experience, addressing impulses and models from abroad, in which every nation and region created, and creates, its own ways of playing with and at modernity. These "spectacular experiments"[7] constituted what Angel Rama called "the momentous second birth of modern Latin America," which took place as *la ciudad letrada,* or the lettered city—the nexus of lettered culture, state power, and urban location that had facilitated the continentwide colonizing process—entered the twentieth century.[8] Albeit intensely engaging with European and, later, U.S. culture, the intellectual sectors Rama dubbed the *letrados* were nevertheless able to define local modernities.

Another crucial sign of Latin American modernity is a kind of temporal warp in which the premodern coexists and interacts with the modern, a differential plotting of time and space, and, subsequently, of history and time. In Anibal Quijano's words, "In Latin America, what is sequence in other countries is a simultaneity. It is also a sequence. But in the first place it is a simultaneity."[9] Rather than a devastating process that plows over the traditional bases of a social formation—all that is solid melting into air—Latin American modernity is produced via an ambiguous symbiosis of traditional experiences/practices and modernizing innovations, such as the technologies of visuality epitomized by the cinema. To quote Brunner again, "Not all solid things but rather all symbols melt into air."[10] This warp has profound consequences for any historical project:

because of temporal ambiguity and asynchronicity, teleological narratives of evolution become mired in dead ends and failed efforts and do not do justice to the circuitous routes of Latin American modernity.

If we are to understand the "indigenization" of the cinema in Latin America, the "spectacular experiments" through which it was inserted into and contributed to the specificity of the experience of Latin American modernity, our conceptual framework must link the national and continental with global practices, tracing the complex and specific negotiations between local histories and globality through differential and overlapping chronologies. Any attempt to superimpose the developmental grid of U.S. and European early film history (albeit with its own discontinuities and heterogeneity) directly on the Latin American experience is doomed to failure and frustration, for the early history of Latin American cinema already points to the complexly intertwined chronologies and multiple branchings that later characterized the development of subsequent media.

Likewise, it is not productive to seek replicas of the technological and narrative experiments associated with early cinema in the developed West, for the history of filmmaking in Latin America is too profoundly marked by differences in global position, forms of social infrastructure, economic stability, and technical infrastructure. Studying this period is made even more daunting by the paucity of available material; most of the films produced in Latin America between 1896 and 1930 have disappeared, victims of the inevitable ravages of time (and fires) and the official neglect of cultural preservation. Scholarship on this period is necessarily tenuous, limited to a few dozen extant films, and for the most part based on secondary materials, especially press coverage. Nevertheless, this history in some countries, especially Argentina, Brazil, and Mexico, has been fairly well documented; conversely, few have attempted transnational comparative studies, since so much of the available material seems bound by "nationness."[11]

The first step befuddling any continental chronology is the cinema's uneven diffusion and development. The cinematic apparatus appeared in Latin America quickly, less than six months after its commercial introduction in Europe. There is journalistic evidence that British Brighton School films (using the Vivomatograph) were premiered in Buenos Aires as early as July 6, 1896 (not surprising, given the ongoing neo-colonial relationship between Argentina and England during this period).[12] Confirmed screenings using the Lumière apparatus (the Cinématographe) took place shortly thereafter: in Rio de Janeiro (July 8, 1896), Montevideo and Buenos Aires (July 18), Mexico City (August 14), Santiago de Chile (August 25), Guatemala City (September 26), and Havana (January 24, 1897). Edison's Vitascope took only slightly longer to arrive. First was Buenos Aires (July 20 1896), followed by Mexico City (October 22), Lima (January 2, 1897), and Rio de Janeiro (January 30).[13] These locations are not surprising, for they follow well-established routes of transatlantic commerce through the most advanced cities of the continent, which were already in the throes of modernization.

Arguably, Buenos Aires was ahead of the pack. Looking at some of the most salient indicators typically used to assess modernization, Buenos Aires was the center of national industrial activity (through its ports flowed the wool, beef, and leather that arrived on the British-sponsored railroad system linking the city to interior production centers; it housed 600,000 of the nation's four million inhabitants); it had an efficient electric streetcar system (since 1890), a reliable electrical infrastructure that serviced business interests, and two telephone companies (with more than 10,000 subscribers by 1900).[14] Furthermore, its population was cosmopolitan; the government-encouraged waves of immigration from Europe, beginning in 1895, had changed the physiognomy of the city, producing a fluid constituency and sumptuous public works and private palaces that coexisted alongside *conventillos* (tenement housing), where laborers and poor immigrants resided.[15] Also quite modern by continental standards, Rio had electric streetcars, telegraphs, telephones, and electricity, although the latter was unstable until completion of a hydroelectric plant in nearby Ribeirão das Lajes in 1905. Like Buenos Aires, Rio's population was cosmopolitan: Rio (and later São Paulo) was a magnet for migrants from the northeast and immigrants from Europe.[16] In contrast, a capital city like Lima was showing only the beginning signs of modernization. Despite urban renewal, funded by the rubber boom that would eventually modernize the city (especially significant was the redesign of the principal urban arteries of La Colmena and the Paseo Colón), Lima lacked a reliable source of electricity and was the center of a quasi-feudal state that historian Jorge Basadre calls the "República Aristocrática."[17] Peru was a nation in which only 5 percent of the population had the right to vote and in which that 5 percent governed and suppressed all peasant protests and urban popular movements. Further, its Europeanized elites, not the nation's majority indigenous population, controlled the country.[18] Thus, it is not surprising that the "modernity" of early cinema echoed more resoundingly—and lastingly—in Buenos Aires and Rio than in Lima, since even the simple films shown at these first screenings already exemplified a particularly modern form of aesthetics responding to the specificity of modern urban life.

Porteños (Buenos Aires residents) took to the medium immediately; there is evidence that the first Argentine film—views of Buenos Aires—may have been produced as early as 1896. By the turn of the century, businessmen specializing in photography had mastered the new medium's technology and begun to produce a steady stream of actualities and proto-fictional shorts. Other impresarios included imported and national films in their popular public entertainment venues (theaters, and in the summer, open-air festivals) and, as early as 1901, had even built dedicated movie houses. *Cariocas* (Rio de Janeiro residents) also became early enthusiasts, but despite a series of "firsts" and the efforts of pioneers, the medium did not become established until reliable electricity was available in 1905. In contrast, the cinema acquired a foothold in Lima much more slowly. Although there is evidence that a national short may have been produced in 1899, the first confirmed filming did not take place in Peru until 1904; newsreel or actuality production was not consistent until 1909–1915; dedicated movie theaters did not appear until 1909, the first fiction film was not produced until 1915, and the cinema did not develop beyond its first documentary impulses until the 1920s.[19]

The diffusion of the cinema throughout the interior of Latin American countries followed a pattern determined by, among other things, the level of development of railroads and other modern infrastructures. In Mexico, for example, where a national railroad system was already well established by the turn of the century,[20] the Edison equipment enchanted Guadalajara, the nation's second-largest city, in 1896, and by 1898 the Lumière apparatus had already appeared in Mérida, San Juan Bautista, Puebla, and San Luis Potosí.[21] Conversely, more inaccessible regions—that is, regions marginal to international trade—were not exposed to the new invention until significantly later. For example, residents of the remote community of Los Mulos in Cuba's Oriente province did not see movies "for the first time" until the mid-1960s, made possible through the auspices of the Cuban film institute's (ICAIC) *cine-móvil* program and documented in Octavio Cortazar's short film *Por primera vez* (For the First Time, 1967).

More significant than the speed of diffusion of the technological apparatus is how it was used at various sites and locales—the process of adaptation, contestation, and innovation in the context of the international cinematic marketplace. The cinema experienced by Latin Americans was—and still is—predominantly foreign. This is a factor of tremendous significance in the complex development of indigenous forms, always caught in a hybrid dialectics of invention and imitation, as well as in the development of the form of experience—mass spectatorship—necessary to sustain the medium.

Peripheral Attractions

The early films that arrived in Latin America alongside the new technology were part of what Tom Gunning and other film scholars have characterized as the "cinema of attractions."[22] Instead of the narrative forms that would later become hegemonic, the cinema of attractions (predominant in the United States until 1903–1904) was based on an aesthetics of astonishment; it appealed to viewers' curiosity about the new technology and fulfilled it with brief moments of images in movement. It was, above all, a cinema of thrills and surprises, assaulting viewers with stimulating sights; in Miriam Hansen's terms, it was "presentational rather than representational."[23]

In Latin America, this aesthetics of astonishment was complicated by the ontological and epistemological status of the apparatus. In fact, the Latin American context, in which, despite all attempts to produce films locally, imported films tended to dominate the market and have usually been the most popular, leads us to pose the question "indeed attracted, but to what?" The cinematic attraction is "attractive" in and of itself *and* as an import. However, beyond any purported fit with the experience of modernity in local urban life, its appeal is—and perhaps first of all—the appeal of the other, the shock of difference. With its vistas of sophisticated modern cities and customs (ranging from Lumière's rather sophisticated workers leaving the factory and magnificent locomotives to Edison's scandalous kiss), the imported views could produce the experience of an *accessible* globality among the urban citizens of Latin America, many of them less than a generation away from the "old world." Fashion, consumer products, other new technologies and different ways of experiencing modern life and its emotions and challenges[24] were suddenly available with tremendous immediacy: "In its earliest days . . . the cinema was an opening to the world."[25] But to the degree that that experience was desired and delightful, it was also profoundly ambivalent and a source of anxiety.

The cinema's complex images of distance and otherness problematized the meaning of locality and self. Where were they to be found, these spectators of the "new world," in this brave new "other" world of specular and spectacular thrills? On the one hand, the cinema fed the national self-confidence that its own modernity was "in progress" by enabling viewers to share and participate in the experience of modernity as developed elsewhere, to respond to the thrill. On the other hand, to do so, the national subject was also caught up in a dialectics of seeing: viewers had to assume the position of spectators and become voyeurs of, rather than participants in, modernity. To the degree that the cinema of attractions depended on a highly conscious awareness of the film image *as* image and of the act of looking itself, it also produced a tremendously self-conscious form of spectatorship that in Latin America was almost immediately translated as the need to assert the self as modern but also and, more lastingly, as different, ultimately as a national subject. Thus, the earliest Latin American films recirculated the parameters of modernity as cinematically experienced elsewhere, while simultaneously enabling viewers to participate in and promote whatever forms of that modernity were available locally.

In its form and content, early Latin American cinema clearly resonates with the technological changes and innovations generally associated with modernization, echoing how the intersection of cinema and modernity was evidenced in Western Europe and the United States while demonstrating the desire to identify "attractions" locally in order to exploit incipient modernity of each site. For example, in response to the great impact of the Lumières's *Arrival of a Train at the Station* (1895), one of the films included in most "first" Latin American screenings, local filmmakers sought in the developed or developing national railroad and transportation systems an equivalent symbol and the duplication of the amazement produced by the French film. One of the first national "views" filmed in Buenos Aires, screened in November 1896, was precisely of the arrival of a train at a local station, described pointedly in the press as "the arrivals of *our* trains."[26] Slightly later, in 1901, Eugenio Py chronicled the *Llegada de un tramway* (Arrival of a Streetcar), undoubtedly seeking a similar effect. In Brazil, Vittorio de Maio filmed *Chegada de um tren a Petrópolis* (Arrival of a Train in Petrópolis) and

Ponto Terminal da Linha dos Bondes (Streetcar Line Terminal) in 1897; their exhibition at the Teatro Casino Fluminense in Petrópolis (a mountain resort city near Rio) in May 1897 was widely advertised.[27]

As in the rest of the world, all modern modes of transport were quickly imbricated with the emerging medium, not only as subject but also by reproducing the perceptual changes they embodied. Railroad travel, in particular, profoundly altered the human sensorium and produced a specifically modern perceptual paradigm marked by what Wolfgang Schivelbusch calls "panoramic perception"—the experience of passengers looking out of a moving train window—as well as a changed temporal consciousness, an orientation to synchronicity and simultaneity.[28] The cinema in Latin America developed a similar natural affinity with this panoramic mode of perception within its first decade; the railroad "view" became the logical predecessor and producer of early traveling shots. For *Los festejos de la Caridad* (The Festivities of St. Charity, 1909), for example, Cuban film pioneer Enrique Díaz Quesada put his camera on a streetcar to produce a traveling shot of festivities in Camagüey province. Affonso Segreto produced a similar, albeit slower, effect with his Brazilian "views" from his ship pulling into the Bay of Guanabara in Rio de Janeiro in June 1898 upon his return from a trip to Europe (where he had purchased equipment from the Lumières).

Mexican filmmakers assiduously followed President Porfirio Díaz's many train trips, beginning with a sojourn to Puebla in 1900; during a later trip to Tehuantepec (to inaugurate a rail line linking the Gulf of Mexico with the Pacific), actualities captured "fugitive" images of the pyramids at San Juan Teotihuacán. In Chile, Arturo Larraín filmed the funeral of President Pedro Montt in 1910 and included an extended sequence shot from the last wagon of the train that carried his remains to the capital from the port in Valparaíso (Montt died in Germany). In *Missão militar e diplomática Alemã* (German Military and Diplomatic Mission), an actuality-newsreel about the 1913 visit of a German diplomatic mission to Rio de Janeiro, shot by Alfredo Musson, what is of greatest interest is not the visiting dignitaries but the extraordinary, elegantly functioning, transportation infrastructure, including the electric streetcar shown climbing the steep Corcovado mountain and the monorail to Pão de Açucar (Sugarloaf Mountain). The vistas shot from inside both vehicles are magnificent.

Sometimes the train effect was pushed to its limits to produce the phenomenological experience of railroad travel (akin to the Hale's Tours popular in the United States from 1906 to 1910); according to the Curitiba (Brazil) newspaper *A República*, to watch the 1910 film *Viagem à serra do mar* (Trip from the Mountains to the Sea), spectators

> enter a simulacrum of a fully outfitted railroad car, including a machine on top providing the noise and vibrations of a moving railroad. . . . Spectators receive a total illusion of a railroad trip, topped by the projection in the front end of the car of the amazing landscapes (visible from) our railroads, especially our marvelous mountains.[29]

Figure 1. Affonso Segreto shows off his equipment shortly after his return to Rio de Janeiro from - Europe (1898).

Figure 2. The German diplomatic mission boards the Corcovado electric car in Missão militar e diplomática Alemã *(Alfredo Musson, 1913).*

Figure 3. Another scene from Missão militar e diplomática Alemã, *shot from inside the monorail climbing Pão de Açucar (Sugarloaf Mountain).*

Mobility in general was a great attraction. In the Brazilian films *Carnaval em Curitiba* (Carnival in Curitiba, 1910) and *Desfile Militar* (Military Parade, 1910), for example, the camera's focus on the various means of transport overwhelms the alleged subject of the shorts (carnival festivities in Curitiba and a military parade in Rio). In both films, we witness a veritable melee of mobility as cars, electric streetcars, and horse-drawn carriages parade in front of the cameras. Here and elsewhere, the earliest Latin American films produce an extraordinary catalogue of mobility; early films privilege travels, races of all kinds of vehicles (from bicycles to airplanes), mechanized journeys, and international visitors and tourists. As epistemologically unstable as the new medium's predominant characteristic (the illusion of movement), these new "visions" offered fleeting (one- to three-minute-long) fragments of the experience of mobility in and around a modern metropolis.

In Latin America, as elsewhere, the early cinema capitalized on the panoply of modern technologies, including urban developments, media, and new amusements. In *Melhoramentos do Rio de Janeiro* (Improvements in Rio de Janeiro, 1908), for example, Brazilian Antonio Leal documented the 1905 opening of the urban artery the Avenida Central (today's Rio Branco), which changed the physiognomy of the city, and other urban improvements. Sophisticated firefighting organizations were the focus of early films in both Chile and Cuba. In Chile, *Ejército General de Bombas* (Firefighters' Corps, 1902) was a three-minute view of the city's firefighters on parade and the first national "view" on record. The first film recorded on Cuban soil, *Simulacro de un incendio* (Simulacrum of a Fire, 1897), was shot by Lumière cameraman Gabriel Veyre; it documented a staged firefighting incident and featured a well-known Spanish stage actress.[30] In the area of communication, the telephone was at the center of the proto-narrative of Argentinian Eugenio Py's *Noticia Telefónica Angustiosa* (Sorrowful Telephone News, 1906), while the popularity of the phonograph suggested a series of experiments in which music and sound were added to films, in particular, Py's thirty-two very popular "sonorized films" for the Casa Lepage (1907–1911).[31]

Meanwhile, the still-in-development fields of public relations and advertising were exploited early in Cuba, following U.S. trends. In José E. Casasús's *El brujo desaparecido* (The Disappearing Witch-doctor, 1898), a trick film in the style of Georges Méliès, a magician "disappeared" to drink a beer. Somewhat later, Enrique Díaz Quesada's *El parque de Palatino* (Palatino Park, 1906) chronicled and reproduced the thrills of the rides at the newly opened Palatino amusement park, a mini-Coney Island that included a movie theater.[32] Influenced by the popularity and foreign novelty of the *bel canto* series at the newly inaugurated Teatro Municipal and other theatrical revues in Rio, Brazilian producers created what is perhaps the "first" Brazilian film genre: the *falados e cantantes* (spoken-and-sung) films, in which actors spoke and sang behind a screen. These films were wildly successful between 1908 and 1912. They began as simple illustrated songs but quickly introduced complicated stagings of operas, zarzuelas, and operettas; eventually, producers developed their own "scripts," using well-known and new songs, as in Alberto Botelho's *Paz e Amor* (Peace and Love, 1910), a thinly disguised parody of the newly inaugurated president Nilo Peçanha.[33] In short, the cinema very quickly became emblematic of modernity, while the specularity and spectacularity of its fragmentary processes came to epitomize local forms of a modern sensibility.[34]

The Novelty of Objectivity

The cinema's impulse toward display and spectacle was ambivalently linked with the technology's purported affinity with science, much lauded in Latin America[35] and aligned with then hegemonic positivist ideologies of progress. Positivism and modernity were themselves inextricably linked; the former was perceived as the theoretical matrix that would permit the achievement of the latter. The idea that "scientific" rational knowledge could control the chaos of natural forces and the reorganization of social life was the intellectual rationale for the ideology of "Order and Progress," the motto of more than one nation and a sublation that condensed the contradictory impulses of the evolving "modern" rationalities of economics and politics in still overwhelmingly traditional societies. In fact, only a few early films documented "scientific" projects. In Argentina, surgical pioneer Alejandro Posadas recorded two of his surgeries—a hernia operation and the removal of a pulmonary cyst—in Buenos Aires in 1900 (both films are extant). In Brazil, the preventive work of Oswaldo Cruz was the subject of *Eradicação da Febre Amarela no Rio de Janeiro* (Eradication of Yellow Fever in Rio, 1909), while a somewhat precarious dental extraction in Venezuela was the subject of what may be the earliest views shot in Latin America. The film, *Un célebre especialista sacando muelas en el Gran Hotel Europa* (A Famous Specialist Pulling Teeth in the Gran Hotel Europa), was made by Guillermo and Manuel Trujillo Durán and shown for the first time in January 1897. The cinema's veneer of scientific objectivity—its ability to display the physical world—perfectly rationalized its more thrilling appeals.

Also linked to the ideology of scientific rationality and progress was the insistence of local inventors on improving and expanding the medium. In 1898 Mexico, for example, someone "invented" the *ciclofotógrafo*, a camera attached to a bicycle for traveling shots, and Luis Adrián Lavie announced his *aristógrafo*, which allowed spectators to see motion pictures in 3-D.[36] In Argentina, three inventors patented a series of machines, among them the *estereobioscopio*, which produced moving images with depth.[37] The cinema was welcomed first and foremost as a sign of and tool for expressing the rationalist impetus of the modern. It was thoroughly aligned with the civilizing desires of the urban modernizing elites and disassociated from the "barbarism" of national "others."

In Mexico, it was, above all, the cinema's purported objectivity that first endeared it to the highly positivist intelligentsia of the Porfiriato, who were fully committed to its leader's "Order and Progress" motto. Linking the cinema with the also new and booming illustrated press and arguing that it was against the medium's nature to lie, early commentators railed stridently against the film *Duelo a pistola en el bosque de Chapultepec* (Pistol Duel in Chapultepec Forest, 1896), a reconstruction shot by Lumière cameramen Bertrand von Bernard and Gabriel Veyre of a duel between two deputies, as "the most serious of deceits, because audiences, perhaps the uninformed or foreigners . . . will not be able to tell whether it is a simulacrum of a duel or a real honorific dispute."[38] The concern over Mexico's image abroad is explicit; after all, the film was shot by Lumière cameramen charged with collecting foreign views for international distribution, at a time when the government was already beginning to organize its pavilion for the 1900 Paris Universal Exhibition. But the paternalism explicit in this commentary—the "uninformed" (i.e., the national illiterate masses)—indicates the unstable relationship between the regime's much-touted "progress" and those it had bypassed. For the majority of Mexico City inhabitants, "progress" was experienced as entertainment, not science; they had already gathered in the streets to watch the installation of electrical power posts and a parade of new bicycles they still could not afford. The cinema was next in line, and, to the degree that it was adopted by the masses and developed its "attractions," it was repudiated by the elites. Thus, the cinema functioned as a modernizing force, not according to positivist scientific parameters but by consolidating the formation of a modern urban audience. Nonetheless, although abandoned by the *científicos*[39] and eventually given over to the masses as spectacle, the Mexican cinema remained bound to the myth of objectivity, to its value as "truth."

Figure 4. Eugenio Py films Viaje del Doctor Campos Salles a Buenos Aires *(1900).*

If at first the illusion of movement necessarily involved the disavowal of the frailty of our knowledge of the physical world, that thrilling anxiety was quickly sublimated into the still-shocking experience of seeing "history"—near and far—as it happened. Stimulated by the surprise of being able to see imported images, whether real or reconstructed, of the Spanish-American War,[40] local filmmakers throughout the continent exploited the ostensible objectivity of the medium to record current events. The attraction of history-in-the-making allowed the still economically unstable medium to continue to attract audiences and develop commercially; as the novelty of the first shocks of movement wore off, the focus shifted to monumental current events. In fact, it has been argued that locally financed and local interest actuality-newsreels constitute the only consistent and unbroken cinematic tradition of early Latin American cinema. Beginning with the chronicling of the visit to Buenos Aires by the Brazilian president—*Viaje del Doctor Campos Salles a Buenos Aires* (Trip of Dr. Campos Salles to Buenos Aires, 1900)—and, the next year, naval operations—*Maniobras navales de Bahía Blanca* (Naval Operations in Bahia Blanca, 1901)—the company of Argentine pioneer Max Glucksmann, Casa Lepage, which specialized in actuality-newsreels, produced an outstanding record of the Argentine public sphere throughout the silent and sound periods. Joining in this endeavor were other entrepreneurs, among them Julio Irigoyen (*Noticiero Buenos Aires*) and Federico Valle. Valle entered the field shortly after his 1911 arrival in Argentina (after working with Méliès in France) and produced, among other films, the *Film Revista Valle* weekly newsreel from 1920 to 1930.

Actualities were also the mainstay of the early film business in Brazil. Antonio Leal in Rio and regional producers (especially in Curitiba) were soon joined by Marc Ferrez and his son Julio, Francisco Serrador, the Botelho brothers, and others in the provinces. In Brazil, however, the novelty of news also took on a spectacular character as sensational crimes, already popularized by the illustrated press, were meticulously restaged and shot on location. Films like *Os Estranguladores* (The Stranglers, Francisco Marzullo or Antonio Leal, 1908) and the two versions of *O crime da mala* (The Suitcase Crime, Francisco Serrador and Marc Ferrez and son, respectively, both 1908) were wildly successful: the audience's familiarity with the crimes enabled the filmmakers to tell their stories efficiently without intertitles or internal continuity.

Another restaging of a news story, Antonio Leal's *O comprador de ratos* (The Rat Buyer, 1908), is of particular interest, as it unwittingly captures the idiosyncrasies of modernity in the midst of underdevelopment, thus serving as a particularly vivid example of the contradictions produced by "misplaced ideas."[41] During the Oswaldo Cruz-led campaign to eradicate yellow fever in Rio, the government announced that it would buy dead rats by the pound. The inhabitants of Rio's poor neighborhoods found themselves in the midst of a thriving industry, breeding and fattening rats to sell to the government. In a brilliant allegory of modernity in Latin America, *O comprador* tells the story of a Niterói native who attempted to sell thousands of rodents until the scam was discovered.[42]

Following the Lumière model, Mexican pioneers also took to current events, perhaps with the greatest enthusiasm after Salvador Toscano exhibited the actualities *Guanajuato destruido por las inundaciones* (Guanajuato Destroyed by Floods, 1905) and *Incendio del cajón de la Valenciana* (Fire at the Valenciana

Warehouse, 1905). In 1906, both Toscano and his principal competitor, Enrique Rosas, rushed to chronicle an official trip to Yucatán by President Díaz, whose image was still of great interest to audiences; their films exhibited a preoccupation with formal structure that pushed them beyond the simplicity of the typical actuality. Following an excruciatingly linear logic dependent on editing, Toscano's film narrated the presidential trip from beginning (Díaz's departure by train from Mexico City) to end (his farewells to Yucatán), thus substituting a chronology that was absolutely faithful to the pro-filmic event for narrative development.

Similarly, the Alva brothers' *Entrevista Díaz–Taft* (Díaz–Taft Interview, 1909), a report of the Díaz–William Howard Taft meetings in Ciudad Juarez and El Paso, employs the chronological "record of a trip" structure, but it is mediated by two additional concerns: a visible effort to record both sides of the event (some of President Taft's trip as well as Díaz's) and a willingness to fiddle with the chronology of the pro-filmic event to augment the narrative impact. As Aurelio de los Reyes demonstrates, the filmmakers altered the sequence of events toward the end of the film in order to have the film end on an apotheosis, with the image of both presidents on the steps of the customs building in Juarez.[43] This image is the visual equivalent of their interview, but it is also strongly marked by an accidental pro-filmic action: as the presidents descend the steps, an observer waves a flag in front of the camera and, for an instant, the screen is filled by the flag and its large slogan, "Viva la República," visually affirming the national despite the alleged impartiality of its treatment. In fact, the cinema's "truth value" was selectively applied: the Porfirian cinema was basically escapist and did not record the more disagreeable aspects of national life, such as the bloody strikes in Cananea (1906) and Río Blanco (1907), the violence and poverty of urban ghettos, or the injustices of rural life.

Beyond the drive to identify "local" modern thrills—almost, but not quite, the same as those of the imported views—or to record current events, the new technology was used for the benefit of the imagined national community, to negotiate precisely the conflicts generated by the dilemmas of a modernity that was precariously balanced between indigenous traditions and foreign influences, between nationalist aspirations and internationalist desires. Thus, the fascination with the epiphenomenal manifestations of modernity and their perceptual thrills was inflected with explicit exaltations of nationness—these are not just "our" railroads but symbols of our national *belongingness*, in a sense as "modern" as the new technological forms themselves—linked in many instances to current events.

Following the nonchronological plotting of time and history suggested earlier, this process occurred both sequentially and simultaneously with the fascination with modern technology and current events described above. In late 1897, for example, a notice in the Buenos Aires newspaper *El Diario* announced not only a filming of local events but the time and location: "The views will be photographed in the morning. The first will be of bicyclists in Palermo park at 7:30 AM. Those who would like to see their figures circulating on the screen of this theater should take notice."[44] Similarly, a few months later, *La Nación* remarked in its column "Vida Social":

> The views shot in Palermo, which will be projected by the marvelous machine next Monday on the stage of the Casino theater, will perhaps be of greater interest than the landscapes and exotic scenes reproduced by the "American Biograph." We are assured that these views are as sharp as the European and that we shall clearly recognize many of our socially prominent citizens.[45]

Clearly invoking another kind of desire or "attraction," these notices posited a spectatorial position predicated on identification and self-recognition, which was but an embryonic form of cinematic nationness. It was also a process markedly aligned with the existing power structure: the appeal was not just that one would see ordinary Buenos Aires citizens but socially prominent ones— metaphorical stand-ins for the nation itself.

In Latin America as a whole, the cinema was, from its earliest moments, closely aligned with those in power, be they wealthy and socially prominent or simply in government, and this alignment was a first step toward nationalist projects. The first films photographed in Mexico, for example, were not landscapes or street scenes but carefully orchestrated views of Porfirio Díaz (recently reelected for a fourth presidential term), his family, and his official retinue shot by Lumière cameramen von Bernard and Veyre in 1898. The young Frenchmen recognized the need to secure the dictator's goodwill to proceed in their commercial enterprises and arranged a private screening of the new technology for Díaz and his family in Chapultepec. During the five months they remained in Mexico, they filmed the president, who quickly recognized the propagandistic value of the new medium, at all sorts of official and familiar events. As one historian has remarked, Porfirio Díaz was, by default, the first "star" (attraction?) of the Mexican cinema:[46] his on-screen appearances were enthusiastically hailed with rousing "Vivas!"[47]

Akin to the Mexican example, the first two views filmed in Bolivia were explicit paeans to the power structure. Both *Retratos de personajes históricos y de actualidad* (Portraits of Historical and Contemporary Figures, 1904) and the very popular *La exhibición de todos los personajes ilustres de Bolivia* (The Exhibition of All the Illustrious Characters of Bolivia, 1909) were designed to align the new technology with those who effectively controlled and defined the nation *and* to display them for the enjoyment and recognition of the new audiences. In Mexico, however, the initial links between cinema and the urban power elites were short-lived. Production/exhibition pioneers, motivated by the 1900 closing down of Mexico City's exhibition sites—primarily *carpas* or tents—because of city safety regulations designed to curb the "uncivilized" behavior of popular spectators and to diminish the risk of fires, became itinerant and left Mexico City, taking the cinema with them (there was only a handful of film exhibitions in the capital between 1901 and 1905).[48] They traveled throughout the national territory showing the films in their repertoires but also regularly producing local views to entice the various regional audiences. These views chronicled the activities of small cities and towns: the crowds leaving church after Sunday Mass, workers outside factories, and local celebrations and festivities. Rather than focusing on modern life and technology, this early cinema took a turn toward the people—positioned in their local landscapes and captured in their everyday activities. Its attraction was self-recognition: "On premiere nights the improvised actors would come to the shows en masse to see themselves on film; the enthusiasm of each and every one when they saw themselves or their friends and relatives on screen was great."[49] But through that self-recognition, these actors also began the process of producing an image of the nation based on its traditional sectors and ways of life—the peoples and customs of the interior rather than the modernity of the capital city—and a more broad-based audience for the cinema.

The linchpin of the cinema-nation symbiosis coincided with the various centennial celebrations around 1910. In Argentina and Mexico (Chile also celebrated its centennial in 1910), filmmakers competed fiercely to record the festivities, and their films were quickly exhibited to great public acclaim. Aurelio de los Reyes reproduces a telling photograph in his book *Filmografía del cine mudo mexicano, 1896–1920*: while President Díaz is placing the cornerstone of a monument to Louis Pasteur, three cameramen vie for the best angle.[50] At least three filmmakers—the Alva brothers, Salvador Toscano, and Guillermo Becerril—competed to record the events that were the apotheosis and swan song of the Porfirian era. Actualities such as *El desfile histórico del Centenario* (The Historic Centennial Parade), *Gran desfile militar del 16 de septiembre* (Great Military Parade of September 16), and *Entrega del uniforme de Morelos* (Presentation of Morelo's Uniform) illustrated the magnificence of the events as well as the exuberance and optimism of the crowds. But the paroxysms of patriotism elicited by the centennials and their preparations also motivated filmmakers in a different direction, away from current events and toward the reconstruction of key patriotic moments, in an effort to further mobilize the new medium in the service of nationhood.

National Narratives

Undoubtedly, Latin American audiences were already quite familiar with the post-1904 productions imported from the United States and Europe—dubbed "transitional narratives"[51] to highlight their status in between the cinema of attractions and full-fledged narrative cinema—and had begun to experience the appeal of a different kind of cinematic identification, one that filmmakers sought to exploit for the national celebrations. Viewers were influenced less by the chase films and Westerns arriving from the United States than by the theatrical adaptations filled with artistic aspirations produced by the Societé Film d'Art and other European producers. The theater was already an art form with an extensive history and of

Figure 5. From the last tableaux of La Revolución de Mayo *(Mario Gallo, 1909). Leader Saavedra addresses a crowd of patriots.*

great elite and popular appeal throughout Latin America. As such, it was a natural source of inspiration for filmmakers seeking to narrativize the medium. This process is most evident in Argentina, where the appeal of actualities of current events waned in comparison to the enthusiasm generated by a new series of proto-narratives, beginning with Mario Gallo's *La Revolución de Mayo* (The May Revolution, 1909).

A perfect example of a transitional film, *La Revolución* has neither a self-sufficient nor an internally coherent narrative. To make sense of the film and understand the motivations linking the various tableaux, the spectator must have extensive knowledge of the historical event being represented, as the intertitles are identificatory rather than expository. Furthermore, the style is thoroughly presentational, ranging from direct address to mise-en-scène (theatrical acting and theatrical backdrops suggesting depth and perspective rather than reproducing it). Its one purely "cinematic" moment occurs in the last tableaux, in which a visual device effectively supplements the film's patriotic enthusiasm: while the patriot leader Saavedra speaks from a balcony to a throng, an image of General San Martín in uniform and wrapped in the Argentine flag appears unexpectedly over a painted backdrop of the Cabildo; the people and the army salute him and shout "Viva la República" (according to the titles). Other Gallo historical reconstructions further developed this patriotic theme and style (utilizing well-known popular stage actors), as seen, for example, in *La creación del himno* (The Creation of the National Anthem, 1909), an homage to the writing and first performance of the national anthem, and *El fusilamiento de Dorrego* (Dorrego's Execution), *Juan Moreira*, *Güemes y sus gauchos* (Guemes and his Gauchos), and *Camila O'Gorman* (all 1910).

Humberto Cairo's *Nobleza gaucha* (Gaucho Nobility, 1915) further developed Gallo's narrative-nationalist impetus. This film most clearly exemplifies the nationalist sentiments and contradictions of the period and was perhaps the first to develop the city/countryside dialectic central to Latin America's modernity debates. Although much closer to a classical style than *La Revolución*, *Nobleza* is still a transitional narrative. Rather than depend on the audience's prior historical knowledge, however, its intertext is cultural; the intertitles cite the great Argentine epic poem *Martín Fierro* to recount the story of a courageous gaucho who saves his beautiful girlfriend from the evil clutches of a ranch owner who abducted her to his palatial city mansion. The ranch owner falsely accuses the gaucho of theft, but dies when he falls off a cliff while being chased by the hero on horseback. Skillfully filmed—with well-placed close-ups, elegant lighting, and diverse camera movements, including tracking shots from trains and streetcars—and acted naturalistically, the story line allowed Cairo to focus on the always appealing folklore of the countryside (songs, ranchos, gauchos, and barbecues), as well as the modernity of the city: shots of Constitución Avenue, Avenida de Mayo, Congress, the Armenonville station, and even nighttime urban illuminations. *Nobleza* simultaneously exalts the traditional values of rural life—indulging in what Rey Chow calls "primitive passions"[52]—while displaying in all its splendor the modern urbanity that would make it obsolete; the gaucho may have been the hero of the narrative, but he was already relegated to the status of a foundational myth like *Martín Fierro*. *Nobleza*'s exploration of the crisis in national identity generated by the conflict between traditional experiences and values and the internationalization endemic to modernity was extraordinarily well received: the film only cost 20,000 pesos to produce but made more than 600,000 from its many national and international screenings.[53]

Thus, transitional narrative styles, in all their diverse forms, were almost naturally linked to the project of modern nation building. Once the cinema had exhausted its purely specular attractions and sought new storytelling possibilities, the task of generating narratives about the nation inevitably led to the problematization of modernization itself. The epidermal modernity of urban daily life—with its railroads, mobility, and technology—had been exalted earlier. Narratives now required the exploration of the contradictions of that process at a national level. With few exceptions, the earliest successful Latin American films identified as narratives were linked to patriotic themes. In Mexico, for example, Carlos Mongrand invoked well-known historical figures in *Cuauhtémoc y Benito Juarez* and *Hernán Cortés, Hidalgo y Morelos* (both 1904); later Felipe de Jesús Haro and the American Amusement Co. produced the elaborate (seven tableaux) *Grito de Dolores* (The Shout of Dolores, 1907), which was usually screened with live actors declaiming the dialogue behind the screen.[54] In Brazil, in addition to addressing historical events and figures (for example, Alberto Botelho's *A vida do Barão do Rio Branco* [The Life of the Rio Branco Baron, 1910], similar to *Nobleza Gaucha*), narrative was aligned with comedy and contrasted with urban and rural lives. Julio Ferrez's *Nhô Anastacio chegou de viagem* (Mr. Anastacio Returned from a Trip, 1908), recognized as the first Brazilian fiction film, presents the misadventures of a country bumpkin newly arrived in Rio, including his encounters with urban modernity (railroads, monuments, etc.) within a mistaken identity love plot. It engendered a series of similar comedies, focused on the conflicts between traditional rural ways and the modernity of cities filled with foreign immigrants and twentieth-century technologies. Throughout these comedies, which attempt to produce the discursive triumph of positivism, the traditional/rural is figured as nostalgically obsolete, a cultural remnant being willed into history, while the modernity of the metropolis is presented as inevitable, "natural," and national.

Although problematized by differential chronologies, similar efforts occurred in other parts of the continent. On the one hand, it is as if developments that took place in, say, Argentina or Brazil, in the early to mid-1910s began to unfold in nations like Chile, Bolivia, and Colombia in the 1920s. On the other hand, the films of the 1920s in Chile, Bolivia, and Colombia were very much produced in the context of 1920s global trends—familiar through always abundant imported films—and had, to some degree, already abandoned the parameters of the 1910s. Thus, instead of rough transitional narratives, the first Chilean, Bolivian, and Colombian fiction films follow very closely the hegemonic representational parameters of the era—continuity editing, self-sufficient internal narration, and feature length—yet return to the nationalistic concerns of the earlier era elsewhere. In Bolivia, for example, the conflict between indigenous/rural existence and urban life was explored in José María Velasco Maidana's *La profecia del lago* (The Prophecy of the Lake, 1925) and Pedro Sambarino's *Corazón Aymara* (Aymara Heart, 1925). In Colombia, we find skillful adaptations of foundational fictions mediated through the conventions of European-inspired film melodrama: *María* (Alfredo del Diestro and Máximo Calvo, 1921–1922) and Di Doménico's *Aura o las violetas* (Dawn or the Violets, 1923). Chile's version of *Nobleza Gaucha*, *Alma chilena* (Chilean Soul, 1917), was directed by Arturo Mario, the star of the Argentine film, while Gabriella von Bussenius and Salvador Giambastiani's *La agonía del Arauco* (Arauco Agony, 1917) contrasted the Mapuche landscape and people with the melodramatic foibles of its urban protagonists, and Pedro Sienna's *El húsar de la muerte* (The Hussar of Death, 1925) chronicled the exploits of national hero Manuel Rodríguez.

The Chilean example highlights a curious characteristic of early Latin American cinema that perhaps explains, in part, its obsessive concern with nationness: throughout the continent, the overwhelming majority of early filmmakers were first-generation immigrants. The evidence to support this assertion is too vast to summarize efficiently, so a few names must suffice: in Brazil, the Segreto family came from Italy, Antonio Leal from Portugal, and Francisco Serrador from Spain. In Argentina, Enrique Lepage was Belgian, Federico Figner Czech, Max Glucksmann Austrian, Eugenio Py French, and Mario Gallo and Federico Valle Italian. In Chile, Salvador Giambastiani was Italian (and had worked in Argentina before arriving in Chile in 1915), and the Argentine actors Arturo Mario and María Padín became producers/directors in 1917. In Uruguay, the branch of Max Glucksmann's Argentine company was the principal producer of actualities between 1913 and 1931. Pedro Sambarino, an Italian, worked in Bolivia and Peru. Originally from Italy, the Di Doménico family was instrumental in establishing the cinema in Colombia and Central America. After immigrating to Panama, they acquired filmmaking equipment from Europe and traveled through the Antilles and Venezuela, arriving in Barranquilla in 1910 and settling in La Paz in 1911, where they established a regional distributor/production company of great significance until the arrival of sound.[55] Thus, the cinema was a medium not only of mobility but also of great appeal to the mobile, to immigrants seeking to make their fortunes in the new world through the apparatuses of modernity yet eager to assert their new national affiliations, and to those who restlessly traveled throughout the continent.

A Nation at War and Beyond

Mexico is a case apart, not only because its cinema pioneers were not foreign immigrants, with a few exceptions (Henri Moulinié and Carlos Mongrand were French), but because its cataclysmic revolution determined a different, although no less nationalistic, path for the cinema between 1910 and 1918.[56] The films of the Mexican Revolution were the direct heirs of the passion for objectivity and reportage of the earlier actualities. Just as Díaz had been the "star" of early Mexican views, Francisco Madero, the other *caudillos*, and the armed struggle became the stars of the next decade. The success of the Alva brothers' *Insurrección de México* (Mexican Insurrection, 1911), one of the first films depicting revolutionary events, demonstrated that audiences were avid for news of the Revolution, and most filmmakers followed the *caudillos* and fighting troops to capture images of the complicated events taking place. Alongside the increase in production, movie theaters mushroomed in the capital to accommodate new capacity crowds, many composed of newly arrived peasants escaping from the fighting and violence in the provinces.

In the first films of the Revolution, filmmakers continued to adapt narrative strategies to the documentation of events. *Asalto y toma de Ciudad Juárez* (Assault and Takeover of Ciudad Juarez, 1911), for example, the third part of the Alva brothers' *Insurrección en México*, was subdivided into four parts and

Figure 6. The Alva brothers—Salvador, Guillermo and Eduardo—take a lunch break from filming (ca. 1910–1912).

consisted of thirty-six scenes, the last of which was the "apotheosis" or grand climax, in which the people acclaim the victory of the hero, Pascual Orozco. Similarly, the Alva brothers' *Las conferencias de paz y toma de Ciudad Juárez* (The Peace Conferences and Takeover of Ciudad Juárez, 1911,) ended with the military's triumphant entry into Ciudad Juárez, and their *Viaje del señor Madero de Ciudad Juárez hasta Ciudad de México* (Mr. Madero's Trip from Ciudad Juárez to Mexico City, 1911) climaxed at the intersection of two parallel narrative lines (Venustiano Carranza and Madero's journeys, culminating in two apotheosis scenes). Finally, Guillermo Becerril Jr.'s *Los últimos sucesos de Puebla y la llegada de Madero a esa ciudad* (The Latest Events in Puebla and Madero's Arrival to This City, 1911) ended with the "apotheosis" image of President Madero and his wife posing for the camera. All these films respected the chronological sequence of the events and simultaneously adopted a clearly dramatic/narrative structure for their representation.

Potentially the most ambitious of all the revolutionary films was the Alva brothers' *Revolución orozquista* (Orozquista Revolution, 1912). It documented the battles between General Victoriano Huerta's and Orozco's troops and was shot under extremely dangerous circumstances. The filmmakers chose to present both sides of the battle with a great degree of objectivity and thus structured the film to tell two parallel stories without providing explanations or justifying the actions of either side: in the first part, we see the activities of the Orozquista camp, in the second the Huertistas. The third part features the battle between the two camps, but we are not shown the outcome—who won is withheld from the report. Believing that the events were powerful enough to speak for themselves, the filmmakers attempted to assume the impartiality required of the positivist historian and thus produced a spectacular transitional form that engaged narrative protocols while remaining wedded to documentary objectivity and that aimed, above all, to inform. This form would be exploited and further developed by all the filmmakers active in this period, especially in the several films dealing with the events of the *Decena Trágica* in February 1913 (the ten days of violence in Mexico City following an armed uprising led by Félix Díaz, Porfirio's nephew, that culminated in Huerta's triumph over Madero).

It is important to note that each of the principal combatants had his "own" camera crews on hand to record his achievements. The Alva brothers followed Madero's activities; Jesús Abitia covered General Obregón—a former friend of his family—and also filmed Carranza; the Zapatistas were filmed by several cameramen; Pancho Villa and Carranza favored the U.S. cinematographers, who rushed across the border to produce newsreels and documentaries. Villa, in particular, signed an exclusive contract with the Mutual Film Co. and was known to stage battles and events such as hangings in the daytime so that they could be filmed.[57]

Huerta's takeover in 1913 had a great impact on the development of the revolutionary documentary; because the films often awakened violent reactions in their already partisan audiences, Huerta approved legislation requiring "moral and political" censorship prior to exhibition. Thereafter, filmmakers gave up striving for "objectivity" and assumed the point of view of those in power: *Sangre hermana* (Fraternal Blood, 1914), for example, is told from a marked federalist and propagandistic perspective. Other films focused on using previously shot materials to produce "reviews" of the Revolution that were then updated regularly and shown in their entirety: Enrique Echániz Brust and Salvador Toscano's *Historia completa de la Revolución de 1910–1915* (Complete History of the Revolution, *1910–1915*, 1915); and Enrique Rosas's *Documentación histórica nacional, 1915–1916* (National Historical Documentation, *1915–1916*, 1916). Eventually, the Revolution disappeared from Mexican screens and was replaced by a new fiction cinema:

Before, filmmakers were pragmatists who had learned their craft by documenting people and events in order to attract audiences . . . National producers had never before dealt with narrative, a term that had been used exclusively to refer to foreign fiction films. . . . Now a different conception of cinema made its way. The "views" had lost their appeal and the desire was for *films d'art* based on foreign models.[58]

An important predecessor was the Alva brothers' *El aniversario del fallecimiento de la suegra de Enhart* (The Anniversary of the Death of Enhart's Mother-in-law, 1912), a short comedy about the "daily life" of two very popular theatrical comedians (Alegría and Enhart) in the style of the French films of Max Linder. Although "fictional," the narrative focuses on the domestic as well as the professional lives of the two comedians. The Alvas apparently had not given up on their use of the medium to capture the real world, and the camera scrutinizes the very real Mexico City locations in which the fictional mise-en-scène takes place. The film is skillfully constructed, with editing that contributes to the narrative coherence by alternating between two parallel story lines, inserts (such as intertitles) that add to the suspense/humor, judicious use of special effects (like the old Méliès magic disappearing trick), and close-ups for comic/performative emphasis. The Alvas were perfecting their technique, only now in the service of narrative entertainment rather than information.

Beginning in 1916, Mexican filmmaking turned to fictional narratives in the style of the French *film d'art* and ignored the revolution and the revolutionary documentary. This change can be attributed to a number of interrelated factors: the political restrictions imposed by the Venustiano Carranza government, a desire to improve the image of the nation (which had been sullied by the Revolution itself but also by how Hollywood films represented it), the popularity of Italian melodramas, and a widespread desire to leave the Revolution behind (especially after the 1917 constitution and the 1919 assassination of Emiliano Zapata).

Two potentially contradictory tendencies were evident in the efforts to develop a Mexican industry: nationalism and the influence of Italian melodramas. The first tendency was exemplified by the work of Carlos Martínez de Arredondo and Manuel Cirerol Sansores, who founded the company Cirmar Films in Mérida. After making some fictional shorts with indigenous themes, such as *La voz de su raza* (The Voice of Your Race, 1914[?]) and *Tiempos mayas* (Mayan Times, 1915–1916), they produced the first Mexican fictional feature film with a clear nationalist spirit: *1810 o los libertadores* (1810 or the Liberators, 1916). Meanwhile, the tremendous influence of Italian film melodramas was perhaps nowhere better illustrated than in Ezequiel Carrasco's *La luz* (The Light, 1917), the second Mexican feature-length fiction film. Clearly plagiarizing the popular Italian film *Il fuoco* (The Light, Piero Fosco, 1915), starring Pina Menichelli, *La luz* featured Emma Padilla, who not only resembled Menichelli but also copied her mannerisms and postures. (Padilla was the first "actress" to become a "star," a position that had previously been occupied by real historical

Figure 7. Emma Padilla imitates the Italian actress Pina Menichelli in La luz *(Ezequiel Carrasco, 1917).*

figures.) The story (a tripartite tale of misguided passions following the trajectory of daily light—dawn, zenith, dusk) followed the melodramatic style of Italian films, although, as Aurelio de los Reyes has indicated, it was set in a very Mexican land-scape, thus pointing to what would become a characteristic of the Mexican cinema throughout the rest of the silent and early sound periods: transforming foreign nar-rative models by setting them in explicitly Mexican mise-en-scènes.[59]

Approximately seventy-five feature-length fiction films were produced in the 1917–1921 period, the most prolific in the history of the Mexican silent cinema. The most significant film of this period, Enrique Rosas's *El automóvil gris* (The Gray Automobile, 1919), evidences the complex negotiations between the almost-forgotten devotion to objectivity of the revolutionary documentary and the more modern narrative film styles from abroad. Originally a twelve-part serial with explicit documentary ambitions, the film tells the real-life story of a band of thieves who pretended to be *carrancista* troops and robbed and kidnapped wealthy families throughout 1915. The members of the band were eventually captured, tried, and sentenced to death. Their execution took place on December 24, 1915, and Rosas had filmed the event for his documentary *Documentación histórica nacional 1915–1916*. Because the band was linked to various military factions, the entire event was politically charged and Rosas's film version, combining historical facts and legends, vindicates and clears the image of the *carrancistas*. Like Toscano's *Viaje a Yucatán* and the Alva brothers' *Revolución orozquista*, however, the cen-

Figure 8. El automóvil gris *(Enrique Rosas, 1919).*

tral structuring element of Rosas's film is the historical chronology of the events: the film presents the various robberies and the subsequent chase by the police in strict chronological order. Like *Aniversario del fallecimiento de la suegra de Enhart*, *El automóvil gris* was shot on location, where the robberies and chases took place (and includes footage of the execution of the gang members previously shot by Rosas). By comparing the two films, we can see how drastically Mexico City had changed in the intervening seven years: whereas in the earlier film we see people walking, interacting, and engaging in commerce in a clean and orderly city, in *El automóvil*, the city is in ruins, dirty, and almost completely empty.

El automóvil gris is the last Mexican silent film to have this kind of documentary feel—the last gasp of the previous documentary tradition—and, in its combination of documentary realism with touches of Italian melodrama and sophisticated Hollywood-style cinematic syntax (i.e., irises, close-ups, the serial structure), it points to the future Mexican sound cinema.

Peripheral Displacements

In complex negotiations between national events/traditions and foreign models and the demands of Westernization, Latin America produced a series of "spectacular experiments" that dialectically inscribed the cinema in national histories while simultaneously recognizing it as the embodiment of always differential dreams of modernity. Parochial yet also of the "world at large," the silent cinema was a key agent of both nationalism and globalization. With few if any proprietary claims to technology (the technology remained primarily an import), early cinema nevertheless contributed to the construction of strong nationalistic discourses of modernity. As evidenced by this comparative analysis, throughout the continent and despite certain regional differences, filmic visuality came to define the necessarily ambivalent position of those caught in the whirlpools of change, whether because of the shift from rural to urban life, displacements caused by immigration, or the cataclysms of civil war. A mechanism for accessible globality, the cinema captured and accompanied the vertiginous modernization of urban sectors, as well as the simultaneous inertia of other zones and territories: in the discursive struggle between the urban and the rural as icons of nationalisms, the cinema—the urban instrument par excellence—actively contributed to the postulation of the nonurban as a folkloric past or an anachronistic vestige.

Throughout the continent, national producers were faced with two significant changes in subsequent decades. The onset of World War I redefined the international cinematic marketplace; U.S. producers "discovered" the potential of the Latin American market, blocked from the usual markets and practices in Europe, and moved in aggressively. They consolidated their presence throughout the continent and, in most instances, effectively precluded national production from prospering commercially. This was quite marked in Brazil, for example, where the end of the *bela época* (circa 1912) coincided with the development of a strong distribution/exhibition sector geared to imports[60] and the subsequent arrival of subsidiaries of U.S. firms.[61]

This shift was soon followed by a far more devastating change: the arrival of sound. Aggressively marketed, sound films from the United States quickly took over the exhibition and distribution sectors, while national producers scrambled for capital, technology, and know-how. In some cases, the arrival of sound severed all cinematic activities: several nations—notably Bolivia, Venezuela, and Colombia—were not able to resume filmmaking until nearly a decade after the introduction of sound. Others—principally Mexico, Argentina, and Brazil—by hook or by crook, invented, adapted, and experimented, producing a different yet resonant version of early cinema. The sound cinema of the 1930s, 1940s, and 1950s would become the principal interlocutor of Latin American modernity—as Carlos Monsiváis says, where Latin Americans went not to dream but to learn to be modern.[62]

NOTES

Funding for research for this essay was made possible, in part, by grants from the Stone Center for Latin American Studies at Tulane University. My thanks to Hamilton Costa Pinto for his constant companionship, astute movie watching, and patient fact seeking over the years.

"Train of shadows" is Maxim Gorky's description of his first encounter with the cinema in 1896; his account is included as an appendix in Jay Leyda, *Kino: A History of the Russian and Soviet Film* (London: Allen & Unwyn, 1960), pp. 407–409.

1. As, for example, Armand Mattelart, *Transnationals and the Third World: The Struggle for Culture* (South Hadley, Mass.: Bergin and Garvey, 1983); Herbert Schiller, *Communication and Cultural Domination* (White Plains, N.Y.: International Arts and Sciences, 1976); and Jesús Martín Barbero, *De los medios a las mediaciones* (Barcelona: Ediciones Gili, 1987).

2. Paulo Antonio Paranaguá, *Cinéma na America Latina: Longe de Deus e perto de Hollywood* (Porto Alegre: L & PM Editores, 1985), p. 9. Unless otherwise noted, all translations from foreign language sources are my own.

3. Ella Shohat and Robert Stam, *Unthinking Eurocentrism: Multiculturalism and the Media* (New York: Routledge, 1994), p. 100.

4. Leo Charney and Vanessa R. Schwartz, "Introduction," in *Cinema and the Invention of Modern Life* (Berkeley: University of California Press, 1995), p. 1.

5. Whereas I use *modernity* to refer to both the idea of the modern as well as a particular disposition toward lived experience that encompasses various ideological and discursive paradigms, *modernization* refers more specifically to the processes of change that result from the introduction of certain technologies into the various spheres of private and social life.

6. José Joaquín Brunner, "Notes on Modernity and Postmodernity," tr. John Beverly, *Boundary 2* 20, no. 3 (fall 1993): 41.

7. This term was coined by Arjun Appadurai in reference to the introduction of cricket to India: "The indigenization [of a cultural practice imported by the colonizers] is often a product of collective and spectacular experiments with modernity, and not necessarily of the surface affinities of a new cultural form with existing patterns in the [new nation's] cultural repertoire." "Playing with Modernity: The Decolonization of Indian Cricket," in *Consuming Modernity: Public Culture in a South Asian World*, ed. Carol Breckenridge (Minneapolis: University of Minnesota Press, 1995), p. 24.

8. Angel Rama, *The Lettered City*, tr. John Charles Chasteen (Durham, N.C.: Duke University Press, 1996), p. 99.

9. Aníbal Quijano, "Modernity, Identity, and Utopia in Latin America," tr. John Beverly, *Boundary 2* 20, no. 3 (fall 1993): 149.

10. Brunner, "Notes on Modernity and Postmodernity," p. 53.

11. With three exceptions: the general comparative study by Paranaguá, cited above in note 2, which begins with the silent period; Paranaguá's subsequent essay on silent cinema, "El Cine silente latinoamericano: primeras imágenes de un centenario," published in *La Gran Ilusión* (Universidad de Lima, Peru), no. 6 (1997): 32–39; and a rather cursory and inadequately documented survey in Anne Marie Stock, "El cine mudo en América Latina: Paisajes, espectáculos e historias," *Historia General del Cine*, ed. Carlos F. Heredero and Casimiro Torreiro, vol. 4 (Madrid: Cátedra, 1997), pp. 129–157. Although the groundbreaking volume, edited by Guy Hennebelle and Alfonso Gumucio-Dagrón, *Les cinemas de l'Amérique latine* (Paris: Pierre L'Herminier, 1981), was the first to attempt to present comparable histories of filmmaking throughout the continent, its format—a national cinema per chapter—and the uneven quality of the research/contributions dilute its comparative usefulness.

12. Guillermo Caneto et al., *Historia de los primeros años del cine en la Argentina, 1895–1910* (Buenos Aires: Fundación Cinemateca Argentina, 1996), pp. 25–26.

13. For Argentine dates, see Caneto et al., *Historia de los primeros años*, pp. 27–28; for Brazil, see Paulo Antonio Paranaguá, ed., "Tableau Synoptique," in *Le cinema bresilien* (Paris: Centre Georges Pompidou, 1987), p. 24; for Mexico, see Federico Dávalos Orozco, *Albores del cine mexicano* (Mexico City: Clio, 1996), p. 12, and Aurelio de los Reyes, *Los orígenes del cine en Mexico* (Mexico City: UNAM, 1972), p. 40; for Uruguay, see Eugenio Hintz, *Historia y Filmografía del cine uruguayo* (Montevideo: Ediciones de la Plaza, 1988), p. 11; for Cuba, see Raúl Rodríguez, *El cine silente en Cuba* (Havana: Letras Cubanas, 1993), pp. 27–31; and for Chile, Peru, and Guatemala, see Paranaguá, *Cinéma na América Latina*, pp. 10–11.

14. See José Luis Romero and Luis Alberto Romero, *Buenos Aires: Historia de cuatro siglos* (Buenos Aires: Editora Abril, 1983); and Richard J. Walter, "Buenos Aires," in *Encyclopedia of Latin American History and Culture*, ed. Barbara Tenebaum et al. vol. 1 (New York: Scribner's, 1996), pp. 480–483.

15. See Charles S. Sargent, "Argentina," in *Latin American Urbanization: Historical Profiles of Major Cities*, ed. Gerald Michael Greenberg (Westport, Conn.: Greenwood Press, 1994), pp. 1–38.

16. See Sam Adamo, "The Sick and the Dead: Epidemic and Contagious Disease in Rio de

Janeiro, Brazil," in *Cities of Hope*, ed. Ron Pineo and James A. Baer (Boulder, Colo.: Westview Press, 1998), pp. 218–239, and Roberto Moura, "A Bela época (Primórdios-1912)," in *História do cinema brasileiro*, ed. Fernão Ramos, (São Paulo: Art Editora, 1987), pp. 13–20.

17. Jorge Basadre, *Historia de la República del Perú, 1822–1933* (Lima: Editorial Universitaria, 1968–1970).

18. See David S. Parker, "Civilizing the City of Kings: Hygiene and Housing in Lima, Peru," in Pineo and Baer, *Cities of Hope*, pp. 153–178.

19. See Ricardo Bedoya, *100 Años de cine en el Perú: una historia crítica* (Lima: Universidad de Lima/Instituto de Cooperación Iberoamerica, 1992); and Giancarlo Carbone, *El cine en el Perú, 1897–1950; testimonios* (Lima: Universidad de Lima, 1992).

20. William E. French, "In the Path of Progress: Railroads and Moral Reform in Porfirian Mexico," in *Railroad Imperialism*, ed. Clarence B. Davis and Kenneth E. Wilbrun (New York: Greenwood Press, 1991), pp. 85–102. By 1911, more than 11,000 miles of track had been laid. Mexico was so thoroughly blanketed by railways that fewer than 2,000 miles of track have been added since the Díaz regime. See also Jonathan Kandell, *La Capital: The Biography of Mexico City* (New York: Random House, 1988), pp. 367–370.

21. De los Reyes, *Los orígenes*, p. 91.

22. See, for example, Tom Gunning, "The Cinema of Attractions: Early Film, Its Spectator, and the Avant-Garde," *Wide Angle* 8, nos. 3–4 (1986): 63–70, reprinted in Thomas Elsaesser and Alan Barker, eds., *Early Cinema: Space, Frame, Narrative* (London: BFI, 1990), pp. 56–62.

23. Miriam Hansen, "Early Cinema, Late Cinema: Transformations of the Public Sphere," in *Viewing Positions: Ways of Seeing Films*, ed. Linda Williams (New Brunswick, N.J.: Rutgers University Press, 1997), p. 137.

24. Aurelio de los Reyes's discussion of how the practice of kissing in Mexico changed after the circulation of explicit cinematic kisses and the innovation of darkened public spaces—movie theaters—in which they could be exchanged is especially relevant here. See his "Los besos y el cine," in *El arte y la vida cotidiana: XVI coloquio Internacional de Historia del Arte*, ed. Elena Estrada de Garlero (Mexico City: UNAM, 1995), pp. 267–289.

25. Caneto et al., *Historia*, p. 31.

26. "Vida Social," *El Diario*, November 7, 1896, cited in Caneto et al., *Historia*, p. 34. Emphasis added.

27. Research by Paulo Henrique Ferreira and Vittorio Capellaro Jr., source unknown, cited in José Carlos Monteiro, *Cinema Brasileiro: Historia Visual* (Rio de Janeiro: FUNARTE, 1996), p. 13.

28. Wolfgang Schivelbusch, *The Railroad Journey: Trains and Travel in the Nineteenth Century*, tr. Anselm Hollo (New York: Urizen Books, 1971), pp. 57–72. See also Lynne Kirby, *Parallel Tracks: The Railroad and Silent Cinema* (Durham, N.C.: Duke University Press, 1997).

29. *A República* (Curitiba, Brazil), January 14, 1911, cited in Jurandyr Noronha, *Pioneros do Cinema Brasileiro*, CD-ROM (1997).

30. Raúl Rodríguez comments on the clearly political intentions of *Simulacro de un incendio*: the firefighters were aligned with the Spanish colonial government and fought against the liberating army, the film featured a Spanish actress, and, in its initial screening, was featured with three other shorts about the Spanish military. Rodríguez, *El cine silente en Cuba*, p. 33.

31. The "sonorization" was accomplished according to the system developed by Gaumont and Pathé in France. First, the sound track was recorded on a disk; later, while playing the record on a gramophone, they filmed the actors or actresses pretending to sing or recite. During projection, the film would be synchronized to the gramophone, whose sound was amplified by speakers near the screen. The equipment to reproduce sound was actually manufactured in Buenos Aires by Eugenio Py. See Caneto et al., *Historia*, p. 85.

32. See Rodríguez, *El cine silente en Cuba*; and María Eulalia Douglas, *La Tienda Negra: El cine en Cuba, 1897–1990* (Havana: Cinemateca de Cuba, 1996).

33. In his 1910 inaugural speech, Nilo Peçanha declared that his would be a government of "peace and love."

34. As early as 1897, for example, the major Mexico City daily *El Mundo* featured a column signed by "Lumière" that presented what can only be described as "fragments" or cinematic views of everyday urban life. An exemplary article from November 28, 1897, is reprinted in de los Reyes, *Los orígenes*, pp. 237–238.

35. All accounts of the new medium describe its *technology* in excruciating detail over and

above its effects, giving precise technical information about how the illusion of movement was produced. See, for example, the description of the cinématographe that appeared in the Buenos Aires newspaper *La Prensa* on April 3, 1896, cited in Caneto et al., *Historia*, p. 23, and the one published in the Mexican daily *El Mundo* on August 23, 1896, reproduced in its entirety in de los Reyes, *Los orígenes*, pp. 217–222.

36. De los Reyes, *Los orígenes*, pp. 174–178.

37. Caneto et al., *Historia*, pp. 47–48.

38. De los Reyes, *Los orígenes*, p. 104.

39. What Porfirio Díaz's closest advisers—the Mexican power elite—called themselves in reference to their conviction that Mexico would be transformed (i.e., modernized) through science and technology.

40. Soon after the sinking of the *U.S.S. Maine* in Havana harbor on February 15, 1998, U.S. Edison and Biograph cameramen began to produce views and shorts of the events unfolding in Cuba. Throughout 1898, and especially after the United States entered the war, they extended the cinema's capacity as a visual newspaper (often in collaboration with the Hearst organization) and, for the first time, used the medium to elicit patriotic sentiments in U.S. audiences, revealing the medium's ideological and propagandistic force. The difficulties of filming in real battles also led to many "reconstructions" of famous events, most notoriously Albert E. Smith and J. Stuart Blackton's reconstruction of the battle of Santiago Bay in New York, using a tub of water, paper cut-out ships, and cigar smoke. Many credit the enthusiasm generated by these films with the revitalization of the lagging motion picture business in the United States; the ongoing production of a few firms set the commercial foundation for the U.S. industry.

41. The term was coined by Roberto Schwarz to explain the juxtaposition of modernizing ideologies such as liberalism within traditional social structures such as the slave-owning Brazilian monarchy. Misplaced or out-of-place "ideas" lead to significant discursive dislocations, which critically reveal the fissures of allegedly universal concepts. See his *Misplaced Ideas: Essays on Brazilian Culture*, tr. John Gledson (London: Verso, 1992).

42. Vicente de Paulo Araújo, *A bela época do cinema Brasileiro* (São Paulo: Perspectiva/Secretaria da Cultura, Ciência e Tecnologia, 1976), pp. 229–279; and Maria Rita Galvão, "Le Muet," in Paranaguá, *Le Cinèma Bresilien* pp. 51–64.

43. De los Reyes, *Cine y sociedad en México, 1896–1930: Vivir de sueños* (Mexico City: UNAM, 1983), pp. 96–98.

44. *El Diario*, December 29, 1897, cited in Caneto et al., *Historia*, p. 35.

45. *La Nación*, February 17, 1898, cited in Caneto et al., *Historia*, p. 35. This is an astounding example of the speed of cinematic diffusion, not only of technology but also of modes of commercialization and spectatorship. According to Charles Musser's research, American Biograph began its overseas expansion in 1897, establishing a London office in March. It was one of the characteristics of the Biograph operators to provide locally shot scenes to theater operators in order to enhance the programs' popularity. Musser, *The Emergence of Cinema: The American Screen to 1907* (Berkeley: University of California Press, 1990), pp. 157, 172.

46. Dávalos Orozco, *Albores del cine mexicano*, p. 14.

47. See press reports cited in de los Reyes, *Los orígenes*, p. 153, and *Cine y sociedad*, p. 54.

48. See de los Reyes, *Cine y sociedad*, pp. 32–34, 55.

49. José María Sánchez García, "Historia del cine mexicano," *Cinema Reporter*, June 30, 1951, p. 18, cited in de los Reyes, *Cine y sociedad*, pp. 53–54.

50. Aurelio de los Reyes, *Filmografía del cine mudo mexicano, 1896–1920* (Mexico City: UNAM, 1986), p. 61.

51. According to Tom Gunning's periodization, after the waning of the cinema of attractions' dominance (circa 1905), early narrative forms developed that enabled filmmakers to experiment with the specific cinematic narrative language that would become standardized as the "classic Hollywood narrative style" around 1915–1917. This "transitional" period of more than a decade was volatile and ambivalent; D. W. Griffith's narrative ambitions of the period were far from the norm. Gunning, "Early American Film," in *The Oxford Guide to Film Studies*, ed. John Hill and Pamela Church Gibson (New York: Oxford University Press, 1998), pp. 262–266.

52. The modernist effort to reconceptualize origins, which typically attributes to indigenous traditions the significance of a primitive past. Rey Chow, *Primitive Passions* (New York: Columbia University Press, 1995).

53. Domingo di Núbila, *Historia del cine Argentino*, vol. 1 (Buenos Aires: Cruz de Malta, 1959), pp. 18–20.

54. De los Reyes, *Filmografía*, pp. 42–47.

55. For a family biography, see Jorge Nieto and Diego Rojas, *Tiempos del Olympia* (Bogotá: Fundación Patrimonio Fílmico Colombiano, 1992).

56. The Mexican Revolution was extraordinarily long and complex. It began in 1910, when Francisco Madero, a wealthy Chihuahuan and opponent of Porfirio Díaz, issued his "Plan of San Luis Potosí" manifesto calling for revolts against the tyrant. The government was unable to defeat the small bands of revolutionaries and, after Díaz resigned in May 1911, Madero headed a provisional regime. In 1913, Díaz supporters in Mexico City staged a coup leading to an artillery duel with the forces of General Victoriano Huerta. Known as the *Decena trágica*, the "tragic ten," the fighting lasted for ten days, during which time hundreds of bystanders were slaughtered. The result was that Huerta toppled Madero and ostensibly arranged for his assassination. This bloody assumption of power had wide repercussions: Emiliano Zapata in Morelos and Francisco "Pancho" Villa in Chihuahua rallied to Venustiano Carranza's call for a drive to unseat the usurper; their coalition became known as the Constitucionalistas. Zapata's movement included the more radical elements; Carranza's, the bourgeois, reform-minded groups; while Villa's group was populist, rural, and without a well-defined political position.

Years of bloody civil wars and complex political maneuverings involving the various factions and the United States and other world powers followed, including the occupation of Veracruz by U.S. troops in April 1914. In July of that year, Huerta escaped and the constitutionalist armies of Obregón and Carranza arrived in Mexico City, where a struggle for power ensued among the victors. After the Aguascalientes convention, General Eulalio Gutiérrez was named provisional president, but Carranza set up a parallel government in Veracruz, which U.S. forces had just evacuated. The following years—1915 and 1916—were possibly the worst years of the struggle, with all the factions fighting each other, derailing trains, issuing currencies, and creating absolute chaos, including Villa's attack on the U.S. town of Columbus, New Mexico, which provoked a punitive expedition led by U.S. General John J. Pershing.

Finally, in February 1917, war with the United States was averted and a new progressive constitution was promulgated. Although Venustiano Carranza was elected president in March, the struggle was not yet over and revolts against Carranza's government soon broke out. Zapata in Morelos had remained insurgent (he was assassinated in 1919); Pancho Villa took up arms again. Finally, in 1920, Alvaro Obregón released the Aguas Prietas Plan, calling for an uprising and backed by Pancho Villa and most of the army. A few weeks later, Carranza was assassinated while trying to flee to Veracruz with a good part of the treasury. Obregón was subsequently elected president and the Revolution was officially over, leaving behind more than a million dead.

57. See, for example, Aurelio de los Reyes, *Con Villa en México: Testimonios de los camarógrafos norteamericanos en la Revolución* (Mexico City: UNAM, 1985); and Margarita de Orellana, *La mirada circular: El cine norteamericano de la Revolución mexicana* (Mexico City: Joaquín Mortiz, 1991).

58. De los Reyes, "The Silent Cinema," in *Mexican Cinema*, ed. Paulo Antonio Paranaguá (London: British Film Institute, 1995), p. 72.

59. Ibid., p. 73.

60. Francisco Serrador, an early entrepreneur, expanded his business and, by the mid-1910s, had created what is often referred to as an "exhibition trust." He created the company Companhia Cinematográfica Brasileira in 1911 with a broad base of investors to focus on distribution and exhibition. It proceeded to acquire or build theaters throughout Brazil, especially in Rio de Janeiro. The company also became the exclusive agent of the principal European producers and featured imports prominently. See Araújo, *A bela época do cinema brasileiro*, pp. 369–370, 396, and Vicente de Paula Araújo, *Salãoes, Circos e Cinemas de São Paulo* (São Paulo: Perspectiva, 1981), pp. 210–225.

61. Fox arrived in 1915, Paramount's Companhia de Películas de Luxo da América do Sul in 1916, Universal in 1921, MGM in 1926, Warner Bros. in 1927, and First National and Columbia in 1929. See Randal Johnson, *The Film Industry in Brazil: Culture and the State* (Pittsburgh: University of Pittsburgh Press, 1997), pp. 34–36.

62. See Carlos Monsiváis, *Mexican Postcards*, tr. John Kraniauskas (London: Verso, 1997).

Julianne Burton-Carvajal

Oedipus Tex/Oedipus Mex: Triangulations of Paternity, Race, and Nation in John Sayles's *Lone Star*

The Dry Bones of History

Like any murder mystery worthy of the name, John Sayles's *Lone Star* (1997) wastes no time in confronting its viewers with a corpse. In the precredit sequence, two middle-aged army buddies dressed in casual civilian clothes comb the desert scrub of an abandoned firing range somewhere in the Rio Grande Valley.[1] The botanically inclined Cliff identifies assorted succulents while bantering to his pal Mikey, an amateur sculptor of found objects engrossed in the sounds coming through the earphones of his metal detector. Interacting at first from opposite edges of wide frames, Cliff scolds Mikey: "The guy knows a hundred-fifty varieties of beer but can't tell a poinsettia from a prickly pear!" When Mikey excitedly summons him over to take a look at his latest find, Cliff sardonically challenges his friend as he approaches, descending a small rise that initially obstructs his view, "Don't tell me! Spanish treasure, right? Pieces of eight from the Coronado expedition!"

What is contemplated at the climax of this opening vignette will, in a subsequent sequence, be classified by the laconic forensics expert from Austin as not in fact a corpse (a "stinky" in his binary system) but a skeleton (a "skinny"). This crucial distinction, a function of the passage of time, establishes the fact of history: the bones Mikey has stumbled across will eventually be revealed to have been baking in the desert sun for nigh on forty years.

Mysteries conventionally tease out viewers' ability to read the signs. When all the signs are rendered legible, when all the clues have been pieced together so that the puzzle finally fits, the film's closure imparts the satisfaction of a universe of meaning rendered coherent once more, reinforcing viewers' confidence in their ability to get a handle on truth. Forensically speaking, when it comes to the human remains that set mysteries in motion, "stinkies" offer more immediate legibility; "skinnies," literally denuded of evidence, require—and sometimes defy—more laborious decoding.

Figure 1. Publicity poster: superimposed lone star and laughing calavera. Sony Pictures.

Encouragingly for *Lone Star* viewers and their prospects of epistemological certitude, alongside these half-buried bones in the south Texas desert Mikey unearths a series of corroded metallic clues that will help to identify the skeleton. First, a Masonic ring. Later, in the presence of Sheriff Sam Deeds once the credits have scrolled by, a star-shaped badge circularly engraved with the legend "Sheriff Rio County." Finally, a day later, a slug from a Colt 45 pistol, so out of place among the ordnance from the abandoned rifle range that Cliff and Mikey decide to place another call to the sheriff. Even across a gap of decades, viewers are led to believe, these remnants and remains can be made to tell their story. One of the virtues of Sayles's tour-de-force screenplay is that the story it unravels turns out to be as deeply embedded in the region, if not quite as elusive, as Coronado's.

Figure 2. Three generations of Texas lawmen: Charley Wade, Buddy Deeds, and Sam Deeds. Sony Pictures. Photos by Alan Pappé.

The film's dialogue is suffused with ironic humor that also pivots on historical allusions. Delivered in close-up, Mikey's comeback to Cliff's sardonic query about Spanish treasure—"Was Coronado in the Masons?"—is the verbal climax of the precredit sequence. At the film's conclusion, it falls to high school teacher Pilar Cruz, embattled defender of "a more complete version" of local history over the vociferous objections of several PTA members, to deliver the film's final, rueful line —"Forget the Alamo"—a phrase that was a provisional title for the film (Smith, 1998, p. 219).

From the film's opening moments, the "fact of history" is also made prominent in the extra-diegetic register, through contrasts in musical accompaniment. When the off-duty soldiers first happen upon the skeleton, the sound track features the evocative strumming of a Spanish guitar. As "the law" in the person of Sheriff Sam Deeds joins them, a Norteño (northern Mexico style) love song carries over from the credits to the sheriff's viewing of the bones. The song provides a sound bridge from the camera's brief hold on the open door of the sheriff's car, with its prominent lone star logo, to the second canted close-up of the gap-mouthed skull emerging from the desert gravel. Repeated later over a montage of forensic operations performed on the evidence, these lyrics, sung as a plaintive lament, convey more than a tinge of irony:[2]

Traigo una pena clavada,	I carry a pain deeply lodged,
una puñalada,	stabbing like a dagger
en mi pensamiento	driven deep in my thoughts,
como carcajada	like a peal of laughter
que se hace lamento,	turning into lamentation,

como si llorando,	as if, through teardrops,
se rieran de mí	they were laughing at me
en la vida pasada queriendo	extending from some past life
reprochar el haber sido así	their reproach for my being this way.

Names of the cast end here. Production credits and, later, the montage of forensic operations are viewed over the remaining verses of the song:

Mi pecado y mi culpa serán	My sin and guilty burden must be
conocer demasiado el dolor,	too much firsthand acquaintance with pain,
y las penas y los desengaños	the hurts and bitter life lessons
que por tantos años	that during all these years
me ha dado el amor	love has given to me.

Por si acaso quisieras volver,	If by chance you might wish to come back,
olvidando tu viejo rencor	forgetting that old grudge you hold,
me hallarás frente a un trago de vino,	you'll find me in front of a wine glass
único camino que me dio tu amor.	the only road left to me by your love.

The melodramatized self-pity of this ballad will find its gendered counterpoint in the lustily yodeled version of "I Want to Be a Cowboy Sweetheart" that accompanies the film's closing credits. The musical selections prefigure and refigure the thematics (and intricate dialectics) of three-way cultural interchange that are the very core of *Lone Star*. In fact, according to its director, the film had its genesis in the musical sound track, which was fully developed before the crew went on location (Carson, 1999, p. 206). Two versions of another song featured in very different afterhours contexts—a lovers' tryst at the Santa Barbara Cafe and a tense father-son reunion at the black roadhouse—illustrate the subtle, historicized dynamics of the *Lone Star* sound track:

> The jukebox holds some of [Sam's and Pilar's] past. The song they [dance to], "Since I Met You, Baby," or "Desde te conozco," is also playing on the jukebox when Del walks into Otis's place, a different version of it. . . . It was a song that was a hit on black stations, and then it was the first hit for Freddy Fender, the first Hispanic rock-and-roll guy. He took rock and roll, black music that was becoming used by white people, and brought it to Latin America. (Smith, p. 231)

The ironic dimension of history seems most tellingly registered, however, by the skull twice profiled in canted close-up on the dusty desert floor in the first moments of the film, its jaws flung open as if venting a great belly laugh.[3] In the film's promotional materials, this same toothy, gaping profile is superimposed on the five-pointed sheriff's badge. Both elegant and macabre, this superimposed image synthesizes the film's story and the confluence of cultures so central to it, while foregrounding the association between power and annihilation. Mysteries prompt the viewer to ferret out a motive for murder; incongruously, this one also challenges us to uncover a motive for the murdered man's mirth.

Questions and Answers, Structure and Style

Several enduring cross-cultural murder mysteries begin by appearing to pose one line of questioning, only to conclude by posing quite another (Orson Welles's *Touch of Evil*) or by abdicating any hope of epistemological certitude (Lourdes Portillo's *The Devil Never Sleeps*, Wayne Wang's *Chan is Missing*). Here, from the outset, Sheriff Sam Deeds questions Mikey's assumption that the corroded sheriff's badge is evidence of foul play when he states, in his characteristically impassive style, "No telling yet there's been a crime, but this country's seen a good number of disagreements over the years."

Six days, seven flashbacks, and several dozen sequences later, when he has finally succeeded in assembling the pieces of the puzzle, an equally nonplussed Sheriff Sam will reassure Charley Wade's killer(s), "I don't think the Rangers are likely to find out any more than they already know. As for me, it's just another one of your unsolved mysteries." By this point, Sam has unraveled a parallel mystery even closer to home.

The original series of questions—Whose skeleton is it? What was the cause of death? If violent, who was responsible?—acquires an all too personal valence for Sam as soon as it is determined that the remains are those of Sheriff Charley Wade, since it is public knowledge throughout Rio County that Sam's now deceased father was one of the last people to see Wade alive. Far from any pious filial impulse to add further luster to the paternal reputation, Sam's quest to solve the mystery of Wade's death seems driven by the reverse—the desire to dethrone his legendary parent.

In the film's fourth postcredit sequence and first flashback, set at the Santa Barbara Cafe, the viewer learns that Buddy Deeds became sheriff after Charley Wade vanished, and that Buddy retained the position for almost thirty years, acquiring a reputation for efficacy and fairness as legendary as his predecessor's reputation for coldbloodedness and corruption. Now that Sam holds the same job, his resentment toward his father may be fueled by the general consensus around town that he falls far short of filling his daddy's boots. As one local woman tells him, "Sheriff Deeds is dead. You just Sheriff *Junior.*" Sam seems to savor the prospect of symbolic patricide: if his suspicions about the identity of Wade's murderer prove correct, he may be able to burst the bubble of the Buddy Deeds legend once and for all.

In the first of several sequences that begin with slow lateral pans, the present moment seamlessly merges with the past "over a basket of tortillas" as the voice-over of present-time mayor Hollis Polk leads the viewer back in time to witness a confrontation between the young Buddy Deeds and the gnarled and snarling Charley Wade. Before the flashback elides, via another lateral pan, back to the film's present tense, each man has threatened to kill the other. Buddy has called the sheriff's bluff, and Wade has risen to the bait, setting the stage for the eventual shoot-out that is the obligatory set piece of any Western. In the flashback, diners suspend their forks in midair as they witness this fateful exchange. Several inter-cut medium close-ups of young deputy Hollis Polk also register the tension as his eyes shift nervously from one adversary to the other.

It is established early on that the remains are Wade's, yet the cause and the agent(s) of death only emerge in the film's penultimate sequence. In *Lone Star's* double finale, the prime suspect is exonerated of one crime only to have another, unsuspected transgression come to light, casting its long, chilling shadow over past, present, and future. The story that Sayles unravels over six days of present time encompasses more than four decades of local history—and invokes as many centuries of the region's past.

Seven flashbacks inject the past into the present. Days one, two, and three contain one flashback each; days four and five, two each; day six, none. The first and final flashbacks sequentially illuminate the events of the same April night in 1957. Flashbacks two, four, and six revert to a prior time. In a strict chronology, Mercedes's illegal crossing of the river constitutes the earliest point of the narrative, followed a full decade later by Sheriff's Wade's murder of Eladio Cruz, the man who welcomed her to the other side. Flashback five, the routing of the teenage lovers from their backseat tryst, is dated by Sheriff Buddy's flashlight beam on the car's license plate. The flashbacks appear in the following order:

1. 1957: Deputy Buddy Deeds confronts Sheriff Charley Wade at the Santa Barbara Cafe, in the presence of Deputy Hollis Polk and numerous diners.
2. 1957: Sheriff Wade publicly taunts, subjugates, and threatens the young Otis Payne, a waiter at the black roadhouse (later, under the latter's ownership, renamed Big O's).
3. 1972: By the river's edge, adolescent lovers Sam and Pilar concur in their rejection of the moral standard imposed by their parents.
4. 1956: Sheriff Wade sets up the young Eladio Cruz on (the Mexican side of) the highway and then shoots him in the back at close range.
5. 1972: Buddy and Hollis search out and violently separate teenage lovers Sam and Pilar at the drive-in movie theater.
6. 1945: A terrified young Mercedes, crossing the river under cover of darkness, is welcomed on the Texas side by Eladio Cruz.
7. 1957: Sheriff Charley Wade is shot at the black roadhouse.

Rather than using an edit to shift between present and past tenses in the first flashback sequence, just described, Sayles employs an elaborate blocking technique.[4] In a continuous and unbroken movement, the camera tilts down, pans right, and then briefly holds in close-up on the basket of tortillas, its significance underlined in the voice-over dialogue. This device allows for alterations to background and substitutions of cast while the camera keeps rolling, its panning motion now revealing a hand that reaches into the basket from the opposite side

Figure 3. Chet, Otis, and Delmore Payne: three generations linked by tensions between father and son. Sony Pictures. Photos by Alan Pappé.

of the table, pulling greenbacks out from between the tortillas. Further panning reveals that the hand belongs to Charley Wade. As the camera tracks back, still in a continuous movement, we see that the surroundings have been modified and cast members substituted; the scene is now nearly forty years earlier, and the story Hollis was telling in voice-over is being enacted before our eyes. This technique of seamless substitution, in which uninterrupted footage bears no trace of a cut or dissolve, engages history as a living presence anchored in place. In this instance, the place is Mercedes's Santa Barbara Cafe, the town's most popular eatery—for whites and Mexicans, at least, since no blacks are seen frequenting it.

The second flashback takes us to the cafe's African American counterpart, Big O's roadhouse. The opening of this flashback hinges on a slightly different device: a track-in to a close-up of Widow Bledsoe as she begins her narration, followed by a lap dissolve to the roadhouse that she and her husband ran for many years, followed by a lateral pan into the past-tense action. Another lateral pan closes this flashback sequence, locating Sam and the now middle-aged Big O in the same tavern in the present tense. All the other flashbacks begin and end with symmetrical lateral pans. Significantly, this same camera movement also inaugurates the film. In the opening sequence, the extreme separation of the two on-screen characters—Cliff prominent in the upper left foreground, Mikey almost unnoticeable in the lower right background, the "barren" scrub streching out between them—accentuates the scope of the presumably empty and unmarked desert space.

This emblematic panning device conveys, through style, the director's sense of the "seamless" interrelationship between past and present and his insistence on how the former infuses and suffuses the latter. Reflecting on the visual style of the flashback sequences, Sayles explains in an interview, "A cut is very much a tear. You use a cut to say there's a separation between this thing and that thing. And so in *Lone Star*, I didn't even want a dissolve, which is a soft cut" (Smith, 1998, p. 230). The intricacies of the film's emplotment and its complex editing structure convey how living on the border implies imbrication over bifurcation. Focusing on the film's inclination to triangulations emphasizes Sayles's interest in reaching beyond the limitations inherent in binarisms. Expressed in the simplest form, Sayles's project in this film is to move his viewers beyond the intrinsic limitations of an "our side" versus "their side" worldview.

Climax: The Seen of the Crime

In *Lone Star*, the scene of the crime turns out to be Big O's roadhouse, the African American saloon on the outskirts of town where a nonfatal shooting takes place in an early sequence. In the prelude to the final flashback, Sam surprises Hollis (current mayor and one-time deputy to Charley Wade) and Big O (saloon keeper and unoffical "mayor of Darktown") in an afterhours confab over drinks at the bar. Sam confronts them —"You two saw it, didn't you?"—and immediately proclaims, with uncharacteristic assertiveness and rancor, "Buddy Deeds was a murderer!"

But to Sam's surprise, if not the viewer's, the suspicions he harbors against his own father turn out to be unfounded in light of the film's flashback visualization of events, initially anchored to the subjectivity of the young Otis, then subsequently corroborated by Hollis in the narrative's present time. Expressionistically angled and edited, this final flashback uncharacteristically masks its dialogue under high-volume blues—until the abrupt arrival of Buddy Deeds reintroduces synchronous sound.

Having literally thrown the young Otis across the backroom floor, Wade instructs him at gunpoint to turn over the monthly payoff. After Otis opens an envelope and spreads a fan of twenty dollar bills atop the bar, Wade points again with his gun barrel, wordlessly directing Otis to locate the weapon that tavern owner Bledsoe kept concealed on a shelf. This element echoes the fourth flashback sequence, when Wade instructed the equally cornered Eladio Cruz to show his "protection" before shooting him in cold blood. Wade's over-the-shoulder wink to young Deputy Hollis, another visual echo of the earlier flashback, cues the viewer that another interracial vengeance killing is about to take place, this one in "retribution" for a poker game run outside the net of Wade's graft. What ensues in the following rapid montage, however, is not quite what the setup primes the viewer to expect.

Just as Wade turns back toward his target, deputy Buddy Deeds bursts through the door, yelling, "Charley WADE!" (The first diegetic dialogue in this sequence, this cry is indistinguishable from "Charley, WAIT!") At this instant, Wade is surrounded by three young men with guns: Otis, behind the bar, removing a pistol from a cigar box; Buddy Deeds at the door, with Colt 45 drawn; and Hollis, between Wade and Buddy, with his own Colt 45 likewise drawn. All three have good reason to kill the sheriff: Otis in self-defense, Buddy to make good on

Figure 4. Elizabeth Peña as Pilar Cruz, a pillar of her community who has an unsuspected cross to bear. Sony Pictures. Photo by Alan Pappé.

his threat against Wade's life, and Hollis out of his finally overwhelming disgust at witnessing one too many cold-blooded murders committed in the name of law.

The intricacy of the quick montage that follows leaves lots of room for confusion; in fact, the editing is riddled with ambiguity. Two shots ring out in quick succession, although in the screenplay, only one bullet was fired (Sayles, 1998, p. 239). Wade's body torques first in one direction, then in another as it sinks to the floor. The montage includes two insert cuts of pistols pointing in opposite directions. The cutting suggests that Otis had no time to shoot the gun he had uncovered, although he well might have intended to do so—but then again, the camera angles keep Otis's hands out of view behind the bar. By the time Buddy reaches Hollis to lower the deputy's stiffly extended, trembling arm, a tilt down past the still-smoking weapon reveals Buddy's own pistol lodged in its holster. In the long shot cutaway to Buddy's entrance, his gun had been drawn; the editing elides his progress from doorway to center of the floor.

The murderer is identified by dialogue only, indirectly, rather than by on-screen action and editing. Hollis acknowledges the two other men as his accomplices and recalls his own state of shock, presumably because he was author of the deed: "The three of us cleaned him up and took him out by the post and put him under. Can't say I was much help." The killing of Charley Wade turns out to have been less an individual crime than a collective act of prophylaxis. This climactic flashback places three white men and one black at the colored tavern. Hollis and

Figure 5. José Guadalupe Posada's "Gran Fandango" broadside.

Otis were united in the past, as they are in the film's present, through the act of shooting Charley Wade, joining forces with Buddy Deeds to dispose of the body, and then keeping the secret for forty years.

In one of the most memorable speeches from this sterling screenplay, Big O tells Sam, "I don't know why I trusted Buddy with it—don't know why he trusted me. The first time I ever talked with him was right there and then with a dead white man leakin' blood on the floor between us." This collaboration across the racial divide clearly breaches the "lines of demarcation" that, according to the pontifications of a redneck bartender in an earlier scene, constitute the last bulwark protecting "advanced [white] civilization." Whether or not Otis actually fired against the sheriff, and notwithstanding the justifiability of such an action on the grounds of self-defense, an ancient tradition of Southern "justice" could have all too easily been invoked to frame him for the death of Charley Wade. Alternatively, had either deputy been as bigoted as the dead sheriff, he might not have hesitated to shoot Otis, thus avoiding the bother of having to dispose of Wade's body.

The showdown restages two previous shooting sequences: one (intraracial) that occurs early in the film (Private Johnson's former boyfriend shooting her dance partner at Big O's) and the other (interacial) that occurs toward the middle (Charley Wade's murder of Eladio Cruz). The axis of the multiple, overlapping plots and subplots pivots on racial as well as generational conflict, and *Lone Star* is exceptional in envisioning racial difference as more than a black/white polarity.

From the second sequence, in which Pilar converses in her schoolroom with the African American wife of the new base commander, the complex racial makeup of this border town is made manifest: "Mexican kids, Anglo kids, black kids. . . . They're our smallest group, except for a couple of Kickapoo [Native American] kids." Two sequences later, Sam feels compelled to remind the contractor, Fenton, that "nineteen out of twenty people in this town are Mexican."

Sayles's script—reportedly written during a two-week visit to the Texas-Mexican border region, but manifestly the product of a more seasoned familiarity—choreographs fifty-three speaking parts. Several parts require two different actors to play young and mature versions of the same character. Eight key members of the cast, along with several more secondary characters, are African American. Ten featured players and several more secondary ones are Mexican American. Another, Wesley, is Native American. Through expert casting and direction, Sayles delineates each of these personages so deftly that, rather astoundingly, their impression lingers no matter how brief their appearance on screen. His method of developing characters is based on firsthand experience:

> having been an actor, one of the things that I do is go through [the script] and play every part, and ask, "Is there a three-dimensional character here? . . . Can I have more than one connection between this character and the rest of the story, thematically and just in terms of plot?" In your average Hollywood movie there are two leads and everyone else is basically an extra—in mine the secondary characters start moving forward and become primary. (Smith, 1998, p. 232)

Although the performances of this ensemble cast mesh with remarkable evenness, most are in fact memorably nuanced, their depth becoming more apparent through repeated viewings.

Triangulating Race and Nation

Lone Star weaves interconnected, trigenerational stories around three local families: Mexicano/Tejano (Mercedes Cruz, daughter Pilar, and Pilar's two children, Amado and Paloma), African American (Otis Payne, son Delmore, and grandson Chet), and Anglo (Buddy Deeds, son Sam, ex-wife Bunny). Far from imposing itself in a mechanical or contrived way, this triangular design emerges slowly and subtly from the intricate human fabric of the Frontera community.

Lone Star both pertains to and transcends the panorama of racialized melodrama that Linda Williams lays out in her recent book-length study of "melodrama in black and white." Following Peter Brooks, Williams defines melodrama as "a central mode of American popular culture," a means of constructing "moral legibility" in a world that has lost the obvious signs of virtue" (p. xiv). She argues that the mechanisms of racialized American melodrama require that the hero also become at some point a victim, since virtue is invested through suffering. She argues that the special category of racialized melodramas gives permission to certain racial groups for actions that they could not otherwise justify. In the classical Hollywood Western, for example, white settlers "deserve" to conquer because they have been beset by hostile Indians and have suffered at their hands. Consequently, melodrama moves in two gendered and mutually imbricated directions: feminized pathos (the suffering that confers virtue) and masculinized action (fight, rescue, chase, flight).

Since the publication of Harriet Beecher Stowe's *Uncle Tom's Cabin*—a novel that Williams characterizes as America's first media event, harbinger of an incipient national culture industry capable of leaping genres and acquiring ubiquity across the cultural landscape—Williams discerns a persistent dialectic, an interpenetrating sequence of "negro-philic and negro-phobic" representations, each reciprocally interdependent (pp. xiv, xv). Her genealogy encompasses *Birth of a Nation*, *The Jazz Singer*, *Gone with the Wind*, *Showboat*, Alex Haley's television saga *Roots*, and the real-life 1990s courtroom dramas surrounding Rodney King and O. J. Simpson. Williams insists that the American melodrama of nationhood is still writing itself in black and white, and that this version of racial polarity retains the function of realism in American culture.

Lone Star poses a challenge to that view. Confounding the established dichotomy of race written in black and white, Big O proudly displays an Exhibition of Black Seminoles in the back room of his roadhouse. In the sequence that inaugurates day five, he explains to his grandson Chet how the Seminole tribe resisted white colonization, were forcibly resettled to Florida, intermarried with escaped slaves, fled to Mexico, fought with Santa Ana in the Mexican/American War, and then, after the War Between the States, migrated north again to become fabled black indian scouts for the U.S. Army's campaign to eradicate the indigenous population in the newly acquired Southwestern territories. The Payne family's blended African-Native American ancestry, a motif in three separate sequences, takes on the quality of metaphor to connote those formative intermixtures buried deep in individual and family pasts.

Sam gets a piece of information crucial to his investigation from a Native American loner, a former Korean War-era friend of Buddy's, who prefers tending his deserted roadside curio stand to living on the reservation. Their encounter concludes with Wesley's impromptu story about being surprised by a rattlesnake. His warning to Sam —"You gotta be careful where you go pokin'. Who knows what you'll find."—can be retroactively read as a reference to the skeletons lurking, unbeknownst to Sam, in his own family closet.

Lone Star gives its characters and viewers two interlocking mysteries, one public, the other private. The key to the public mystery reveals an extra-legal black/white alliance that has endured and remained secret for four decades (although without effectively breaching the functional ghettoization of the town's African American community, still confined to "Darktown" and the soon to be closed army base). The private mystery hinges on another cross-ethnic (cross-racial, cross-cultural, cross-class) alliance, outside of both legality and morality. Rather than cover up a demise, this second crossing conceals origins and masks identity.

Lone Star's concluding sequence reveals that Pilar is the unknowing off-spring of Buddy Deeds and Mercedes Cruz, a kind of "black Seminole" unawares. The intense love that Pilar and Sam consumated in their early teens and again in the film's present time, in the aftermath of her widowhood and his divorce, is revealed to be incestuous. Wearing the mantle (badge) of his father's kingship (the office of sheriff), Sam consults the oracles and attempts to unravel the skein of the past. Unknowingly, he sleeps (again) not with his "saintly" mother (long deceased) but with his half-sister, offspring of his father's sustained adulterous relationship with an immigrant from "the other side." Having attributed the severity of the original parental prohibition to racist bias, Sam and Pilar realize too late that their parents' attempts to keep them apart derived from an alto-gether different kind of taboo.

In this Tex/Mex spin on the oedipal triangle, the sins of the father con-tinue to wreak revenge upon his descendants long after the father's demise. Like *Touch of Evil*, the Orson Welles masterpiece to which it pays tribute, *Lone Star*'s slyly ambiguous ending compels its viewers to choose. The romantically inclined will opt to believe that Sam and Pilar can manage to pull up stakes and start fresh elsewhere, leaving Frontera and their entangled personal histories behind. Less sanguine viewers will ponder how the pair could live out their attachment to one another under the shadow of this unwelcome new knowledge. Choosing the con-ventional happy ending in which the embattled lovers are forever reunited sub-scribes to a more naive, more characteristically "American" penchant to deny history and "start fresh"; it construes the private sector as quasi-independent of the social realm. The alternative, pessimistic view subscribes to the more world-weary, more characteristically "Mexican" sense of characters burdened and entrapped by the malice of the past; it views the radius of personal agency as delimited by social forces beyond individual control.

The come-on featured in the film's advertising campaign—"John Sayles invites you to *return* to the scene of the crime" (my emphasis)—suggests that the setting is familiar (in both senses of the word) and that the border's story (Fron-tera, a made-up place name, means "border" in Spanish) is *everyone's* story. As Sayles himself says, "One of the reasons why I chose Texas for this thing is because [it] has a compressed history that is like a metaphor for the history of the United States"(Smith, 1998, p. 232). Among the lingering questions that *Lone Star* bequeaths its audience is this one: When will Americans collectively recognize how many of us are the figurative if not literal equivalent of "black Seminoles"?

Denoument: "Forget the Alamo"

Lone Star's final sequence returns characters and viewers to a location visited once before: the long-abandoned drive-in movie theater where Sam and Pilar, as teenage lovers, tried in vain to elude the omnipresent Buddy Deed and his determination to keep them apart. This ill-starred couple is helplessly condemned to repeat the past even at the juncture when, as mature adults, they should finally be out from under it. Perched on the hood of his car and staring at the patched and missing panels of an empty screen, Sam waits for Pilar at the weed-strewn El Vaquero (The Cowboy). The sound of another car approaching does not prompt him to turn his head; he doesn't look toward Pilar until she has entered the frame, boosted herself up beside him, and inquired brightly, "When's the picture start?"

In a very different key, he responds by posing another question, the primal one for their particular context: "You gonna tell your mother we've been seeing each other?" Like disobedient children, these two middle-aged adults are still sneaking around behind other people's backs: the deserted riverbank, the empty high school parking lot, Mercedes's locked cafe, Sam's place in the wee hours, the decaying drive-in outside of town. As the full-grown Sam said sardonically (and prophetically) at the recent dedication of the local courthouse to the memory of his father, "I used to think there was nowhere in this town to hide from my dad, and now I'm sure of it."

Neither Pilar nor the unsuspecting viewer realizes until this concluding sequence that the sins of the all-powerful Buddy indeed leave the lovers no place to hide. Once all the obstacles to their union have been removed—through Pilar's widowhood, Sam's divorce, the solution to Charley Wade's disappearance, and the related theft of town funds—the deceased father has the last laugh after all.

The reason that Buddy and Mercedes so adamantly nixed the attraction between their teenage offspring has not been rendered inconsequential by the passage of time. Instead, in a twist worthy of the most involuted Mexican melodramatic tradition, Sam confronts Pilar with the evidence that they are siblings. Gently, he shows her a photo of Buddy embracing a young Mercedes at the beach, then reveals that Buddy paid the hospital bills when Pilar was born and that Mercedes, in the love letters she wrote to the married Buddy, referred to "our beautiful daughter." However devastating, this evidence resonates with Pilar's own uncomfortable memory of Buddy's persistent stare, of how he would single her out among the children in the schoolyard. "Funny what you remember," she had told Sam as they strolled by the river's edge after the dedication ceremony, "I thought he was going to arrest me."

Indeed he did. The powerful surveillance of the father's gaze "arrested" the future of his offspring—and even his offspring's offspring. One final, fateful time in this "Texican" reworking of the oedipus story, the son is bested by the father, the daughter by her hard-shelled mother. First incredulous and outraged, then tearful and supplicating, Pilar assimilates the terrible knowledge that she is the product of Buddy's extended extramarital affair with her widowed mother, now the respected and circumspect owner-manager of the Santa Barbara Cafe—thanks to the $10,000 in "widow's benefit" funds that Buddy stole from the town council in order to make Charley Wade's disappearance look less like foul play. The earnest, hardworking, sympathetic Pilar is the product of adultery; her education, however indirectly, is the fruit of the theft of public funds designed to cover up a murder.

Using a combination of musical, literary, and cinematic examples, José Limón has traced the genealogy of "racialized sexuality" and in particular the Anglo male's ambivalent attraction to the Mexican female through nineteenth- and twentieth-century popular culture. In contrast to Rosa Linda Fregoso, who has analyzed the intraracial attachment between Sam and Pilar as a colonialist rein-scription, Limón credits Sayles with "radically revising the history of this iconography" (p. 610). Citing social historian David Montejano on the emergence of a new historical juncture in which "the politics of negotiation and compromise have replaced the politics of conflict and control" (p. 306), Limón recognizes "the implied ending of the colonial order" in *Lone Star* and concludes that it "has much to do with the sexualized kinship twist that Sayles has given his story" (p. 613). Like Sayles himself in a number of interviews, Limón's analysis casts a positive light on Pilar's proposal to abandon historical consciousness in favor of what Limón terms "productive forgetfulness" (p. 613).

"They can't pull this on me; it isn't fair," is Pilar's intial response to Sam's revelation. Then this champion of a more complete version of history does an about-face and renounces history altogether: "We'll start from scratch. All that other stuff, all that history, to hell with it, right? Forget the Alamo." Her assertion that she is unable to have any more children and the prospect of starting over again somewhere else resound rather unconvincingly at the end of a film that has so compellingly exposed the intricate network of mutual imbrications underlying past and present, person and event in the highly permeable cultural sediment of the border region. Even though they might succeed in keeping this new knowledge from everyone beyond Mercedes, Pilar and Sam will always have that socially unspeakable and emotionally destabilizing genetic bond between them. Script, setting, direction, camerawork, and editing all coalesce to underline the ambivalence of this concluding sequence, which inevitably remits us to the opening—to the long lateral pan across the desert scrub and its eventual object, the grinning *calavera*.

Contrasting Cultural Icons: The Laughing *Calavera*, The Lonesome Cowboy, and the *Gran Chingón*

In the arbitrary exercise of his power, the figure of the father in the Mexican tradition merges with the *cacique* (chief) and the *patrón* (boss).[5] Octavio Paz, in the most important chapter of the most definitive twentieth-century essay on Mexican identity, expounds upon the composite masculine archetype of the father/macho/conquistador, asserting that Mexican representations of masculinity emphasize the wrathful, tyrannical, devouring aspect of masculinity. Paz observes that masculinity's "aggressiveness, insensitivity, invulnerability and other attributes" are condensed into arbitrary power wielded with an absurdist sense of humor that relishes "unforeseen acts that produce confusion, horror and destruction." This violence "puts things in their places, by reducing them to dust, to misery, to nothingness. The humor of the macho is an act of revenge." Paz dubs this prototype of Mexican masculinity *el gran chingón* (awkwardly but most accurately rendered in English as the Big Fuckover-er), derived from a common verb (*chingar*) with a particular set of culturally specific meanings and associations for speakers of Mexican Spanish. Paz uses this label to denote the sexualized paternal power figure who elevates himself through the subordination and debasement of others:

> The essential attribute of the macho—power—almost always reveals itself as a capacity for wounding, humiliating, annihilating. Nothing is more natural, therefore, than his indifference toward the offspring he engenders. He is not the founder of a people . . . His power is isolated in its own potency . . . He is pure incommunication, a solitude that devours itself and everything it touches. (1961, pp. 81, 82)

The corroded lone star sheriff's badge from which the laughing skull emerges in the film's advertising logo could belong to either Charley Wade or Buddy Deeds. Likewise, the vengeful mirth expressed in the grotesque skeletal grin is potentially as much Buddy's as Charley's. Voraciousness could account just as well for this gape-jawed expression. Indeed, the unlamented sheriff Charley Wade was known for "taking a bite" out of everything that came through Rio County, but since he would have grinned broadly while doing so, the distinction turns out to be moot. In a double sense, this controlling last laugh comes from "the other side"—the other side of the grave, obviously, but also from the other side of the border.

About to pull out of the parking lot behind the jail in a brief, transitional sequence, Sam tells one of his deputies that he is "going over to the other side." The deputy, focused on the upcoming local election and his own aspirations to Sam's job, asks uncomprehendingly, "The Republicans?" In fact, Sam's excursion to "the other side" is no laughing matter. From that location, the abhorrent underbelly of Texas "law enforcement" comes starkly into focus when Sam hears a firsthand account of Eladio Cruz's murder. Before retelling the tale, used-tire dealer Chucho Montoya, *"el rey de las llantas,"* gives Sam a lesson in the arbitrariness and irrelevance of notions of the border as "a line drawn in the sand."

On Chucho's side of the Rio Grande, the laughing *calavera* still reigns as the supreme icon of Mexican popular culture, thanks to the inspired artistry of

José Guadalupe Posada (1852–1913), who has been called "Mexico's most beloved and most truly national artist." Printmaker, lithographer, and engraver, Posada produced broadsides for the barely literate at the end of the nineteenth and beginning of the twentieth centuries. His illustrated news sheets "commemorat[ed] all sorts of crimes, disasters and miracles, . . . reporting on political or social current events . . . from a proletarian or lower middle class point of view" (Berdecio and Applebaum, 1972). His *calaveras*, cartoon prints in which the characters are skeletons miming every conceivable human activity, are the most imaginative and celebrated facet of his extensive output. Admired and visually quoted by twentieth-century Mexican artists of the stature of Diego Rivera and José Orozco, Posada's inspiration continues to channel through Mexican and Chicano art in all its contemporary manifestations.

A typically Mexican syncretic form, the *calaveras* merge Spanish and indigenous sources into the stoic, but far from humorless, view of death that has become a hallmark of Mexican culture, whether oral, literate, plastic, musical, or cinematic. The symbolic prominence of this laughing skull, a quintessentially Mexican motif, suggests from the outset that John Sayles's north-of-the border movie is finely attuned to south-of-the-border essentials. The iconographic fusion, in the film's publicity, of a laughing *calavera* and the silvered star of the Texas lawman, familiar emblem of the lone star state, mates two fundamental symbols while juxtaposing two diametrically opposed traditions: on the Mexican side, irreverently playful social and political satire for the masses, viewed "from the bottom up"; on the Texas side, the towering individualism and infamously arbitrary authority of the lone frontier lawman.

In the universe of Frontera, Texas, as evoked by *Lone Star*, traditional male authority is seen as opportunistic, repressive, and anchored to a political hierarchy—whether local (the sheriff and his deputies), organizational (Colonel Payne and his subordinates on the army base), or governmental (the white power structure in army private Athena's egotistical calculus of military life). In Frontera, history impacts how paternal authority manifests itself. The blatant, one-on-one corruption of Sheriff Charley Wade contrasts with the more subtle, sophisticated corruption of Sheriff Buddy Deeds. Charley Wade extracted a kickback from all legal and extralegal commerce transacted within his domain. The price of "independence" under his regime was humiliation or death—or both. Mrs. Bledsoe recalls that "people didn't complain, not if you was colored or Mexican, not if you wanted to keep breathin'."

When Buddy coolly refused to do part of Charley's collecting, the patricidal nature of their confrontation set the stage for a changing of the guard, a new regime of power. Sam learns that Buddy, in contrast to his predecessor, "was more a part of the big picture: county political machine, chamber of commerce, zoning board." As Sam realizes throughout the film's unfolding, his progenitor/predecessor's corruption was of a different magnitude: guaranteeing whole voting blocks, reducing jail sentences in exchange for private services, engineering a real estate transaction that left him holding coveted "lake front" property after submerging a working-class Mexican community under a new dam. Despite their different legacies and the different "generations" of law enforcement that they represent, despite their personal enmity, Charley and Buddy merge into a specter of abusive male authority, the *gran chingón* who thrives on the havoc and suffering that he causes.

As for Sam, he proves to be a good detective but a lousy hero. He never wields a weapon, much less shoots one. He springs someone from jail (Pilar's teenage son Amado) but puts no one in. Sober and dedicated, even-tempered and even-handed, Sam has a wry sense of humor with a self-deprecating edge. In a "post-Western" like *Lone Star*, a hero is beside the point and the cowboy a residual image, more ironic than iconic—as indicated by the derelict "El Vaquero" movie marquee and by the fading admonition painted on the old barnside behind Wesley's roadside curio stand: Woa, Cowboy / Stop and See / Genuine.

The intrinsically Mexican/Hispanic origins of the figure of the "quintessentially American" cowboy are not irrelevant to Sayles's theme of cross-cultural (re)articulation. Hollywood tradition notwithstanding, the Yankees borrowed this colorful ride-the-range lifestyle (and all its accoutrements except the six-gun) from the Mexicanos and Californios whose horse-and-cattle culture was a thriving part of the landscape before the U.S. takeover of California and the Southwest in the late 1840s. Although dazzled by the virtuoso displays of horsemanship that they witnessed on their newly conquered frontier, the Yankees made their pervasive attitude of superiority apparent when they translated *vaquero* into the belittling "cowboy" rather than the neutral "cowhand" or "cowherder."

If Sam doesn't fill the bill as hero, what about victim? Is the suffering evoked in the melifluous lament of the opening credits an echo of his? The yodeled aspirations of the final song, "I Want to Be a Cowboy Sweetheart," can be read, complementarily, as Pilar's equally ironic, equally futile lament. Yet Sam's character fails to evoke the virtue/victim paradox characteristic of American racialized melodramas as Linda Williams analyzes them. Rather than winning a prize through his suffering, he leans toward "the other side," placing himself within a characteristically Mexican melodramatic tradition according to which the "prize" he wins *is* his own suffering, the costly contamination of too much knowledge, a diligently deciphered past that puts the hoped-for future to rout.

Frontera's "last Anglo sheriff" shares a kinship with the hapless Juan Preciado in the novel of patriarchy that is the fountainhead of much of the best Mexican (and Latin American) fiction of the twentieth century, Juan Rulfo's *Pedro Páramo* (1955), in which the apparent protagonist journeys home to claim his patrimony only to be absorbed and permanently infantilized by a pervasive past in which his dead father still reigns in brutal supremacy. In both these revisionist, Mexicanized oedipal tales, even death does not diminish the father's power or limit his predatory reach.

Genre and Paternity

In generic terms, *Lone Star* turns out to be as much a quest narrative as a mystery, as much a family-centered drama as a love story, and above all, in light of its ending, as much a (retro-)melodrama as a (post-)Western. Fatherhood, siblinghood, and nationhood are the film's dominant (dis)organizing tropes. *Lone Star* fits within and poses challenges to both the hypothetical Mexican subgenre of patriarchal melodrama and the emergent American category of race melodrama. The final showdown crystallizes the film's deliberately vexed connection to the Hollywood Western. While foregrounding certain icons and restaging certain set-pieces associated with the classical Western, Sayles keeps his eye (and his viewer's) on the subjective, historicized filter through which the action is recounted:

> The answers Sam is given are always going to be influenced by the person who's giving them ... but I also wanted the emotional state of what was being told. ... When Hollis [first] tells the story, he is going to embellish it and make it into a real showdown. And so the shooting [sequence used] very much the same cuts and lines you would get if it were a Western showdown. And it had all the fetishistic items: the guns, and the hats, and the badges. (Smith, 1998, p. 230)

Film critics persist in the quest for a suitable typology of the Western. In his landmark 1975 structuralist analysis, Will Wright identified four categories: the classical plot, the vengeance plot, the transition theme, and the professional plot. Writing two decades later, Peter Babiak proposed a tripartite typology: classical, revisionist, and post-revisionist:

> The Classical Hollywood Western tends to ascribe the community's potential for positive moral growth to established social institutions, such as "The Law" or "Big Business." ... The Revisionist Western of the sixties and seventies tended to reverse the roles of the players while preserving the notion of a moral universe. ... The Post-Revisionist Western ... refuses to provide us with any clear moral viewpoint from which the actions of its characters may be assessed. (1998, p. 57)

In his comparative study of hybridized genres, Del Jacobs uses *Lone Star* as a prime example of the neo-Western, a term he chooses in order to emphasize the film's recycling of nostalgia and tradition. In my reading, *Lone Star*'s revisionism is "post-" rather than "neo-" in that it clearly marks the various recycled elements of the Western genre as vestigial. Stylistically, narratively, and generically, *Lone Star* insists on "the presence of the past." By emphasizing individual situatedness and the inevitable filtering of subjectivity, the film foregrounds the imprint of history and acknowledges that history itself is filtered through locations of culture and power. *Lone Star* gives its revisited vengeance plot an oedipal spin that resonates differently across the border. It persists in posing questions about public and private morality and critiques the unsavory underside of the

Western tradition (in the various senses of the word). Through the very intricacy of its generic engagements, this revisionist, multiethnic, transculturated post-Western questions and illuminates the complexity of cultural location.

The roots of *Lone Star*'s thematic and generic complexity tap deeply embedded "Mexican" as well as "American" substrata. (I put these two labels in quotations to suggest the tenuousness of their claims to univocal status as categories.) In contrast to the facile overlay applied by too many American filmmakers when they work across cultures, Sayles manages to have Mexican elements pervade his film on multiple levels—from the signal prominence, in the opening sequence, of the nopal (prickly pear cactus), a revered symbol of origins emblazoned on the Mexican flag, to the filters and gels that give "patriotic" red and green tonalities to much of the footage; from the sense of the border as arbitrary and artificial divide to the view of history as pervasive shaper of both present and future.

One of the ways that Sayles anchors his project in the border experience is by acknowledging paternity within his own creative trajectory. In its refractory reconstruction of deceased individuals through the disparate filters of those who knew them, *Lone Star* manifests homage to *Citizen Kane*. Sayles's debt to Orson Welles is doubled in *Lone Star*'s echoes of another Welles's classic, *Touch of Evil*, an analogous murder mystery that also emphasizes its border setting as a transformative multicultural space of moral and epistemological realignment.[6] Both films go to some lengths to represent the border as a polycultural rather than simply bicultural space. Both thematize border-crossing as more metaphysical than physical, more grounded in personal morality and ethics than in geography. Both not only narratively evoke but also stylistically reproduce the destabilizing convergence of different subjectivities and modes of perception that lies at the core of the border-crossing experience. Both films deal centrally with truth and justice, revealing these values to be contingent on their relationship to power and cultural location.

The final sequence of *Touch of Evil* takes place in a wasteland of oil derricks and detritus surrounding a brothel. However incongrously, that gingerbread whore house, with its old-fashioned pianola and tawdry Victorian decor, is "home" to Quinlan even though his accrued pounds and years initially prevent the world-weary but still beautiful Tanya from recognizing him. As long as Quinlan remains inside, he is safe from the machinations of his antagonist Mike Vargas (Charlton Heston); once he lets himself be lured out, he is lost, since his future, as Tanya's cards have revealed, "is all used up." The final sequence of *Lone Star* also involves a second visit to a site of escape and long-lost love, a homecoming reunion that is also deceptively short-lived. The drive-in movie theater where Sam and Pilar meet on a Sunday morning is as shabby, timeworn, and deserted as Tanya's place, and just as much a remnant of a bygone era. Likewise, *Lone Star*'s climax has the "good cop" taking on the behavioral coloration of the "bad cop" whom he has so doggedly pursued, ostensibly *because* of the latter's corruption. In both films, it turns out to be the disillusioned lawman's partner (Hollis/Menzies) who pulls the trigger on his boss (Wade/Quinlan). In both climactic sequences, intricately ambiguous editing and a highly expressionistic shooting style challenge and undermine perceptual confidence about the true agency of the crime. In the U.S.-Mexican border setting, both Welles and Sayles found an apt frame for their greatest talents, perhaps in part because both have more than a superficial knowledge of the culture "on the other side." Upon completion of *Lone Star*, John Sayles "crossed over" the border, making *Men with Guns*, a project that he wrote in Spanish and filmed in Mexico with a Spanish-speaking cast.

Cleaving Frontera(s)

Part of *Lone Star*'s lingering fascination has to do with its timely relocation of the narrative crux of U.S. nationhood to the Southwest. For at least one pivotal cultural critic, however, that gesture is, at its core, yet another colonizing one. Rosa Linda Fregoso notes how representations of the border in both Mexican and U.S. film traditions tend to render the region an abject other against which both nations "define [and] shape their national identities" (p. 178). Initially crediting Sayles with a more complex, nuanced, and multidimensional representation, one at least superficially in tune with the writings of Chicana/o border theorists, her fascinating essay "Recyling Colonialist Fantasies on the Texas Borderlands" ends up censuring the film as an "overture" that is not "truly" multicultural but instead "driven by a deeply colonialist and phallocentric project" (p. 180) and intent on "erecting the borders of its own racial purity and masculine privilege" (p. 186). Fregoso deplores *Lone Star*'s failure to "decenter whiteness and masculinity," and delineates how the film "refigures race relations in Texas yet again in patriarchal terms" (p. 184) by maintaining maleness as "the key, privileged signifier of the narrative" (p. 181). In a forthcoming essay that pursues this line of analysis in a continuing dialogue with her "Tejano paisano" José Limón, fellow offspring of the Texas borderlands whom she believes is "seduced by the patriarchal visual economy" of *Lone Star*, Fregoso further develops her analysis by focusing on the unresolved conflict between mother and daughter and reiterating her contention that the film "privile[ges] the father while rendering the mother invisible in the reproduction of Texas history" (p. 202).

Fregoso's reading of *Lone Star* rigorously analyzes the mechanisms through which the film offers "history metaphorized in patriarchal patrimony" (p. 185), yet *Lone Star* can also be understood as detailing the demise of white male authority through its narrative design and through the characterization, casting, and direction of its protagonist. The reading that I have attempted to develop here, perhaps tangential to the ongoing debate between the two Tejano border theorists, views *Lone Star*'s essential project as the critique of patriarchal masculinity across ethnicities—a critique that includes the African American Paynes, omits the matriarchal Cruz family, and focuses most pointedly on white masculinity as the lynchpin of a version of Texas history that is now losing its hegemonic status.

Sayles's protagonist shares his author's privileged subject position as a white male in a society where whites are losing racial (pre)dominance.

Chris Cooper's subsequent performance in *American Beauty* showed him to be fully capable of smouldering frenzy; his restrained embodiment of the deliberate and understated Sam Deeds makes for a striking contrast. Sam's sense of self has been repeatedly compromised by overweening models of paternity. He has been ground under the heel of not one but two fathers—the overpowering Buddy as well as a domineering and belittling father-in-law, recalled to him when his ex-wife volunteers: "Daddy hired a pin-head to take your job. Says so himself. Says 'Even my son-in-law was better than this pin-head I got now.'" In Frances McDormand's brilliant cameo as Sam's football-obsessed ex-wife Bunny, her repeated references to "Daddy" and her fascination/revulsion at the idea of sustaining a 350-pound weight intimate that her "tightly wound" condition (Daddy's euphemism for her obvious mental instability) might be the product of an incestuous father-daughter bond. With this shadow doubling of the incest motif (here in a much more disturbing key), Sayles layers into his script yet another instance of abusive paternal authority.

Lone Star's triad-based narrative design attempts to get beyond the pernicious oversimplification of the binary: three trigenerational family sagas, each representing a different racial/ethnic formation; the succession of three sheriffs; three people who know the truth behind the death of Charley Wade; the love triangle that, once revealed, confronts Pilar with her origin. The three-stage genealogy of the lone Texas lawmen also manifests a hollow, destructive model of paternity. Neither Charley nor Sam has offspring whereas Buddy, in contrast, has two: one whom he squelches, the other whom he fails to acknowledge. Buddy's memorial sculpture, unveiled at the courthouse midway through the film, is a loaded monument to self-aggrandizing Anglo paternalism: the cast bronze sheriff rests his hand on the shoulder of a small Tejano boy who looks up at (to) him. A bystander quips: "I think he's gonna run that Mexican kid in for loiterin'." (Not the least of the several layers of irony here is Buddy's actual paternity of a "Mexican kid," female, a revelation deferred to the end of the narrative.)

In this patriarchal succession of lone-wolf lawmen, Charley Wade is symbolic father to Buddy Deeds, whose biological son Sam chooses to be the end of this line: genetically (the walls of his apartment are bare because he has "no kids' pictures to put up" and, reunited with his "one true love," he will produce no offspring with her); behaviorally (his low-key personality and painstaking procedures are not the stuff of lawman legend); and professionally (uninclined to stand for reelection, he expects to be succeeded by a Mexican American). Scarred by the excesses of patriarchal power, Sam has never "committed" (to) fatherhood. Repulsed by the abuses of Anglo rule, he welcomes a realignment of the local power structure to correspond to the town's predominantly Mexican demographic.

In interviews, Sayles himself has subscribed to the idea that "[Sam] and Pilar at the end of the movie are basically embarking on a new life" (Smith, 1998,

p. 225). Yet when projected beyond the frame of the film's conclusion, the coupling of Sam and Pilar does not announce a new national/regional formation via the pending emergence of the next (hybridized, allegorized) generation. *Lone Star* flirts with the trope, all too familiar in narratives of national (re)construction, of symbolic synthesis mortgaged upon a future literally in embryo, but in the end rejects this device via the insistence on Pilar's postoperative sterility. The final track-back onto El Vaquero's derelict marquee suggests patchy layers of historical sedimentation that are irrelevant to the successor generation already in existence. Chet, Amado, and Paloma will project their own stories onto their own screens; both the stories and the screens will be essentially different.

Even while refusing closure and underlining the ambiguity of its final sequence, *Lone Star* projects a certain tentative optimism for the future. Army commander Delmore Payne has effected a tentative rapprochment with both his father and his son. The unbending Mercedes Cruz, prototype of the assimilated "Hispanic" who jealously guards her own hardwon place in the socioeconomic hierarchy, has shown compassion for a young couple who have risked life and limb, as she herself did so long ago, for a new start on the other side of the river. Although the Buddy Deeds legend remains intact and the mystery of Sheriff Wade's murder remains officially unsolved, the regime of the patriarchal white lawman, dismantled from within, is but a tattered remnant of a bygone era. That particular history will have no successors to haunt.

Borders bespeak a cleavage that aligns and reconfigures even as it separates. The cleaving together of individuals across (social, ethnic, racial, economic) borders of difference—Otis and Hollis, Mercedes and Enrique, Delmore and Athena, Cliff and Priscilla, Sam and Pilar—is the warp and woof that sustains the fabric, not just of *Lone Star*, but of the present and future of us all. Like Allison Anders's *Mi vida loca* (1994), *Lone Star* has provoked debate among border constituencies and has been the object of pointed critique. Yet like the more consecrated *Touch of Evil* and Lourdes Portillo's still underrecognized masterpiece *The Devil Never Sleeps* (1994), these more controversial films also warrant recognition as bold, intelligent, cross-culturally oriented, and stylistically illuminating invitations to reflect on and re(de)fine the borders of our mutual understanding.

NOTES

David Bolam coined the phrase "Oedipus Tex" while a student in my 1999 "Movies on the Border" course at the University of California, Santa Cruz. David also made perceptive comments on the first draft of this essay, Zuzana Pick at an intermediate stage, and Margarita de la Vega Hurtado on the final draft. Daniel Burton-Rose's careful reading sent me back to the computer for one "post-final" set of revisions. Rosa Linda Fregoso's long-delayed comments reached me as I was literally dropping the completed essay into the mail pouch. Sincere thanks to one and all.

1. Shot in various south Texas locations, including Eagle Pass. Frontera and Rio County are both fictitious names.

2. My transcription and translation. Without sacrificing literal meaning, and making no attempt at rhyme, I have adjusted the translation so that its meter approximates that of the song.

3. Sayles's final cut differs significantly from his original screenplay: "CU: Bones. Sticking

out from the sand bank are the skeletal bones of a man's hand. There is a ring on one finger" (Sayles, 1998, p. 108).

4. I am grateful to another student in the above-mentioned course, Max Terronez, for explaining the mechanics of this technique.

5. For a sustained discussion of the historical and symbolic roots of Mexican patriarchy as related to film, see my essay, "Mexican Melodramas of Patriarchy: Specificity of a Cross-Cultural Form."

6. These two directors have several other things in common. Both came to movies via theater. Both are actors as well as directors—actors who often appear in their own films. Welles's role as the corrupt and bloated Quinlan in *Touch of Evil* is one of his most indelible; Sayles preferred to leave his own *Lone Star* character—Zack, one of Sam's deputies—on the cutting room floor, although the role still appears in the published screenplay. Both directors wrote their own material, assuming the risk and embracing the challenge of extremely diverse projects. Both worked independently of Hollywood for the most part—whether by exclusion, by default, or by choice. Sayles occasionally works as screenwriter (and actor) for television and as a "script doctor" in Hollywood: *The Lady in Red* (1979), *The Howling* (1980), and *Men of War* (1994).

WORKS CITED

Babiak, Peter E. S. "Rewriting Revisionism: Clint Eastwood's *The Unforgiven*," *CineAction* 46, The Western Then and Now, (1998): 57–63.

Berdecio, Roberto, and Stanley Appelbaum, eds. *Posada's Popular Mexican Prints*. New York: Dover Publications, 1972.

Brooks, Peter. *The Melodramatic Imagination*. New Haven: Yale University Press, 1975, 1996. Cited in Williams.

Burton-Carvajal, Julianne. "Mexican Melodramas of Patriarchy: Specificity of a Cross-Cultural Form." In *Framing Latin American Cinema: Contemporary Critical Perspectives*, ed. Ann Marie Stock. Minneapolis: University of Minnesota Press, 1997.

Carson, Diane, ed. *John Sayles Interviews*. Jackson: University of Mississippi Press, 1999. Interview cited is by Megan Ratner, *Filmmaker Magazine* (summer 1996).

Comito, Terry, ed. *Touch of Evil: Orson Welles, Director*. New Brunswick, N.J.: Rutgers University Press, 1985.

Fregoso, Rosa Linda. "Recycling Colonialist Fantasies on the Texas Borderlands." In *Home, Exile, Homeland: Film, Media, and the Politics of Place*, ed. Hamid Naficy. New York: Routledge, 1999.

———. "Reproduction and Miscegenation on the Borderlands: Mapping the Maternal Body of Tejanas." In *Chicana Feminisms: Disruptions in Dialogue*, ed. Aída Hurtado, Olga Nájera Ramírez, Norma Klahn and Pat Zavella, Duke University Press. Forthcoming 2002. This essay will also appear in Rosa Linda Fregoso, *Mechicana Encounters: Essays on Culture, Politics and Representation*. Forthcoming, University of California Press.

Jacobs, Del. *Revisioning Film Traditions: The Pseudo-Documentary and the Neo-Western*. Lewiston, N.Y.: Edward Mellen Press, Studies in History and Criticism of Film no. 3, 2001.

Limón, José. "Tex-Sex-Mex: American Identities, Lone Stars and the Politics of Racialized Sexuality." *American Literary History* 9, no. 3 (fall 1997): 598–616.

Montejano, David. *Anglos and Mexicans in the Making of Texas, 1836–1986*. Austin: University of Texas Press, 1987.

Paz, Octavio. "The Sons of La Malinche." Chapter 4 of *The Labryinth of Solitude*. New York: Grove Press, 1961. (Original Mexican edition, 1950)

Sayles, John. *Men With Guns & Lone Star*. London: Faber and Faber, 1998.

Smith, Gavin, ed. *Sayles on Sayles*. Boston: Faber and Faber, 1998.

Williams, Linda. *Playing the Race Card: Melodramas of Black and White from Uncle Tom to O.J. Simpson*. Princeton: Princeton University Press, 2001.

Wright, Will. *Sixguns & Society: A Structural Study of the Western*. Berkeley: University of California Press, 1975.

Binita Mehta

Emigrants Twice Displaced: Race, Color, and Identity in Mira Nair's *Mississippi Masala*

The relationship between nonwhite minority groups in the United States today is an issue that requires our immediate attention. To recognize the gravity of the situation, one has only to look at such disputes in Brooklyn as the 1990 black boycott of two Korean grocery stores and the clashes between the Hasidic and African American communities in the Crown Heights neighborhood. The much-publicized April 1992 riot in South Central Los Angeles following the Rodney King verdict was not simply a black versus white incident, but one that involved members of African American, Korean American, and Latino communities. Peter Kwong explains the complex nature of the violence in "The First Multicultural Riots": "The fixation on black versus white is outdated and misleading—the Rodney King verdict was merely the match that lit the fuse of the first multiracial class riot in American history." Many Korean American stores located in Koreatown, north of South Central Los Angeles, were looted and burned down by Latino, mostly Central American, immigrants who lived in the area. The Korean American community was mobilized by the riots and came to see themselves—for the first time—as victims of white racism when neither the local nor state police came to their aid.[1]

With the influx of immigrants from Latin America, Asia, and the Caribbean to the United States, American society has become more complex. The black/white dichotomy no longer provides an analytical model for the problematics of race, color, and identity. Many historians and cultural critics recognize the need for new coalitions, especially among marginalized communities and peoples of color. Manning Marable speaks of a new stage of black freedom in the United States that no longer involves blacks but includes all people of color: "We must find new room for our identity as people of color to include other oppressed national minorities—Chicanos, Puerto Ricans, Asian/Pacific Americans, Native Americans, and other people of African descent."[2] Taking a broader perspective, philosopher and theologian Cornel West expresses the need for unity between different groups of people—

regardless of race, class, gender, or sexuality—while maintaining individual identity. The new cultural politics of difference "affirms the perennial quest for the precious ideals of individuality and democracy by digging deep in the depths of human particularities and social specificities in order to construct new kinds of connections, affinities and communities across empire, nation, region, race, gender, age and sexual orientation."[3] Like Marable and West, Edward Said suggests that binary oppositions rooted in imperialism have disappeared and that "new alignments made across borders, types, nations, and essences" have challenged the notion of identity: "Just as human beings make their own history, they also make their cultures and ethnic identities."[4] Contemporary debates on race and color in the United States must necessarily include relations between nonwhite minorities.

In her 1991 film *Mississippi Masala*,[5] Mira Nair depicts the complex relations between two nonwhite minorities in the United States, the Indian and the African American, prompting a reflection on issues of race, color, and identity.[6] The Indian family depicted in *Mississippi Masala* has migrated via England from Uganda, East Africa, to Greenwood, Mississippi. Expelled from Uganda by General Idi Amin in 1972, they are twice displaced: Indians by culture and tradition, Ugandan by birth, they move to the United States to live in a motel owned by relatives, themselves immigrants from India. The narrative includes many vignettes about the family's social and cultural adjustments in a small southern town, but the main thrust of the film is the violent opposition of the parents, father Jay (Roshan Seth) and mother Kinnu (Sharmila Tagore), to the relationship of their daughter Mina (Sarita Choudhury) with Demetrius (Denzel Washington), an African American who owns a rug-cleaning business. Mina and Demetrius's relationship brings to the surface the prejudices of the extended Indian family toward African Americans, rendered particularly poignant by the fact that they are both minority communities in Greenwood, as well as by their peculiar status with respect to the white community.

Preceding a detailed analysis of the film, some background information about Ugandan Indians is in order.[7] Mercantile and commercial ties between the East African coast and India date back a thousand years, when Indian merchants lived in Zanzibar and traders from Karachi and Bombay did business regularly with Madagascar. Soon the Indians moved inland, and by 1900 they "controlled wholesale trade along a two-thousand-mile stretch of coastline."[8]

The British used Indians first as soldiers, then as labor to help build the Ugandan railway. The railway opened up remote areas of the country, paving the way for more Indian immigrants, who arrived in large numbers, opened shops, and soon controlled most of the retail trade in Uganda. Although the British encouraged the prosperity of the Indians, real power in Uganda remained in British hands. As the Indians prospered, however, the black African population was relegated to the bottom rung of society: "Indians created a second-class [stratum] for themselves, while the Africans were automatically relegated to the third, and lowest," according to G.S.K. Ibingira. As the business class in Uganda, Indians controlled most of the wealth, excluding Africans from the economic structure. Soon Indians were involved in every aspect of the country's economy, from laborers to the professional classes; they hired Africans as servants, making them work long hours and paying them low wages. Africans resented the Indians not only for their wealth but also because they "lived an isolated communal life, they never mixed with Africans, and their interracial dealing never went beyond business matters."[9] In addition, Indians were not concerned with social change, preoccupied as they were with making a living, educating their children, and planning suitable marriages for them. The relationship between Indians and Africans deteriorated further with the growth of African nationalism and worsened after Ugandan independence. These social and economic conflicts were among the reasons invoked by General Idi Amin when he decided to expel all Ugandan Asians during a ninety-day period in 1972.

The Indian community in Uganda comprised a mixed group of Hindus, Muslims, Christians, and Sikhs. Most came from the states of Gujarat, Kathiawad, and Kutch on the northwest coast of India, plus some from the Punjab. In their social structure the Hindus were divided into caste and subcastes (*jati*), and the Muslims into two principal sects, the Sunnis and the Shias (which were further divided into subsects). Although Indian immigrants wanted to prosper in Ugandan society and were willing to become Ugandan citizens, they were unwilling to give up caste and cultural differences. They were not able to transfer to Uganda the traditional hierarchy of the caste system as it existed in India, but caste exclusiveness still remained."[10] For example, marriage within one's caste or subcaste was rigidly followed, and needless to say, marriage between black Africans and Indians was completely out of the question. (Members of the Muslim Ismali sect, however, were encouraged by the Aga Khan, their religious leader, to become Ugandan citizens and to assimilate into Ugandan society.) Indians from Uganda and other African countries retained caste and kinship ties, maintaining customs such as endogamy, in the countries they migrated to after expulsion—England, Canada, and the United States.[11] In a study of East African Gularatis in Britain, Maureen Michaelson observes: "Despite the double migration of Gujaratis from India to East Africa, and thence to Britain, Hindu Gujarati castes have retained remarkable resiliency and in many important aspects continue to operate according to traditional restraints."[12] The historical and social context of the Ugandan Indian family is set up in the first frame of *Mississippi Masala* and continues by means of flashbacks throughout the film. Beginning and ending in Uganda, the film opens with an attempt to enunciate the rationale for Idi Amin's expulsion of Indians. The grim precredit sequence in Kampala, set in November 1972, shows Jay and his childhood friend Okelo (Konga Mbandu) in a car stopped at a roadblock, where a policeman shines a flashlight in their faces. After a tense moment, the policeman allows them to leave. We later learn that Jay, a lawyer, had been jailed for denouncing Idi Amin as an evil man during a BBC interview, and that Okelo had bribed the police in order to obtain Jay's release. Reluctant to leave the land of their birth yet realizing that they have no choice, Jay, Kinnu, and Mina pack up whatever belongings they can carry, abandoning their home to their African servants. During the bus ride to the airport, Mina's mother Kinnu is forced out of the bus by Ugandan policemen who jeer at her and throw a photograph depicting her husband in lawyer's robes into the mud. In a final humiliating act, one policeman tears a gold chain from around her neck with a rifle. Mira Nair based this scene on one of the many reports of harassment and mistreatment by Ugandan officials related by Ugandan Indians who had left during the expulsion period.[13]

We meet Mina's family again in Greenwood, Mississippi, in 1990. Moving from the lush landscape of the Kampala hills overlooking Lake Victoria, the camera scans the North American concrete jungle of motels, highways, supermarkets, and automobiles. From the drumbeats of Africa to the rhythm of Mississippi blues, the sound track reflects the change of scene.[14] The adult Mina fills her supermarket shopping cart with gallons of milk. The camera follows Mina outside and slowly pans from an Indian woman counting dollar bills to a black teenager loading groceries into the trunk. Suggested here are the class differences between a typical middle-class Indian immigrant who has attained material success in the United States and a black teenager who is relegated to menial labor. Mina's own nuclear family, however, does not fit neatly into the stereotype of the successful immigrant. In a major change from their comfortable upper-middle-class existence in Uganda, in the United States they are forced to live in a motel, the Monte Cristo, owned by relatives. Mina's father spends his time filing lawsuits against the new Ugandan regime for the restoration of his property and possessions. Her mother runs a liquor store, purchased with money borrowed from relatives and located in a black neighborhood—much to the horror of other Indian women in Greenwood. Mina works as a maid in the motel, cleaning bathrooms and helping out at the front desk.

The motel motif is significant in *Mississippi Masala*. Motels are quintessentially American: convenient, inexpensive, and linked to working-class life both as rest stops for traveling families and as sites of illicit sexual encounters. Driving through South Carolina and Mississippi during research for the film, Mira Nair found a number of Indian-owned motels. Many of the owners were sponsored and financed by relatives and, like Korean grocers, employed family members who needed only a limited knowledge of English to carry on their daily business.[15] In this "no-man's-land" of "truck drivers or prostitutes or lovers having a tryst," says Nair, the Indians continue to preserve their way of life, their religion and food habits.[16] Moreover, because motel chains are standardized nationwide, many have no character, no style; by and large they look the same everywhere. It is precisely this lack of identity, this standardization, this neutrality, which acts as a symbolic backdrop of a paradoxical nature for the Indian family seeking to maintain its identity. The motel creates a natural community for immigrants like Jay and his family. Nuclear families have their own living quarters and share certain areas during social events such as weddings. Because the motel is self-contained, it is an ideal setting where the Indian family can practice social and religious customs without fear of interference from the outside world and maintain their exclusiveness, their separateness from other ethnic groups. History and tradition are preserved; family ties are strengthened. Yet at the same time the motel serves as a site of transition. For Jay, Kinnu, and Mina, the chintzy environment of the Monte Cristo stands in stark contrast to their life of elegant comfort in Uganda.[17]

The scenes of leave-taking from Uganda, as well as scenes of the extended family in the motel in Mississippi, symbolize the temporary and the transitional, emphasizing the binary structure of rootednesss/rootlessness that operates throughout the film. The ghettoization of immigrants suggested by the motel is not particular to Indian immigrants but typical of immigrant communities in general for whom the ghetto becomes not only a space for maintaining their culture but also a space of empowerment in hostile surroundings. The motel in *Mississippi Masala* has allowed the Indians to maintain their cultural exclusiveness, but Mina's relationship with Demetrius forces them to leave that security and to confront not only questions of their own identity as Ugandan Indian immigrants in the United States but also their feelings toward other communities in Greenwood, especially the black community.

Despite the fact that Nair's treatment of representation identity and displacement is complex and nuanced and has the potential for suggesting productive coalitions between Indians, and African Americans, bell hooks and Anuradha Dingwaney are severe in their critique of the film, denouncing it as a stereotypic portrayal of blacks, Indians, and whites and lacking in political commitment.[18] Calling Nair's work "another shallow comment on interracial, interethnic, transnational 'lust,'" hooks writes, "Nair's film compelled commentary because spectators in the United States have never had the opportunity to see a Hollywood narrative about Africa, India, and African-American cultures" (p. 41). Dingwaney reports that fellow Indians found it "the only film that dared to represent working class Indian culture in the United States." They praised the film for conveying so much realism, but both hooks and Dingwaney question the portrayal of a "real" that is already a selection by the director: "Often stereotypes are used to embody the concept of the 'real,' or the everyday" (p. 41). These critics admit that *Mississippi Masala* shows familiar images, but assert that the familiar "need not embody the stereotypical," which only confirms "hegemonic Western notions of Indian traditionalism or the parochialism of both the black and white in the deep South" (p. 41). They also claim that although black and Indian viewers were uncritical in their enjoyment of the film—because they felt that it did indeed explore Indo-black relationships—nevertheless, the film's exploration of that relationship was "shallow, dishonest, and ultimately mocking" (p. 41). Their critique, less valid in some cases than in others, nevertheless facilitates the introduction of critical questions for the film in particular and for interminority relations in the United States in general.

The issue of filmic "truth" and "realism" in ethnic or racial representations is a highly contested one. It is obvious that Nair makes a choice in her depiction of the Indian family and offers her version of the "truth," based on interviews with Ugandan Indians who had settled in the United States and were mostly in the business of operating motels in South Carolina and Mississippi. To that extent it is real. Although representations can have a real effect on the world, Ella Shohat and Robert Stam observe that they can also lead "to an impasse in which diverse spectators or critics passionately defend their version of the 'real.'"[19] hooks and Dingwaney's complaint that the film "offers only stereotypical portraits of southern whites and blacks" (p. 43) is, however, valid to a certain extent. It is true that the film has its share of black, brown, and white stereotypes. Demetrius's brother Dexter (Tico Wells) is depicted as a wastrel spending his time on the streets with his friends and listening to rap music. In keeping with images of the sexual prowess of black males, much is made of the unbridled sexuality of Demetrius's partner Tyrone (Charles S. Dutton). The white motel owners depicted in the film hate the Indians yet hate the blacks even more. Some Indians, such as motel owners Anil (Ranjit Chowdhry) and Kanti (Mohan Agashe), are portrayed as greedy vultures. Yet it must be acknowledged that the film has its share of nonstereotypical, multifaceted characters: Mira Kinnu and Jay among the Indians; Demetrius and his Aunt Rose (Yvette Hawkins), with her heightened sense of self, among the blacks.[20] hooks and Dingwaney do not allow sufficiently for the multiplicity and plurality of Indian immigrant experiences, or for the complexities and diversities of the African American experience presented in the film. In contrast, while Shohat and Stam understand the importance of "the study of stereotyping in popular culture," they are aware of its downfalls: "First, the exclusive preoccupation with images, whether positive or negative, can lead to a kind of essentialism. . . . This essentialism generates in its wake a certain ahistoricism; the analysis tends to be static, not allowing for mutations, metamorphoses, changes of valence, altered function."[21]

Nair is careful to present a family situated in a very particular historical context; the film portrays the experiences of one Indian family that emigrated from Uganda. The temptation to read this family as representative of all Indian immigrants in the United States may be understandable in light of the paucity of Indian images in the American media; it may be more useful, however, to attempt to understand the complexities in their lives and the important issues that surface with regard to race relations in representing that family.

When hooks and Dingwaney remark that "there is little interaction between the two cultures when the focus is the United States" (p. 41), they point to a lack that is all too exemplary of the huge gap that exists between minorities in this country. Mina and Demetrius's attempt to bridge this gap emphasizes both the gap and the difficulties that attend their effort. Mina does have dinner with Demetrius's family for the birthday of his father, Williben (Joe Seneca), however, and Demetrius meets Mina's father on one occasion. Whereas Mina is very warmly received by Demetrius's family and they, especially his brother Dexter, are intrigued by her African-Indian roots, Demetrius's meeting with Jay as confrontation encounter must be understood in light of Jay's experiences in Uganda as well as his observations about race relations in the United States; no less important to the confrontation are Demetrius's own experiences with racism among minorities and the long history of African American struggles for recognition and acceptance. Jay's reaction to Demetrius, complicated by his love/hate feelings for Uganda, brings multiple and conflicting histories to the fore. In a conversation early in the film, Jay agonizes over being forced to leave the country of his birth: "I've always been Ugandan first and Indian second," he exclaims to Okelo. "I've been called a bootlicker and traitor by my fellow Indians." He asks, "Why should I go, Okelo? Uganda is my home." Okelo sadly replies, "Not any more, Jay. Africa is for Africans—black Africans." hooks and Dingwaney claim that Jay "never reflects on the power relations between Indians and blacks in Uganda that the film so skillfully erases and. denies" (p. 43).

On the contrary, Jay is fully aware of the exploitative relationship that existed between Indians and blacks in Uganda, and this understanding is depicted in one of the flashbacks: on their last night in Uganda Jay is in a bar drinking with some Indian friends and reminiscing about their lives. When one of them raises the toast, "Uganda, you have been so good to us until this madman [Idi Amin] came," Jay responds that it was the Indians who had created the "madman." Noting the failure of the Indian community to make itself a meaningful part of Uganda, he says, "Most people are born with five senses. We are left with only one, sense of property." Unlike the prejudices of other members of his extended family, there is a good amount of self-reflection on Jay's part as to the unequal relationship between Indians and Africans in Uganda. Jay's character in the film is much more nuanced than it appears at first glance. Although he can easily be dismissed as prejudiced against blacks because of his rejection of Demetrius, he had, unlike other Indians in Uganda, established professional and social ties with blacks there, as his close ties with his childhood friend Okelo reveal.[22] There develops a definite strain in the relationship when he is forced to leave Uganda, perhaps because he unconsciously blames Okelo for Idi Amin's decision.

Yet although Jay's feelings toward blacks are definitely embittered after his expulsion and the loss of the social and economic status he had enjoyed, Jay still has mixed feelings about Ugandan blacks. When a fellow Indian in the United States comments that Jay was "a champion defender of blacks" in Uganda and that the "same blacks kicked him out," Jay insightfully remarks, "Cruelty has no color." Nevertheless, despite his liberal ideas (he also tells Demetrius that Mina is free to love whomever she wants to), he warns Mina that, ultimately, "people stick to their own kind. You are forced to accept that when you grow older. I'm only trying to spare you the pain." It is precisely because the power relations between the races cannot be denied that Jay is sensitive both to exploitative relations between Indians and blacks in Uganda and to the struggle in store for those who abandon "their own kind." Influenced by his own experience in Uganda ("After thirty-four years that's what it came down to, the color of my skin"), Jay expresses his misgivings about Demetrius's relationship with Mina, saying that he does not want his daughter to struggle as he did.

Demetrius, in turn, is obliged to invoke the history of black men in the South. On hearing the word *struggle,* he explodes: "Struggle, struggle, look, I'm a black man, born and raised in Mississippi, not a damn thing you can tell me about struggle." He continues, "You and your folks can come down here from God knows where and be about as black as the ace of spades, and as soon as you get here you start acting white and treating us like we're your doormats. I know that you and your daughter ain't but a few shades from this right here [points to his skin], that I know." Demetrius's scathing critique reflects the Indian community's tendency to affiliate with the dominant rather than minority cultures in the United States. Discussing Indian attitudes toward race and racism, Mira Nair says that when asked if he had experienced racism, an Indian motel owner is reported to have said, "'I'm just a white person who stayed in the sun too long,'" thus identifying with the whites and implying that he considered himself light enough to be accepted by white society.[23]

Attitudes toward skin color in the film likewise show that the Indians identify with the whites rather than the blacks; the preference for light skin color is frequently stressed. Mina makes light of her dark skin in talking with her mother, who wants her to go out with the lighter-skinned Harry Patel, an eligible young Indian. Color also becomes the subject of gossip between two Indian women, who discuss the probable effect of Mina's skin color on her marriage prospects with Harry. One of them sardonically remarks, "You can be dark and have money or fair and have no money but you can't be dark, have no money, and expect to get Harry Patel." The concern with gradations of skin color is something Indian culture shares with African American culture, but it serves to drive them apart rather than bring them closer.[24] Near the film's conclusion, as Mina and Demetrius try to reestablish their relationship after the scandal (which ensues when they are found in a motel room together), he asks Mina why she had not warned him that her family had "trouble with black folks." "You didn't ask," responds Mina, implying that her family was perhaps transferring its social segregation from blacks in Uganda to their American situation. Shohat and Stam suggest that Spike Lee's *Do the Right Thing* (1989), which deals with the tensions and affinities between Italian American and African American communities, "calls attention to how some members of recent immigrant communities have used Blacks as a kind of 'welcome mat,' as a way of affirming. Through anti-Black hostility, their own insecure sense of American identity," so also racist behavior toward blacks, may have been learned by the Indian family in *Mississippi Masala* after arrival in the United States, or reinforced if already present.[25]

The Indians' relationship with the whites in Greenwood is also conflicted. They may wish to maintain physical and social distance from the blacks and to identify with the whites, but white attitudes toward Indians are founded on racism and ignorance. Neighboring working-class white motel owners confuse the

Indian family with American Indians. When one of them remarks, "Send them back to the reservations where they belong," the other responds, "How many times have I told you they are not that kind of Indian!" The very same white motel owners—who resent the Indians encroaching on their territory and complain to the police about the family making too much noise during wedding festivities—express a sense of solidarity with the Indians after learning of the Mina–Demetrius scandal; they call up Anil's father Jammurebhai (Anjan Srivastava) and ask in a conspiratorial chuckle, "Are ya'll having nigger problems?" The whites in this incident are blatantly racist, and the "conspiracy" involves their assuming that the "brown" Indians share their virulent racist feelings against blacks. Another scene reinforces the stereotype of Indians as cow worshipers. As Mina is buying gallons of milk and buttermilk for Anil's wedding, the supermarket clerk jokes, "Holy cow! Are you opening a dairy?" Seeing that Mina is not amused, he apologizes for his flippant remark. White racist attitudes toward the black family are more overt, especially when the white bank manager threatens to repossess Demetrius's van. The discrimination suffered, albeit to varying degrees, by both Indians and blacks fails to create alliances between them and paradoxically widens the gulf that separates them.

That the community at large is unable to imagine the possibility of alliance with the African American community is underscored in a mock-coalitional scene—long before the confrontation between Demetrius and Jay—when members of the extended family fake a move to ally themselves with the blacks for selfish reasons. Mina first meets Demetrius when she accidentally runs into his van while driving a car to Anil, the relative who owns the motel her family lives in. Afraid of a lawsuit, Anil seeks the help of fellow motel owner Kanti, whose motel carpets are also cleaned by Demetrius and his partner Tyrone. In an attempt to find out if Demetrius is going to sue Anil, Kanti expresses solidarity with African Americans as members of nonwhite minorities: "Black, brown, yellow, Mexican, Puerto Rican, all the same. As long as you are not white, means you are colored." He concludes with "United we stand, divided we fall." Kanti's pat rhetoric is transparent in its slickness; we are not surprised to learn later that he was merely paying lip service to ethnic solidarity, using his color and minority status only to curry favor with Demetrius.

In fact, the gulf between the groups is only reinforced by Kanti's mouthing of a "lime" that rings well but means nothing. Showing the Indians feigning friendship with the blacks, hooks and Dingwaney argue, only downplays "the significance of political bonding between people of color" and does not promote the coalition building among minorities "that subverts the status quo" (p. 42). On the one hand, they point out that the film does not emphasize enough that Indians in Uganda mediated between the oppressed blacks and the oppressing imperialist class; on the other hand, they criticize Nair's representation of Indians as conniving hustlers.[26] But not all the Indians in the film are portrayed as conniving hustlers, any more than all the blacks or whites are. By placing minorities on the high ground, the critics can be faulted for reverse stereotyping. Should the Indians be judged by different standards because of their minority status? This critique in fact diverts attention from the possibility that Kanti's failure to internalize the values he so glibly musters might be read as a powerful comment on the larger failure of minorities to find common cause with one another. Later, when Mina and Demetrius are discovered in a Biloxi motel room by Anil and his friends, both African American and Indian communities defend their mutual isolation. Tyrone, when he bails Demetrius out of jail after that fiasco, observes bitterly, "Leave them fuckin' foreigners alone. They ain't nothing but trouble." He repeats with irony, "United we stand, divided we fall. Ain't that a bitch! Yeah, but fall in bed with one of their daughters, your ass gonna swing," referring both to the cultural value of female chastity in the Indian community and the false promise of unity that is destined to be belied.

If Jay is haunted by the ghosts of racial difference that constitute his betrayal by Uganda, and the Indian community is obsessed with maintaining its distance from blacks, Mina herself identifies more with the blacks than with the whites in Greenwood. In one incident, when Mina has a date with Harry Patel, they go to a club where she is perfectly at ease socializing with the predominantly black crowd, dancing with some black friends and later with Demetrius, but Harry becomes so uncomfortable that he angrily leaves the club without her. As an Indian who has never been to India, Mina also shares a common history with African Americans who, as Dexter explains, are Africans who have never been to Africa. Moreover, Mina also has fond memories of her childhood in Uganda and of her father's friend Okelo. She chastises Jay for his refusal to bid Okelo goodbye. "Okelo risked his life to save yours," she reminds him. "I don't know what more proof you need of his love. I remember his face when he came to say goodbye. You would not even look at him."

It may be true, as hooks and Dingwaney suggest, that Mina "is no civil rights activist in the making" (p. 43), but she is acutely sensitive to the racism around her. She recounts to Demetrius the racism faced by Indian motel owners: "You know how many people come to the motel. They look at us and say, 'Not another goddam Indian.' Makes me so mad."[27] Moreover, although Mina is not given to making political speeches on racism and equality, her leaving Greenwood with a black man in a society where blackness has come to be feared and loathed is nothing less than radical. Breaking the social taboos of both her own community and the larger society around her, she is engaged in a revolutionary act for an Indian woman under any circumstances.

Although Mina's relationship with Demetrius is an attempt to transcend a devastating racial divide, after their actual sexual union the chasm between the two cultures gapes wider. Yet hooks and Dingwaney assert that the film's message is one of romantic love that breaks down racial barriers, a message that "deflects from the very real politics of domination that underlies our inability as individuals to bond and form sustained community while simultaneously embracing our difference" (p. 41). They object to the use of romantic love as a means of bonding between the two groups. Mina and Demetrius are not blinded by the love that brings them together, however; they have a realistic view of the problems they are likely to face. When Demetrius ironically asks Mina whether they will live on fresh air if they leave Greenwood, Mina responds, perhaps not so unrealistically, "I could be your partner. I know how to clean rooms." Demetrius is also fully aware of his financial responsibilities. The couple's departure demonstrates that they can be together despite their differences, thus rendering their bonding more challenging and circumspect.

Still more egregious to hooks and Dingwaney is the fact that whereas the film portrays the sexual frustrations of a newlywed Indian couple, it shows Mina and Demetrius's sexual encounter as so "intense and so fulfilling that it empowers them to abandon familial ties" (p. 42). These critics exaggerate the impact of the one sexual encounter shown in the film; the narrative structure does not allow for more sexual trysts, or even for the development of the relationship, especially since Mina's relatives prevent her from meeting Demetrius after they are discovered together. Only when she finally slips away from her family's watchful eye to find him do they have a brief moment to connect emotionally and discuss their true feelings for each other. Admittedly, Nair may have forfeited the opportunity to represent a more complex and layered relationship between Mina and Demetrius; however, the sexual aspect of it is liberating for Mina, given her restrictive background and the repression of female sexuality within Indian society. The sexual difficulties experienced by the newlywed Indian couple may be perceived as an indictment of a certain Indian middle class, which treats sex as taboo and does not educate men and men, especially women, in sexual matters. Often Indian women (and on occasion, Indian men) are thrust into arranged marriages with little or no knowledge of sex, or of their future spouses.

Disapproval of Mina and Demetrius's sexual exuberance must be framed by another claim that appears in hooks and Dingwaney's review, that Nair mocks Indian traditions such as prayer and traditional weddings. They point to Jammubhai's during his son's wedding reception: "Even though we are ten thousand miles away from India, we should not forget our roots, our culture, traditions, our gods." "By making these moments comedic," the critics remark, "Nair seems to stand with white Americans who insist that ethnic jokes poking fun at non-white cultures is harmless and not meant to undermine respect for difference" (p. 42). Yet they never question what aspects of Indian culture are being portrayed in the film. The social customs depicted are a potpourri of Hindu religious ritual and pop culture: family members gather for daily prayers, celebrate a traditional Hindu arranged marriage, listen to Indian music, watch commercial Hindi films on video, and wear Indian clothes. When hooks and Dingwaney speak about the film's lack of respect for "Indian" culture, they refer to Nair's depiction of a Hindu culture, thus conflating "Indian" and "Hindu" identity. They do not consider the religious, regional, caste, and class differences within Indian culture itself.

Indeed, Nair appears to ridicule not the customs themselves bust the manner in which they are conducted, underscoring the pompous tone of Jammubhai's declaration, followed by his leading a Hindu *bhajan* or hymn in which many of the younger Indians participate only halfheartedly. The practice of rituals may help the older generation maintain a sense of identity, but the rites are perhaps meaningless to the younger generation. In fact, given that many of the Indians either left India a long time before or have never been there at all, the practice of certain customs may be anachronistic in a contemporary Indian context. For Mina, who has never been to India and who left Uganda as a child, these so-called traditions are merely symbols devoid of significance.

In their eagerness to affirm culture and tradition as sacrosanct institutions, hooks and Dingwaney do not acknowledge that Indian customs such as arranged marriages can be oppressive to Indian women. Anxious to see twenty-four-year-old Mina married, Kinnu encourages her to go out with Harry Patel. She admonishes Jay, who is less concerned about Mina's marriage prospects: "You want your daughter to be a thirty-year-old spinster, running a liquor store?" The sexual politics of propriety and shame are evident in Kinnu's remark. Both parents,. although "Westernized" enough to encourage Mina to go out with eligible young Indian men, are shocked when she and Demetrius are discovered in bed together. Kinnu and Jay feel that she has brought dishonor to her family, although it is unclear whether they are upset because she has slept with a man before marriage or because Demetrius is American or because he is black. The film's allowing Mina a measure of sexual liberation constitutes less an instance of sex at the expense of family than an arraignment of a sexual economy that uses the female body as currency for cultural survival.

Moreover, far from celebrating Mina and Demetrius's "self-chosen homelessness," as hooks and Dingwaney contend (p. 43), the film shows that the decision is wrenching for the couple as well as their families. Mina and Demetrius call their parents before they leave; Demetrius receives his father's blessing, and Kinnu tearfully accepts Mina's decision, but Jay receives the news in stoic silence, refusing to speak to his daughter once he learns that she is with Demetrius.[28] Mina and Demetrius do not wish to leave their families. It is the families and the community that force their departure by refusing to accept their relationship. Moreover, they decide to leave Mississippi for a more practical reason: ostracized by Greenwood society. Demetrius is unable to find work; moving to another state offers him more employment opportunities. It is important to emphasize here that it is not they who fail the family, but the family and community that fail them.

Nevertheless, hooks and Dingwaney see in *Mississippi Masala* the suggestion that "personal fulfillment cannot be found within the context of nation or family where one is able to reconcile the longing for personal autonomy with the desire to function within community" (p. 43). Their comment echoes that of Demetrius's ex-girlfriend Alicia (Natalie Oliver); observing that there is no shortage of black women in Greenwood, she accuses Demetrius of letting down his family, his community, and his entire race. Dismissing the couple's decision as a manifestation of "bourgeois white western . . . individuality" (p. 41), hooks and Dingwaney do not allow for the complexity of the role of immigration, whose very nature complicates notions of "identity," "family," "community," and "nation," which are nuanced and not monolithic concepts. Mina was born in Africa of Indian parents, and raised in the southern United States. She cannot deny her "Americanness" any more than she can deny her "Africanness" or her "Indianness"—if it were possible to identify an essential Indian, African, or American. Therefore, Mina does not reject her identity but accepts her multiple identities. Because of her unique experience she is forced to create her own space, which does not necessarily imply rejection of tradition and family. Mina describes herself as a *masala,* or mixture, a "bunch of hot spices." For Mina, *masala* is a social construction, a means of explaining her Indian/Ugandan/American identities, an amalgamation of her ethnic roots, as well as her immigrant past.

The term *masala,* literally a blend of spices, has various connotations in the film. At times it refers to the hybrid nature of the family, which is Indian, Ugandan, and now North American. Nair herself defines *masala* in a more postcolonial sense as a "polyglot culture of the Indians who were colonized in their own nation by the British and then forced by poverty to seek survival elsewhere."[29] Shohat and Stam comment that culinary terms like *masala* have a metaphorical meaning for filmmakers: "'creating something new out of old ingredients'—as a key to their recipe for making films."[30] For several male characters in the film, however, *masala* is reduced to a description of Mina's sensuality and earthy good looks, a means of objectifying her as sexual object. Demetrius describes her as "hot and spicy." To Tyrone, Demetrius's oversexed business partner, Mina is "just ripe for plucking." He even mistakes her for a Mexican at first, reinforcing the Hollywood image of Latin American women as sex objects. When she corrects him and identifies herself as an Indian, he assumes she means a Native American (the only "Indian" he is familiar with) and refuses to believe her. Even the *New York Times* film critic Vincent Canby emphasizes Mina's sensual appeal as if it were the only thing that determines her relationship with Demetrius: "Her voluptuous presence defines the urgency of the love affair."[31]

hooks and Dingwaney's observations with regard to family and nation raise a number of important questions: Is the Ugandan Indian (Hindu) family in the film typical of all Indian immigrant families in the United States? What constitutes Mina's Indian identity, given the fact that she has never been to India? In their concluding paragraph the critics write, "Exile is not homelessness, rather a deep engagement with 'home'" (p. 43). The very question of "home" is central to the film, but what is "home" to the Indian family in the film—Uganda? India? The United States? What does Mina consider home?

There are no simple answers to these questions of identity and home. Cultural historians have discussed these very issues as they pertain to emigrant groups. Stuart Hall speaks about the notion of migranthood and the attitudes of migrants who know deep down that they are not going home, because migration is a one-way trip. "There is no 'home' to go back to. There never was."[32] Ashis Nandy observes that South Asians in the diaspora "cling to the memories of [a] South Asia which no longer exists and to a myth of return to the home land which is no longer shared by their children or grandchildren." Even Jay comes to realize that his home is now in North America, and that neither the India nor the Uganda of his memories exists anymore. "Home is where the heart is, and my heart is with you," he writes to Kinnu from Uganda, using a well-worn cliché to attain perhaps a reasonable compromise in his own mind to his personal dilemma. Jay's resolve signals an important moment of commitment, to his wife and, by extension, to the "home" he must build with her in their new domicile, thereby recalling Nandy's suggestion that "the diaspora must work towards dismantling links with the mother-country and entering the political realm of their new country."[33] In this context one might say that whether or not Mina and Demetrius's departure is a celebration of individualism, more urgently it is a call for minority communities to recognize and begin to resolve their differences in their immediate surroundings. That the film ends not with the couple's departure but with Jay in a Kampala marketplace holding an African child in his arms and swaying to the beat of African drums suggests that despite the admittedly mawkish display, it points to a more hopeful future—or at least a longing for a better world in which such hopes need no longer be quixotic.

The film demonstrates how essential migration and displacement are to an understanding of the behavior of the twice-displaced Indians as Mina's family transfers its attitudes and behavior toward black Africans to black Americans. It ends on a note of uneasy reconciliation: all conflicts appear to have been resolved, at least temporarily. Mina and Demetrius have left Mississippi for an uncertain future, but there is the "possibility" that the love relationship will work out. Both families have accepted the couple's decision, albeit with difficulty, and it becomes clear that the Ugandan Indian family must forge a new identity: a combination linking their Indian and Ugandan past with their present life in America.

Although *Mississippi Masala* does not have a radical political agenda, the film nonetheless makes a political statement by raising the necessary question of interiority politics, so rarely addressed by the mass media. Given that minorities often seem preoccupied with making political statements of representation in opposition to the majority culture, the film creates a space where we can refine black/white issues in order to study the more subtle shades of relationships between minority groups in the United States. Indeed, the film urges that connections be made between different nonwhite minorities, old taboos broken, and new identities created. In a broader context, *Mississippi Masala* shows that hinary oppositions such as black versus white, victim versus victimizer, are not necessarily the most significant oppositions in American society. The film declares that people of color must overcome mutual prejudice if they are to unite in a collective space of their own.

NOTES

I thank Deepika Bahri, George McClintock, Pia Mukherji, and Francesca Sautman for their helpful suggestions and patient reading of earlier drafts of this essay.

1. Peter Kwong, "The First Multicultural Riots," *The Village Voice*, June 9, 1992, pp. 29, 32. Edward T. Chang similarly titles his article tracing the historical roots of the riots "America's First Multiethnic 'Riots,'" in *The State of Asian America: Activism and Resistance in the 1990's*, ed. Karin Aguilar-San Juan (Boston: South End Press, 1994), pp. 101–117.

2. Manning Marable, "Race, Identity and Political Culture," in *Black Popular Culture*, a project by Michele Wallace, ed. Gina Dent, Dia Center for the Arts, Discussions in Contemporary Culture 8 (Seattle: Bay Press, 1992), p. 302.

3. Cornel West, *Keeping Faith: Philosophy and Race in America* (New York: Routledge, 1993), p. 29.

4. Edward Said, *Culture and Imperialism* (New York: Knopf, 1993), pp. xxiv–xxv, 336.

5. *Mississippi Masala*, dir. Mira Nair, with Denzel Washington, Sarita Choudhury, Roshan Seth, Sharmila Tagore, Michael Nozik, and Mira Nair, Samuel Goldwyn Company, 1991.

6. I use "African American" and "black" almost interchangeably, but I specifically use "black" when I want to stress the issue of color.

7. This historical background of the Ugandan Indians derives from four principal sources: Grace Stuart K. Ibingira, *The Forging of an African Nation: The Political and Constitutional Evolution of Uganda from Colonial Rule to Independence, 1894–1962* (New York: Viking Press, 1973); Jane Kramer, "Profiles: The Ugandan Asians," *New Yorker*, April 8, 1974, pp. 47–93; J. S. Mangat, *A History of the Asians in East Africa, 1886–1945* (Oxford: Clarendon Press, 1969); and H. S. Morris, *The Indians in Uganda* (Chicago: University of Chicago Press, 1968).

8. Kramer, "Profiles," p. 48.

9. Ibingira, *Forging*, pp. 69, 107–108. It is important to note that Ibingira's stance is an official one. He played a major role in the independence movement of Uganda, was a founding member of the Uganda People's Congress (UPC), and served as both minister of justice and minister of state after Uganda became independent.

10. Morris, *Indians in Uganda*, p. 27.

11. Within the United States, Suvarna Thaker's "The Quality of Life of Asian Indian Women in the Motel Industry" confirms that most of the Asian Indian women she interviewed (who had come to the United States from England and Africa) said they hoped to marry off their children within their "small caste," and some who said that their children might not marry in their own caste "would certainly appreciate it if the other partner were at least Indian" (*South Asia Bulletin* 2, no. 1 [1982]: 72).

12. Maureen Michaelson, "The Relevance of Caste among East African Gujaratis in Britain," *New Community* 7, no. 3 (1979): 350.

13. Bert N. Adams and Mike Bristow have written about Ugandan Asians' expulsion and later resettlement in their adopted countries; see, e.g., "Ugandan Asian Expulsion Experiences: Rumour and Reality," *Journal of Asian and African Studies* 14, no. 3–4 (1979): 191–203, for the experiences of refugees they interviewed in 1973.

14. The move from Africa to the United States, part of the narrative of *Mississippi Masala*, is reminiscent of Indian commercial films where, in the course of a song sequence, for example, the protagonists change both costume and locale.

15. In her introduction to Suvarna Thaker's "Quality of Life," p. 68, Sucheta Mazumdar observes that a high percentage of Asian Indians in the United States invest in the motel industry. When asked why, some cite the security of investment in real estate; others, the fact that it provides jobs for newly arrived immigrants. For still others, a motel provides a living area for the extended family, bringing in higher returns on investment than house ownership; in addition, the family also provides the labor to run the motel. Michaelson, "Relevance," pp. 350–351, mentions similar settlement patterns of East African Gujaratis in Britain. Those who purchased homes in certain areas affected later settlement patterns: first, their homes served subsequent migrants from East Africa; second, they were "nuclei around which later immigrants clustered in specific suburbs or centres of Britain."

16. Quoted in Samuel G. Freedman, "One People in Two Worlds," *New York Times*, February 2, 1992, p. H14.

17. In contrast to the role of the motel in the film helping to preserve a sense of history for the Indians, James Clifford (*Traveling Cultures in Cultural Studies*, ed. Lawrence Grossberg, Cary Nelson, and Paul A. Treichler [New York: Routledge, 1992], p. 106) quotes Meaghan Morris, "At Henry Parkes Motel," *Cultural Studies* 2, no. 1 (1988): 1–47: "Motels, unlike hotels, demolish sense regimes of place, locale, and history."

18. bell hooks and Anuradha Dingwaney, "*Mississippi Masala*," *Z Magazine*, July–August 1992, pp. 41–43. Quotations from this review are cited by page number in the text.

19. Ella Shohat and Robert Stam, *Unthinking Eurocentrism: Multiculturalism and the Media* (London: Routledge, 1994), p. 178. For further discussion, see the introductory section (pp. 78–82) to the chapter entitled "Stereotype, Realism, and the Struggle over Representation."

20. Rose is quick to point out that her brother owes nothing to his white employers, given that they had only recommended Demetrius to the bank for a loan: "All you and the rest of them want is that he [Demetrius] know his place and stay in it. But the days of slavery, they're over, Williben."

21. Shohat and Stam, *Unthinking Eurocentrism*, pp. 198, 199.

22. hooks and Dingwaney observe that Nair makes the relationship between Okelo and Jay ambiguous. At no point, however, does the film explicitly indicate, as they suggest, that Okelo is Jay's servant. Although one might concede that Nair perhaps waits too long to reveal that he is a schoolteacher, there are several instances in the film where we see the two men drinking and talking on equal terms.

23. Quoted in Freedman, "One People," p. 14.

24. Although color is not really presented as an issue for the black family in *Mississippi Masala*, it has played an important role in films by black Americans, such as Spike Lee's *School Daze* (1988), whose plot revolves around the tensions between the lighter and darker-skinned African Americans, as well as his *Jungle Fever* (1991).

25. Shohat and Stam, *Unthinking Eurocentrism*, p. 237.

26. Mark A. Reid, "Rebirth of a Nation," *Southern Exposure* (winter 1992): 27–28, disagrees. He says that three films, one of them being *Mississippi Masala* (the two others, *Daughters of the Dust* and *Fried Green Tomatoes*), "suggest that there is an alternative vision of Southern race relations gradually finding its way into mainstream media. . . . The community represented in each film represents the uneasiness of a society faced with emerging coalitions fighting the privileges of the status quo." These films "resist beliefs, socio-cultural customs, and detrimental ideas and practices which would inhibit the growth of their central characters." Mina and Demetrius, Reid argues, fight the forces that say love between people of different colors is unacceptable.

27. Sonia Shah, "Presenting the Blue Goddess: Toward a National Pan-Asian Feminist Agenda," in Aguilar-San Juan, *The State of Asian America*, p. 157, says that Mina is portrayed as "unconcerned with issues of race, history, culture and gender"—yet we have seen that Mina is aware of issues of race, history, and culture although she may not be taking an obvious feminist position. I also disagree with Shah when she says that Nair hurts the South Asian American cause by portraying Mina as one of those "little more than exotic, browner versions of white women, who by virtue of a little color can bridge the gap between black and white." Nair, by virtue of her portrayal, is just presenting her own view on the subject and not protecting some South Asian American cause. Given the diversity among the South Asian Indian community, what "cause" is she hurting? Again, what would be an appropriate portrayal of an Indian character? Mina is considered "white" by Shah, because she is not political and socially conscious enough. In literal terms Mina is more "black" than "white" and feels closer emotionally to the blacks than to the whites in Greenwood.

28. R. Radhakrishan, "Is the Ethnic Authentic in the Diaspora?" in Aguilar-San Juan, *The State of Asian America*, pp. 225–226, sees in *Mississippi Masala* a "commodification of hybridity" as "the two young adults just walk out of their 'prehistories' into the innocence of physical heterosexual love." He remarks that the term *masala* (see below) "trivializes histories" by allowing for "individualized escapes." "Just think of the racism awaiting the two lovers," cries Radhakrishnan. Yet the decision to leave their families is not an easy one for either Mina or Demetrius, and neither is blind to the problems ahead, racial or otherwise. Nor do I believe that the film trivializes the histories of any of the countries it discusses. On the contrary, both Mina and Demetrius are conscious of their roots and heterogeneous identities.

29. Quoted in Freedman, "One People," p. 13.

30. Shohat and Stam, *Unthinking Eurocentrism*, p. 314. There is a resemblance between *masala* and Gloria Anzaldua's definition of the "new mestiza" in her *Borderlands La Frontera: The New Mestiza* (San Francisco: Aunt Lute, 1987). Anzaldua describes her Mexican American heritage as a hybrid mixture resulting from living on the "borderlands." Despite certain liabilities, the mestiza is seen as a positive, empowering force that strengthens rather than weakens: "This mixture of races, rather than resulting in an inferior being, provides hybrid progeny, a mutable, more malleable species with a rich gene pool" (p. 77). The "new mestiza consciousness" is the creation of a new self, the amalgam of the different parts. It has political and feminist overtones, resulting in "a conscious rupture with all oppressive traditions of all cultures and traditions" (p. 82). Implicit in *Mississippi Masala* is the notion of hybridity, but without the political and feminist agenda.

In Srinivas Krishna's film *Masala* (1991), the term has multiple meanings. It refers not only to the various story lines but, at another level, to the narrative structure, which borrows from video, television, and popular Hindi film. *Masala* is also used literally to mean the spices ground by the grandmother for a curry. Finally, it describes the hybrid quality of the Indian Canadian families portrayed in the film who live their lives in a hodgepodge of Indian kitsch (Hindu gods and idols, Indian food, arranged marriages) and the reality of a racist Canada (the protagonist, Krishna, is stabbed to death by a white teenager at the end of the film).

31. Vincent Canby, "Indian Immigrants in a Black and White Milieu," *New York Times*, February 5, 1992, p. 19.

32. Stuart Hall, "Minimal Selves," ICA Document 6 (1987): 44.

33. Nandy quoted in Nikos Papastergiadis, "Ashis Nandy: Dialogue and Diaspora—A Conversation," *Third Test: Third World Perspectives in Contemporary Art and Culture* (special issue: "Beyond the Rushdie Affair") 11 (1990): 103, 105.

Brian Larkin

Itineraries of Indian Cinema: African Videos, Bollywood, and Global Media

The tape recorder, the device that conveys love between the two main characters in the Nigerian (Hausa) video film *In Da So Da K'auna* (The Soul of My Heart, Ado Ahmad, 1994), is a mediating device, filtering, on several levels, the physical and symbolic boundaries among characters, societies, and technologies. Sumayya sits in her bedroom as a boy brings in a tape from her lover, Mohammed. The camera zooms in to a medium close-up as she turns on the tape recorder and hears her lover announce he will sing to her "Lambun Soyayya," (The Garden of Love). She sits still, for a full three minutes, as the camera moves to an extreme close-up on an immovable face. There is no reaction, no expression, and the viewer is forced to contemplate the unspectacular practice of listening. In this sensual, physical scene, a visceral declaration and acceptance of love occurs and in the intimacy of a bedroom lovers share the same space but only by virtue of the mediating capacity of the tape recorder. The tape recorder allows the presence of love, but preserves the segregation of the sexes as Mohammed, the lover, is only present by prosthesis. And in doing so the tape recorder also mediates between Indian films and Nigerian Hausa videos, enabling the declaration of love through song, so central to Indian films and their popularity in Nigeria, while preserving the sexual segregation necessary to Hausa Islamic values.

The adoption of song-and-dance sequences in Hausa videos is one of the Bollywood-influenced intertextual elements that distinguish them from the Yoruba- and English-language videos, also made in Nigeria. For over forty years, Indian films,[1] their stars and fashions, music and stories, have been a dominant part of everyday culture of northern Nigeria. The rise of Hausa videomakers who borrow plots and styles from Bombay cinema are part of a proliferation of cultural forms that have resignified the global flow of Hindi cinema within Hausa culture. Here I will use the rise of a new genre of Hausa love films as an example of how transnational flows of Indian films can spawn a range of cultural phenomena as they are reworked in local settings. I use this example to rethink the idea of global media and the ways in which global cultural politics of identity are contested.

Figure 1. Nigerian poster of Indian film stars. From the collection of Brian Larkin.

While Indian film is a hugely successful global media form that has been strikingly successful in competing with, and sometimes dislodging, Hollywood in the global arena, the specific and diverse reasons why Indian film travels have rarely been analyzed. For some, Indian film represents tradition, a space outside of, and alter to, the cultural spread of Western modernity; for others, the cultural address of Indian film is future-oriented, modern, and cosmopolitan. To understand the varying reasons why Indian film provides amenable spaces for global cultural imagining means taking seriously a decentered media theory, one whose premises start from the specificity of why media travel and the social context of their operation.

The popularity of Indian films with Arabic, Indonesian, Senegalese, or Nigerian youth reveals the mobilization of desire and fantasy that animates global cultural flows. These moments of borrowing are the choices individuals and cultures (in the case of extended, elaborated genres of music or film) make out of the range of mass-mediated cultural goods available to them in order to make those cultural goods do symbolic work locally. Stressing this range of cultural goods is important because discussions of global media are often structured around the dichotomy of the dominance or resistance to foreign (Western) media. This dominance is clear, but in many societies Hollywood *and* Indian films are popular; Egyptian *and* Indian *and* Hollywood *and* Hong Kong films are popular (in the case of the Middle East, for instance). If we take into account that most societies live in a diversified media environment, then we must shift our critical questions. What pleasures do Indian films offer that Hollywood films do not? What cultural work do Hollywood films accomplish that is different from Hong Kong films? The presence of one media flow—such as mainstream American films—does not mean the obliteration of others, as people take diverse meanings and different pleasures from various types of media available to them.

By examining the migration of Indian film outside of India, I will begin to analyze the diverse and often long-standing reasons Indian film travels. Following a more general discussion I will analyze the import of Indian film styles into Nigerian Hausa video. I argue that Indian film offers a "third space" for Hausa audiences that mediates between the reified poles of Hausa Islamic tradition and Western modernity (a false dichotomy to be sure, but one that remains deeply meaningful to people's political consciousness). Indian film offers Hausa viewers a way of being modern that does not necessarily mean being Western. This multifacetedness is key to their success and to their popularity. For Nigerian Hausa, Indian film offers a space that is alter to the West against which a cultural politics (but not necessarily a political one) can be waged. The story does not stop there, however, because Indian film also offers Hausa a cultural foil against other Nigerian groups, to wit, Igbo and Yoruba. The popularity of Indian film with Hausa audiences is so great that, in the north of Nigeria at least where Hausa are based, they are used by both Hausa and their others as means of defining identity and locating the temporal and political nature of that identity. When Hausa videomakers incorporate elements of Indian films into their videos they are thus engaging a complicated series of cultural hierarchies external and internal to the nation, setting our understanding of the operation of transnational media within a more complicated terrain.

The Global Flow of Indian Films

The popularity of Indian film in Nigeria reflects the extraordinary global reach of Bollywood—a cinema that has successfully marginalized Hollywood in certain world markets. Understanding this phenomenon is a means of revising the ways in which we understand what we conceive of as global media. In certain areas of the world Indian films have succeeded in establishing a cultural and aesthetic style outside the dominant genres of American media. In many cases audiences engage with Indian films as a means of establishing distance from the ideologically loaded presence of American film. This last statement needs careful contextualization so that the popularity of Indian films is not reduced to a simplistic notion of "resistance" to America, (although in many cases this is a self-conscious part of the process). Rather, this popularity is complexly grounded in history and cultural difference. Hausa videomakers, for instance, borrow from Indian films as a means of addressing an urban Hausa audience that is emphatically not Western and, just as important, not southern Nigerian, suggesting that some of the popularity of Indian film lies here in specific political and cultural relations well outside the knowledge of Indian filmmakers. If we examine this process we can see the diversity of audiences Indian films attract globally and suggest reasons for how it is that Indian films create narrative forms and modes of address and narrative that draw viewers in large numbers.

Indian Film and the Cultural Production of Diaspora

Perhaps most famously, Indian films have followed in the wake of Indian migration across the globe. In countries from England to the United States, Tanzania, Trinidad, Fiji, and elsewhere, these films play a complicated role in producing diasporic belonging, cultural knowledge, and even language training (for Fijian Indians, see Ray, 2000; for England, see Dhondy, 1985; Gillespie, 1995; Tyrell, 1998; Sardar, 1998). For many Indians, who are often internally divided by region, caste, and class, the archive of images, memories, and narratives produced by Hindi cinema creates a common cultural nostalgia in the diaspora, a cultural lingua franca that has the possibility to transcend difference. This role of Hindi film in mediating the connection between the diaspora and the homeland revolves around the tropes of loss, nostalgia, and pastness, where for diasporic Indians, India represents a way of life once present but now gone and film the means to reconnect with it. For second-generation diasporic Indians, Indian films play a role as ethnographic and cultural texts "teaching" migrant youth cultural knowledge about India. One British Asian woman commented that being taken as a child to see Indian films taught her "just about everything I know about religion, about India and my family traditions" (Tyrell, 1998, p. 20). Manas Ray argues that for Fijian Indians, separated from India by the historical rupture of indenture under British colonialism, this process of cultural ethnography is even more stark in that for Fijian Indians, the India represented in Indian films is a wholly imagined way of life (2000). The concept of India being mobilized here is one about transport, about using the images and narratives of film as a conduit back to the idealized world of India itself.

But while the link between Bollywood and Indian diasporic identity is growing stronger, Manas Ray warns against assuming that the reasons for this intensification are stable (2000). In his study of Fijian Indian migrants to Australia he argues that the consumption of Indian films in the diaspora varies greatly according to class, caste, and national origin. Whereas for some Bollywood might be a means of reconnecting with a homeland, Ray argues that for Fijian Indians (or Tanzanian or Trinidadian Indians) India remains an imagined entity and Indian films function as introduction to a whole way of life about which they know little and have experienced even less (2000). This points to what he terms the historical subjectivity of particular diasporic groups like Fijian Indians, for whom the mass culture of Hindi film provides a cultural repertoire of Indianness.

In recent years the style and nature of the way in which Hindi films have mediated the relation between the diaspora and the homeland have changed considerably. The introduction of liberalization in India, the rise of the diaspora abroad, the increase of middle-class incomes in India, and their ability to consume the same sorts of technological and cultural goods available to their diasporic cousins have heightened the shared cultural context between urban India and Indians overseas. This process has been mediated through satellite television, through the renewed interest in filmgoing among diasporic audiences, and through the emergence of a vibrant diasporic South Asian youth culture in the United States and especially in England. Indian films have in their turn recognized this cultural convergence in the production of a new genre of films centered on the diasporic experience and an increased awareness of the economic strength of the Indian market abroad. These changes exhibit a relation between the diaspora and India that is not based on issues of nostalgia and pastness, where India and Indian films represent the repository of enduring cultural values threatened by the modernity of Western diaspora. As Manas Ray argues, the dichotomies of past and present, inside and outside, are beginning to lose their analytical purchase. Rather, the relation is now one of cultural convergence and contemporaneity in which Indians in New York, London, Sydney, and metropolitan centers such as Mumbai and Delhi are engaged in the production of a transnational diasporic culture.

The renewed success of Indian films in the diaspora is signified by the return of diasporic audiences to cinematic exhibition and the rise of Bombay films specifically oriented toward a diasporic audience. *Dilwale Duhaniya Le Jahenge* (Braveheart Will Win the Bride, dir. Aditya Chopra) was one of the first films to include a character from the diaspora at the center of the film; its huge success prompted the producer Yash Chopra to establish his own distribution company in the United States and United Kingdom. This opening up of the overseas market entailed a reorganization of the infrastructural distribution of Indian film. In an interview with *Business World India*, Chopra said that previously blockbuster Indian films had to appeal to a range of class, caste, and regional tastes (October 23, 2001). Now, the opening up of the diaspora market meant that Chopra could perfect a genre of light romantic comedy that addressed a cosmopolitan urban audience without worrying about how the film would play in the Indian hinterland. These films presume a mobile viewing subject equally at home in Mumbai, London, or New York. Chopra's first film after the opening of this distribution company was the massive hit *Dil to Pagal Hai* (1997, dir. Yash Chopra), a film that Rachel Dwyer argues set a new cool, urban visual style for Hindi films (1999).

Indian films have always been hugely popular on video. But because video is limited to the domestic sphere, the popularity of Indian films in the diaspora has rarely impinged on the mass cineplex public. That, however, is beginning to change. As cineplex managers, particularly in Britain, realize that Indian films can outperform Hollywood at the box office, there has been a movement of Indian films out of the dilapidated "flea pits" of old and into the best facilities available. These are often new multiplexes showing a mix of American and Indian releases. Major new releases of Indian films in Britain now premier at the Odeon, Leicester Square, the most prestigious cinema in Britain and formerly the site only of American and British film premiers. In 2000, the hosts of the Film Fare Indian film awards used the Millennium Dome in Greenwich, London (Britain's homage to fin de siecle, spectacle) as the site for the first ever Indian film awards ceremony held outside of India, an event broadcast on mainstream British TV. This demonstrates how Indian film has migrated from the realm of the family, the domestic, and the marginal in British society to a much more public arena, carrying with it a palpable sense of cultural self-assertion and self-confidence.[2]

Bollywood without Indians

While diasporic Indian engagement with Bollywood is a significant and intensifying phenomenon, perhaps more striking is the long-standing popularity of Indian films with non-Indian audiences in Asia, the Middle East, Africa, and Europe. It is this reach across the boundaries of nation, language, culture, and religion that makes Hindi films true global media. By the 1950s, Indian films were beginning to be exported all across the socialist world and into much of the Third World as a whole. In Russia, Bulgaria, Poland, and elsewhere, as relations with the West settled into the structured estrangement of the Cold War, Indian films found favor with socialist states.

It is this same fantastic, extra-real engagement with Indian films that we see mobilized in the continuing popularity of Bollywood in Africa and the Middle East, where the films' popularity was established outside of any meaningful connection with India itself (with the notable exception of the substantial Indian populations in parts of East and South Africa). Work on Indian film in African studies has stressed the ways in which Indian films offer a space for imaginative play for African audiences in which melodrama, love, and even action constitute spaces of alterity free from both Western media and local generational and gender hierarchies. Fugelsang (1994) and Behrend (1998) both argue that in Lamu, Kenya, love relations depicted in Indian film offer youths a subversive alternative to the control of relationships by elder kin. This was an important element in my own study of Hausa love literature in northern Nigeria and the intertextual borrowing from Indian films (1997). I argued that the imaginative investment of Hausa viewers with Indian films comes about because of the possibilities of narrative as a means of allowing readers to explore imaginatively social tensions in multiple connotations. The mass culture of Indian films, Hausa love literature, or Hausa videos develop this process of ambiguity by presenting various resolutions to similar predicaments in thousands of narratives extending over many years. Indian films become an attractive site for this investment. The massive popularity of Indian films in northern Nigeria stems, in part, from their ability to offer Hausa viewers a "third space," a way of engaging with forms of tradition different from their own while at the same time conceiving of a modernity that comes without the political and ideological significance of that of the West.

The work of the Kenyan photographer Omar Said Bakor presented and explored by Behrend (see Behrend, 1998; Wendl and Behrend, 1999) is a spectacular example of this identification. Bakor, a Swahili of Yemeni descent living in Lamu Island off of Kenya, worked as a street photographer before opening his own studio in 1962. He developed a style of portrait photography involving the superimposition of Indian film actresses over portraits of local Lamu men. In one photograph the film star Sridevi is superimposed next to a young Lamu man who is reaching over to embrace her (see Figure 2). Another portrait shows Sridevi reclining against what looks like the hills of Kashmir (notable as the setting for legions of love songs). Superimposed over her heart is the portrait of another Lamu man (see Figure 3).

These portraits play with themes of presence and absence, desire and imagination, in which Bakor sutures the fantasy space of Indian film into the indexical reality of portrait photography. Behrend argues that in the strict Islamic society of Lamu, images of Swahili women were seen as illicit and so the genre of lovers having their pictures taken together never developed. In this absence, she suggests, fantasy images of female Indian stars acted as substitutes. If this is the case, this intensifies the play between transgression and conformity, where the technological medium of photography allows imaginative transgression through disembodied representation. Photographs sutured together represent a mixing of images, not bodies, preserving the Islamic separation of the sexes. This preservation occurs, however, only if one follows the letter of Islamic law. In Lamu, Islam

Figure 2. Photomontage with Indian film star Omar Said Bakor, Lamu, 1980. From the catalogue *Snap Me One! Studiofotografen in Afrika*, ed. Tobias Wendl and Heike Behrend. Munich: Prestel, 1998.

is syncretically mixed with older forms of magical practice. Photographs are often used for magical purposes by people who wish to secure the love and affection of the person photographed (Behrend 1998; Fugelsang 1994). This magical use often depends on the indexical and iconic qualities of the photographic image that insist on *connection* between the representation and the represented. Under Islamic law montage works because it keeps the sexes separate physically while uniting them

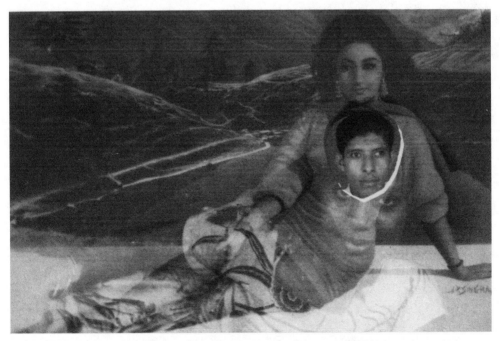

Figure 3. Photomontage with Indian film star Omar Said Bakor, Lamu, 1980. From the catalogue *Snap Me One! Studiofotografen in Afrika*, ed. Tobias Wendl and Heike Behrend. Munich: Prestel, 1998.

visually. Local practices of love magic threaten to transgress those boundaries where magic worked upon the image will have consequences on the person to whom the image is tied. Behrend makes the fascinating point that the portrait of a man's head superimposed over a reclining Sridevi also has another ghostly image. Superimposed over Sridevi, but underneath the image of the man is the spectral, hard-to-see image of a second, African woman. Behrend argues this suggests love magic and the mixing of a real with an ideal partner. Who can say? But the use of the photographic space to bring into one field love and transgression, the (mass) mediated and the spirit world, the local and the global, makes it a rich site of imagination and transgression.

In Nigeria, Indian films offer ways of being modern and traditional that create a template for exploring the tensions of postcoloniality. In the Indian diaspora, Bollywood can be both a conduit into an essentialized, traditional past and the site for the production of a hip, hybrid present. Indian films betray a love/hate relation with both the West and a mythic India and in doing so open up interstices in which heterogeneity and ambivalence flourish, allowing the films to be both Westernized and traditional; corruptor of local values and a defender of them. Vasudevan (2000) analyzes the ways Indian films create a politics of cultural difference by reinventing themselves to establish dialogue with and assert difference from universal models of narration and subjectivity. He analyzes these workings internally to India, but the same process operates on a global stage. Indian films travel because they become a foil against which postcolonial identity can be fashioned, critiqued, and debated. They allow an alterity to Hollywood domination but offer their own aggressive commercialism in its stead that is at the same time traditional and modern. The reasons for the global popularity of Indian films—crucial to the ability to map and understand the phenomenon of global popular media—lie in this interwoven process where Western media, Indian media, and local cultural production interact, at times coalescing and at other moments diverging.

Before I turn to the relation between Indian film and Nigerian Hausa videos, I first wish to make a brief detour in order to contextualize the rise of Nigerian videos in the past ten years and what this means for our understanding of that discursive construct "African cinema."

Nigerian Video Films and the End of African Cinema?

By *cinema* in this heading I refer not just to a body of films but to the critical cultural project that is inherent to the idea of African cinema (see Cham and Bakari, 1996; Diawara, 1992; Pines and Willemen, 1989; Ukadike, 1994). This is clear in the overt political and aesthetic project of "third cinema" (Pines and Willemen, 1989) but more important has informed state media policy and practice in many postcolonial nations. The concept of "national cinemas" derives from a legacy where the nation-state is posited as the definer and defender of cultural values (cf. Meyer, 1999). The Nigerian state sponsored "Nigerian" cinema to preserve "Nigerian" values, and so on. The video industry, by contrast, emerged outside of state participation, frequently in opposition to it and driven largely by commercial rather than political motives.

In what is truly a remarkable cultural renaissance in Africa, in the past eight years or so a mass media genre—Nigerian video film—has come to dominate local media production and to become regionally hegemonic in exporting media to other nations in West and East Africa. Over 3,500 of these video films have been released in the general market. These "films," shot and released on video but known locally as films, can be broadly broken down into three main categories according to language (and culture): Yoruba, English, and Hausa (for an introduction, see Haynes, 2000). The appearance of these films is remarkable in that the industry developed outside of state or foreign support, in a time of intense economic deprivation and based wholly on a mass viewing audience.

These films nearly all exhibit the qualities that Vasudevan (2000) associates with the cinema of "transitional" societies negotiating the rapid effect of modernity: the cinematic address is to a world governed by kinship relations; the plot is driven by family conflict; melodrama predominates, relying on excess, Manicheanism, and privileging the moral over the psychological. In "Nigerian" videos, the term used to refer to English-language videos (as opposed to Hausa or Yoruba videos), this melodrama is intensified by the use of horror and the supernatural. Here magic mixes with the world economy, and capitalist accumulation is only possible through occult means. Husbands sacrifice their wives to become rich, mothers bewitch their children, and the devil, through his intermediaries, is ever present in Nigerian life. In dramatizing the work of witches and the prevalence of human sacrifice, video films move from the world of melodrama into the suspense and gore associated with horror. Nigerian films, in particular, are known for their special effects, as humans transform into animals, witches fly through the night, and money is magically produced (for similar issues in Ghanaian film, see Meyer, forthcoming). It is the mixing of melodrama with horror and magic and the linkage of financial with sexual and spiritual corruption that makes the melodrama of Nigerian and Ghanaian video film distinctively African. In contemporary postcolonial West Africa, where the everyday suffering of the vast majority stands in stark contrast to the fantastic accumulation of the small elite, the tropes of sorcery, witchcraft, and supernatural evil have provided a powerful way to express the inequalities of wealth.

African cultural heritage here is rarely represented as the valued cultural patrimony we are familiar with from the debates around African cinema. Rather it is frequently represented as evil, a place where the forces of darkness operate unchecked, a representation that is the outgrowth of the emergence of what Meyer has termed (in another context) a Pentecostalist public culture (Meyer, forthcoming; Marshall-Fratani, 1998; Ukah, n.d.) in which styles of Pentecostalist discourse have proliferated in a variety of popular cultural forms. Nigerian videos address a cosmopolitan public in which the modern and the Pentecostalist, consumption and Christianity, are intertwined. The realist verities of modernist development and cultural authenticity are rejected, as is any attempt toward a progressive political project. These videos represent the working out of a specific form of Nigerian melodrama in a society that is both modern and sacred. Peter Brooks's argument that melodrama rises when the traditional hierarchies of a sacred society are dissolved captures the sense of spiritual insecurity and permanent transition that marks Nigerian melodrama, but God, the devil, and the supernatural are the everyday forms through which modernity emerges (on melodrama as a postcolonial project, see Abu-Lughod, 2002).

The rise of these videos highlights several ironies inherent in the concept of African cinema. African cinema, for instance, has tended to refer to the films Africans *produce* rather than those they *watch*. Films that travel under the sign of African cinema are still much more readily available in festivals in London, Paris, and New York, than they are in Abidjan, Lagos, or Mombasa. The calls by African filmmakers for a "popular" film practice glossed over the fact that this cinema referred first and foremost to an auteur artistic practice that rarely had to rely upon the marketplace or a mass audience for its funding and survival. This now stands in stark contrast to the rise of local video film industries in countries such as Ghana and Nigeria that, while accused of being much more "Westernized," are successful in an African marketplace. Video filmmakers have been much less concerned with ideas of cultural authenticity and cultural value. Most clearly, Nigerian videos have indeed fashioned aesthetic forms and modes of cultural address based on the experiences of the societies they address rather than those of the West—a prime concern of third cinema—but this fashioning has emerged not so much in opposition to Hollywood and Western cultural values, but *through* and *out* of the history of that engagement.

So far I have used the term *Nigerian videos* or *Nigerian film* without unpacking the regional hegemony that is built into this concept. As Jonathan Haynes (2000) has pointed out, the scholarly and film festival circuits that have deployed the concept of "African cinema" have found it extremely difficult to deal with the issue of ethnicity and of subnational difference. This is in part the legacy of the struggle against colonialism and, later, against a cultural imperialism that downplayed ethnic allegiance in favor of identification with the nation-state. In part, it also has to do with the history of cinema studies, which has tended to concentrate on the dynamics of national rather than ethnic cinemas. Nigerian videos, however, are divided into Yoruba-, English-, and Hausa-language films. The term *Nigerian films* in fact often refers to *English*-language films primarily made by Igbo and minority group producers who address their productions to a pan-Nigerian, English-speaking urban subject.[3] This means the claim to "Nigerianness" has been constructed through exclusions, as a specific form of urban culture and experience serves as the sole basis of a a pan-Nigerian address. This is an urbanism marked by fast-growing capitalism, consumption, Pentecostalist Christianity, the occult, temptation, and corruption, the central themes around which the abstraction of "national" cinema and national subject is constructed.

If these videos address a cosmopolitan "modern," urban subject, then Muslim Hausa are the internal other against which that modernity is imagined. Hausa cosmopolitanism, focused as it is on dynamics in the Muslim world more than in the West, is readily stigmatized as "backward," "traditional," and "ignorant," in southern Nigerian stereotypes. For Hausa viewers and Hausa filmmakers, the melodramatic form of southern Nigerian videos—their focus on sexual and magical excess, their unrelenting materialism, the frequent stereotyping of Pentecostalist pastors as culture heroes—makes these videos an ambivalent space for cultural imagining. As one Hausa video storeowner said to me, while he sold southern videos, he wouldn't allow his family to watch them. This is not to say that southern Nigerian videos are not popular in the north, where they do sell well, but the form, content, and even distribution of Hausa videos have developed along strikingly different lines. And it is here that Indian films have proved to be a powerful intertexual presence.

Hausa Video Films

While magic, materialism, and corruption are all present to a certain extent in Hausa video films, perhaps the primary narrative difference is the focus on love and romance and the spectacular development of this through song-and-dance routines (*waka da rawa* in Hausa)—a generic convention rarely seen in English-language videos. The focus on love comes about for a number of reasons. Most obviously, the first Hausa videos evolved from a literary genre of local Hausa-language love stories, *soyayya* books (see Furniss, 1996; Larkin, 1997). These became hugely popular among youth just at the time that the first Nigerian videos were being produced in the south of Nigeria. The first Hausa videos tended to be adaptations of these "best-selling" books and maintained their preoccupation with love. This tendency was intensified, however, by several producers who sought to make films that were explicitly *not* like southern Nigerian videos and were closer to Hausa culture. In this search for alterity producers fell back on familiar cultural forms that were separate from southern Nigeria: *soyayya* books and Indian films.

Indian Films and Hausa Viewers

First imported by Lebanese cinema owners in the 1950s, by the early 1960s Indian films were, perhaps, the dominant film form in the north.[4] Since that time Indian films have remained an integral part of the Nigerian media landscape and form the everyday media environment through which people move. Stickers of Indian stars emblazon trucks, cars, and bikes of the north. Popular stars are given Hausa

Figure 4. *Indian film stickers*. From the collection of Brian Larkin.

nicknames, such as *Sarkin Rawa* (King of Dancing) for Govinda, or *Dan daba mai lasin* (licensed hooligan—in the same way that James Bond is licensed to kill). Indian jewelry and clothing have influenced Hausa fashions and Indian film songs and stories have penetrated everyday Hausa popular culture (see Larkin, 1997).

In northern Nigeria there is a familiar refrain that Indian culture is "just like" Hausa culture. While indeed, there are many similarities between Hausa and "Indian culture" (at least how it is represented in Indian films) there are many differences, most obviously the fact that Indians are predominantly Hindu and Hausa are Muslim. The popularity of Indian films rests, in part, on this dialectic between difference and sameness—that Indian culture is both like and quite unlike Hausa culture. It is the gap between difference and sameness, the ability to move between the two, that allows Indian films to function as a space for imaginative play in Hausa society. The intra–Third World circulation of Indian film offers Hausa viewers a way of imaginatively engaging with forms of tradition different from their own at the same time as conceiving of a modernity that comes without the political and ideological significance of that of the West. Moreover, when Hausa youth rework Indian films within their own culture by adopting Indian fashions, by copying the music styles for religious purposes, or by using the filmic world of Indian sexual relations to probe the limitations within their own cultural world, they can do this without engaging with the heavy ideological load of "becoming Western."

The sense of similarity and difference is produced by the iconography and mode of address of the films themselves as well as by the ways in which Bollywood deploys a reified "culture" that acts as a foil against which Westernization in its myriad forms can be defined. Bollywood films place family and kinship at the center of narrative tension. Traditional dress is remarkably similar to that of Hausa: men dress in long kaftans similar to the Hausa *dogon riga* over which they wear long waistcoats much like the Hausa *palmaran*. Women dress in long sarees and scarves that veil their heads in accordance with Hausa moral ideas about feminine decorum. Indian films, particularly older films, express strict division between the sexes and between generations. Hausa audiences are not familiar with the main tropes of Indian religion, but they realize that the visual portrayal of Hindu religion and Indian tradition provides a cultural field that is frequently opposed to the spread of "Westernization" or modernity. It is this reified sense of tradition that Hausa refer to when they say that they "have culture" in a way that American films seem to lack. Britain and America are the structuring absences here and form the Other(s) against which Hausa can define their relation to Indian culture as similar. Hausa recognize the similarity in traditional dress; more, they realize the relational value of how one wears traditional dress. When characters code-switch from English to Hindi, when they elect to wear Western instead of Indian clothes, when they refuse to obey parents and follow their own desires, Indian films create a narrative in which action is based on moral choice. Ashis Nandy recognizes a communal mode of address in this moral choice in Indian film, arguing that commercial Indian cinema tends to "reaffirm the values that are being increasingly marginalized in public life by the language of the modernizing middle classes, values such as community ties, consensual non-contractual human relations, primacy of maternity over conjugality, priority of the mythic over the historical" (1995, p. 202). In short, the battle is against the values associated with Westernization.

It is the discourse around love, especially the tensions between arranged and love marriages, that has most influenced Hausa viewers. Indian films provide Hausa youth with an alternative style of sexual interaction, a different pattern of speech and bodily affect between the sexes. As these patterns of behavior have migrated to Hausa videos, the effect has been exhilarating. This migration is, of course, a matter of translation and accommodation and not merely copying. Like Indian films themselves, the act of borrowing plots, dance style, or visual effects entails detailed processes of rejection and addition, a stripping of superfluous detail and insertion of culturally relevant matter. Jeremy Tunstall's (1977) argument that Indian films were a dream factory locally assembling dreams manufactured 10,000 miles away (in America) has recently been decisively countered by the work of Tejaswini Ganti, who traces the transformations of narrative and form that go into the "copying" of an American film by an Indian one (Ganti, 2002). In the next section, I turn to this work of translation in the Hausa context, tracing the global flow of Indian film to Nigeria through the adoption of themes of love and song and dance sequences in Hausa video, concentrating on a transitional video, *In da So Da K'auna* (The Soul of My Heart, 1994) by the author/producer/director Ado Ahmad.

The introduction of new media forms always brings with it moments of ambivalence as the potential possibilities of the medium have to be reconciled within existing social and cultural norms. *In da* is a fascinating example of this ambivalence, especially when compared to the subsequent evolution of Hausa films. When *In da* was released in 1994, it was one of about four or five Hausa videos (there are less then ten Hausa feature films). In contrast, in 1999 alone, 125 Hausa videos were released in the market. *In da* inaugurates a new cultural form in a society where previously none existed, and introduces visual and narrative themes that have strong overlaps with Indian films. But because it is an innovation it foregrounds an uncertainty about how these themes should be handled and what the reception of this new form will be. *In da* treads delicately over themes that later videos represent unproblematically and is interesting because it is a transitional video that reveals the cultural *work* that goes into the process of cultural translation.

In da So Da K'auna

In da is set among the world of the urban elite in Kano, Nigeria. It follows the relationship between a rich girl, Sumayya (Ruk'ayya Mohammed), and a poor man, Mohammed. The theme of love and the sexual precociousness of the heroine signify the intertextual presence of Indian film. Sumayya initiates contact and pursues Mohammad, against his admonitions that their difference in status can never be overcome. In reality, as director Ahmad told me in an interview,[5] Hausa women are expected to be sexually modest, and such an open pursuit would be socially unacceptable. His dilemma as a director was how to invoke the desire and romance of Hindi cinema, while at the same time preserving a Hausa moral universe. The film treads delicately through the rituals of courtship in ways that seem unimaginable when compared to contemporary videos.

In one of the central scenes of the film, Mohammed declares his love for Sumayya. Until this point he had resisted her advances, wary of the gulf between them in terms of wealth and status. The scene consists of a series of parallel edits between the two. It opens with the lovers separated in space and time. Mohammed is in his dormitory at school; Sumayya is in her bedroom writing a letter to Mohammed. Music plays in the background as Sumayya writes. As the film cuts to Mohammed reading her letter, the same music continues to play, linking the lovers across the rupture of space and time. As the scene continues, Mohammed writes back. Their experience of each other is mediated by writing. The scene heightens when, as Sumayya receives her letter from Mohammed, his face is superimposed over the letter. As his voice-over reads the contents, the camera zooms in on Sumayya and his face appears again, superimposed over an extreme close-up of Sumayya.

Ahmad here preserves sexual segregation in the diagetic space of the film. While Mohammed's body is absent from Sumayya's room, his physical presence is made manifest through his voice and his superimposed face, permitting the lovers to share the same cinematic frame. This is a careful game that allows Ahmad to allude to the intimacy and sexual interaction familiar to Hausa viewers from Indian films while keeping its sexual excess safely separate. Ahmad repeats this narrative device frequently in the film, separating lovers in space and establishing that separation through a series of parallel edits and the a mediating device—a letter, a tape, or even dreams—to create a space for the lovers to unite through sound and montage.

The bedroom is a key space here. Sumayya first spies Mohammed as she passes him sitting outside with a group of friends. This is a male activity forbidden to Hausa women, especially wealthy ones, who are expected to remain inside the domestic space. Sumayya is narratively identified with her bedroom: this is where she writes her letter to Mohammed telling him she loves him; it is where she plays his tapes and where she returns to and listens to them after (later in the film) he tells her they should separate. Spatially and visually, then, Sumayya stays where a proper Hausa woman should be, restricted to the interior space of the house where men rarely are allowed to visit. It is only the fantasy of the film that allows her to move out of that space.

Visually these scenes are marked by restriction and immobility. In the song sequence I described in the introduction and in the scene where Sumayya

Figure 5. Poster for the video In Da So Da K'auna. From the collection of Brian Larkin.

first reads Mohammed's letter Sumayya is confined by both her bedroom and by the extreme close-up on her unmoving face. This restricted consummation of love is in stark contrast to the kinetic freedom of the dancing in Indian films. Here, the Hausa film stays within the bounds of cultural realism, adopting moral and bodily codes of Hausa expression, yet it always threatens to transgress that boundary with its constant mimetic reference to a fantasy world outside of local Hausa norms. This transgression was noted frequently by a group of young Hausa friends I watched the films with. The muted, minimalist nature of the love scenes seemed, to me, to bear little relation to the excess of Indian films, but for them the song scene was hilarious and immediately seemed culturally false. "Indian song!" one friend shouted as the scene began, "How can someone sing songs to a woman?" he asked in amused disgust.[6] Hausa viewers know that a sequence such as this, or scenes in which couples openly declare their love for each other or even spending unchaperoned time together, go against the conventions of Hausa sexual interaction. For them, such scenes are obviously derived from the style of courtship in Indian films.

In da, in its emphasis on love and relationships, and on the spectacular use of song-and-dance sequences, represents an early attempt at what is rapidly becoming an elaborate genre in Hausa cultural life. In contemporary films, song-and-dance sequences are common and few betray the cultural and religious delicacy of this transitional film. To take one example, the film *Daskin da Ridi* (dir. Aminu Mohd. Sabo) includes a love song sequence between Indo (Hauwa Ali Dodo) and her lover Yarima (Nasir Ismail). The song sequence opens with a medium shot of the couple splashing each other at a lakeside. It then cuts to them holding hands and running toward the camera and then, cutting again, to the two of them, still holding hands, running up a small hill. Still in medium shot, they begin to dance and sing to each other. As the sequence progresses, Indo dances away from Yarima. He follows, chasing her playfully, and they splash each other again. Here the use of Indian film style is blatant and unashamed: the lovers change clothes frequently during the song sequence; Indo sings in a high-pitched voice more reminiscent of the famous Indian playback singer Lata Mangeshkar than of a Hausa singer,[7] and the teasing, playful chasing is associated strongly with Hindi film.[8] The difference from Ahmad's delicate balancing act seems immense. When Ahmad adapted *In Da* from his book he changed one of the scenes so that Sumayya *dropped* a ring into Mohammed's hand rather than putting it on his finger as she did in the book. Unsure if Hausa audiences would tolerate physical contact of any kind, he developed a style that allowed sharing of filmic space while preserving strict physical separation.[9] In contrast, instead of being separated in space and time, nearly the entire *Daskin* sequence is filmed as a two-shot with both lovers constantly present in the frame.

In da and *Daskin* are revelatory of the deep intertextual influence that Indian films have had on the evolution of Hausa video film form. As I suggested elsewhere (Larkin, 1997), this influence has emerged because Indian films are useful repositories for Hausa audiences to engage with deeply felt tensions over the nature of individual freedom and familial responsibility, providing a safe imaginative space outside of the politicized contexts of western and southern Nigerian media. Indian films work for Hausa because they rest on a dialectic of presence and absence culturally similar to Hausa society but at the same time reassuringly distant. These films have allowed Hausa filmmakers to develop a genre of video films that are strikingly different from those of their southern Nigerian compatriots. This is not to say that the success of Hausa videos does not generate its own controversy. The engagement of Hausa with Indian films involves a sort of mimicry that carries with it the ambivalence of border crossing. As Hausa videos have boomed so has criticism of their cultural borrowing, leading in 2001 to a state ban on mixed-gender song sequences.[10] Interestingly the intense criticism has not focused on Indian films (which are unaffected by any censorship) but on the Hausa written and visual forms that are accused of translating their themes into Hausa social life.

Conclusion

Contemporary Indian film theorists have insisted on the "Indianness" of Hindi film. Chakravarty (1993) has elaborated on structuralist film theory to argue that Hindi film has developed a "communal" mode of address that interpellates an individual spectator as part of a wider national or religious community rather than as an isolated viewer. Vasudevan (1993, 2000) and others have examined the concept of the "darsanic" mode of vision enacted in Indian film. They argue that the formal construction of filmic meaning depends upon mobilizing extra-filmic cultural and ritual modes of knowledge in the (Indian) audience—at least in certain genres. These arguments emerge from the long-standing struggle against cultural imperialism and a desire to establish the cultural logics of a film form not totally subsumed by the Hollywood narrative and form. Studies of non-Western film therefore derived from the need to explicate the alterity and particularity of national cinemas partly, as Willemen has argued, to resist the "projective, universalizing, appropriation" that situates the Western experience of media as the model for the rest of the world (Willemen, 1991, p. 56; see also Shohat and Stam, 1994).

Similarly, in this essay, I have sought to decenter the Western experience of media, not by insisting on the alterity of Nigerian video but on its thoroughgoing intertextuality. At the same time, I have tried to place the historical and geographic spread of Hindi films at the center of an analysis of global media, rather than on the margins of a theory centered around Hollywood and the West (for a similar argument, see Ginsburg et al., 2002). Timothy Mitchell has recently argued that modernization continues to be commonly understood as a process begun and finished in Europe, that to be modern is to take part in a history defined

by the West and against which "all other histories must establish their significance" (2000, p. 6). The privileging of Western media as the only "global" media
has had a similar effect, downplaying the social significance of other long-standing global flows. By highlighting the global flow of Indian films, I do not mean to
downplay the cultural and financial hegemony of Western media, especially since
Indian films travel, in part, precisely because they counter Western media. I do
want to suggest, however, that we must shift our focus to analyze the cultural
flows of goods that do not necessarily have the West at their center.

The reasons Indian films travel and have traveled are diverse, evolving,
and culturally specific. While southern Nigerians cite the popularity of Indian
films among Hausa audiences as evidence of the northerners' "backwardness,"[11]
for young British Asians sampling dance beats with Hindi film tunes, Indian films
can be the source of a hip hybrid modernity (Sharma et al., 1997). Analyzing Indian
films as global media entails revising the ways in which media scholars have
tended to conceptualize national and transnational media. It necessitates revising
our concept of African cinema to understand Indian films as part of *African* media.
Similarly, the excellent work on the cultural particularity of Indian cinema, specifying the *Indianness* of Indian cinema, only goes partway in helping us to understand the phenomenal popularity of Hindi films in cultures, religions, and nations
whose grasp of Indian and Hindu realities is weak. Central to this project should
be the acceptance of diverse media environments in which audiences engage with
heterogeneous cultural forms. Hausa youth, who listen to fundamentalist Islamic
preaching, admire Steven Seagal, are captivated by the love tribulations of Salman
Khan, and are voraciously consuming emerging Nigerian videos are part of a postcolonial media environment in which the Western domination is only a partial
and contingent facet of global media flow.

NOTES

This chapter benefited from critical comments by Meg McLagan and Birgit Meyer. Many of
my ideas and knowledge about Indian films came from innumerable conversations with Teja
Ganti. Likewise my work on Nigerian video has emerged in dialogic relation with Jon Haynes
and Birgit Meyer. All three will recognize their presence here. I thank Ado Ahmad for his gen-
erosity and help in this research and I thank Ibrahim Sheme, Abdullah Uba Adamu, and Yusuf
Adamu for their insights on Hausa video and for their untiring efforts to stimulate a critical cultural debate about Hausa media and culture. I also thank the editors for the careful work they
put into this essay.

1. In recognition of local Hausa usage, I will use *Indian film* interchangeably with the more
specific term *Hindi film* in this essay.

2. When the film *Taal* (dir, Subhash Ghai) was released in the United States in 1999, it
entered the *Variety* list of the top grossing American films at number 20. The New York/New
Jersey-based *Asian Variety Show* that caters to the South Asian population announced the news
with the title: "Bollywood invades Hollywood." A few months later, when *Hum Saath Saath
Hain* (dir. Sooraj Barjatya) was one of the top grossing English films, the London *Times* reported,
"Bollywood knocking Hollwyood for six" (November 20, 1999).

3. It may be that the term *Nigerian* video came about from the popularity of English-language videos *outside* Nigeria in countries such as Ghana and Kenya.

4. To give an example, in May 1962, 33 Indian films were screened in Kano, the main city of northern Nigeria. This compared to 21 American films and 3 English ones. In June the numbers were 32 Indian, 23 American, and 1 English. In July there were 30 Indian films, 19 American, and 3 English (figures taken from the *Daily Comet, Kano*). Until the rise of Hausa Indian films videos were shown 5 nights a week on Kano screens compared to 1 night for American and 1 night for Hong Kong films.

5. Interview with Ado Ahmad, July 1996.

6. This is ironic give that only a few years later Hausa video films became famous precisely because of men singing love songs.

7. The credits for the video include listings of "Play Back Singers" (Fati Abubakar is the female singer) and "Music Director."

8. The radical novelty of this mode of romance was brought home to me during a discussion with an older Hausa (male) friend. He said that, as a youth in the 1970s, he went to see many Indian films at a time when they were mainly restricted to the cinema and thus to men. He said this caused problems when he got married, as in Indian films women openly declare their love for their partners and are passionate in their relations. In the 1970s, he continued, Hausa men were expecting, or wanting, this behavior from their wives but when he got married his wife, acting with the modesty that a "proper" Hausa wife should have, was initially reluctant to talk with him, or even spend much time with him alone, creating disappointment and friction in the relationship. He saw the problem lying in the fact he wanted the relationships he was used to in Indian films, but that this sort of relationship could not be realized within traditional Hausa gender relations.

9. Ibid.

10. For three months all filmmaking was prohibited., After intensive lobbying by the film industry, filmmaking was resumed but placed under the control of a new censorship board.

11. This was a common observation made to me by southerners living in northern Nigeria. They emphasized their participation in Western culture and especially what Gilroy calls a "black atlantic" world, listening to rappers like Tupac Shakur and Puff Daddy and watching Hollywood films. For them, Indian films were a marker of temporality, an index of marginalization from a history that is centered around the West. Abadzi makes the similar point when she argues that the popularity of Indian films waned in Greece at the moment during the 1960s when Greeks wished to emphasize their Westernness and their distance from the Eastern heritage.

BIBLIOGRAPHY

Abadzi, Helen, and Emmanuel Tasoulas. *Indoprepon Apokalypsi* (Hindi-style Songs Revealed). Athens: Atrapos, 1998.

Abadzi, Helen. "Hindi Films of the 50s in Greece: The Latest Chapter of a Long Dialogue." http://www.sangeetmahal.com/journal_hindi_films_greece.asp.

Abu-Lughod, Lila. "Egyptian Melodrama, Technology of the Modern Subject?" In *Media Worlds: Anthropology on New Terrain*, ed. Faye Ginsburg, Lila Abu-Lughod, and Brian Larkin. Berkeley: University of California Press, 2002.

Armbrust, Walter. 'When the Lights Go Down in Cairo: Cinema as Secular Ritual." *Visual Anthropology* 10, no. 2–4 (1995).

Behrend, Heike "Love A La Hollywood and Bombay in Kenyan Studio Photogrpahy." *Paideuma* 44 (1998): 139–153.

Chakravarty, Sumita. *National Ideology in Indian Popular Cinema 1947–1987*. Austin: University of Texas Press, 1993.

Cham, Mbye. "Introduction." In *African Experiences of Cinema*, ed. Imruh Bakari and Mbaye Cham, pp. 1–14. London: BFI, 1996.

Cham, Mbye, and Imruh Bakari. *African Experiences of Cinema*. London: BFI, 1996.

Dhondy, Farukh. "Keeping Faith: Indian Film and its World." *Daedalus* 114, no. 4 (1985):125–40.

Diawara, Manthia. *African Cinema: Politics and Culture*. Bloomington: Indiana University Press, 1992.

Dwyer, Rachel. *All You Want is Money, All You Need is Love.* London: Cassell, 1999.

Eck, Diana L. *Darsan: Seeing the Divine Image in India.* New York: Columbia University Press, 1998.

Fugelsang, Minou. *Veils and Videos: Female Youth Culture on the Kenyan Coast.* Stockholm: Studies in Social Anthropology, 1994.

Furniss, Graham. *Poetry, Prose and Popular Culture in Hausa.* Edinburgh: Edinburgh University Press, 1996.

Ganti, Tejaswini. "The (H)Indianization of Hollywood by the Bombay Film Industry." In *Media Worlds: Anthropology on New Terrain*, ed. Faye Ginsburg, Lila Abu-Lughod, and Brian Larkin. Berkeley: University of California Press, 2002.

Gillespie, Maria. "Sacred Serats, Devotional Viewing, and Domestic Worship: A Case Study of Two TV Versions of *The Mahabarata* in a Hindu Family in West Lond." In *Soap Operas Around the World*, ed. Robert C. Allen. London: Routledge, 1995.

Ginsburg, Faye, Lila Abu-Lughod, and Brian Larkin, eds. *Media Worlds: Anthropology on New Terrain.* Berkeley: University of California Press, 2002.

Haynes, Jonathan. *Nigerian Video Films.* Athens: Ohio University Press, 2000.

Larkin, Brian. "Indian Films and Nigerian Lovers: Love Stories, Electronic Media and the Creation of Parallel Modernities." *Africa* 67, no. 3 (1997): 406–440.

Marshall-Fratani, Ruth. "Mediating the Global and the Local in Nigerian Pentecostalism." *Journal of Religion in Africa* 28, no. 3 (1998): 278–315.

Meyer, Birgit. "Popular Ghanaian Cinema and 'African Heritage.'" *Africa Today* 46, no. 2 (1999): 93–114.

———. "Ghanaian Popular Cinema and the Magic in and of Film." In *Magic and Modernity: Dialectics of Revelation and Concealment*, ed. B. Meyer and P. Pels. Stanford: Stanford University Press, forthcoming.

Mitchell, Timothy. "The Stage of Modernity." In *Questions of Modernity*, ed. Timothy Mitchell. Minneapolis: University of Minnesota Press, 2000.

Nandy, Ashis. *The Savage Freud: And Other Essays on Possible and Retrievable Selves.* Princeton: Princeton University Press, 1995.

Pendakur, Manjunath, and Radha Subramanyam. "Indian Cinema Beyond National Borders." In *New Patterns in Global Television: Peripheral Vision*, ed. John Sinclair, Elizabeth Jacka, and Stuart Cunningham, pp. 67–82. Oxford: Oxford University Press, 1996.

Pines, Jim, and Paul Willemen, eds. *Questions of Third Cinema.* London: British Film Institute, 1989.

Ray, Manas. "Bollywood Down Under: Fiji Indian Cultural History and Popular Assertion." In *Floating Lives: The Media and Asian Diasporas*, ed. Stuart Cunningham and John Sinclair. Queensland: University of Queensland Press, 2000.

Sardar, Ziauddin. "Dilip Kumar Made Me Do It." In *The Secret Politics of Our Desires: Innocence, Culpability and Indian Popular Cinema*, ed. Ashis Nandy. London: Zed Books, 1998

Sharma, S. A. Sharma, and J. Hutnyk. *Disorienting Rhythms: The Politics of the New Asian Dance Music.* London: Zed Books, 1997.

Sheme, Ibrahim. "Zagon Kasar da Finfanan Indiya Ke Yi Wa Al'Adunmu" (The Danger of Indian Films to Our Culture.) *Gaskiya Ta Fi Kwabo* May 15, 1995, p. 5.

Shohat, Ella, and Robert Stam. *Unthinking Eurocentrism: Multiculturalism and the Media.* London: Routledge, 1994.

Tunstall, Jeremy. *The Media Are American: Anglo-American Media in the World.* London: Constable, 1977.

Tyrell, Heather. "Bollywood in Britain." *Sight and Sound* (1998): 20–22.

Ukadike, Nwachukwu Frank. *Black African Cinema.* Berkeley: University of California Press, 1994.

Ukah, Asonzeh F-K. "Advertising God: Nigerian (Christian) Video Films and the Power of Consumer Culture." Paper delivered to the Consultation on Religion and Media in Africa, held at Ghana Institute of Management and Public Administration (GIMPA), Greenhill, Accra, Ghana, May 20–27, 2000.

Vasudevan, Ravi. "Shifting Codes, Dissolving Identities: The Hindi Social Film of the 1950s as Popular Culture." *Journal of Arts and Ideas* 23/24 (January 1993).

Brian Larkin

———. "The Political Culture of Address in a Transitional Cinema." In *Reinventing Film Studies*, ed. Christine Gledhill and Linda Williams, pp. 130–162. Oxford: Oxford University Press, 2000.

Wendl, Tobias, and Heike Behrend. *Snap Me One! Studiofotografen in Afrika*. Munich: Prestel Books, 1999.

Willemen, Paul. "Negotiating the Transition to Capitalism: The Case of *Andaz*." *East-West Film Journal* 5 no. 1 (1991): 56–66.

Manthia Diawara

The "I" Narrator
in Black Diaspora Documentary

It is customary to define diaspora as the voluntary or involuntary dispersion of a social or ethnic group. Diaspora studies therefore look for the stability or discontinuity of the identity of individuals or groups from their origins to their present location. In thinking about the black diaspora and its representation, some of the issues of retention of African cultures or rupture with origins and traditions commonly come into play. However, identity politics notwithstanding, the quest for modernity for the group and the individual in the diaspora also constitutes the main motivation of the people who insisted upon the concept. Diaspora subjects such as W.E.B. Du Bois, Aimé Césaire, Langston Hughes, Patrice Lumumba, and Kwame Nkrumah were interested in removing obstacles from their people's path toward modernization, in opening access to the tools of Enlightenment, and in valorizing their people's contribution to universal civilization.

The representation of these figures on film by Louis Massiah, Raoul Peck, and John Akomfrah has resulted in different subjective strategies in the documentary genre. One can even say that these filmmakers have reshaped the documentary genre in their attempt to reconcile identity politics with the universal message of modernity in their films. To film the African diaspora is to represent that which is African about the subjects in the first place; on the other hand, it is also about the depiction of what is modern and liberating about the diaspora subjects.

The intersection between the two poles of diaspora thematics, identity politics and modernist liberating aesthetics, has resulted in first-person documentary narratives by Raoul Peck, John Akomfrah, and Louis Massiah. The first-person point of view enables these directors to build and validate their own identity through the identities of the diasporic subjects of their films. Another measure of the merit of first-person narratives lies in their ability to demonstrate, through such poetic devices as irony, realism, or allegory, the significance of the life of the diasporic subject to present conditions. It is therefore possible to define the first-person narrative in diasporic cinema as the filmmaker's revisionist construction of history in which the narrator is as central to the film as the film's object, or what I call the diasporic subject. In fact, there is a blurring between the identities of the filmmakers and/or narrators and the diasporic subjects which

From *Struggles Over Representation: African American Documentary Film and Video*, edited by Phyllis R. Klotman and Janet K. Cutler (Indiana University Press, 1999).

transcends the different poetic languages of the films to constitute a thematic cluster in diasporic documentary.

The Allegorical Mode: Raoul Peck's *Lumumba*

In Raoul Peck's *Lumumba: The Death of a Prophet*, an allegorical film about the myth of Lumumba, the director-turned-first-person-narrator poses as the ghost of Lumumba to haunt the streets of Brussels and its high society. The allegorical narrative is imposed on the documentary genre from the beginning, when we learn that the director cannot go to Zaire (present-day Democratic Republic of Congo) to make his film. To produce the documentary, he had therefore to rely on home-movie footage, archival material in Europe, and interviews with journalists, Belgian colonial officials, and family and former collaborators of Lumumba. It is allegory that provides this film with its magic, inasmuch as it constitutes the power in the voice-over poetry that makes the viewer believe that Brussels is Kinshasa (formerly Leopoldville and the capital of Congo).

Lumumba: The Death of a Prophet is a challenging documentary not only because the director was unable to go to Zaire and film the "real" places Lumumba inhabited and the people he died for. The challenge also comes from the voice-over, which is poetic and mythical instead of objective and balanced in the tradition of the classical documentary. In fact, Peck's *Lumumba* can be seen as an indictment of the objective documentary style in the way it debunks so-called facts about Lumumba's character. This is most effectively executed in the film through Peck's juxtaposition of Lumumba to Mobutu (the former dictator of Zaire) and the past to the present. Peck uses newsreel footage and newspapers to show how Lumumba was depicted as a communist, a devil, and a harbinger of violence. Mobutu, on the other hand, was called a hero who saved the nation and promoted peace. The Belgians, meanwhile, are portrayed as saints whose only task was to educate the Congolese and prepare them for independence. We soon learn that these images are no more objective than the action-packed films that we see on the television screen in the director's hotel room. From a new perspective imposed by the end of the Cold War, we now see Lumumba as the hero and Mobutu as a traitor to the Pan-African revolution and as an evil dictator-president. As for the Belgians, they liked their Africans as long as "they remained stupid." At the time of the independence of the Congo in 1960, "there was one bishop for the country and no one with a bachelor's degree." So much for the objective documentary.

In Peck's *Lumumba*, images mean nothing without the words that define them. To paraphrase Jean-Luc Godard, a good documentary for Peck does not depend on just the right image, but on the *mot juste*, a poetic language with the power to invent meaning for the images. In fact, it is a measure of Peck's genius in this subjective documentary to have succeeded without the "real" images of the Congo, to have created a documentary account of the life and myth of

Lumumba out of what Peck himself calls *"ces trous noirs"*—these black holes—which are "images in our heads. Forbidden and harmless images." Mobutu is afraid of these forbidden images: could it be, the narrator asks himself, that these "black holes are more corrosive than the images that they hide"?

The documentary pleasure—by which I mean the desire to know who Lumumba is—is inextricably linked to our desire to know what the black holes in the narrator's head are hiding. We want to know who Raoul Peck is, what his class position is, and why he is making this documentary on Lumumba. We learn at the beginning of the film that Peck's parents are expatriates from Haiti who came to the Congo at the time of independence to replace Belgian colonial technocrats where there were few university-trained Africans. His mother worked as a secretary in different transitional governments, from revolutionary leaders to coup d'état organizers to dictators. We see Peck's class position from the home movies of his childhood. He grew up privileged in a country where the majority was exploited and kept illiterate and where Lumumba was killed for trying to bring a revolution. Peck himself explains his position in the home movies as ambivalent: "We were *Mundele*—white people—when it was convenient, and Africans when it was convenient."

Making a film on Lumumba is therefore a process of self-examination for Peck. Even though we learn about Mobutu's betrayal of Lumumba and Belgian racism toward the people of Congo, what concerns us most in the film is how Peck feels about Lumumba. We identify with Peck's guilt for growing up privileged in Congo at a time when it would have been better to have been a revolutionary like Lumumba. We empathize with him for wishing that his parents had left Congo before the betrayals and the coups. Why did they stay in Congo for so long? So that they could be among the first black bourgeois to take vacations in Europe? And why didn't Lumumba leave before he was assassinated?

The film takes on additional importance when the viewer realizes that Peck holds him or her responsible as well for Lumumba's death. He compares the massacre in Congo to other crimes against humanity, such as the Holocaust and the A-bomb dropped on Hiroshima, in order to reveal to us that our neutral position vis-à-vis these horrendous crimes is a form of guilt. To drive this point home, the narrator takes his camera to a black-tie party in Brussels. As he passes by people drinking cocktails, the voice-over states that the ghost of Lumumba was everywhere in the room, and that the destinies of the people at the party are forever linked to his.

It is remarkable that *Lumumba: The Death of a Prophet* begins in a street in Brussels called *Place des martyrs*. Peck is searching for Lumumba in a place dedicated to the martyrs of the two great wars. This scene is soon followed by archival footage of a jungle; the voice-over reads a poem by Henri Lopes entitled "Du Côté du Katanga," which goes as follows: "Near Katanga, they said that a giant had fallen during the night." The same poem is recited toward the end of the film over images of deserted Brussels streets. As Peck interchanges images of Africa and Europe while reading the same poem, one gets the sense that the myth of Lumumba is everywhere—everywhere there is oppression. One understands finally that Peck did not need to go to Zaire to make his film on Lumumba.

By linking his destiny and ours to Lumumba's quest for freedom, Peck creates an original space for black diasporic expression through the documentary genre. His allegorical style is well suited to describing the dispersion and transfiguration of African identity and motifs in the modern world. The presence of both Peck and Lumumba as diasporic subjects in the film, or the blurring of the identities of the filmmaker and the object of the film, underlines the important role of identification in the documentary genre. This subjective relation between subject–object, Peck–Lumumba, which is taken for granted in diaspora studies, is often ignored in the classical documentary in favor of objectivity, "realness," and impartiality. In diaspora studies, identification with the hero is therapeutic and a function of the cultural worker or researcher coming into consciousness from a liminal space or a space of indeterminacy. That is why Peck rejects objectivity earlier in the film and borrows from the techniques of experimental filmmakers. One can read *Lumumba: The Death of a Prophet* sometimes as a video-diary, sometimes as a surrealist film in which the images and the sound enter into conflict, and sometimes as a historical documentary.

The Ironic Mode: John Akomfrah's *Testament*

I would like to turn now to *Testament* by John Akomfrah (Black Audio Film Collective) to address another style in first-person narratives in black diasporic cinema. Narratologically speaking, *Testament* is more complex than *Lumumba*. The voice-over commentator is a woman who also refers to herself as another character in the film. She uses the narrating "I" to comment on the documentary, and yet she is treated in the story/history as "Abena" or "she" instead of "I." These confusions of characters are further complicated by the use of time in the film. For Abena, the "I" narrator, time is static; the coup d'état that overthrew Kwame Nkrumah in 1966 is at the origin of her trauma. On the other hand, Abena, the character in the film, has to count time. She has returned to Ghana twenty years later on assignment as a reporter for British television. She has to produce reportage on a film that Werner Herzog is making on slavery in Ghana, and is therefore bound by time.

Whereas I describe the poetical style of *Lumumba* as allegorical, I would call *Testament* an ironic or deconstructivist documentary. As I will show, the film derives its poetics of irony from the way history is *mise en abîme* by the loss of memory. Abena the narrator is traumatized by the 1966 coup; history no longer has a meaning for her. On the other hand, Abena the character in the film is forced to make sense of history; not only does she have to make her report before Herzog finishes shooting his film with Ghana as a backdrop, but she has also to piece together her own identity and to remember history as a critical assessment of the present.

The film draws its poetic irony from these embedded and contradictory narratives. Herzog's film within the film is the first sign of narrative irony. The narrator exposes Herzog's film as historically inaccurate and obsessed with images of cannibalism and violence. As Herzog ignores the slave castle of Almina and builds his own setting, stereotypes and clichés take the place of history. Abena's reportage is a document that ironizes Herzog's setting as fake history and an inauthentic testament. The irony in Abena's reportage is reminiscent of the ending of Chinua Achebe's classic novel *Things Fall Apart*, where a colonial administrator turned African historian (like Herzog turned African filmmaker) pushes aside the history of the Africans in order to emphasize the civilizing mission of the British. The director of *Testament* deconstructs Herzog's film just as Achebe reveals the naiveté of the colonial administrator in his novel.

Another ironic language in the film concerns Abena's relation to her former comrades from Nkrumah's ideological school. After the coup, the soldiers destroyed the school and burned the books. Nkrumah and his regime were soon demonized as the enemies of the people, while the coup leaders were transfigured as the saviors of the nation. Abena herself left the country "like a thief in the night," while her comrades stayed to face the consequences. Rashid, Danzo, and Mr. Park now consider Abena an outsider. Rashid believes that the conditions in Ghana are too hard for Abena and that she should move into a hotel where it is more comfortable. He dismisses Abena's criticism of the coup as "exile talk." Danzo, for her part, refuses to talk to Abena. She is seen throughout the film as either turning her back, rolling her eyes, or pursing her lips at Abena's questions. As for Mr. Park, he has embraced numerology as a way of coping with reality. He explains the different coups in Ghana as determined by the coincidence between the first names of the coup leaders and the day of the week they were born. "They were all born on a Sunday: Kwasi Acheampong (coup of 1966), Kwasi Akuffo (1972), and Kwasi Rawlings (1981)." Abena's reliance on Rashid, Danzo, and Mr. Park to document the past ironizes the film's claim to truth, or, for that matter, the claim to truth in any documentary film.

In *Testament*, Akomfrah realizes the ultimate dream for every diaspora subject: the return home. We have seen that part of the frustration of the narrator in *Lumumba* was not to have been able to return to Congo. It is always desirable in the diaspora experience to visit the home that one was forced to leave. This kind of return operates as a guarantee for the diasporic subject's identity. That's why Peck talks about black holes in his mind that needed to be filled with the repressed images of Lumumba. The camera represents the mind of the first-person narrator in diasporic films, and the images that the camera takes are images of "home" that fill the black hole in the narrator's mind.

In *Testament*, the return narrative is complicated by two factors, one experiential and historical and the other mythological and psychological. To find Ghana and the Nkrumah revolution again, Abena has to find her comrades Danzo, Rashid, and Mr. Park. But as I have already shown, Abena's comrades have changed, and they no longer believe in the ideals of the past. When we see flash-backs of Nkrumah addressing a jubilant crowd, or of students at the ideological school, we know that only Abena is interested in these images. Her friends do not even share with her the memories of torture and rape at the hands of the soldiers during the coup. Unlike Abena, who wants to go back to 1966, they have erased everything from their minds except for the challenges that they have to face daily.

Abena is a theoretical character in the film who wants to find a synthesis between the past and the present, between tradition and modernity. Like Peck in *Lumumba*, she prefers the images in her mind to reality. She tries to find Ghana in traditional folk songs, in the ideological writings of Nkrumah's party, and in poetry. For example, she is often distracted from her reportage or from interacting with her friends by flashbacks or subjective images of women dressed in tradi-tional clothes and singing revolutionary songs. One such song calls upon the gods and the ancestors to help Ghana free herself from foreign control. Another song summons the people to rise up and punish those responsible for the crimes com-mitted against Ghana. At the end of the film, Abena recites a revolutionary poem which goes as follows: "There is victory for us in this struggle for the Convention People's Party / Sons of Ghana, rise and fight. / Daughters of Ghana, rise and shine." One realizes at the end that Abena has brought the traditional songs up to date and inserted them in the larger cause of the Ghana revolution. The film reclaims Nkrumah as the true hero and the soldiers as those who have commit-ted a terrible crime. The transfiguration of traditional songs into modern revolu-tionary poetry reminds one of Richard Wright's *Black Power*, a classic diasporic return narrative. *Black Power* is also about the Ghana revolution. In the book, Wright shows his impatience with reactionary traditional customs, and he urges Nkrumah to modernize them and use them in his revolution.

Finally, one must also look at the psychological impact of return in *Tes-tament*. I call this the trauma of diasporic subjects. We have seen Abena's strug-gle to recapture the past and to belong to the present of Ghana. But her former comrades treat her as an outsider and a tourist. We also know that Abena left Ghana "like a thief in the night." She feels guilty for abdicating her responsibil-ity to her country in the same manner that Peck feels guilty toward Lumumba and the Congo. In fact, the search for identity in diaspora films is as much an expression of guilt as it is an exercise in self-empowerment. Both Peck and Abena feel guilty for siding with the victimizers by abandoning African shores.

Testament goes deeper in exploring the trauma caused by the separation of the diasporic subject from Africa. The film begins with Siamese twins on an operating table: "I've always thought that two bodies could be one, live together, believe in the same thing, live for life." But later in the film, after the operation is completed, one of the twins survives and the other dies. By taking us from the unitary moment, the moment of the Lacanian imaginary where everything is fluid, amorphous, and connected like the Siamese twins, to a symbolic moment and a transition to identity formation, the film delineates the diasporic trauma.

The Atlantic slave trade that took Africans away to distant shores, and the coups during the Cold War that caused new dispersions and genocides, are like the surgical "splitting" of the twins. The return narrative, insofar as it enables Abena to revisit this original moment of splitting, is important to the discourse of the diaspora. They are the ones through which the diasporic subject discovers her identity and difference. Abena cannot go back home again, but she can build a new relationship with Rashid, Danzo, and Mr. Park.

At another level of the film, Abena's trauma is more personal and precedes diasporic return narratives. When she was a child, she used to be afraid of a ditch in her parents' yard. She imagined wolves coming out of it and taking her away. She had dreams of being covered in a blanket of leeches. She therefore had to fill the ditch with bricks and rocks to prevent the little beasts from coming out. Of course, Abena associates this form of death with Nkrumah's death and the political death of Ghana. To survive the trauma and to exorcise her fear of empty holes, Abena has to face her childhood memories. She has to follow the traces of her father, who blamed his political failures on the river gods and turned his back on his family and society. Abena too spends much of her time on the river when she cannot find answers to her questions in society. She and Danzo revisit their elementary school, hoping to find out where things went wrong. Abena sees flashbacks of soldiers destroying effigies of Nkrumah, of open graves in the cemetery. She sees images of folk dances and mobs burning books. It is only then that she is able to look without fear at the empty holes, the diasporic holes born in violence. She can now give Nkrumah a proper burial and continue the struggle begun by him and other diasporic subjects.

The Symbolist Mode: The Films of Louis Massiah

Louis Massiah's films *The Bombing of Osage Avenue* (1986) and *W.E.B. Du Bois: A Biography in Four Voices* (1996) are special because they provide a historical explication of the past through the voices of ordinary people and artists, incorporating poetic and subjective diction as parts of the historical documents (hence my reference to them as symbolic films). We have seen that in *Testament* Akomfrah uses a woman as first-person narrator, but also to take his own place as filmmaker in the diaspora. Massiah too uses voice-over or on-screen narrators as mediators between himself and the diasporic subjects of his films (the MOVE people and W.E.B. Du Bois). Insofar as these narrators stand in sometimes as the voice of Massiah, and sometimes as the voice of his diasporic subjects, they become the symbols simultaneously of the subject and the object of the diaspora.

The Bombing of Osage Avenue is unusual as a documentary because it is less about the actual bombing of the MOVE house or the assignment of blame than it is about community and identity. The film opens with a definition of Cobbs

Creek Park community through images. There are kids riding bikes, the elderly talking in familiar spots; everybody knows everyone else. As Toni Cade Bambara puts it in her poetic voice-over, people are at home in the rituals and rhythms of the place. Everybody belongs and "You don't have to know that you are on the margins of the community." One of the ordinary voices says that the neighborhood was self-sufficient before the bombing; "you didn't have to go to Center City for your shopping." Other people, black and white, come to repeat more of less the same vision of the Cobbs Creek Park neighborhood. In fact, for Louis Massiah, repetition is a narrative style which becomes as effective for the documentary genre as it is for fiction. For example, we are told several times that Mother's Day is a family tradition that started in Philadelphia, that the siege of the MOVE compound began on Mother's Day, and that the bombing violated the aesthetic contract which is symbolized by Mother's Day.

The MOVE family is a post–civil rights social movement which settled on Osage Avenue after being forced out of different neighborhoods in Philadelphia. Clearly, therefore, the MOVE people's struggle is a struggle for belonging, citizenship, and justice. The film documents the MOVE family's relation to their neighbors in the predominantly black working- and middle-class community in order to bring out the shortcomings of each side. For example, the presence of the MOVE family in the community reveals that the civil rights gains have not borne fruit for everybody to gain access to citizenship and economic emancipation. As the conflict between some of the community members, who are concerned about their image and the market value of their houses, and the MOVE family reveals, the black middle class has constructed the lower class as a different race to be avoided at all cost. The film also shows that the MOVE people, with their barricades, obscene language, and foul odors, may have been stuck in the resistance politics of the 1960s, without any recourse to modern strategies and dialogue with the community. In fact, the MOVE family was using the community as hostage in their struggles against the police and City Hall. The film shows that, when the final confrontation takes place between the police and MOVE, it is really the community that loses. The people realize their helplessness against MOVE and the fire bombs of the police; their neighborhood is transformed into a war zone; things will never be the same again. *The Bombing of Osage Avenue* reveals the psychological loss and the political disempowerment of a community that is unable to take care of its own. Massiah brings out the best in Toni Cade Bambara, who comments on the images of Cobbs Creek Park and its community. The collaborative work between Massiah and Bambara forces the filmmaker to occupy the place of the writer and vice versa, producing a result that is nothing less than a rearticulation of the documentary genre in a poetics of symbolism.

W.E.B. Du Bois: A Biography in Four Voices is Louis Massiah's latest collaborative work with four major writers—Wesley Brown, Thulani Davis, Toni Cade Bambara, and Amiri Baraka—who are used as both characters and voice-over narrators of the film. The first part of this four-part documentary is told from the point of view of Wesley Brown. It deals with Du Bois's formative years at Harvard and in Germany, discusses the publication of *The Souls of Black Folk* in 1903, and culminates with the creation of the Niagara Movement in 1905 and the NAACP, the first civil rights organization, in 1909. Brown's narrative highlights Du Bois's clash with Booker T. Washington, whom Du Bois accused of neglecting the full civil rights of black people through his emphasis on technical training at the expense of the liberal arts. Du Bois was committed to the intellectual as well as the physical freedom of black people; it was for this reason that he and other black leaders such as Monroe Trotter and Ida B. Wells formed an alliance called the Talented Tenth to lead the race into modernity, and to fiercely oppose Washington's attempt to only channel the energies of black people into manual work. In these early years, Du Bois also published a book entitled *The Philadelphia Negro*, in which he interviewed more than 3,000 people in an attempt to document the new types of black workers emerging out of the industrial revolution. Most people see in this book, which resembles the European physiologies of the nineteenth century, the cardinal elements of the discipline of sociology in America.

Thulani Davis, the second narrator, picks up the thread of Du Bois's life from 1919 to 1929, date of the stock market crash and possibly of the end of the Harlem Renaissance. Davis focuses on Du Bois's activities as a full-time leader of the NAACP, the creation of *Crisis*, the most important journal on race in America, and the challenge created by Marcus Garvey, a black nationalist with a separatist and populist agenda. At the time, Du Bois was enjoying a bourgeois cultural existence, having married his daughter to Countee Cullen, a well-known poet of the Harlem Renaissance and son of a prominent family in Harlem. However the marriage did not last, because Countee Cullen was also gay, a fact to which Du Bois was oblivious. Davis's narrative is most attentive to culture as it reveals Harlem as the capital of the black world, where people were free to participate in the cosmopolitanism and modernism of jazz music and the other arts of the Harlem Renaissance movement. This moving part also shows Du Bois's puritanism toward the more extrovert members of the Harlem Renaissance, and his vulnerability against the populism of the race pride advocate and nationalist Marcus Garvey.

Toni Cade Bambara, in the third section of the film, 1934–1948, rationalizes Du Bois's attempts to broaden the basis of the NAACP among black people and to create a relief organization as a reaction to Garvey's criticism. But Du Bois's interest in black economic self determination is seen by the elitist members of the NAACP as an exercise in self-segregation and Garveyism. Walter White emerged as the new leader of the NAACP, causing Du Bois to resign from the organization and to return to Atlanta University as professor. Other fascinating moments of this section include Du Bois's publication of *Black Reconstruction*, which is Marxist in its approach and instrumentality; the creation of *Phylon*, a journal of race and culture, at Atlanta University; the beginning of a major project entitled *Encyclopedia of the Negro*; and the Manchester Congress of 1945, which was attended by many Africans determined to take their destinies into their own hands.

Amiri Baraka's narrative occupies the fourth and last part of *W.E.B. Du Bois*. It is mainly concerned with Du Bois's efforts to internationalize the black struggle, his relation to the Communist Party, and his indictment by the U.S. government. Baraka is pained by the number of times Du Bois is betrayed by his friends, the NAACP, and McCarthyism. But there were also moments of victories, such as the speech Du Bois delivered at the Waldorf Peace Conference, his decision to join the Communist Party after the indictment, and—the most celebrated of all the return narratives—the trip in 1961 to Ghana, where he lived until his death in 1963.

Louis Massiah's skill as a director is apparent through his ability to work with four very different writers in the Du Bois project, and to keep all of them focused on the theme of the film. His skill as a filmmaker is manifest in the plot structure, which never ceases to intrigue the spectator. The narrative is built around tensions which oppose Du Bois to Booker T. Washington, Marcus Garvey, Walter White and the NAACP, and finally the McCarthyites. In each case Du Bois learned from his opponent and grew stronger. For example, he organized the Niagara Movement to fight Washington, and he steered the NAACP toward a broader economic and cultural base as a result of Garvey's criticism of the assimilationist position of the Talented Tenth.

W.E.B. Du Bois: A Biography in Four Voices is a tour de force of documentary filmmaking, presenting evidence and maintaining a self-reflexive film style at the same time. From Grierson to Leacock and Rouch, objectivity has dominated the packaging of information and evidence in the documentary genre. As a reaction to this logocentrism, postmodern documentarians such as Trinh T. Minh-ha have deployed a fragmentary film language in order to put into question the validity of information in documentary films. Massiah's strategy is different because he does not challenge the fact that documentary films are capable of conveying verifiable information. But he redefines the documentary genre by presenting the evidence on a subjective grid. He places other artists or characters between himself and the evidence presented. By effacing himself in this manner, Massiah is able to show the evidence from different points of view. In other words, in Massiah's films the evidence is built intersubjectively.

This is not to say that Massiah's work is without any echo in the documentary world. On the contrary, the reflexive and repetitive narrative style of *The Bombing of Osage Avenue* reminds the viewer of *Handsworth Songs*, a film about the riots of Handsworth (U.K., 1985) by John Akomfrah and the Black Audio Collective. Massiah's films are part of an international diasporic documentary emergence about major black leaders which includes *Lumumba: The Death of a Prophet* by Raoul Peck, *Testament* by John Akomfrah, *Looking for Langston* and *Frantz Fanon: Black Skin, White Mask* by Isaac Julien, and *Langston Hughes: The Dream Keeper* by St. Clair Bourne. Louis Massiah should be recognized for being, more than anyone else, the connecting thread for this movement. *W.E.B. Du Bois: A Biography in Four Voices* is the most important film in scope and artistic achievement so far in the movement.

Hamid Naficy

Phobic Spaces and Liminal Panics: Independent Transnational Film Genre

We are living in an increasingly global media environment. Access to multiple channels and types of transnational media is problematizing our received notions of, and demanding new approaches to, questions of national cultures and identities, national cinemas and genres, authorial visions and styles, and audience reception and ethnography. This essay takes as its point of departure Arjun Appadurai's forceful statement that "The image, the imagined, the imaginary—these are all terms which direct us to something critical and new in global cultural processes: *the imagination as social practice* . . .. The imagination is now central to all forms of agency, is itself a social fact, and is the key component of the new global order."[1] In this essay I attempt to identify and theorize "something critical and new" in current global media practices by proposing a genre of independent transnational cinema, a genre that cuts across previously defined geographic, national, cultural, cinematic, and meta-cinematic boundaries. I will develop two aspects of this genre here: transnational filmmakers as interstitial authors and configuration of claustrophobic spaces as one of the chief iconographies that characterizes this genre.

    The important contribution that transnationals, exiles, émigrés, refugees, and expatriates have made to the literatures and cinemas of the West is undeniable. Indeed, "foreigners and émigrés" have dominated the pinnacles of modern English literature.[2] Filmmakers from Eastern Europe and Russia in the early twentieth century to those from Germany in the second to the fifth decades dominated both the studio system and the master genres of Hollywood cinema. Despite acknowledging their contributions, however, little sustained and systematic attention has been paid to theorizing the expatriate or exile genre, particularly in cinema. Recent shifts in the global configuration of capital, power, and media, however, have made such an attempt necessary. In addition, vast global economic and structural changes since World War II have ushered in the postmodern era characterized in part by massive displacement of peoples the world over, creating a veritable "other worlds" of communities living outside of their places of birth

From *East-West Film Journal* 8:2, July 1994: 1–30. Reprinted by permission of the East-West Center.

and habitus. Transnational filmmakers not only have given expression to these other worlds but also have enriched the cinemas of their home and adopted lands.

How films are conceived and received has a lot to do with how they are framed discursively in both their production and exhibition. The films that transnationals have made are usually framed within the "national cinemas" of their host countries or the traditional and established cinematic "genres." Thus, the films of F. W. Murnau, Douglas Sirk, George Cukor, Vincent Minnelli, Jacques Tourneur, Fritz Lang, and Alfred Hitchcock are usually considered as exemplars of the classical Hollywood cinema or of such genres as melodrama, noir, and spy-thriller. Of course, the works of these and other established directors (such as Andrey Tarkovsky) are also discussed under the rubric of "auteurism." Alternatively, many independent transnational filmmakers who make films about their homelands and its peoples, cultures, and politics (such as Abid Med Hondo, Michel Khleifi, Fernando Solanas, and Ghasem Ebrahimian) are often marginalized as merely "ethnic," "national," "Third World," or "third cinema" filmmakers, unable to reach mainstream audiences in either their country of residence or origin. Others, such as Jonas Mekas, Mona Hatoum and Trinh T. Minh-ha, are placed within the "avant-garde" category.

While these classificatory categories are important methods for framing and positioning films to target markets, distributors, exhibitors, reviewers, and academic studies, they also serve to overdetermine and delimit the films' potential meanings. Genres are not neutral structures but are "ideological constructs masquerading as neutral categories."[3] The undesirable consequences of overdetermination of meanings and ideological structuration are particularly grave for films made in diaspora. By classifying these films into one of the established categories, the very cultural and political foundations which constitute them are limited, negated, or effaced altogether. Such traditional schemas also tend to lock the filmmakers themselves into "discursive ghettos" which fail to reflect or account adequately for the filmmakers' personal evolution and stylistic transformations over time. Once labeled "ethnic" or "ethnographic," transnational filmmakers remain so even long after they have moved on.

Like all genres, of course, the independent transnational genre also attempts to reduce and channel the free play of meanings in certain predetermined manners. But, in this task, the genre is driven by its sensitivity to the production and consumption of films in conditions of transnationality, liminality, multiculturality, multifocality, and syncretism. This new generic designation will allow us to classify certain hitherto unclassifiable films. It will also allow us not only to classify new transnational films but also to reclassify and thereby to reread certain existing films by loosening them from their traditional generic moorings. Thus, Jonas Mekas's massive film *Lost, Lost, Lost* (1976), which has been variously classified as documentary, avant-garde, or diary film, will yield new insights if reclassified as transnational cinema. Transnational films are here considered as (1) belonging to a genre of cine-writing and self-narrativization with specific generic and thematic conventions and (2) products of the particular transnational location of filmmakers in time and place and in social life and cultural difference. By linking genre, authorship, and transnational positioning, the independent transnational genre allows films to be read and reread not only as individual texts produced by authorial vision and generic conventions, but also as sites for inter-textual, cross-cultural, and translational struggles over meanings and identities.

One of the values of such an undertaking is that it forces us to reconcile three different approaches to film studies that are usually kept separate for fear of contaminating one other: generic, auteurist, and cultural studies. By problema-tizing the traditional generic and authorial schemas and representational prac-tices, such an approach blurs the distinction, often artificially maintained, between types of films: fictional, documentary, ethnographic, and avant-garde. Because it considers the relationship of all types of cinemas to their filmed sub-jects to be one of representation not presentation, the independent transnational cinema is an inclusive and integrative genre, encompassing various types of films. More, this genre considers the relationship of the transnational filmmakers to their subjects to be a relationship that is filtered through narratives and icono-graphies of memory, desire, loss, longing, and nostalgia. Memories are fallible, playful, and evasive, and the narratives and iconographies that they produce—in whatever type of film—are palimpsestical, inscribing ruptures, fantasies, and embellishments as well as ellipses, elisions, and repressions.

To delimit the topic and to differentiate the current moment of transna-tional and its cinematic figuration from previous moments in the twentieth cen-tury, my examination of the transnational film genre is focused on the films made in the past two decades by transnational filmmakers who live or make their films in Europe and the United States. By and large these filmmakers are from the so-called Third World, and they operate independently, that is, outside the studio sys-tems and the mainstream film industries of the host countries. As a result, they are presumed to be more prone to tensions of exile, acculturation, and transna-tionalism, and their films should and do encode these tensions. These are impor-tant factors that set apart recent transnational filmmakers from European filmmakers who emigrated to the United States from the 1920s to the 1940s and who were often absorbed by the studio system and were in fact instrumental in its consolidation as a hegemonic transnational cinema of another kind.

Now, what kinds of generalizations can one make about the films pro-duced by the late-twentieth-century liminars, transnationals, and exiles? First of all, this: each of their films is a product of the particular location of its maker in time, place, and culture. As such, each is a new and different film, a product of authorial vision, contextual politics, and cinematic practices. Yet, each expresses the personal vision and "location" of its maker in terms of themes and styles that are indicative of the independent transnational genre as a whole. There is a reci-procal relationship between genre formation and society. Each epoch creates its own narratives about itself and its own genres, and each act of self-narrativization and generic formation influences the perception of the age and the formation of its cultures. Transnationality and its shared features are experienced through and are expressed as never before via the mass media that span the globe and penetrate all communities, necessitating the formulation of not only one but a series of transnational genres.

We could define a genre as the recurring patterns in a film of expectations and their frustration and fulfillment. Such recurring patterns must be repeated in a number of films to form the corpus of the genre. Genres are not immutable *systems*, however; they are *processes* of systematization, structuration, and variation which function to produce regularized variety.[4] Further, a one-to-one relationship between genre and reality does not exist. As such, genres are not reflections of reality; rather, they are a means of processing and structuring reality through narrative conventions, industrial practices, and authorial decisions.

In genre cinema, spectatorial pleasure is not derived entirely from newness but from the play, or the slippage, between the old and the new. Pleasure is obtained from the familiarity and comfort of repetition and from the recognition of the conventions and deviations from them. However, since it is impossible to bridge the gap between repetition and difference, the desire to repeat in hope of obtaining pleasure does not exhaust itself. In theory exhaustion occurs only when bliss or death is reached! In practice, exhaustion occurs when over a period of time the formulae are repeated with only minor differentiations or slippages (such as was the case with the Western in the past couple of decades). Difference and slippage, however, are essential to generic economy, and they are inscribed by filmmakers not only as authorial visions or stylistic variations but also as markers of ethnic, gender, national, racial, or class differences.

Genre cinema thus rests on the existence of an implied contract among four parties: filmmakers/authors, film texts, individual spectators and interpretive communities, and the film industry and its practices. In the remainder of this essay, I will explore two of the terms in this quadruple contract: the transnationals as filmmaking authors and one aspect of the transnational film texts, the claustrophobic configuration of space in films made in exile by Turkish and Iranian filmmakers.

Transnational Filmmakers as Authors

Traditionally, exile is taken to mean banishment by governments for a particular offense, with a prohibition of return, either for a limited time or for life. Depending on the location to which one is banished, it could be called "internal" or "external" exile. If internal exile were to be defined as "isolation, alienation, deprivation of means of production and communication, exclusion from public life,"[5] then many intellectuals, women, artists, religious and political figures, and even entire communities have suffered from it within their own countries. These deprivations may be social or economical, and they may be sought by the exiles themselves or imposed upon them by the state. To this constellation of deprivations and repressions, literary critic Paul Ilie applied the term *deculturation,* which on the surface appears apt but by implying no culture, it posits the state of being in internal exile as an empty space.[6] In fact, however, many filmmakers flourish under internal constraint and deprivation and fail to prosper in their absence.[7] Since the "fall" of communism, for example, many successful east-central European filmmakers have began to covet the restrictions (on what they can say) and the incongruities (between private life and public propaganda) of the communist era, which drove them to develop personal "auteurist" styles and hermeneutically rich texts. In the absence of such restrictions and incongruities, they now find themselves "dislocated, unable to complete projects, even abandoning filmmaking altogether."[8] Of course, this withdrawal may be temporary as new restrictions and incongruities— of the free market system—will emerge, forcing them to develop fresh themes and styles appropriate to their new realities. Under communism in Hungary, for instance, political repression inspired a rich symbolic and satirical cinema that made fun of the regime that financed it. Now, deprived of "paymaster and punching bag," Hungarian cinema must struggle to find other ways of telling stories that compete with Hollywood films and appeal to a broad spectrum of audiences—not just to the local elite or festival audiences.[9] The tremendous toll that internal restrictions, deprivations, and various forms of censorship prevalent in totalitarian countries have taken on filmmakers has been widely publicized. What has been acknowledged less is the way such constraints become loyal and reliable oppositions against which many filmmakers define themselves and develop their style. The continued creativity of some of the filmmakers who stay in repressive societies (such as Bahram Baiza'i of Iran) must be partly sought in the inspiration and certainty that these harsh conditions provide.

In the age of internationalized capital and tourism and exposure to globalized mass media and electronic links, it is not necessary to leave home to enter the spaces of liminality and transnationality. In this way, not only filmmakers but people the world over are always already transnational.[10] However, those filmmakers who journey beyond their homelands constitute more fully the type of exilic transnationals whom I have in mind. While most definitions of external exile consider it to be a dystopic and dysphoric experience, stemming from some form of deprivation, exile must also be defined by its utopian and euphoric possibilities, driven by wanderlust or, better yet, by what in German is called *Fernweh,* which means not only wanderlust but also a desire to escape from one's own homeland. In its Germanic sense, for those in their homeland this wanderlust for other places is just as insatiable and unrealizable as is the desire for return to the homeland for those who are in exile.

To be in transnationality is to belong to neither of the two modes of dystopia or utopia. The authority of transnationals as filmmaking authors is derived from their position as subjects inhabiting transnational and exilic spaces, where they travel in the slip-zone of fusion and admixture.[11] What results is an agonistic liminality of selfhood and location which is characterized by oscillation between extremes of hailing and haggling. This turns exile and transnationalism into a contentious state of syncretic impurity, intertextuality, even imperfection. They become moments of dialectical vision, of sameness in difference, of continuity in discontinuity, of synchronicity in diachronicity. Emotionally, they are characterized by zeniths of ecstasy and confidence and nadirs of despondency and doubt. Finally, exile and transnationality are highly processual, discursive, and ambivalent.[12]

For exilic transnationals the descent relations with the homeland and the consent relations with the host society are continually tested. Freed from old and new constraints, they are "deterritorialized." Yet, they continue to be in the grips of both the old and the new, the before and the after. Located in such a zone, they become interstitial creatures, liminars suffused with hybrid excess. On the one hand, like Derridean "undecidables" they can be "both and neither": the pharmakon, meaning both poison and remedy; hymen, meaning both membrane and its violation; the supplement, meaning both addition and replacement.[13] On the other hand, they could aptly be called, in Rushdie's words, "at once plural and partial."[14] As partial subjects and undecidable multiple objects, these filmmakers are capable of producing ambiguity and doubt about the absolutes and taken-for-granted values of their home or host societies. They are also capable of transcending and transforming their own individual, cultural, and other affiliations in order to produce hybrid, syncretic, or virtual identities. If Rushdie himself were to be taken as an example of exilic hybridity, F. M. Esfandiary may be considered to be an example of exilic virtuality. Esfandiary wrote novels in the 1960s from exile about the horror of life in his home country, but in the late 1980s changed his name to FM-2030 and developed the concept of transhumanism which, in the interest of discontinuity and provisionality, dismissed all usual markers of continuity and identity—such as descent, homeland, religion, language, nationality, ethnicity, race, and gender.[15] To be a transhuman is to be a universal "evolutionary being."[16]

Not all transnationals, of course, savor fundamental doubt, strive toward hybrid self-fashioning, or reach for utopian or virtual imaginings. However, for those who remain in the enduring and endearing crises and tensions of transnational migrancy, liminality becomes a passionate source of creativity and dynamism that produces in literature and cinema the likes of James Joyce and Margaret Duras, Joseph Conrad and Fernando Solanas, Ezra Pound and Trinh T. Minh-ha, Salman Rushdie and Andrey Tarkovsky, Gárcia Márquez and Atom Egoyan, Vladimir Nabakov and Raúl Ruiz.

Transnational cinema is concerned with the output of filmmakers who not only inhabit interstitial spaces of the host society but also work on the margins of the mainstream film industry. As a result, these filmmakers are multiple not only in terms of their identity and subjectivity but also in the various roles they are forced to play in every aspect of their films. As independent filmmakers, they have to search for financing and co-financing from national and international institutions and from private (particularly ethnic, religious, and nationalist) sources, state agencies, and television companies. What this means is that like many independent filmmakers in the Third World they are forced often to write their own scripts and even act in a principal role in them in order to control the film and keep the cost down.[17] By editing their own films, many transnational filmmakers not only save money but also control the film's vision and aesthetics. And, after the film's completion, these filmmakers must either spend extra effort to distribute their films themselves or be satisfied with limited distribution in art-house cinemas or TV transmission at non-prime-time hours. A large audience for their films is not a given; they must be created and sought after. One consequence of the difficulties of making and exhibiting films under conditions of transnationality is the very meager output of most transnational filmmakers. Sometimes, years pass without a new film being made: Argentinean filmmaker Fernando Solanas made his second film in exile (*Tangos: Exile of Gardel*, 1986) eight years after his first (*The Sons of Fierro*, 1975–1978). Iranian filmmaker Parviz Sayyad made his second film in the United States (*Checkpoint*, 1987) only four years after his first (*The Mission*, 1983). Another accomplished Iranian director, Amir Naderi, emigrated to the United States in 1986 to make films. But it took him seven years to produce his first English-language film (*Manhattan by Numbers*, 1993), which he directed, wrote, and edited. Likewise, despite constant efforts, Marva Nabili has directed only one feature film (*Nightsongs*, 1984) in the past dozen years in her adopted land. Sometimes it takes years to shoot a single film: Mauritanian exile filmmaker Abid Med Hondo relates how it took him a year and a half to film *Soleil O* (Sun Oh) and three and a half years to film *Les Bicots-Nègres, Vos Voisins* (The Nigger-Arabs, Your Neighbors).[18]

For transnational filmmakers thus, the dream of transcendence and transformation that their liminality promises must constantly be checked against the realities of fierce competition in the free market. Some of their output is entertaining even though ironically and parodically critical of the host society. But as artists who often make distressing and dystopian films, transnational filmmakers inhabit a realm of incredible tension and agony, as Iranian exile filmmaker in Germany, Sohrab Shahid Saless, has sarcastically noted:

> People like us who make somber and hardly entertaining films are not fortunate. They write letters, come up with treatments, put together scripts that are never filmed and once in a while a good soul appears, gestures to them and says—just like in Kafka—it's your turn now. You too can have a chance.[19]

Straddling more than one culture, sometimes transnational filmmakers are in a position to play funding agencies from different countries against each other to receive financing. Sometimes, transnational filmmakers attempt to get ahead by cashing in on the newsworthiness of their country of origin. Such efforts pay off more when newsworthiness is based on positive attributes, but they can backfire badly if negative connotations are involved. The case of *Veiled Threat* (1989), made by Iranian-American filmmaker Cyrus Nowrasteh, may be cited briefly. The film was scheduled to premiere at the American Film Institute's Los Angeles International Film Festival in April 1989, but the festival organizers canceled the screening on account of a bomb threat. Much furor ensued and many issues such as responsibility for public safety and First Amendment rights were discussed, but it was difficult to sort out definitively the real reasons behind the bomb threat itself or the cancellation of the show. The festival director claimed that the producers had brought on the threat themselves as a publicity stunt by publicly linking their film and its anti-Islamist content to the Ayatollah Khomeini's *fatwa* against Salman Rushdie. The producers, on the other hand, claimed the threat was real enough for the FBI to take it seriously. This low-budget, low-velocity, lowbrow thriller finally opened in Los Angeles theaters to dismal reviews and attendance. Trying to recoup their loss by downplaying its Islamic connotations, the producers dropped the "veil" from the title.[20]

The Kafkaesque situation that Shahid Saless speaks about is certainly real, and it becomes more personally painful when it comes to national representation in festivals, raising anew for transnational filmmakers such questions as which country they belong to and which "national cinema" they represent. Since the 1973 military coup, Chilean exile filmmakers have produced over 250 feature and documentaries—far more films than were produced in Chile itself up to 1973.[21] Much of this work constituted a "Chilean cinema of resistance." The classification excluded certain films made in exile, for example, the works of Raúl Ruiz after *Dialogue of Exiles* (1974), which critiqued the exiles.[22] The politics of exilic filmmakers, which is usually against their government at home, often force them into painful positions that highlight both the liminality of their status as exiles and the problematic of their national identification as artists. For example, the Turkish government revoked Yilmaz Güney's citizenship after he escaped his country to complete his film *Yol* (The Way, 1982), which powerfully critiqued the Turkish society under military rule. Thus, the most famous Turkish filmmaker and a very popular actor could not represent his own country abroad. Sayyad, too, could not enter in Cannes Film Festival as an Iranian product *The Mission* (1983), a sharply anti-Islamic Republic film. Unwillingly, he entered it as a U.S. production.[23] By doing so, he was forced in effect to admit that he did not represent Iran and Iranians. This was a painful admission for him who, like many Iranian exiles, claimed the clerics were destroying the "true" Iranian culture at home and who faced increasing social hostility in her adopted land. Unable to represent his own and unwilling to represent the host country, he was in essence made "homeless."[24]

It is this homelessness and unbelonging and the filmmakers' split subjectivity and multiple involvements in every aspect of production that turns them from "auteur directors" (implying benefiting from mainstream institutions of cinema) to "filmmaking authors" (implying individual efforts and involvement at all levels of production and distribution). As authors of their texts (and to some extent of their lives), their biography is not just implicitly coded in their films. Often autobiography and self-reflexivity are the forces that drive the narratives and the tropes through which the films are conceived and structured.[25] Any cultural space such as the transnational liminality described here is capable of generating films that inscribe at a fundamental level their makers' station in life and their location in culture, marking their films with narrative and iconographic hybridities, doublings, and splittings.

Space in Transnational Cinema

Genres are often spatially overdetermined by gender and sexuality. From Elsaesser to Mulvey,[26] melodrama has been considered to be a feminine and domestic genre, characterized by "emotion, immobility, enclosed space and confinement." Such a configuration is postulated in opposition to a masculine space, which is outside and is characterized by "adventure, movement, and cathartic action."[27] Generically, this masculine space most defines the American Western. Every society and social condition creates its own space. In the transnational cinema genre, the inside and outside spaces express not only gendered subjectivity but also often national or ethnic imaginings and longings. Western critics have associated the domestic, enclosed spaces with women and heralded the disappearance of nature. However, many non-Western and preindustrialized civilizations still live in nature and although they often confine women to inner quarters, they associate the external, particularly the wilderness and the sea, with the female and the maternal. Transnational filmmakers bring to their films these different styles of spatial inscription. In addition, they further destabilize the traditional gendered binarism of space since in transnationality the boundaries between self and other, female and male, inside and outside, homeland and hostland are blurred and must continually be negotiated. Moreover, spatial configuration in their films is driven not only by structures of identification and alienation but also by eruptions of memory and nostalgia and the tensions of acculturation. The inside and outside spaces are thus not only, as it were, transnationalized but also nationalized and ethnicized.

It has been noted that the emotional high and low points of many classic Hollywood melodramas are staged against the vertical axis of the staircase, where the staircase becomes the site not only for the presentation but also the representation of emotional extremes.[28] In transnational genre, it is the enclosed claustrophobic spaces, often in the form of prisons, which both express and encode the (melo)drama of transnational subjectivity. These phobic spaces are often played off of spaces of immensity. Space in transnational cinema, therefore, mediates between cosmos (order) and chaos (disorder).

To examine the dynamics of the closed and open spaces, I must take a moment to bring in the allied concepts of agoraphobia and claustrophobia—only in so far as they have a bearing on the configuration of space in this genre. My intention here is not to establish a pathology of transnational cinema or of its spaces but to use the medical language and paradigms suggestively and heuristically to discover the specificities of the experiential and allegorical uses of space in this genre.

In 1871 a Berlin neurologist, Carl F. O. Westphal, described three male patients who shared common symptoms which he termed agoraphobia.[29] All three became extremely anxious when crossing empty streets or large open spaces. Today, agoraphobia is understood to be a complex complaint, involving fear and avoidance of public places whether mobile (trains, elevators, buses, and subways) or stationary (streets, tunnels, movie houses, restaurants). It is also associated with "panic attacks" consisting of breathlessness, air hunger, heart palpitation, and fear of going insane or of dying. Other symptoms germane to this context include fear of being away from home and from familiar places and people who provide psychological comfort and security.[30] Light aggravates agoraphobia as does social interaction. Finally, agoraphobia also usually involves claustrophobia, or dread of enclosed places—which most of the public places noted above are.

Although the first patients characterized as agoraphobic by Westphal were all men, the majority of agoraphobes today are women. The onset of agoraphobia is often preceded not by a single trauma but by "excessive adverse life events," among them relationship disruptions, loss, bereavement, and separation anxiety.[31]

To gain control over these clusters of fearful symptoms, agoraphobes withdraw to "safe zones" by confining themselves to their place of residence or sometimes to a single room or even to their bed. They draw comfort not only from "housebondage" but also from the company of "phobic partners" such as a trusted person or an object (such as an umbrella and a suitcase). They prefer dark places and when they venture outside they tend to wear dark glasses. Erecting such physical and visual barriers and withdrawing to confining places, of course, can aggravate their claustrophobia. Thus, the affected individual may oscillate between agoraphobia and claustrophobia, between feeling secure and feeling trapped.

Such contradictory states have been linked by sociocultural critics such as Simmel and Kracauer to the pathology of living in modern cities.[32] Other social critics have written treatises on various enclosed spaces of urban excess and commerce—from arcades to shopping malls—which engender both agoraphobia and claustrophobia and recuperate them in the service of increasing consumption.[33] With the onset of postmodernism and the postindustrial global economies, such enclosed spaces of economic, social, and psychic excess have become practically universal.[34] In addition, "societies of control" have gradually replaced the old "disciplinary society" about which Foucault theorized.[35] If the disciplinary society was characterized by central institutions such as prisons that molded "individuals," the new societies of control are dispersed networks of domination that serve to modulate "dividuals." Thus, schools are replaced with perpetual training, watchwords by passwords, discipline with control, and factories with corporations—all in the interest of "universal modulation."[36]

For many transnationals, the voluntary or forced separation from homelands, the state of seemingly permanent deterritorialization, and the pervasive controlling modulations that postmodernist late capitalism has engendered may constitute sufficiently "excessive adverse life event" to lead us to expect to see in their films agoraphobic and claustrophobic spatiality. As independent, even marginal, filmmakers, they are less apt to follow the conventions of established genres or the styles of dominant cinemas than to inscribe in their films their own experience of liminality and multifocality. The inscription of phobic spaces, which is often based on their own experience of incarceration in their indigenous disciplinary societies, also reflects the conflicting and confining social and political conditions in their homelands. Such phenomenological and allegorical inscriptions of space may serve therapeutic as well as strategic purposes. They not only express the psychic tensions of transnationalism (thus therapeutic) but also assist transnationals in working out new individual and collective identities in the new societies (hence strategic).[37]

Phobic Spaces and Liminal Panics

A sense of claustrophobia pervades the worldview, mise-en-scène, shot composition, and plot development of many transnational films.[38] These are films of liminal panic, of retrenchment in the face of what is perceived to be a foreign, often hostile, host culture and media representation. This perceived (and at times very real) threat is dealt with by invoking confining but comforting claustrophobic spaces. A variety of strategies are used to create such spaces, including the following: closed-shot compositions, tight physical spaces within the diegesis, barriers within the mise-en-scène and the shot that impede vision and access, and a lighting scheme that creates a mood of constriction and blocked vision. Often many of these strategies are condensed in the site in which the film unfolds. Such locations are self-referential, but since at the same time they refer to other places, they are also symbolic.

Turkish Transnational Films

A review of films made by Turkish filmmakers in Europe shows that for them the key spatial symbol seems to be the prison. One of the ironies of transnationalism is the way in which key symbols are manipulated by political adversaries of the nation-states and by transnationals themselves. This is the case with prison as a key symbol for Turkey. According to Turkish film critics, no film has damaged the public image of Turkey as a nation more than did Alan Parker's powerful but

Figure 1. Patriarchy keeps relentless check on citizens in Yilmaz Güney's Yol. Frame enlargement.

hysterical and ethnocentric prison movie, *Midnight Express* (1978).[39] And yet, it is the image of the prison that Yilmaz Güney deployed in his film *Yol* to critique his own society. In fact, from his prison cell in Turkey, Güney obtained permission to direct this film by proxy under the pretext of combating the negative portrayal of *Midnight Express* by focusing on the liberal Turkish prison policies, including a furlough program.[40] The film was shot on his behalf by his associate Serif Goren.[41] Afterward, Güney escaped from prison (and the country) using the very furlough program depicted in *Yol*. He edited the film in Switzerland. The film tracks the harrowing stories of five prisoners released on a five-day leave from their small jail cells into the larger prison of the Turkish society, where the modern military and bureaucratic apparatuses and the traditional feudal patriarchy keep relentless check on all citizens. In this film, the space of the nation becomes a claustrophobic, repressive panopticon dispersed throughout the country transforming Turkey from a disciplinary society into societies of control. By highlighting the stories of a woman—wife of the main protagonist—and a Kurd—a significant minority in Turkey (20 percent of the population)—Güney genders and ethnicizes his spaces and emphasizes the double oppression of women and ethnic minorities in his homeland. Because of a sexual relation with another man during her husband's absence, the wife is held captive by his family. Awaiting certain death, she is confined to a dark, damp barn, where she is chained and starved. The most confining metaphors are reserved for the woman while the most libratory are reserved for the Kurdish prisoner on furlough. Himself a Kurd, Güney portrays the Turkish army's ruthless massacre of the Kurdish rebels caught in their walled village homes and alleys. But in the midst of these claustrophobic spaces of the village and the dominating spaces of the state's assertion of Turkish nationalism, Güney introduces a new space of immensity which he encodes as the space of the longed-for Kurdish homeland achievable by means of exile. These points are underscored by the Kurdish prisoner who, wooed by love for a Kurdish girl and passion for a Kurdish nation, decides to join the rebels in the hills beyond Turkey's borders.

With the release of this scathing film, Güney was sentenced in absentia in Turkey to twenty additional years in prison and all his films (including those he directed and scripted and those in which he acted) were confiscated and banned.[42] Understandably, Güney never returned home. A year after *Yol*, with financial aid from the French government, he directed his last film, *Duvar* (The Wall, 1983). About a prison in Turkey, it is shot entirely within the walls of a single prison, itself divided into other walled prisons housing women, boys, and anarchists. In a more insightful and nuanced way than *Midnight Express*, this film demonstrates the Foucauldian structures of vision and division so necessary for coercion and control. However, perhaps because of the specific microeconomics of control and the cultural characteristics of Turkish society, the prisoners are not totally atomized and neutralized. There is much life and happiness even though these moments are tinged with irony and tragedy. A male prisoner and a female prisoner awaiting execution are prepared by other prisoners for an elaborate wedding. They are wed but also shot, with the palm-print of the bride's hennaed hand on the prison wall the only reminder of their moment of joy. There is an uprising by anarchists, ironically not to be freed, but to be transferred to another prison, which turns out to be no better than the one they left. Although there is reference to the Kurdish aspiration for political independence, this theme is muffled in the interest of returning to the metaphor of Turkey as a total phobic space. The meticulous portrayal of life's routines (including a birth), the wide spectrum of social strata incarcerated, and the high angle shots that dramatically capture the entire prison system with its subdivisions—all these work together to turn the diegetic prison into a metaphor of Turkish society itself as a total prison.

As is true of all key symbols, Güney's relation to prison was complex and appears to have hardened with the militarization of his homeland and his own exile. When he was imprisoned before the military coup in 1981 on the charge of murdering a judge, he appeared to have had a benign view of prisons and, indeed, the prison system itself was benign to him. When film director Elia Kazan interviewed Güney in prison in 1979, jail did not represent to Güney just a brutal and traumatic confinement but also a place of security, where he was given a study from which he was able to run his successful production company, directing by proxy at least three features. At the time, the prison rules were so lax that Güney could have escaped but, as he told Kazan, he felt safer where he was.[43] The military takeover at home and exile seem to have transformed this rather mild view into a totally pessimistic one, disallowing any possibility of escape or change. In a short on-camera statement that appears at the beginning of the print of *Yol* in distribution in the United States, he says that some people are imprisoned by the state but all are prisoners of their own mind.

In Güney's case we can observe the dynamics of the transnational genre at work, where the filmmakers' liminal subjectivity, their own memories and biographical experiences at home, and the genre's spatial configuration intersect. For Güney the prison was partly an allegorical rumination on the real stifling social conditions of his homeland, especially under military rule. It also expressed and reworked Güney's own life experiences before exile, so much of it spent in jail: of the twenty years he had been active in cinema, he spent twelve in jail, two in the military service, and three in exile.[44] Finally, creating phobic spaces and safe zones for Güney was also a reaction against exilic deterritorialization and chaos (and possibly against the surveillance of European societies of control, especially against the "undecidable" guestworkers). An inflexible vision of the homeland as a total prison may be appealing when caught in the flux of transnationality and when you are not there in the belly of the beast, so to speak, where you might be forced to consider other tainted options involving compromise.

Güney is the most celebrated of the Turkish filmmakers abroad (he died of cancer in France in 1984). There are, however, a number of others whose collective output can be said to have created a kind of Turkish cinema in exile. These directors include Tunç Okan, Erden Kiral, Tuncel Kurtiz, and Tevfik Baser. To demonstrate that claustrophobic spaces, especially prisons, are not just an authorial preoccupation of Güney but also a feature of transnational location and subjectivity, I will examine briefly three films made in Europe over a period of a dozen years by two of the directors named above.[45] Unlike Güney's exile films, which deal with Turkish society and are "located" at home, these three films each deal with Turkish immigrants living in Europe. Yet, despite the shift in location, the metaphor of encapsulation and the key symbol of imprisonment are equally strong and pervasive in them. *Otobüs* (The Bus, 1977), directed by Tunç Okan, deals with a group of Turkish migrant workers who, swindled by a Turkish con man, are abandoned without passport, food, or money in their battered bus in the middle of a square in Stockholm. Although comic at times, the metaphor of prison is grimly multilayered here. At one layer, the bus—a means of mobility, even freedom, and a safe haven for the migrants who fear the foreign society—is transformed into its opposite—an immobile and confining edifice. At another level, those who venture out of the bus discover that the host society which they feared is not always hostile; more often, it is just indifferent to their presence. The claustrophobic space in *Otobüs* is parasitically transnational in that a Turkish microorganism (the bus and its inhabitants) is inserted under the skin of the Swedish body politic. As an encysted ethnic organism, this foreign body must be expelled, symbolized by the demolishing of the bus at the film's end.

In Baser's two films made in Germany, the claustrophobic space of Turkish immigrants is inscribed not so much as ethnic or national but as feminine. *40 m² Deutschland* (40m² Germany, 1986) portrays a wife who is literally locked by

Figure 2. Turna whittles her space as a strategy of resistance by withdrawing from her husband in Tev-fik Baser's 40 Meter² Germany. Frame enlargement.

her cruel and distraught husband inside their apartment every day that he goes out to work. Her access to Germany is limited to what she sees and hears from her window. Her strategy of denying herself to the man by refusing to speak or show emotions reduces her space even farther. She possesses neither 40 meters *of* Germany nor 40 meters *in* Germany.[46] All she has is the space of her own body and her memories of her childhood home.[47] In this film, the closed space is totally gendered and, although both man and wife practice denial against each other, it is the woman who is its chief victim. As a victim, however, she is empowered with subjectivity, able to escape the gendered confinement by imagining spaces of childhood's immensity. For many transnationals, especially poor migrant workers, men and women alike, the phobic personal space of the body here and now is enlarged by the nostalgia for and the memories of the elsewhere and other times. Together, claustrophobia and immensity constitute the space of transnationality.

In his *Abscheed vom Falschen Paradies* (Farewell to a False Paradise, 1988) Baser puts a different spin on his meditation on confinement and control. In most of the transnational films I have seen, closed spaces are coded negatively, as prisons that trap individuals. In this film, the coding is reversed, turning the prison into a haven. The protagonist is serving a jail term in Germany for killing her abusive husband, but as her release becomes imminent, the fear of what freedom means engulfs her. The film posits that for Turkish immigrants, particularly women, confinement to a prison in Germany and protection by German laws are preferable to life outside the prison in either Germany or Turkey. Prison provides for women a safe haven from the racist attacks of German neo-Nazis and the severe patriarchal retributions should they return home. In insisting on the security of confined spaces, this film echoes an Iranian director's film, *Utopia*, also made in Germany (see below).

Iranian Transnational Films

The configuration of closed spaces in the Iranian transnational cinema is similar to the Turkish exile cinema, yet there are certain key national, historical, and individual differences. Iranian transnational filmmakers have been among the most active in the past two decades, completing over two dozen feature fictional films in Europe and North America.[48] Here I will focus on a few outstanding examples that deal with configuration of closed spaces. Parviz Sayyad's last film in Iran, *Bonbast* (Dead-end, 1977), was completed a year before the revolution which drove him into exile to the United States.[49] In this film—a treatise on the stifling prerevolution conditions—a young girl is pursued by a man she thinks is a suitor but who turns out in the end to have been a security agent tailing her brother. The man, dressed in a dark suit, always watches from across the street the girl's house which is located in a cul-de-sac. Looking out of her window, she (mis)reads with disastrous consequences the surveying gaze of the state police as the desirous look of a potential suitor. The film's structure of confinement is both national and gendered. It is national because the girl is posited as a metaphor for all Iranians condemned to live in a panoptic disciplinary society; it is gendered because the girl's confinement to a room overlooking the dead-end alley is itself a haunting metaphor for women's lives in Iran. While her window promises freedom, the cul-de-sac suggests an obstacle to freedom.[50] Most of the story in Sayyad's second film made in the United States, *Sarhad* (Checkpoint, 1987), takes place in a bus during the so-called Iranian hostage crisis (1979–1981), when Americans were held hostage in their own embassy in Tehran. Although the specific circumstances of this Iranian bus are very different from that of the Turkish bus discussed earlier, as an allegory of exilic liminality they are nearly identical. The bus is carrying Iranian and American students on a field trip to Canada. While there, President Carter, in retaliation for hostage-taking, revokes the student visas of all Iranians in the United States. Attempting to reenter the United States, the bus is caught in a spatial and legal no-man's-land at the Canadian-U.S. border. The passengers can neither return to Canada nor pass into the United States. The liminal place of the border and the claustrophobic space of the bus produce a tremendous emotional flare-up among the passengers. The transnational space in this case is interstitial in that the bus is caught in between and astride two liminal zones, the physical Canadian-American border and the discursive Iranian-American politics. In this interstitial location, the phobic space of the bus provides neither security nor comfort. They are obtained only when the bus is allowed to return to the United States and the students gather at the home of one of the passengers, an Iranian-American. The sympathetic portrayal of this Iranian, who has moved from exilic liminality into ethnic stability, appears to recuperate all tensions and differences in the interest of acculturation.

Jalal Fatemi's video feature, *The Nuclear Baby* (1990), is a futuristic work about a postnuclear holocaust world, where a woman on the run gives birth to a child in a desert. Much of the story, however, unfolds in the claustrophobic spaces of her memories and the nightmare narrative created by a nightmare-mercenary hired by the Ministry of Nightmares. Not only the narrative but also the mise-en-scène is extremely claustrophobic. In several protracted sequences, characters wear terribly confining face masks. The girl—given birth to in the desert—is never seen without her mask. Here again the claustrophobic space is gendered, but it is also encoded with a humanist Iranian nationalism and an ironic reading of American society.

For Iranian exiles, cage and suitcase have become "phobic partners" and confinement to them has taken on the symbolic value of exile.[51] This confinement is often gendered, as in the film *Ghasem Ebrahimian* (The Suitors, 1989) where several parallels are drawn between a captured sheep being readied for slaughter, a Persian cat confined to an airline carrying cage, and the female protagonist caught in the snare of persistent suitors. The suitcase is a potent symbol of exilic subjectivity because it contains souvenirs from the homeland, denotes travel and living a provisional life, and connotes a pervasive sense of being closed in, profound deprivation, and diminution of one's possibilities in the world. It became a multifaceted symbol of national, transnational, and gendered subjectivity for Iranians as a result of a tragic and sensational event in the early 1980s involving a young Iranian couple. The husband was a permanent U.S. resident but his wife, who was in Europe, was not. Unsuccessful in obtaining a visa for his wife, the desperate husband

Figure 3. Claustrophobic spatiality is inscribed in the child character who wears a gas mask throughout her performance in Jalal Fatemi's The Nuclear Baby. Frame enlargement.

attempted to smuggle her into the United States inside a suitcase. Upon discovering in the San Francisco airport that she was asphyxiated and crushed to death, he committed suicide. This story became a cause célèbre in the exile media, and years later it was restaged, albeit with a different ending, in the *Ghasem Ebrahimian*. As the suitcase containing the woman is being carried by a conveyor belt in its slow and seemingly inevitable journey toward the aircraft the screen goes black. We are inside the suitcase and can hear her troubled breathing and her quiet desperation, which builds into a panic. At that point, few exiles would fail to grasp the connotations of constriction and diminution that exile spawns. Just before being loaded into the cargo bay of the plane, the woman unzips the suitcase and steps out. The last shot shows her from above, flagging a cab, heading not toward constriction and claustrophobic spaces but toward the full immensity of American society, with the multiple choices and the uncertainties it offers.

Amir Naderi's visually stunning film, *Manhattan by Numbers*, picks up where *Ghasam Ebrahimian* leaves off. It deals with the widening uncertainty and the deepening homelessness and panic of an unemployed journalist, George Murphy, in New York City. Having lost his wife, child, and job and having pawned or sold most of his belongings, he has become practically deterritorialized in his own country. To forestall his certain eviction from his apartment, he begins a search for a moneyed friend, a journey that carries him first through a Kafkaesque residential building where none of the rooms are numbered or bear any names and later from one end of Manhattan to another.[52] The filming strategy inside Murphy's apartment and in the streets tends to emphasize the sense that the world is closing in—physically, psychologically, and discursively. Telephoto shots collapse large physical places into compressed visual spaces, turning trains into eerily undulat-

Figure 4. Phobia and panic attack in the streets in Amir Naderi's Manhattan by Numbers. *Frame enlargement.*

ing caterpillars and high-rises into ominous steel and glass canyons and craters. Much of Murphy's search is conducted underground, where the ever-speeding and overcrowded subway trains create classic claustrophobic and agoraphobic conditions. Overground he travels from the physically decrepit buildings and neighborhoods of Harlem to the impersonal splendor of Wall Street. Psychologically, he traverses in the opposite direction. As he passes through each overcrowded or desolate neighborhood without finding his friend, his desperation surges into visible moments of panic, resembling Westphal's description of his patients' panic attacks in 1871. The attacks are exacerbated by posters, giant video screens, billboards, neon signs, and huge advertisements everywhere which create a discursive consumerist claustrophobia, from which he finds no escape.[53] Almost sick with panic, blurred vision, and disorientation, Murphy resorts to the safety of a wall as a phobic partner—only to have the camera career across it and ominously turn the corner, leaving him behind. To be sure, *Manhattan by Numbers* is a "city symphony" film not only in its deft orchestration of images and sounds but also in the way it is propelled forward in movements. However, in its dystopic vision it differs from almost all the other exuberant and renowned exemplars of the genre—from Paul Strand's *Mannahatta* (1921) to Alberto Cavalcanti's *Rièn Que les Heures* (Only the Hours, 1926), from Walther Ruttmann's *Berlin: Sinfonie der Grosstadt* (Berlin: Symphony of the City, 1927) to Dziga Vertov's *Cheloveks Kinoapparatom* (Man with the Movie Camera, 1929), and from Ralph Steiner and Willard Van Dyke's *The City* (1939) to Francis Thompson's *N.Y., N.Y.* (1958).[54]

That claustrophobic spaces, narratives, and aesthetics are informed by the conditions of exile and not just by the subject matter or place of production is evident when similar claustrophobic tendencies are noticed in the Iranian transnational films which are not about Iranian topics and are not made in the United States. Sohrab Shahid Saless's despairing and powerful film *Utopia* (1982), made in Germany, takes place in the confining spaces of a house of prostitution run by a ruthless male whoremaster. Although the life of the female prostitutes inside the house is miserable and demeaning, they are bound to it and when one of them dares to leave to experience the outside, she returns disappointed. The security that confinement represented for her far surpassed the choice that freedom posed. Claustrophobia both expresses and for a time being constitutes life itself in exile. That which it encloses is a womblike haven promising security. Yet, as I have tried to show, in transnational cinema the enclosed space is more often than not inscribed as a prison, trapping the individual. In a sardonic short write-up, Shahid Saless calls cinema a "whore's milieu," one that does not do "much for one's potency."[55] If *Utopia* is read through this comment, the analogy of transnational filmmakers as whores working in a society in which they do not fully belong and from which they cannot truly escape becomes more poignant (the option of going back is closed to many of them).

In the unipolar, postmodern world of today, globalized capital, deterritorialization, fragmentation, and uncertainty are all immanent and imminent.

Figure 5. Claustrophobic spatiality as embodied in the formal arrangement of prostitutes after they have stabbed their pimp to death in Sohrab Shahid Saless's Utopia. *The subtitle reads "we are free."* Frame enlargement.

Under such circumstances nations and communities everywhere seem to be involved in creating an other(s) against whom they can best (re)define themselves. The ideologies and practices of a "United Europe," "American firstism," Serbian "ethnic cleansing," "Islamic fundamentalism," and what we might call "heimatism," following Morley and Robin's formulation,[56] are all instances of not only (re)creating actual, material borders but also of drawing new discursive boundaries between the self and its others. Transnationals living in postindustrial societies are constantly in the process of redefining themselves against encroaching abstraction and semiotic manipulation which the reduction of all life's spheres to sign systems promises. Under such circumstances, space becomes untrustworthy. Place, however, becomes attractive and emplacement a viable option. The emphasis on negatively coded phobic spaces in transnational cinema is perhaps part of transnationals' attempts to turn the abstraction of the space in their lives into the concreteness of the place in their representation. It is an attempt to create ontological security and a place-bound identity. When in place, the space is mine— even if it is only 40 m².

Capitalism continually reterritorializes its liminars and transnationals through strategies of assimilation and co-optation, transforming them into ethnic subjects and productive citizens. By barricading themselves, however, these liminars reterritorialize themselves as exiles, as refusniks—psychically and socially. As a result, they become neither the society's others against whom its overarching identity could be formed nor its full citizens who could be pressed into servicing its values. Proactive psychic denial and social refusal and insistence on inscribing phobic spaces differ from passive alienation and the production of alienating spaces ascribed to modernity. They are part of the transnationals' strategies of haggling with and against the hailing efforts of the prevailing capitalist imperium. Ultimately, however, refusal and emplacement may reveal themselves to be forms of entrapment. It is then that the space of liminal panic described here may give way to the space of paranoia—so characteristic of the postmodern science fiction—or of liberation—so promised in third cinema.

NOTES

I thank Melissa Cefkin for her comments on parts of this essay. I also appreciate Kathryn Milun sharing with me her thoughts on agoraphobia and modernity.

1. Arjun Appadurai, "Disjuncture and Difference in the Global Cultural Economy," *Public Culture* 2, no. 2 (1990): 1–24.

2. Terry Eagleton, *Exiles and Emigrés: Studies in Modern Literature* (London: Chatto & Windus, 1970), p. 9.

3. Rick Altman, *The American Film Musical* (Bloomington: Indiana University Press, 1989), p. 5.

4. Stephen Neale, *Genre* (London: BFI, 1983), pp. 48–50.

5. William Rowe and Teresa Whitfield, "Thresholds of Identity: Literature and Exile in Latin America," *Third World Quarterly* (January 1987): 233.

6. Paul Ilie, *Literature and Inner Exile: Authoritarian Spain, 1939–1975* (Baltimore: Johns Hopkins University Press, 1980), p. 19.

7. For the potential cultural richness of internal exile films, see Coco Fusco, *Internal Exiles: New Films and Videos from Chile* (New York: Third World Newsreel, 1990).

8. Catherine Portuges, "Border Crossings: Recent Trends in East and Central European Cinema," *Slavic Review* 51, no. 3 (1992): 531.

9. Carol J. Williams, "New Picture for Hungary's Filmmakers," *Los Angeles Times*, March 3, 1992, p. 5.

10. See, for example, Lazlo Santhás's film, *Inner Movie*, in which Hungarian movie lovers recount and display the power of American films over their imagination and individual identity. See also Hamid Naficy, "Autobiography, Film Spectatorship, and Cultural Negotiation," *Emergences* 1 (1989): 29–54, which examines the self-othering power of Western films for Third World audiences.

11. Indeed, all great authorship is predicated on taking a distance, in essence, banishment and exile of sort, from the larger society. The resulting tensions and ambivalences produce the complexity and multidimensionality so characteristic of great art. In the same way that sexual taboo permits procreation, transnational banishment encourages creation.

12. I have incorporated these and other attributes of otherness and alterity to formulate a paradigm of exile and transnationality. See Hamid Naficy, *The Making of Exile Cultures: Iranian Television in Los Angeles* (Minneapolis: University of Minnesota Press, 1993).

13. Zygmunt Bauman, "Modernity and Ambivalence," in *Global Culture: Nationalism, Globalization and Modernity*, ed. Mike Featherstone (London: Sage, 1991), pp. 145–146.

14. Salman Rushdie, *Imaginary Homelands: Essays and Criticism 1981–1991* (London: Granta, 1991), p. 15.

15. In his *The Identity Card* (1966), the protagonist, an expatriate, loses his identity card on returning to his homeland, Iran. Unable to prove who he is, he feels imprisoned in a society he does not belong to and cannot leave.

16. FM-2030, *Are You a Transhuman?* (New York: Warner Books, 1989), p. 205.

17. Lizbeth Malkmus and Roy Armes, *Arab & African Film Making* (London: Zed Books, 1991), p. 60.

18. Abid Med Hondo, "The Cinema of Exile," in *Film & Politics in the Third World*, ed. John D. H. Downing (New York: Praeger, 1987), p. 75.

19. Sohrab Shahid Saless, "Culture as Hard Currency, or, Hollywood in Germany (1983),"

in *West German Filmmakers on Film: Visions and Voices,* ed. Eric Rentschler (New York: Holmes and Meir, 1988), p. 56.

20. For more on the controversy surrounding this film, see Nina J. Easton, "Threats Spur Police Aid for Film Maker, " *Los Angeles Times,* April 4, 1989, part 6, p. 1. On the impact on Latin American exile films of the politics of the home front, see Zuzana M. Pick, "The Dialectical Wandering of Exile," *Screen* 30, no. 4 (1989): 48–64.

21. Richard Pena, "Images of Exile: Two Films by Raoul Ruiz," in *Reviewing Histories: Selections from New Latin American Cinema,* ed. Coco Fusco (New York: Hallwalls, 1987), p. 137.

22. Zuzana M. Pick, "Chilean Cinema in Exile (1973–1986)," *Framework* 34 (1987): 41.

23. The ambivalent and often negative attitude of Iranian exile filmmakers toward American foreign policies vis-à-vis Iran since the 1950s has prevented some of them from wanting to identify their films as products of the United States. Yet, as filmmakers needing recognition and wide exhibition of their films, they have little choice but to do so.

24. This kind of homelessness of course, is not limited to Third World films. A recent European example is Angieszka Holland's *Europa, Europa* (Hitlerjunge Solomon, 1991) made in Germany. The German Export Film Union refused to nominate the film for an Academy of Motion Picture Arts and Science foreign film Oscar, claiming it was too "international." According to the Union, the film's Polish director, French cofinancing, and Russian assistance disqualified it as a German entry. Critics, however, felt that the Germans were uncomfortable with the film's depiction of a young Jew who opportunistically survives in the Hitler Youth. For more on the controversy, see Karen Breslau, "Screening Out the Dark Past," *Newsweek,* February 3 1992, p. 30, and Joseph McBride, "Foreign Oscar Hopeful Tongue-Tied," *Variety,* October 28, 1991, p. 3.

25. Good examples of transnational autobiographies are *Lost, Lost, Lost, The Great Sadness of Zohara* (Nina Menkes, 1983), *Measures of Distance* (Mona Hatoum, 1988), and *Manhattan by Numbers.*

26. Thomas Elsaesser, "Tales of Sound and Fury: Observations on Family Melodrama," in *Film Theory and Criticism: Introductory Readings,* ed. Gerald Mast, Marshall Cohen, and Leo Braudy 4th ed. (New York: Oxford University Press, 1992). Laura Mulvey, "Pandora: Topographies of the Mask and Curiosity," in *Sexuality and Space,* ed. Beatriz Colomina (Princeton: Princeton University Press, 1992).

27. Mulvey, "Pandora," p. 55.

28. Elsaesser, "Tales of Sound and Fury," p. 528.

29. For an English translation of Westphal's original article, see Ted Curmp, "Westphal's Agoraphobia," *Journal of Anxiety Disorders* 5 (1991): 77–86.

30. Diane L. Chambless, "Characteristics of Agoraphobia," in *Agoraphobia: Multiple Perspectives on Theory and Treatment,* ed. Diane L. Chambless and Alan J. Goldstein (New York: John Wiley & Sons, 1982), p. 2. Issac M. Marks, *Fear, Phobias, and Rituals: Panic, Anxiety, and Their Disorders* (New York: Oxford University Press, 1987), pp. 323–324.

31. Marks, *Fears, Phobias, and Rituals,* p. 360; Chambless, "Characteristics," p. 3; and Maryanne M. Garbowsky, *The House without the Door: A Study of Emily Dickinson and the Illness of Agoraphobia* (Rutherford: Fairleigh Dickinson University Press, 1989), p. 58.

32. Anthony Vidler, "Agoraphobia: Spatial Estrangement in Georg Simmel and Siegfried Kracauer," *New German Critique* 54 (Fall 1991): 31–45.

33. On the arcade *(passage)* and the allied concept of the strolling spectator *(flaneur),* see Susan Buck-Morss, *The Dialectics of Seeing: Walter Benjamin and the Arcades Project* (Cambridge: MIT Press, 1990). On the relationship between shopping malls and cinema, see Anne Friedberg, *Window Shopping: Cinema and the Postmodern* (Berkeley: University of California Press, 1993).

34. The following scholars have fruitfully elaborated on this topic: David Harvey, *The Condition of Postmodernity: An Enquiry into the Origins of Cultural Change* (Cambridge and Oxford: Blackwell, 1992); Henri Lefebvre, *The Production of Space,* trans. Donald Nicholson-Smith (Oxford: Blackwell, 1991); Fredric Jameson, *The Geopolitical Aesthetic: Cinema and Space in the World System* (Bloomington: Indiana University Press, 1992); Edward Soja, *Postmodern Geographies: The Reassertion of Space in Critical Social Theory* (London: Verso, 1989).

35. Michel Foucault, *Discipline and Punish: The Birth of the Prison,* trans. Alan Sheridan (New York: Vintage, 1979).

36. Gilles Deleuze, "Postscript on the Societies of Control," *October* 59 (Winter 1992): 7.

37. Some feminists have argued that the higher incidents of agoraphobia among women and the act of women secluding themselves are both symptoms of patriarchy and resistance against its restrictions on women: see Garbowsky, *House without the Door*, p. 133, and Chambless, "Characteristics" p. 3.

38. In exile literature, we have a number of powerful inscriptions of phobic spaces. In Esmail Fassih's *Soraya in a Coma*, the Soraya of the title is an Iranian patient who remains in a coma in a Paris hospital throughout the novel. In Kafka's *Metamorphosis*, Gregor Samsa is trapped in the body of a beetle, forced to crawl under the couch and hide in the interstitial spaces of an enclosed room. In Ariel Dorfman's *The Last Song of Manuel Sendero*, all the unborn children decide not to be born as a protest against the world adults have created. For a similar reason, in Gunther Grass's *Tin Drum* Oscar decides not to grow physically, trapping himself inside his three-year-old body. In Albert Camus's *The Plague*, whole sections of the town are closed off and many people confined to rooms in order to prevent spread of the disease. However, such denials and phobic configurations are not all innocent protests, they are also skewed by ideological and political projects of their authors. Fassih uses the girl in the coma as a metaphor to condemn Iranians who after the Islamic revolution went into exile in Europe. Kafka denounces the modernist bureaucratization of the unconscious. Although the protest of Dorfman's children is against an unnamed country, it is clear that the country is to be read as the author's homeland, Chile under Pinochet. Oscar's protest against Nazism may be read as Grass's warning against the reemergence of a reconfigured form of Nazism. Although, Camus's protest may be construed as a humanist voice against modernist alienation, as Edward Said has noted ("Narrative Geography and Interinterpretation," *New Left Review* 180 [1990]: 81–97), the staging of the plague in Algeria (Camus's place of birth and rearing) makes the author complicit with French colonialism.

39. Atilla Dorsay made this remark during a conference on images of the East in Western films, Hawaii International Film Festival, December 1992. A similar point is made by Mehmet Basutcu, "The Power and Danger of the Image," *Cinemaya*, nos. 17–18 (1992–93):16–19.

40. John Wakeman, ed., *World Film Directors, Volume II, 1945–1985* (New York: H.W. Wilson Company, 1988), p. 407.

41. Clandestine filming or filming by proxy is not unknown in the Third World. A celebrated example is Miguel Littin's four-hour film *Acta General de Chile* (Chile: A General Record, 1986), shot by five foreign film crews, each entering Chile under the guise of filming innocuous documentaries. Littin himself, as the head of one crew, entered Chile incognito as a businessman, and he appears as such in the film.

42. Ersan Ilal, "On Turkish Cinema," in *Film & Politics in the Third World*, ed. John D. H. Downing (New York: Praeger, 1987), p. 125.

43. Elia Kazan, "The View from a Turkish Prison" *New York Times Magazine*, February 4, 1979.

44. Roy Armes, *Third World Film Making and the West* (Berkeley: University of California Press, 1987), p. 271.

45. That the closed configuration of space is also not limited to cinema is indicated by the confrontational performances of the Turkish-German-American choreographer, Mehmet Memo Sander, who calls himself "HIV+ and Queer choreographer from Istanbul" (Lewis Segal, "Young Turk," *Los Angeles Times Calendar*, July 12, 1992, p. 52). He constructs relentlessly oppressive and claustrophobic physical processes and spaces that test his own and his dancers" endurance, even survival skills. In one dance, Sander is confined within a 6-by-6-foot box, where he climbs the walks, eventually emerging on top. In other dances, a dancer is found hanging inside a wooden box or squeezed within a transparent plastic cube. Sander's use of phobic spaces may be due not only to his transnational status but also his activist queer politics. For gays, being inside the closet or coming out of the closet always entails and unleashes claustrophobic and agoraphobic spatialities and sensibilities. The film *Agora* (Robert and Donald Kinney, 1992), about a gay agoraphobe paralyzed by fear of being found out, represents gayness as agoraphobia. The film also demonstrates that coming out of the closet often forces gays and lesbians to hole themselves in the undesirable interstices of society.

46. The choice of the forty meters may be a reference to Islam and to Turkish cultural beliefs vis-à-vis women. In some traditions in Turkey, women are to remain indoors for forty days after giving birth.

47. In *Passages* (1992), directed by Yilmaz Arlan, a Turkish-born filmmaker with polio, con-

finement is also mapped onto the body. However, the actors in this semi-documentary, which takes place in a German rehabilitation center, are confined to incomplete, missing, or mutilated bodies. Their limitation is not just metaphorical, but also real.

48. See Naficy, "Autobiography" 1993.

49. This film and Güney's *Yol* demonstrate that external exile is often preceded by a form of internal exile.

50. Jamsheed Akrami, "The Blighted Spring: Iranian Cinema and Politics in the 1970s," in *Film & Politics in the Third World*, ed. John D. H. Downing (New York: Praeger, 1987), p.147.

51. For Iranian exiles, the caged bird as a metaphor of imprisonment and exile appears in songs, TV programs, and films. That this type of imagery might be associated with clinical agoraphobia is indicated by the prevalence of metaphors of cage and prison in the poetry of Emily Dickinson who suffered from agoraphobia and was housebound for the last twenty-five years of her life.

52. The protagonist's search for money can be read as a powerful metaphor for all independent filmmaking, but particularly for filmmakers of the transnational genre, who spend much of their time in such searches.

53. The film *Agora* insightfully links agoraphobia to fear of not only the public marketplace but also of consumerism itself. Labels for consumer products dominate the public sphere and the screen and colonize the dreams and consciousness of the gay make agoraphobe.

54. In the case of Iranians, too, as with the Turkish exiles, it can be demonstrated that closed spatiality is not limited to transnational cinema or to the confinement of only straight women. The powerful theatrical performances of Iranian-American director Reza Abdoh may be cited. In one recent confrontational in-your-face production, *Bogeyman* (1993), the audience witnesses through the windows of a three-story apartment house violent discussions and activities among various gay and other sexually "transgressive" people. Soon, the entire front of the building is lifted away to reveal the disturbing interiors of these little confining worlds. What comes across strongly is the explosive desire to break out of the socially predefined spatial, gendered, and sexual categories and roles. The lifting of the building's facade can be read as a metaphor for coming out of the closet to face and to expose oneself to a hostile homophobic world.

55. Shahid Saless, "Culture as Hard Currency," p. 56.

56. David Morley and Kevin Robins, "No Place like Heimat: Images of Home(Land) in European Culture," *New Formations* 12 (1990): 1–23.

Robyn Wiegman

"My Name is Forrest, Forrest Gump": Whiteness Studies and the Paradox of Particularity

Let me begin with the story of two museums. In Laurens, South Carolina, John Howard built one in the old Echo Theater, which is located, as they say, just a stone's throw from the County Courthouse in the center part of town. "The World's Only Klan Museum" blares the marquee. Inside, there are robes and books, Confederate flags, pocket knives, "White Power" sweatshirts, even T-shirts declaring "It's a White Thing. You Wouldn't Understand." When the local authorities denied Mr. Howard a business license to sell souvenirs in the Redneck Shop, he threatened to take his case to court. Suzanne Coe, lawyer for Shannon Faulkner of the Citadel controversy, became his legal counsel; like that earlier case, she said this one too was about civil rights.[1]

In Alabama, the Birmingham Civil Rights Institute is located across from the Sixteenth Street Baptist Church, site of multiple bombings in the 1960s, including the now famous one that killed four black girls. Inside the museum are replicas and remnants from the period of official segregation: public bathrooms marked "white" and "colored," pieces of a yellow school bus, a segregated street scene. In the gift shop, patrons can purchase African American history books, posters, postcards, T-shirts emblazoned with the image of Dr. Martin Luther King.

For Mr. Howard, as for his civil rights lawyer, the existence of the Alabama museum—and the legal protections that enabled it and other such projects to come into being—established the legitimacy of, if not the legal precedent for the Klan Museum, guaranteeing Howard's right, in his terms, to display pride in being white.[2] So many of the characteristics of U.S. racial discourse in the 1990s are exhibited in John Howard's story. Most notably, the language of civil rights is mobilized to protect whiteness, which is cast not only as a minority identity, but as one injured by the denial of public representation.[3] In asking the apparatus of the nation to adjudicate this "minority" injury, Mr. Howard sought the universal and hence abstractly disembodied ledger of rights that are understood as part of the promise of democratic citizenship.[4]

From *Boundary* 2, 26:3 (fall 1999), pp. 115–50. Copyright © 1999, Duke University Press. All rights reserved. Reprinted with permission.

Since the case was settled out of court in Mr. Howard's favor, can we still understand him as injured? This might seem like an odd question, but I ask it in order to advance three interrelated claims about whiteness. The first is historical: that the distinctiveness of southern white supremacist identity since the Civil War hinges on a repeated appeal to the minoritized, injured "nature" of whiteness.[5] To be injured—by the economic transformations of Emancipation, by the perceived loss of all-white social spaces, by the reformation of a national imaginary of white citizen-subjects—provides the basis of white supremacist collective self-fashioning, which has and continues to function by producing the threat of its own extinction as the justification and motivation for violent retaliations.[6]

The second claim, drawing on the first, is theoretical: to the extent that critical race theorists have assumed that the power of whiteness arises from its appropriation of the universal and that the universal is opposed to and hence devoid of the particular, we have failed to interpret the tension between particularity and universality that characterizes not simply the legal discourse of race (where early documents enfranchise the "white person"), but the changing contours of white power and privilege in the past three centuries. Richard Dyer, for instance, has argued that making whiteness visible works "to dislodge them/us from the position of power," and it is now this assumption that governs much of the interrogation of whiteness in academic discourse.[7] In assigning the power of white racial supremacy to its invisibility and hence universality, Dyer and others underplay the contradictory formation of white racial power that has enabled its historical elasticity and contemporary transformations.[8] Apartheid structures, both slavery and Jim Crow segregation, indeed universalized whiteness through the entitlements of the citizen-subject, but they simultaneously mobilized a vast social geometry of white particularity, as the declarative warning "For Whites Only" ominously suggested.[9] While for Mr. Howard, the postsegregation era has put such supremacist white particularity to the test, new and quite powerful strategies of particularization have emerged, with the arsenal of anti-affirmative action legislation since Bakke taking the lead. To begin to discuss the ways in which white power has and continues to reconstruct itself in the context of segregation's demise leads to my third and final claim. But first, I need to tell you more about Mr. Howard's story.

In Laurens, a multiracial town of about 10,000, Mr. Howard is not a popular man. People, both black and white, want him, the museum, and the Redneck Shop out. This is a town with a violent history. "For decades," Rick Bragg writes, "a piece of rotted rope dangled from a railroad trestle, just outside this little town, a reminder of the last lynching in Laurens County. It was back in 1913, but people still talk of the black man wrongly accused of rape, and the white mob that hanged him." The lynch rope was not removed until 1986 when the trestle was destroyed, which means that little more than a decade went by without the public display of violent white supremacy. It also means that no one was compelled, in the course of seventy-three years, to take that rope down. Town rumor said that it was a crime to remove it, and African Americans have been quoted as saying that they well understood the rope's threatening stay-in-your-place message.

While no whites were moved to undo the master sign of their privilege over the years, its resurrection in the downtown Klan Museum was met with an outpouring of white alarm. Why one response and not the other? One answer has to do with the politics of social space: the museum is located in the center part of town, in the most public of public spaces, while the lynch rope hung outside of town, along the road to and from Laurens's historically black section. The lynch rope thus signified the panoptic power of whiteness—always present but never fully visible; it racialized and embodied blackness through its memorialization of terroristic death. The Klan Museum, on the other hand, embodies whiteness in an open public display, marking its presence and visibility and thereby fixing it in an implicit narrative of both local and national violence. To protest the museum means, for whites, protesting the particularizing pact between segregationist ideologies and white embodied identity. It also means participating in—indeed actively forging—a counter whiteness whose primary characteristic is its disaffiliation from white supremacist practices.

It is this disaffiliation that might be thought of as the pedagogical lesson for whites of civil rights reform, where the transformation from segregation to integration reconstructed not only the materiality of black life in the United States, but the national imaginary of race and race discourse within which white identity since the 1960s has emerged. Integration, no matter how failed in its utopian projections of a nation beyond race division, nonetheless powerfully suspended the acceptability of white supremacy's public display, so much so that the hegemonic formation of white identity today must be understood as taking shape in the rhetorical, if not always political register of disaffiliation from white supremacist practices and discourses. This does not mean that racism and white supremacy have been dissolved or that their consequences today are less damaging, exclusive, or exploitative than they were under official national segregation, but it is to remark upon the success of black liberation struggle to deterritorialize the public imaginary and social geography of segregation through critiques of degrading language, segregated social services, and mass circulated stereotypic images. Such success has not been total, nor has it remained exterior to the reproduction of white power in the past three decades. Indeed, throughout the late 1990s, segregationist practices and their Klan-esque defenses served as the referential framework for understandings of white supremacy in general, which means that many white Americans could join efforts to undo civil rights reform without recognizing their activities or opinions as participation in the contemporary reconfiguration of white power and privilege.[10]

This split in the white subject—between disaffiliation from white supremacist practices and disavowal of the ongoing reformation of white power and one's benefit from it—is constitutive of contemporary white racial formation, underlying what Howard Winant calls "white racial dualism."[11] What interests me most about this dualism is how it lends itself to a wide range of political positions and agendas. In "Behind Blue Eyes," Howard Winant describes the postwar era as one in which "the problematic of whiteness . . . has emerged as the principal source of anxiety and conflict" (p. 49), with such anxiety being played out today in five "racial projects": the far right, new right, neo-conservative, neo-liberal, and new abolitionist (p. 43). According to Winant, only the far right deploys a biologist explanation of race that overtly identifies with supremacist practices and discourses. All other projects, no matter how fundamentally neo-racist or antiracist, frame themselves within the official national discourse of integrationist equality. While one might want to argue with Winant's descriptive schema of the contemporary political terrain, his observation that white supremacist discourses in the familiar style of pre–civil rights struggle were decentered from the national lexicon is crucial. It allows us to understand the ways in which disaffiliation from white supremacy founds late-twentieth-century white identity formation for the majority of Americans and further how that disaffiliation can be—and has been—put to multiple and contradictory political purposes.

In the U.S. popular public sphere, for instance, which is to say in the commodified circuits of contemporary identity production, white disaffiliation takes shape as "liberal whiteness," a color-blind moral sameness whose reinvestment in "America" rehabilitates the national narrative of democratic progress in the aftermath of social dissent and crisis. Such liberal whiteness has dominated the popular imaginary for more than a decade, in narratives that feature whites as the soldiers of civil rights (such as *Mississippi Burning* and *A Time To Kill* or television's "Fences"), in spectacular fantasies of a postracist U.S.-based new world order (*Independence Day*), in sentimental renderings of cross-racial relations (*Boys on the Side*), and in filmic celebrations of fundamental white male goodness (*Forrest Gump*). Simultaneously evoking a postracist society and a newly innocent whiteness, representations of liberal whiteness put a seemingly benign touch on those material transformations that have accompanied the twentieth century's long and complicated transition from Jim Crow to official integration to the new multiculturalism. Indeed, we might say that even as liberal whiteness oversaw the rise of "diversity" in the popular public sphere, the nation-state's capitulation to capitalism—in the deaths of welfare and affirmative action on one hand and the heightened regulation of immigrant populations and borders on the other—has extended the material scope of white privilege. While the histories of these issues are complicated, it is nonetheless significant how seemingly "benign" is the popular cultural rhetoric of whiteness today and how self-empowering its consequences. Or to put this another way, until recently, seldom has whiteness been so widely represented as attuned to racial equality and justice while so aggressively solidifying its advantage.

My third claim, then, is simultaneously a descriptive and a prescriptive one: that much of the force of contemporary white racial power arises from the hegemony of liberal whiteness, whose dominance in the popular imaginary must be examined as both provocation and context for the emergence of the academy's latest and—in nearly everyone's opinion—rather confounding antiracist venture: whiteness studies. Journals have devoted special issues to the topic (the *Minnesota Review* and *Transition*), conferences on whiteness have received national network coverage, and both faculty and graduate students have begun to list "whiteness studies" as an area of research and teaching expertise. Often defined as a self-styled response to various demands for whites to quit studying "the other" and study themselves, whiteness studies as a phrase is typically deployed to reference a very recent scholarly archive, with the texts of Theodor Allen, Jesse Daniels, Michelle Fine, Ruth Frankenberg, Mike Hill, Noel Ignatiev, Ian F. Haney Lopez, Eric Lott, Annalee Newitz and Matt Wray, Fred Pfeil, David Roediger, Alexander Saxton, Mab Segrest, and Vron Ware as foundational.[12] Among these texts, three trajectories of inquiry might be said to form the critical project of whiteness studies, all of which take social constructionist renderings of race as their theoretical assumption: the race traitor school (which advocates the abolition of whiteness through white disaffiliation from race privilege), the "white trash" school (which analyzes the "racialization" of the permanent poor in order to demonstrate the otherness of whiteness within), and the class solidarity school (which rethinks the history of working-class struggle as preamble to forging new cross-racial alliances).

Key to all three trajectories is David Roediger's groundbreaking 1991 study of the creation of the white working class in the nineteenth century, *The Wages of Whiteness*, which rehearses the history of the "whitening" of Irish immigrants as a kind of paradigmatic case for understanding whiteness as a social construction. For the Irish immigrant, whiteness was a compensatory "wage" that worked to disrupt black-Irish or Chinese-Irish identifications in the context of industrial exploitation, thereby pitting race against class identifications in ways that have haunted working-class struggle for two centuries. While Roediger's project is quite specifically a rearticulation of class struggle as an antiracist project, his historical account of white racial formation has come to define the political horizon of whiteness studies by imagining for contemporary white people a political (as opposed to biological or cultural) identity beyond the conflation of power and privilege with white skin. The social constructionist project of whiteness studies, we might therefore say, takes shape in a gesture of historical retrieval of not-yet-white ethnics whose experience in the New World can be characterized not as one of "being," but of "becoming" white. In this gesture, which I would call the foundational gesture of whiteness studies, the texts heralded in the academic press as a "new humanities subfield" coalesce as a kind of ethnic studies formulation, but one profoundly divided by the need to destroy its object of study—whiteness—as well.

Whiteness studies thus evinces its own version of the contradictions inscribed in Winant's concept of racial dualism. On one hand, it responds to the contemporary leftist desire to produce an antiracist white (or postwhite) subject, one whose political commitments can be disaffiliated from the deployments of white supremacy and refunctioned as cross-race and cross-class struggle. In doing so, it encounters, on the other hand, the critical difficulty of that antiracist subject, whose self-conscious and willful self-production can only reconfirm a universalist narcissistic white logic, mobilized now through the guise of an originary discursive blackness that simultaneously particularizes and disidentifies with the political power of white skin. These moves, colliding with and contesting the reformulation of whiteness in the public sphere, demonstrate what George Lipsitz calls "the impossibility of the antiracist white subject," thereby necessitating not an oppositional analysis between academic anti-racist projects and the popular public sphere, but one that seeks to link their mutual, if contradictory, critical limits.[13]

This essay addresses itself to such a task by turning first to the film that one month before the Oklahoma City bombing garnered best picture honors for 1994. In *Forrest Gump*, the symptomatic anxieties of contemporary white racial dualism are set into play, with the narrative performing a series of strategic reinventions of a postsegregationist antiracist whiteness as part of a broader claim to rejuvenate "America" for a transnational capitalist order. While the film's overall trajectory is of the most reactionary political kind, it fulfills the cultural desire to forget what we don't know how to remember by remembering in haphazard and incoherent ways the images of racial trauma and social dissent that we can't yet forget—the physical violence that attended desegregation, the street protests of the 1960s, the bloodbath of the Vietnam War, the murder of national political leaders. Through its use of television images and in the passive construction of our model spectator—Forrest Gump, who neither can nor wants to "know"—the film participates in the contemporary struggle to reform whiteness by moving its protagonist through a range of antiracist positions.

Early in the film, Gump is rendered "discursively black" through the analogy between disability (mental and physical) and black social disenfranchisement; later, he becomes a race traitor by innocently participating in desegregation and in interracial male friendship; still later, his antiracist whiteness is forged by the repayment of a compensatory debt to the black family and black community. In these and other ways, *Forrest Gump* takes aim at the segregationist imaginary of white identity formation, demonstrating less a political affinity with the emerging project of whiteness studies than a series of tense and contradictory convergences. From these convergences, we can explore what the emergent theoretical structure of whiteness studies seems unconsciously intent on constructing: namely, a history of racial origin—and a contemporary social analytic—tied to minoritarian positionings (the racialized ethnic, the permanent white poor). By reading the film as precursor to further discussion of whiteness studies, this essay explores the emerging disciplinary apparatus that might be said to produce and define the study of whiteness as an academic field. Call it, if you will, an analysis of the compulsion to form a disciplinary endeavor called whiteness studies in the first place.

Back to the Future

At the Civil Rights Institute in Birmingham, Alabama, visitors begin their tour by taking a seat on one of the narrow white benches that fill a rather small, darkened room behind the admissions booth. As the lights fade, an entire wall comes to life with documentary footage narrating the history of the state and its long and bloody battle to desegregate. A city founded during Reconstruction, Birmingham played a key role in the civil rights struggle by organizing one of the most successful uses of consumer power to grieve forms of inequality sanctioned by the state in U.S. history.[14] The Birmingham bus boycott drew widespread media attention as African American residents turned to other means, most notably walking, to navigate their city. The Civil Rights Institute thematizes this mass resistance by installing its visitor in a space organized around issues and images of mobility. When the documentary ends and the lights return, the movie screen wall rises dramatically to reveal the space of the museum on the other side. Every visitor to the museum must walk through that screen, so to speak, into rooms and corridors that contain artifacts of the material culture of segregation and the fight to undo it. At nearly every turn, there are more screens—a mock 1960s storefront where boxy televisions broadcast images of encounters between Freedom Fighters and the police; a video wall where multiple contemporary televisions juxtapose racist commercials, political interviews, and the speeches of Martin Luther King. In a grand gesture where history and the present meet, the visitor is positioned in front of a picture window that looks out onto the Sixteenth Street Baptist Church across the street.

Forrest Gump, you might remember, is set at a bus stop, and one of its main technological innovations is its clever insertion of the protagonist into nationally recognizable television scenes.[15] In the most famous instance, Gump becomes a participant in George Wallace's failed attempt to block black entrance to the University of Alabama following the court order to desegregate. Positioned initially as a member of the crowd, Gump symbolically joins the students when he retrieves one of their dropped books; in his movement from witness to role player, Gump is strategically disaffiliated from the racist whiteness that Wallace so viciously stands for, but the violence and anger of that historical moment are flattened by the innocence of Gump's unknowing gesture. In the spatializing logic of segregation, Gump is here a race traitor. He crosses the lines of racial demarcation, disengaging from a white racist social body to join the black students, but the innocence of his action crucially depoliticizes the whole scene. It is this kind of race trait-ing that most characterizes the film, as Gump's movement in personal moral terms not only displaces the necessity of conscious identifications as precursors to collective political action, but it consigns the entire realm of the "historical" to television, which installs a consumptive spectator as the ultimate witness—and postracist subject—of political change itself.

In its extraction of Gump from the legacy of southern segregationist identity, the film, we might say, deessentializes the relationship among white skin, white privilege, and white racism, answering (or so it seems) the clarion call of contemporary theory to render race a social construction. But *Forrest Gump* can only imagine a nonessentialist whiteness by shifting the signification of segregation from emblem of black oppression and white material privilege to a form of white injury. This shift enables segregation to serve not only as the historical form of white particularity that must be disavowed, but also as the means for crafting a liberal whiteness that is now, rhetorically speaking, kin to blackness. The film's preoccupation with the resignification of segregation is apparent at the outset, where the narrative tellingly offers a black woman to serve as the bus stop audience for the childhood portion of Gump's tale.[16] Without recognition of the meaning of her only words, "my feet hurt," Gump remembers his first pair of shoes, or I should say he remembers through his *desire for* the woman's shoes his own personal history of mobility as a series of restrictions. The first was physical, as Forrest was forced to wear leg braces to correct his curvature of the spine; the second was social, as Forrest endured ridicule and exclusion because of his physical and mental disabilities. If the analogy between segregationist racialization and Forrest's restricted mobility, ostracism, and physical "difference" isn't clear, the narrative locates the scene of Forrest's social exclusion on a school bus, where his classmates eagerly refuse him a seat. (Later in the film, he will again be refused a seat on a bus by his fellow inductees in the army.) These scenes perform two functions: they rewrite segregation as a discourse of injury no longer specific to black bodies, which installs whiteness as injury, and they define that injury as private, motivated not by a social system but by the prejudices and moral lacks of individuals who seem simply not to know better. That Forrest can "know better" without ever *knowing* is of course the deep irony of this film; from this antiepistemological position, he gets to utter the sentimental punch line: "I may not be a smart man, but I know how to love."

If *Forrest Gump* is a liberal white rendition of the history of segregationist apartheid, if the film can be said to be a walk through the archive of popular national memory, its project does not end with white occupation of injury. That would be a version of Mr. Howard's story. *Forrest Gump* has a more pedagogical mission: to demonstrate that difference and injury, even intellectual deficient, are not impediments to the American way of life. The plot thus advances through scenes in which Forrest gains mobility, thereby exchanging injury for liberation and transcendence. As a kid being chased by his classmates, he magically breaks free of his leg braces; as a teenager being harassed by boys in a truck with a Confederate flag license plate, his flight across a college football field results in a scholarship and All-American athletic career. In Vietnam, his ability to run saves his life and the lives of others, and in the film's oddest and longest segment devoted to mobility, Gump spends three years running from shore to shore, redrawing the boundaries of the nation's geographic identity and demonstrating that no region (no state, no neighborhood, no city street) is off limits or out of reach. All of this mobility critically recasts the segregationist history of the bus stop, even though that too must be left behind. In the final segments of the film, Forrest discovers that he doesn't need the bus to get where he is going, as he is only blocks away from his destination where marriage, the domestic scenario, and miraculously a completed paternity ("Little Forrest") await. He can easily walk there.

In his exodus from the bus stop and its symbolic evocation of national struggle and racial strife, Gump is extricated from the public domain of the political in favor of an insulated private and domestic realm. Such a movement inscribes the cultural logic of what Lauren Berlant calls today's "intimate public sphere," where the family "usurps the modernist promise of the culturally vital, multiethnic city. . . . [and] public life . . . [becomes] ridiculous and even dangerous to the nation."[17] That the family is imagined and indeed popularly imaged as white underscores the conservative racial agenda of this new public intimacy; in the case of *Forrest Gump*, it gives to the protagonist's incessant movement a final resting place: in the last scene, outside his ancestral home on an Alabama country road, the white father will board his now motherless but perfectly intelligent son on a school bus where, the film promises, little Forrest will never be denied a seat. This resolution, in which a sentimentalized white paternity ensures the survival of the nation-as-family, is predicated on Gump's celebrated failure to register cognitively or narratively the events he witnesses—predicated, that is, on Gump's native inability to forge anything but the most narcissistic and personalized of identifications, first with the mother who bore him and later with the child who utopically doubles him. The film's commitment to a protagonist unable to read the historical archive he is moving through demonstrates the prevailing assumption of the Reagan years where, as Berlant puts it, "[the normal American] sees her/his identity as something sustained in private, personal, intimate relations; in contrast, only the abjected, degraded *lower* citizens of the United States will see themselves as sustained by public, coalitional, non-kin affiliations" (p. 185).

The shift to the private and familial carries a certain risk, however, for a film whose protagonist is a southerner, an Alabaman, and the named descendant of the founder of the Ku Klux Klan, Nathan Bedford Forrest. Under these conditions, too much familial intimacy risks sustaining a white identity that the film is sentimentally invested in undoing, the identity, that is, of the overtly racist American: the white southerner.[18] As I have already suggested, liberal whiteness is characterized by its disaffiliation from segregationist forms of white identity and identification. For this reason, the first flashback narrative of the film, told to the black female witness, features Gump's Confederate hero ancestor, a man who was born in poverty but grew rich as a slave trader and planter and who garnered both fame and shame during the Civil War as a brilliant, unconventional battle tactician who incited his men to massacre surrendering black troops at Ft. Pillow. But the film's Nathan Bedford Forrest is ludicrous, not powerful; in Gump's mind, he would "dress up in . . . robes and . . . bed sheets and act like . . . ghosts or spooks or something." Gump's mother chose the name to remind her son that "sometimes people do things that just don't make no sense." The film's parable of naming displaces the intimate family relations that attach Gump to a genealogy of masculine aggression and segregationist white supremacy, and in doing so it importantly diffuses any feminist reading of the violence of patriarchal forms of inheritance.[19] As if to emphasize this point, the patronymic, Forrest, is shifted to Gump's first name, and the repetition of the line, "My name is Forrest, Forrest Gump,"continually reminds us of this foundational displacement. In the liberal white fantasy of *Forrest Gump*, the descendant of the founder of the Klan can emerge at the end of the twentieth century shorn of his damaged patriarchal inheritance, which is to say that the intimacy of familial, personal relations has now been successfully separated from the past and tied instead to a prototypically American future. In the process, white power and privilege are displaced from any inherent relation—historically, ideologically, politically—to white skin.[20]

The liberal whiteness formed from these narrative displacements offers a subtle but telling commentary on one of the most volatile issues of the 1990s, affirmative action. In "Whiteness as Property," Cheryl Harris distinguishes between corrective justice, which seeks "compensation for discrete and 'finished' harm done to minority group members or their ancestors," and distributive justice, which "is the claim an individual or group has to the positions or advantages or benefits they would have been awarded under fair conditions."[21] According to Harris, the goals of affirmative action—to address the harms done to those minoritized by racial (or gendered) oppression—are undermined when corrective justice is the interpretative frame because here not only is the harm assumed to be finished, but the practices through which harm has been done are individualized, confined to the one who perpetrated it and the one who endured it. In this context, whites can claim to be innocent and therefore in need of counter legislative protection because they have not individually perpetuated harm. This is the logic of Bakke as well as California's recent Proposition 209, and of course it is the model of compensation being worked out in *Forrest Gump*. Gump's mother, you might recall, supports her family by running a rooming house out of the old plantation that is the ancestral home in Greenbough, Alabama, a narrative convenience that renders the family's historical connection to the economics of slavery if not deficient, at least not materially advantageous. Whatever harm slavery inflicted is finished and the privileges of economic gain that garner for white identity a material advantage have been narratively swept away. This does not mean that Gump will have no racial debt to pay, but that his debt is first, not historical, not about the ongoing economic privilege of whiteness as a material effect of slavery and segregation, and second, not collective, not about a social identity enhanced and protected by the law as an economic investment.

What, then, is Gump's debt? And why must there be a debt at all in a film so clearly devoted to the fantasy of humanist transcendence? To answer these questions, we need to consider Gump's accumulation of wealth and to return, in time, to the issue of shoes, specifically the red and white Nike running shoes that serve as visual cues of the diegetic present time of the film. Gump's accumulation of wealth has two primary forms: shrimp and computers. The shrimping business is born of an interracial male confederation with Bubba, who gives Forrest a seat in the film's second passage through the scene of the school bus and who also gives to Gump all his knowledge about the shrimping business. When Bubba dies in the Vietnam War, Gump returns to the South and shrimp, only to make it big when a hurricane conveniently destroys every other boat in the black-owned industry. Gump's knowledge is quite literally African American knowledge, but the conversion of that "labor," if you will, into accumulation is effected through nature, not society. Any debt to be paid is thus a personal one arising from Gump's friendship with Bubba and not from the material advantages accorded to whiteness as an economic privilege. In this parable of the economics of contemporary black-white relations, the debt to be paid by Gump to Bubba's family—of half the profits of the shrimp business—is defined not by hierarchy or history, but as an honor to intimate male friendship.

What's significant about *Forrest Gump*, of course, is its inability to imagine the black male as surviving the trauma of the racial history that Gump will supersede.[22] This is especially striking since the other form of debt that the film imagines for Gump is likewise born of a male friendship and features Gump playing a role of compensation that has likewise been detached (in the film) from the responsibilities of the state: in his relationship with Lieutenant Dan, whose patriotic family has lost a son in every war since the Revolution, Gump both rescues and redeems the multiply injured white Vietnam veteran. Not surprisingly, this redemption is thematized through mobility as Lieutenant Dan, initially disabled by the loss of his legs in the war, comes finally to walk again (albeit with artificial limbs) in his last appearance in the film. Set at Gump's wedding to his childhood love Jenny, the symbolic reconstruction of Lieutenant Dan's traumatized white male body is accompanied by his own heterosexual completion, as he announces his impending marriage to Susan, an Asian American woman. Where Jenny has functioned as the traumatized female body who is rescued through Gump but not saved because she *is* contaminated sexuality, Gump's ability to save Lieutenant Dan is figured as a restoration of masculinity via the agency of interracial heterosexuality.

But there is more to Susan's appearance than the predictable circulation of woman as emblem of a rejuvenated masculinity. Susan is the only person of Asian descent in a film that devotes significant narrative time to the Vietnam War and its aftermath, and yet the film's commentary on the war is never able to reverberate beyond the sphere of intimate private relationships among U.S. men. Gump's debts, after all, are to black and white American men, which confines the racial discourse of the film to the traumatic resolutions of antiblack white supremacy. Susan evokes both a history and racial discourse which the film has no mechanism or motive to speak, even as it requires her presence as both witness and accomplice to Lieutenant Dan's remasculinization.[23] Her insertion into the scene of heterosexual intimacy privatizes the national narrative of war in Southeast Asia, thereby displacing the economics of accumulation that have followed U.S. interventions in the region. By this, I am referring to the significance of Gump and Lieutenant Dan's investment in Apple Computers, an industry whose transnational circuits of production and distribution are indelibly linked to postwar capitalist expansion in Southeast Asia. If the Vietnam War cost Lieutenant Dan his legs, his economic mobility is nonetheless enabled by it, as is Gump's, and yet it is precisely this that the film's thematic focus on segregation, mobility, and the resurrection of a privatized U.S. nation occlude. In moving the sites of the accumulation of wealth from shrimping to computer investments, *Forrest Gump* depicts without commentary capital's contemporary mobility from local, regional forms of industry to transnational practices of production and exchange.

With this in mind, we can return now to the opening scene of the film where a feather floats gently from the sky to land on Gump's red and white Nike running shoes. As the first material detail offered of the protagonist, Gump's running shoes are simultaneously his signature and personal trademark, evincing not simply his hard-won physical mobility, but his symbolic ability to move beyond the detritus of historical trauma.[24] More than this, however, the Nike shoes "ground" Gump's magical movement in an unconscious relation to a commodity that has itself become associated in the 1990s with the worst aspects of transnational modes of production. In the context of media revelations about Nike's exploitative working conditions in Southeast Asia, the corporation's commodity presence in *Forrest Gump* seems quite overtly engaged in a project of resignification. Through Gump, Nike can seek the reification of all material relations that is the effect of Gump's mode of narration, which means participating in the film's celebration of the detachment of state from nation. This celebration is demonstrated in two moves: first, in the way that the televisual archive that Gump moves through works to disavow the power of presidents and other state leaders, and hence to undermine not simply the authority but the value of contestation at the level of the state; and second, in the way the film endorses the "shore to shore" logic of nation as geographical entity that underlies Gump's seemingly motiveless three-year run across the United States.[25] With the state represented as the site of traumatic instability, loss of decorum, or simple comic incomprehensibility, the nation arises in illustrious geographical wholeness. Transporting Gump there, beyond the historical problematic of the bus stop, are his Nike running shoes; their resignification as a private commodity relation fulfills Nike's own corporate fantasy of an innocent (that is to say, nonexploitative) historicity.

In the figure of the shoes, then, lies the film's investment in the simultaneous transnational accumulation of capital in the aftermath of imperial war and the reinvigoration of a national symbolic, rescued now through the individual's pedagogical identification with the commodity (and conversely, the commodity's identification of the individual). As Gump is marked quite literally first and foremost by the trademark, the trademark becomes the film's earliest mechanism for ascribing to Gump a particularizing identity. It is, importantly, an identity that situates him from the outset beyond the specific national contestations of the bus stop, beyond any recognition or reception of the lingering meaning of the black woman's utterance, "my feet hurt." Gump's debt, after all, has been paid; compensatory justice, imaginable only at the individual level, has been achieved; all that remains is the telling of the tale. If, in the film's formula, that telling takes shape as a walk through the archive of segregation and black-white racial relations, Gump's innocence, which is to say his rescued whiteness, "stands" on his inexhaustible and dematerialized relation to the commodity.[26] As Gump declares about his chocolates, "I could eat about a million and a half of these."

White Studies in Forrest Gump's America

Forrest Gump's celebration of the white race traitor who defies the logic of segregation and the history of southern racism in order to participate innocently in the new order of global capital is certainly a far cry from the ideals of whiteness studies, which focuses on an object of study whose power and privilege it hopes to critically undo. And yet, even as the popular and the academic move toward different political goals, they both begin their projects of rearticulating a postsegregationist white identity at the site of the historical. In *Forrest Gump*, this entails rendering the history of violent white power incomprehensible, if not comic—the Klan leader, remember, liked "to dress up in . . . robes and . . . bed sheets and act like . . . ghosts or spooks or something." Thus refunctioning the present as the origin for a new America no longer held in grief or guilt to a violently unredeemable past, the film confirms the ideological architecture of the contemporary anti-affirmative action movement. That is, it offers a white subject who becomes "particular" through a claim to social injury, thereby affirming not only that all historical racial debts have been paid (and hence that the historical is itself irrelevant), but that there is finally no privileged linkage between the protocols of universality and white racial embodiment. At the same time, of course, Forrest Gump, like John Howard of the Klan, can only be injured as a white (and male) subject from the symbolic location of the universal since it is the negation of the expectation or actuality of privilege that makes social injury for whites conceivable in the first place. By this, I mean that only from an implicit and prior claim to the universal can the particularity of white injury (and I am tempted to say the particularity of white identity itself) ever be articulated. Passing as a minoritized subject through the "non-sense" of the historical, the white subject thus reclaims its transcendent universality on the far side, we might say, of civil rights reform.

Whiteness studies, in contrast, turns with urgency to the historical to serve as the critical construction site for constituting a postsegregationist, antiracist white subject. In four regularly cited texts—David Roediger's *The Wages of White-ness* and *Towards the Abolition of Whiteness*, Theodor Allen's *The Invention of the White Race*, and Noel Ignatiev's *How the Irish Became White*—social histori-ans chart the effects of industrialization and with it wage labor on the racialization of ethnic immigrants in the nineteenth century. In doing so, they locate whiteness not in the epidermal "reality" of white skin, but in complex economic and politi-cal processes and practices. Key to the demonstration of the historical construc-tion of whiteness is the story of the Irish who left their homeland as racialized subjects of British colonial rule to become white in the course of nineteenth cen-tury U.S. life. As W.E.B. Du Bois diagnosed nearly a century ago in *Black Recon-struction*, whiteness emerges as the compensatory psychological and public "wage" that enabled various groups, especially the Irish—often called the "black Irish"—to negotiate a social status simultaneously distinct from and opposed to that of the slave or ex-slave. For Roediger this negotiation is a tragic failure of insur-gent class consciousness, since much of the force behind the discursive racializa-tion of the Irish as black arose from their large occupation of unskilled and domestic labor. "Whiteness was a way in which white workers responded to a fear of dependency on wage labor and to the necessities of capitalist work discipline" (*Wages*, p. 13). By paying close attention to the Irish's own struggle against the neg-ative racialization that accompanied their lower class status in the United States, Roediger demonstrates how "working class formation and the systematic devel-opment of a sense of whiteness went hand in hand for the US white working class," so much so in fact that the very meaning of "worker" would be implicitly under-stood as "white" by the end of the century (*Wages*, p. 8).

While some scholars disagree with Roediger's tactic of emphasizing the Irish's active pursuit of white identity—Allen, for instance, says the Irish were "bamboozled" by the ruling class (p. 199)[27]—much of the work in the proliferating archive of whiteness studies depends for its political force on the disciplinary legacy of labor history put into play by Roediger. Taking conscious political action and the centrality of the subject as an agent and not simply an object of history, labor his-tory, Roediger explains, "has consistently stressed the role of workers as creators of their own culture [and therefore] it is particularly well positioned to understand that white identity is not merely the product of elites or of discourses" (*Abolition*, p. 75–76). In this retrieval of the historical as the site of human agency, Roediger jump starts, we might say, the critical project of imaging an antiracist white subject in the present, for if whiteness is historically produced and if its production requires something more than the physical characteristic of skin color, then whiteness as a form of political identification, if not racial identity, can be abolished. As James Baldwin puts it, in a line that has become a banner for whiteness studies as a field, "As long as you think you are white, there's no hope for you."[28]

This stress on the active process of "unthinking" whiteness as a structure of power and privilege is certainly a compelling counter to the unconscious white subject celebrated in *Forrest Gump* and it offers, through the political project mapped by labor history, a means to refunction working-class struggle as cross-racial alliance. But once the theoretical precepts of labor history become installed as the governing disciplinary apparatus of whiteness studies—that is, once the historical retrieval of agency and the story of prewhite ethnics who choose whiteness in the tense interplay between race and class come to define the possibility of the antiracist white subject—the field begins to generate a range of contradictory, sometimes startling effects. The most critically important include: (1) an emphasis on agency that situates a theoretically humanist subject at the center of social constructionist analysis; (2) the use of class as the transfer point between looking white and believing you are white; (3) a focus on economically disempowered whites, both working class and poor, as minoritized white subjects; and (4) the production of a particularized and minoritized white subject as vehicle for contemporary critical acts of transference and transcendence, which often produces a white masculine position as discursively minor. Each of these effects must be read further in the context of the contemporary academy, where the assault against affirmative action has been aggressively pursued in a climate of employment scarcity and corporate downsizing. Such economic constrictions are crucial to understanding why the critical apparatus being forged in whiteness studies bears the unconscious trace of the liberal whiteness its reclamation of history so strenuously seeks to disavow. For in the particularity of the prewhite ethnic, whiteness studies reverses the historical process of white construction, offering for the contemporary white subject a powerful narrative of discursively black ethnic origins. History, in other words, rescues contemporary whiteness from the transcendent universalism that has been understood as its mode of productive power by providing prewhite particularity, which gets reproduced as prewhite injury and minoritization.

To trace the critical turns I have narrated above, where the social construction of whiteness is located at the historical origin of "discursive blackness," I want to begin with a brief passage at the end of Roediger's introductory comments in *Towards the Abolition of Whiteness*. Here, in an economist language of investment and divestiture, Roediger hopes to inspire working-class whites to give up the compensatory psychological and public wage of whiteness by forging class-based political identifications with people of color:

> we cannot *afford* to ignore the political implications [that] . . . whites are confessing their confusion about whether it is really *worth* the effort to be white. We need to say that it is not *worth* it and that many of us do not want to do it. Initiatives [should] . . . expos[e] how whiteness is used to make whites settle for hopelessness in politics and misery in everyday life. . . . Our opposition should focus on contrasting the *bankruptcy* of white politics with the possibilities of nonwhiteness. We should point out not just that whites and people of color often have common economic *interests* but that people of color currently act on those *interests* far more consistently . . . precisely because they are not burdened by whiteness. (pp. 16–17, emphasis added)

Casting whiteness as the burden that prevents working-class whites from identifying their real interests, Roediger differentiates identity from identification in order to redirect the "possessive investment in whiteness" toward political allegiances with those designated as "nonwhite."[29] Such identificatory mobility is central to the social constructionist project, countering what we might think of as the political and theoretical *immobility* of an essentialized subject. For when looking white and being white are collapsed, white identity becomes saturated with, if not wholly indistinguishable from, political identifications with white supremacy. To pry apart this essentialized relation, Roediger emphasizes the mobility of political identifications, and in doing so he claims economic marginality as the political location for the production of the antiracist subject. Such marginality is a space of prior occupation, where those "unburdened by whiteness" already, epistemologically speaking, live. Working-class whites need to "cross over" there, to trade against the faulty essentialist confederacy between white power and white skin, in order to discover the class "interests" that are already theirs. In using class as the mechanism for this transportation, Roediger's critical model passes through the prewhite ethnic to a complex citing of cross-racial economic affinities to secure a future of postwhite working-class struggle.

In the context of my conversation about the trope of mobility in *Forrest Gump*, the theoretical moves articulated here reverse the political investment but not the spatializing logic that accompanies the popularized race traitoring white subject in the postsegregationist era: it is the white subject who crosses the segregationist boundaries of both knowledge and political identification, while people of color remain politically identified with the social margins where the relation between race and class is more intimately, one hesitates to say more essentially, interested. The force of social construction as a theoretical vocabulary for agency thus posits the agency of people of color as an effect of their social position as marginal; hence identifications and identities are identical. For the antiracist white subject, it is the incommensurability between racial identity and political identification that bears the fruit of the constructionist enterprise, enabling a claim to particularity that rewrites the universal as a burden that must be shorn. Marked as the difference within whiteness, the antiracist white subject becomes particular by asserting a political difference from its racial "self." Roediger names this difference "nonwhiteness," and in doing so, not only reconvenes an essentialized elision of white with racist, but demonstrates how overwritten is the antiracist subject by universal privilege itself. After all, the white subject's claim to nonwhite particularity can only be asserted from the position of the universal, as it is in the space of the universal and never the particular that the theoretical mobility of political identification by definition takes place. This is not to charge Roediger with the failure to provide us with a seamless model of the anti-racist subject, but to remark upon the way that the desire to combat white privilege seems unable to generate a political project against racism articulated from the site of whiteness itself.[30] In other words, only in becoming "nonwhite," only in retrieving a prewhite ethnicity can the antiracist subject be invented, and this is the case in much of the productions of both the popular and academic realms.

It is not a surprise, therefore, that the activist quasi-academic journal *Race Traitor* locates its antiracist project in "abolish[ing] the white race from within" (p. 2). Troping the emphasis on conscious agency drawn from labor history and finding political sustenance in individual narratives of race traitoring, the various authors collected in *Race Traitor* posit white abolitionism as necessary to "solving the social problems of our age" (p. 10). In the opening editorial to the Routledge volume which collects the first five issues of the journal, editors Noel Ignatiev and John Garvey describe the *Race Traitor* project: "The existence of the white race depends on the willingness of those assigned to it to place their racial interests above class [or] gender. . . .The defection of enough of its members . . . will set off tremors that will lead to its collapse. *Race Traitor* aims to serve as an intellectual center for those seeking to abolish the white race" (pp. 9–10). Guided by the principle *"treason to whiteness is loyalty to humanity"* (p. 10), *Race Traitor* envisions treason on a number of fronts, from verbal retorts to racist jokes or commentaries to interracial marriage to cross-racial identifications in politics, fashion, and music. "What makes you think I am white?" is the quintessential race traitor question, and its deployment in the face of the police is one of the most heralded abolitionist acts. As Garvey and Ignatiev write in "The New Abolitionism,"

> the cops look at a person and then decide on the basis of color whether that person is loyal to or an enemy of the system they are sworn to serve and protect . . . The cops don't know for sure if the white person to whom they give a break is loyal to them; they assume it . . . What if the police couldn't tell a loyal person just by color? What if there were enough people around who looked white but were really enemies of official society so that the cops couldn't tell whom to beat and whom to let off? . . . With color no longer serving as a handy guide for the distribution of penalties and rewards, European-Americans of the downtrodden class would at least be compelled to face with sober sense their real condition of life and their relations with humankind. It would be the end of the white race. (pp. 105–106)

In thus forging a "new minority determined to break up the white race," *Race Traitor* joins Roediger in constructing a model of the mobile antiracist subject whose conscious political production not only particularizes whiteness by citing its power, but does so in order to craft for economically disenfranchised whites a generative and ultimately antiracist class politics.[31]

If this description of *Race Traitor* suggests a coherent intellectual and activist project, it is important to stress that contributions to the journal vary widely in political content. This is due in part to the collective nature of the journal and to its mediation between activist and academic political sites. It is also a consequence, it seems to me, of the difficulties that abound in transposing nineteenth-century antislavery abolition into the paradigmatic site for constructing a contemporary antiracist subject. By affirming as heroic and antiwhite the work of such abolitionists as John Brown, leader of the failed slave revolt at Harper's Ferry, *Race Traitor* reinscribes the centrality of white masculine leadership even as it posits such leadership as historical evidence for the abolition of the white race. "How many dissident so-called whites would it take to unsettle the nerves of the white executive board? It is impossible to know. One John Brown—against a background of slave resistance—was enough for Virginia" (p. 13). Overly drawn to masculine models of armed retaliation, *Race Traitor* effectively evacuates altogether the feminist trajectory of nineteenth-century abolitionism, reproducing instead the white male Rebel as the affirmative subject of antiracist struggle. Such affirmation, situated in the context of essays about the Irish and prewhite immigrants, symptomatically demonstrates the oscillation between universal privilege and minoritized particularity that characterizes not only the history of white subject formation in the United States, but the critical apparatus of whiteness studies itself.

Race Traitor's implicit response to its own critical contradiction of abolishing whiteness in a frame of white masculine heroic narrativity is to situate the African American as the quintessential American. Ignatiev writes, "The adoption of a white identity is the most serious barrier to becoming fully American . . . The United States is an Afro-American country . . . Above all, the experience of people from Africa in the New World represents the distillation of the American experience, and this concentration of history finds its expression in the psychology, culture, and national character of the American people" (pp. 18, 19). Thus defining the abolition of whiteness as the precondition for becoming American, Ignatiev retrieves an American exceptionalist logic that displaces the historical white subject as the national citizen-subject for a narrative of national origin cast now as black.[32] In doing so, a metaphorical "America" of national longing supplants the materialist "America" through which state violence—physical, economic, and ideological—has guaranteed the juridical privileges of whiteness. Leaving aside the many ways this formulation eradicates a range of groups and experiences, it is significant how important to *Race Traitor* is the resignification of the nation as part of a reclamation of the "human." "It is not black people who have been prevented from drawing upon the full variety of experience that has gone into making up America. Rather, it is those who, in maddened pursuit of the white whale, have cut themselves off from human society" (p. 19). The abolition of whiteness reclaims the democratic possibility of human sociality, itself a characteristic of the resignified nation.

My focus on the language of nation and national identity is meant to recall the ideological work of *Forrest Gump* and its mobile protagonist, whose fantastic projection of a postsegregationist America entailed the literal and symbolic remapping of the American territorial nation. In Gump's claim to what Berlant calls "the normal," the white male subject reconstructs itself on the grounds of a fabled sentimentality, with all state-based debts paid and a reproductive future of politically uncontaminated subjectivity guaranteed. In *Race Traitor*, the editors seek not so much the normal but the "ordinary" as the contrast to the state: "the ordinary people of no country have ever been so well prepared to rule a society as the Americans of today" (p. 4). This is because, in Ignatiev's words, "few Americans of any ethnic background take a direct hand in the denial of equality to people of color" (pp. 16–17). The conscious agency that defines the becoming white of the prewhite ethnic is strategically dissolved in the present, where the ordinary person is theoretically divested of taking a committed interest in the perpetuation of white racial privilege. Indeed, whiteness, while the object under investigation and ultimate destruction, is exteriorized to such an extent that the conscious agency heralded as necessary to undo it has no theoretical hold on the interior constitution of the subject. In contrast to Roediger's work, there is here no psychological depth to whiteness as a social construction, merely an interpretative inscription based on skin that can be consciously refused:

> The white race is a club, which enrolls certain people at birth, without their consent, and brings them up according to its rules. For the most part the members go through life accepting the benefits of membership, without thinking about the costs. When individuals question the rules, the officers are quick to remind them of all they owe to the club, and warn them of the dangers they will face if they leave it. *Race Traitor* aims to dissolve the club, break it apart, to explode it. (pp. 10–11)

In dissolving the club, in revealing the "costs" of membership to be the failure of whites to be fully American, *Race Traitor*'s postsegregationist antiracist subject emerges, against the power of the state, as emblem of a coherent nation.

The construction of the antiracist subject in *Race Traitor* thus goes something like this: whiteness is understood as the consequence of a universalizing pact between white skin color and white club privilege, one that deprives white people of both a positive relation to humanity and to American national identity. White supremacy is less an effect of individual activities and ideologies than the consequence of institutions of state power, which themselves alienate the ordinary citizen who is neither directly nor enthusiastically involved in the oppression of people of color. In this way, *Race Traitor* assumes, as does Roediger, that cross-racial class alliance is the locus of more urgent and identifiable political interests for the majority of whites, although *Race Traitor* is dedicated to the possibility of a "minority" of traitors—not, as in Roediger, a mass class movement—to perform the work of abolishing white supremacy. This work involves making whiteness visible as a racial category by interrupting the "natural" assumption that people who look white are invested in being white. Race traitors must thus mark whiteness as a racialized particular in order to perform their disaffiliation from the universality that underwrites the category, where such performance is understood as the necessary claim to an antiracist subjectivity. This is, it seems to me, the performative force of the race traitor question, "what makes you think I am white?" which simultaneously and paradoxically refuses the position of the universally unmarked by ultimately claiming to no longer be marked by it. In asserting the particularity of white racial identity as preamble to refusing it altogether, the race traitor passes through both the universal and the particular in order to found a new minority of former white people. Counting on the power of individual disavowal of the juridical white subject of state power, *Race Traitor* reimagines an empowered humanist subject whose intent to repeal its own whiteness is consecrated as the central practice of antiracist struggle.

In *White Trash: Race and Class in America*, Annalee Newitz is especially critical of the reliance on self-consciousness that underwrites the new abolitionism in her essay "White Savagery and Humiliation." When *Race Traitor*, for instance, asserts its aim to abolish the white race by hailing those who are dissatisfied with the terms of membership in the white club, Newitz questions the self-congratulatory mode that enables whites "to critique themselves before anyone else does."[33] From her perspective, the problem with the abolitionist project is its spectacularization of white humiliation as a mode of political insurgency, since it is finally the specter of self-destruction that enables the abolitionist's heroic refashioning. As a counterstrategy, Newitz seeks to disaffiliate white racial identity from the practices and institutions of white supremacy:

> We are asked [by the abolitionists] to demonize whiteness rather than to deconstruct it . . . Social problems like unequally distributed resources, class privilege, irrational prejudice, and tyrannical bureaucracy which we associate with whiteness are just that—*associated* with whiteness. . . . They are not essential to whiteness itself, any more than laziness and enslavement are essential to blackness. . . . Informing whites that their identities are the problem, rather than various social practices, makes it sound like whites should die rather than that white racism should. The ideologies of white power which make some white people socially destructive are the symptoms of American inequality and injustice, not its principal causes. (pp. 149–150)

Disembodying white racial power by differentiating it from identity, Newitz pursues a deessentialized whiteness, one that can hold its own, so to speak, in the same grammatical gesture as the antiessentialist analysis of blackness. In the process, the empowered privileges of whiteness and the stereotypes that degrade blackness take on an analytical equivalency as whiteness is situated as an identity object in need of the same resignification that has accompanied civil rights and the black power struggle over and in the name of blackness. "While whiteness is undeniably linked to a series of oppressive social practices, it is also an identity which can be negotiated on an individual level. It is a diversity of cultures" (p. 148). Such diversity points toward the possibility, as Newitz writes with co-editor Matt Wray in the anthology's introduction, of "a more realistic and fairminded understanding of whiteness as a specific, racially marked group existing in relation to many other such groups" (p. 5).[34]

The desire for a critical paradigm that can approach both black and white on quite literally the same terms—in a mode of theoretical equal opportunity—shapes *White Trash* at a number of levels. For instance, when the editors write that whiteness is "an oppressive ideological construct that promotes and maintains social inequalities, causing great material and psychological harm to both people of color and whites" (p. 3), they inadvertently construct a mutuality-of-harm hypothesis that powerfully appends whites to the harmed position of people of color. This move co-joins the rendering of "white trash" as "not just a classist slur—it's also a racial epithet that marks out certain whites as a breed apart" (p. 4). The double reading of "white trash" as classist and racist is fundamental to *White Trash*'s articulation of itself as an antiracist project:

> Our anthology is intended as an intervention in this field [of whiteness studies], offering a critical understanding of how differences within whiteness—differences marked out by categories like white trash—may serve to undo whiteness as racial supremacy, helping to produce multiple, indeterminate, and anti-racist forms of white identity. (p. 4)

But how does one arrive at a notion that the class oppression that poor whites experience is also a racial oppression, and further that the very category of "white trash" can serve as a model of antiracist forms of white identity?

Wray and Newitz begin by noting that the term has been traced to African American origins, being deployed by slaves as a mode of insult and differentiation in relation to white servants. This origin story, they write, "in the context of black slavery and white servitude speaks to the racialized roots of the meaning of ["white trash"]" (p. 2). Racialized in what sense? As a mechanism of institutional power? As a force of subordination? The authors don't say, and it is in this failure to explore the nexus of power embedded in the origin story that allows "white trash" to be cast as a racialization with minoritizing effects. This becomes fully clear, it seems to me, in the introduction's quick turn to the "Eugenic Family Studies" of the late nineteenth and early twentieth centuries, where poor whites were medically investigated on models of genetic defect previously used to define black inferiority. But the authors do not cite the relationship between eugenics and the long traditions of scientific and medical renderings of biologically based ideas of African and African American racial difference; instead, their descriptive language of the consequences of eugenics on the enduring stereotypes of poor whites replicates—and comes to stand in for—stereotypes explicitly connected to racist images of blackness:

> The eugenic family studies . . . [were] used . . . as propaganda . . . [for] call[s] to end all forms of welfare and private giving to the poor . . . The stereotypes of rural poor whites as incestuous and sexually promiscuous, violent, alcoholic, lazy, and stupid remain with us to this day. Alarmingly, contemporary

conservative[s] . . . have resurrected this line of biological determinist thinking, blaming white trash for many of the nation's ills and . . . call[ing] for an
end of the welfare state. Indeed, the widespread popularity of Hernnstein and
Murray's *The Bell Curve* speaks to a renewed interest in U.S. social Darwinism as an explanation for cultural and class differences. (pp. 2–3)

The political valence of "white trash" in a slave economy in which servitude has
very different meanings for blacks and whites is compressed under the weight of
the eugenics model, and "white trash" begins to take on the significatory power
of a racialized minority itself: "Because white trash is a classed and racialized identity degraded by dominant whiteness, a white trash position vis-a-vis whiteness
might be compared to a "racial minority" position vis-a-vis whiteness" (p. 5).

The consequences of these critical moves are multiple: the insistence on
"white trash" as a minoritizing racialization simultaneously disarticulates racism
from institutionalized practices of discrimination based on a group's designated
racial status, while crafting for poor whites a position structurally comparable to
that of the racial minority. In doing so, an antiracist project for whites is inaugurated at the site of a harmed and discriminated whiteness. As the editors declare
at the outset: "Americans love to hate the poor. Lately, it seems there is no group
of poor folks they like to hate more than white trash" (p. 1).[35] In an important contrast to *Race Traitor* and the critical tradition offered by labor history, the eluci-
dation of the white permanent and working poor does not function here to
establish a mobile antiracist white subject who can transfer, through the inter-
estedness of class position, identification from the wages of whiteness to collective antiracist struggle with people of color. Instead, the model forged in *White
Trash* is one in which the psychological wages of whiteness defined by Du Bois
and taken up by Roediger are supplanted by emphasizing whiteness as a material
privilege—and one whose security has decidedly lessened:

As the economy and unemployment figures in the U.S. worsen, more whites
are losing jobs to downsizing and corporate restructuring, or taking pay cuts.
While it used to be that whites gained job security at the expense of other racial
groups, whiteness in itself no longer seems a sure path to a good income. (p. 7)[36]

In the context of the introduction's larger and at times deeply contradictory framework, the above assertion functions to produce the power of whiteness as a fully
(and seemingly only) materialized economic relation, hence when material advantage does not exist, one becomes a racialized minority, albeit within whiteness.
In measuring the comparable worth of marginality in this way, *White Trash's*
intervention into whiteness studies produces, we might say, a white identity formation that has no compensatory racial debt to pay.

What generates this compulsion for a minoritized whiteness that is not
"expensive" to people of color? Or more precisely, why does the production of a
minoritized whiteness become the seemingly necessary precondition for an
antiracist project? Part of the answer to this question is lodged, as this essay has

been suggesting, in the contradictions between universality and particularity that characterize contemporary postsegregationist racial formation, especially as particularity has become the invested sign for the creation of antiracist equalities. But particularity is not essentially antiessentialist, nor does it guarantee the white subject's disaffiliation from the powers and pretensions of universality. There is, it seems to me, no theoretical, historical, or methodological escape from the impossibility of the antiracist white subject, partly because the very focus on the subject has far too much of the universal at stake.

Objects of Study in Times of Scarcity

To think about whiteness studies as a field means, then, addressing its own social construction, which is to say that we need to consider how the various formulations of whiteness (as mobile class identification, as self-conscious becoming, as the minority within itself) are situated within contemporary formations of identity, politics, and knowledge. For if, in the Right's version of the popular realm, white men are rescued from a narrative of U.S. history contaminated by their privilege, whiteness studies seems to offer the Left's *hyperconscious* other side, likewise particularizing whiteness in order to transcend it. This is not to suggest a faulty analogy between whiteness studies and the liberal whiteness of Forrest Gump's America, nor is it to deny the enabling possibilities of forging a distinction between having white skin and identifying with white skin privilege. It is neither a dismissal of the significance of reading the historical record of immigration, labor, and slavery in ways that allow us to define seriously the social construction of whiteness, nor an endorsement of a monolithic rendering of whiteness that fails to attend to the complicated local practices through which ethnic identity has been racialized in majoritarian or minoritarian ways. It is rather an interest in the powerful complicities of disciplinary knowledge that leads me to question how the study of whiteness has taken shape, why it has become so invested in figures of disadvantaged whites, why it has been silent about the materiality of its own production in the academy, and why it emerges as a recognizable field in its own right—worthy now of a name that signifies off of and seems to form a symmetry with ethnic studies—at that point in its development when white scholars turn their critical gaze onto whiteness as an object of study.

I raise these issues not to dismiss the political desire that motivates so much academic labor on whiteness as an object of study but to emphasize that the possessive investment in whiteness, as Lipsitz calls it, has institutional form and force. Whiteness studies emerges, after all, in the midst of a devastating lack of employment in the academy, one that many commentators connect to the denationalization of education that has accompanied the dissolution of the Cold War. In the downsizing of the university and the proletarianization of its intellectual workforce, many of the privileges that have ensured the white hegemony of the intellectual elite have been called into question. New doctorates, especially in the humanities and social sciences, are finding themselves accepting part-time and nontenure track appointments, and it is not rare to hear both white faculty and graduate students declare that only people of color have escaped the employment crisis of higher education.[37] In addition, many of the disciplines that have upheld the centrality of the Anglo-European tradition (German, French, and Italian) are now under duress, so much so that a few universities are actually considering the possibility of collapsing these departments into a European area studies program. This, combined with the fact that the academy is leading the way in the institutional dismantling of affirmative action, necessitates not a dismissal of the university as extraneous to the political project of abolishing or transforming whiteness, but heightened attention to it.

Such attention begins, as this essay has suggested, by linking the discourses of the academy with the popular public sphere and by tracing the disciplinary discourses and methodological assumptions that have mobilized whiteness studies as an emergent field. I have done the former in order to evoke the historicity of the present that governs the representational forms of white supremacy and to trace those contradictions that reveal how critical explanations of the present are not inoculations against it but effects of and struggles with the present's insidious power. I have focused on the disciplinary discourses that have shaped the scholarly archive on whiteness and the subsequent field formulation of whiteness studies in order to establish a critical perspective on a seemingly new object of study, one whose status as such has been cited as its antiracist political guarantee. This critical perspective is necessary to disrupt the institutional knowledge investments that accompany every disciplinary gesture—those investments whereby the authority of knowers is established by the reproducibility of a chosen object of study. Legitimate objects are never exhaustible; they do not become knowledge objects as a means for their destruction. To consecrate the study of white racial identity and power as a field formation called whiteness studies (as opposed to its earlier operation within ethnic studies) is not to divest whiteness of its authority and power but to rearticulate the locus of its identity claims from the universal to the particular. It is this rearticulation that I have defined as the project of "liberal whiteness" in the popular sphere, and it has been its logic of intellectual and identitarian mobility that I have critiqued as the theoretical foundation of whiteness studies as an emergent field. For neither the epistemological status of whiteness as the implicit framework for the organization of what we know as the human sciences nor the epistemological status of white scholars as the authorized agents of institutional knowledge is called into question by a field called whiteness studies.

To render whiteness the object of study from within the province of a humanist subject now hyperconscious of itself thus mistakes the way that even radical traditions within modern knowledge formations are not innocently prior to but decisively and unpredictably implicated in the histories and inequalities of racial asymmetries and oppressions. The political project that generates knowledge formations and the political consequences of their generation cannot be unequivocally coordinated, which is to say that the social construction of white racial identities and ideologies that is the object of study in whiteness studies arises in the context of ongoing historical processes. These processes have reworked the relation between universality and particularity that constitutes the negotiated hegemony of white power and made possible new and powerful attacks on civil rights legislation—all as part of a contradictory reconfiguration of the public discourse of race and white racial identity in the postsegregationist era. Far from operating as the opposite or resistant counter to the universal, then, the particular is the necessary contradiction that affords to white power its historical and political elasticity. In this context, the political project for the study of whiteness entails not simply rendering whiteness particular but engaging with the ways that being particular will not divest whiteness of its universal epistemological power.

NOTES

1. I've drawn my information about the original Laurens controversy over the Klan Museum from Rick Bragg's "In a South Carolina Town, a Klan Museum Opens Old Wounds" (*New York Times*, November 17, 1996, p. 1:16). Subsequent twists and turns of the story are fascinating. Apparently, John Howard sold the Echo Theater to his Klan protégée, Michael Burden who, through his fiancée, was converted into an antiracist. When Burden sold the theater to the local black preacher, Rev. David Kennedy, Howard was given a lifetime guarantee that he could continue to run, rent-free, his museum. The museum is thus now housed in a building owned by an African American and it is his church that has taken in Burden, who has been routinely thwarted in his attempts to find steady employment in Laurens. See "Converted by Love, a Former Klansman Finds Ally at Black Church," *Washington Post*, Sunday, July 27, 1997, p. A3.

2. That being white is here a transaction of "race" into a money making business lends further credence to George Lipsitz's suggestion that white identity primarily constitutes itself through propertied investments, whether literal or imaginary. See "The Possessive Investment in Whiteness: Racialized Social Democracy and the 'White' Problem in American Studies," *American Quarterly* 47, no. 3 (September 1995): 369–387, for a discussion of how national policies in the twentieth century furthered the political agenda of white racial supremacy. For instance, FHA housing programs funneled money toward white Americans in the suburbs instead of into multiethnic urban neighborhoods, thereby restructuring in more segregated ways the racialization of social space in the second half of the twentieth century. See also George Sanchez's useful response to Lipsitz's article in the same issue, "Reading Reginald Denny: The Politics of Whiteness in the Late Twentieth Century" (pp. 388–394). In a somewhat different vein, see Cheryl Harris, "Whiteness as Property," *Harvard Law Review* 106, no. 8 June 1993: 1710–1791.

3. In *States of Injury: Power and Freedom in Late Modernity* (Princeton: Princeton University Press, 1995), Wendy Brown discusses the replacement of rights for freedoms in the national political lexicon, which has produced what she means by her title, political inclusion as a state of injury. Analyzing the broad scope in which injury-based claims have come to supplant conversations about freedom, she notes that even leftists have become "disoriented about the project of freedom," concerning themselves "not with democratizing power but with distributing goods, and especially with pressuring the state to buttress the rights and increase the entitlements of the socially vulnerable or disadvantaged" (p. 3).

4. On citizenship, abstraction, and the promise of the universal, see especially Michael Warner, "The Mass Public and the Mass Subject," in *Habermas and the Public Sphere*, ed. Craig Calhoun (Cambridge, Mass.: MIT Press, 1992), pp. 377–401.

5. In the period of nineteenth-century Reconstruction, the ranks of white supremacy swelled from the shared belief in the ascendancy of a new privileged blackness and with it white injury. See Edward L. Ayers, *Vengeance and Justice: Crime and Publishment in the 19th Century American South* (New York and Oxford: Oxford University Press, 1984), especially "The Crisis of the New South," pp. 223–265; and Glenda Elizabeth Gilmore, *Gender and Jim Crow: Women and the Politics of White Supremacy in North Carolina, 1896–1920* (Chapel Hill: University of North Carolina Press, 1996), especially pp. 77–89 and 94–99.

6. Jessie Daniels's *White Lies: Race, Class, Gender, and Sexuality in White Supremacist Discourse* (New York and London: Routledge, 1997) provides an analysis of the documents of contemporary white supremacist organizations, exploring in particular the language of "victimization." See especially pp. 35–43.

7. Richard Dyer, *White* (London and New York: Routledge, 1997), p. 2.

8. And yet, in seeking for whiteness a particularity that can counter its universal status, Dyer also figures whiteness as "too specific." He writes, "white people—not there as a category and everywhere everything as a fact—are difficult, if not impossible, to analyse *qua* white. The subject seems to fall apart in your hands as soon as you begin. Any instance of white representation is always immediately something more specific—*Brief Encounter* is not about white people, it is about English middle-class people; *The Godfather* is not about white people, it is about Italian-American people; but *The Color Purple* is about black people, before it is about poor, southern US people" ("White," *Screen* 29, no. 4 [Autumn 1988]: 46). To the extent that Dyer's description of the function of the ideology of whiteness as infinite particularity counters the theoretical assumption grafted from it—that whiteness is the category of invisibility and nonparticularity—the theoretical articulation of whiteness has been stalled in the collapse of two registers of analysis: (1) the description of the effect of white identity formation that improperly served as its theoretical formulation and (2) a theoretical formulation that cannot render the historical specificity and material production of its description.

9. Two decades ago, Stuart Hall provided the theoretical language for this observation in his writings about the Caribbean: "Most societies with complex social structures achieve their 'unity' via the relations of domination/subordination between culturally different and differential strata. What we are required to 'think' is the nature of the differences which constitute the specific 'unity' and complexity of any social formation. The 'unity' of a social formation is never a simple, undifferentiated unity. Once we grasp the two ends, so to speak, of this chain—differentiated specificity/complex unity—we see that we are required to account, not simply for the existence of culturally distinct institutions and patterns, but also for that which secures the unity, cohesion and stability of this social order in and through (not despite) its difference" ("Pluralism, Race and Class in Caribbean Society," in *Race and Class in Post-Colonial Society: A Study of Ethnic Group Relations in the English-Speaking Caribbean, Bolivia, Chile and Mexico* [Paris: UNESCO, 1977], p. 158).

10. Many of the more reactionary reformations of white power and privilege currently go undetected by whites, from white suburban flight and the proliferation of gated communities to the privatization of institutions of higher learning and the growth of the prison industry, from the English-only movement to the resurrection of states' rights, from bans on public welfare for immigrants to pro-capital international trade agreements. Instead Mr. Howard's Klan and its spawn are taken as *the* American practice of white supremacy in total, which is just one of the many ways that the reconstruction of civil rights Reconstruction has been accomplished.

11. See Howard Winant, "Behind Blue Eyes: Whiteness and Contemporary U.S. Racial Politics," in *Off White: Readings on Race, Power, and Society*, ed. Michelle Fine, Lois Weis, Linda C. Powell, and L. Mun Wong (New York and London: Routledge, 1997), p. 40. Subsequent quotations will appear parenthetically in the text.

12. See Theodore Allen, *The Invention of the White Race* (London and New York: Verso, 1994); Jessie Daniels, *White Lies: Race, Class, Gender, and Sexuality in White Supremacist Discourse* (New York and London: Routledge, 1997); Michelle Fine, Lois Weis, Linda C. Powell, and L. Mun Wong, eds., *Off White: Readings on Race, Power, and Society* (New York and London: Routledge, 1997); Ruth Frankenberg, *White Women, Race Matters: The Social Construction of Whiteness* (Minneapolis: University of Minnesota Press, 1993); Mike Hill, ed., *Whiteness: A Critical Reader* (New York: New York University Press, 1997); Noel Ignatiev, *How the Irish*

Became White (New York: Routledge, 1995); Noel Ignatiev and John Garvey, eds., *Race Traitor* (New York and London: Routledge, 1996); Ian F. Hanny Lopez, *White By Law: The Legal Construction of Race* (New York: New York University Press, 1996); Eric Lott, *Love and Theft: Blackface Minstrelsy and the American Working Class* (New York and Oxford: Oxford University Press, 1993); Fred Pfiel, *White Guys;* David Roediger, *The Wages of Whiteness: Race and the Making of the American Working Class* (London: Verso, 1991) and *Towards the Abolition of Whiteness* (London: Verso, 1994); Alexander Saxton, *The Rise and Fall of the White Republic: Class Politics and Mass Culture in Nineteenth-century America* (London and New York: Verso, 1990); Meg Segrest, *Memoir of a Race Traitor* (Boston: South End Press, 1994); Vron Ware, *Beyond the Pale: White Women, Racism, and History* (London and New York: Verso, 1992); and Matt Wray and Annalee Newitz, eds., *White Trash: Race and Class in America* (New York and London: Routledge, 1996).

The genealogies being constructed for the field by the academic press and within some of the scholarship are interesting in their omissions. Whiteness studies tends to be described as a project devoted to dismantling whiteness from a white perspective, which disturbingly disassociates scholarship from the various ethnic studies areas as being part of the scholarly archive on the social construction of whiteness. Early feminist work, as in *Yours in Struggle* by Elly Bulkin, Minnie Bruce Pratt, and Barbara Smith (Brooklyn, N.Y.: Long Haul Press, 1984), is also jettisoned from the new multidisciplinary scheme. These moves reconvene the logic of white masculinity as the generic subject even as the ideological hold of that subject is supposed to be under abolition. See especially David W. Stowe, "Uncolored People: The Rise of Whiteness Studies," *Lingua Franca* (September/October 1996): 68–77.

13. In private correspondence, August 18, 1997. My thanks to George Lipsitz for his thoughtful and thorough consideration of the issues raised in this essay.

14. For a fascinating analysis of black resistance to public transportation segregation in Birmingham during World War II, see Robin D. G. Kelley, "Contested Terrain," in *Race Rebels: Culture, Politics, and the Black Working Class* (New York: The Free Press, 1994), pp. 55–75.

15. I visited the Civil Rights Institute while in Birmingham to deliver the earliest version of this piece, which means that the juxtaposition between it and *Forrest Gump* originate in a kind of fruitful accident, as opposed to a definitive intertextual exchange. But it was in that museum, with its window—both a screen and a frame—looking out at the Baptist church that the implications of the film's technological mastery of television, its use of television memory as the vehicle for encoding and deflecting national crisis and struggle, and its long incomprehensible narrative deliberation on Gump's running trek across the nation began to make sense as tropes/motifs in the renarrativization of segregation from the vantage point of white masculinity.

16. As the red, white, and blue buses intermittently obstruct the camera's view of the bus stop, Forrest's narrative advances from his early childhood through his college career, his tour in Vietnam, his various business adventures which render him a millionaire, and back to the film's final resting place, the heterosexual reproductive domestic sphere. Each person who listens to Gump is keyed by race and gender to the significant events of his narrative: the black woman gets the story of Gump's physical and mental difference, the discriminatory treatment handed him, and his final transcendence of the leg braces; the white women each hear portions of the romance narrative, which culminates in Gump's marriage to Jenny; and the white male listens to the episodes of war and economic accumulation. Notable here is the absence of the black male as audience as well as the schematic representation of race as a singularly black/white affair.

17. Lauren Berlant, *The Queen of America Goes to Washington City: Essays on Sex and Citizenship* (Durham, N.C.: Duke University Press, 1997), p. 5. All subsequent quotations from this work are cited parenthetically in the text.

18. It's interesting to consider the backhanded compliment that the film offers to white southern men: on one hand, they are crafted as the bearers of a history which they can in somewhat heroic terms negate, but that negation is effected through a stupefying return to native unintelligence. This characteristic "stupidity" is itself a well worn stereotype of the southerner, playing a role in the ongoing tension between white particularity (constructed this time along the axis of region) and a normative liberal whiteness whose political, geographical, and ethnic origins are displaced.

19. The most extensive reading of *Forrest Gump* in the context of feminist analyses of gender is Thomas B. Byers's "History Re-membered: *Forrest Gump*, Postfeminist Masculinity, and the Burial of the Counterculture," *Modern Fiction Studies* 42, no. 2 (Summer 1996): 420–444.

20. This point is explicitly reinforced in the film through Gump's parodic commentary on the white bed sheets worn by members of the Klan. As the figure of white skin, the bed sheets can be cast off by Klan descendants, which means that the materialization of privilege symbolized by and invested in white skin has itself no necessary historical lineage. My thanks to Eva Cherniavsky for suggesting this reading of white skin.

21. Quoted in Cheryl Harris, "Whiteness as Property," *Harvard Law Review* 106 (1993): 1781.

22. More crucially, I am struck by the absence of the black male as a witness to Gump's story at the bus stop. Why this evacuation of the black male from the scene of the bus stop, this denial of his participation as audience for Gump's national tale? Why the spectacular use of the black male as the protagonist's twin, buddy double—Bubba—who seems destined to die? On one hand, the film's failure to imagine the black male as a witness to Gump's tale demonstrates the function of black male embodiment as the signifying means for constructing white liberal morality. Bubba's death offers to Gump the rationale for white retribution, a debt that can be paid. On the other hand, the film's positioning of Bubba symbolically feminizes blackness, as he comes to occupy the place of Jenny in the second scene of exclusion and outsider bonding on the school bus. It is Jenny, after all, who allows Gump a place to sit on the bus in the earliest scene when all the white boys have denied him room; when this racialized site is plumbed a second time, Bubba occupies the narrative space initially held by Jenny, and both of them by the end of the film die (Jenny from an illness implicitly framed as AIDS and Bubba in the Vietnam War). These deaths, as the deaths of the feminine and of the black male buddy, are crucial to *Gump*'s simultaneous claim to and transcendence of injury, since they mark specific bodies as the bearers of national trauma—Jenny, we see, travels through the antiwar and drug cultures of the 1960s and 1970s, while Bubba becomes the fallen emblem of the war—and they do so within a context that disaffiliates white masculinity from the historical power and privilege of its social and economic position.

23. On the broader contexts of the remasculinization of the white Vietnam veteran, see Susan Jeffords, *The Remasculinization of America: Gender and the Vietnam War* (Bloomington: University of Indiana Press, 1989).

24. Gump wears other kinds of shoes in the film, but the meditation on shoes that opens the film—and subsequent meditations on his mobility—revolve around the Nike running shoes. Even the advertisements for the film, both in theaters and on video, feature Gump in his Nike running shoes.

25. Gump's run, while denied an explanation in the film, begins the day after July 4—the day after Jenny has "run off" without explanation. In the final moves of the narrative, we will find out that it was their encounter on the Fourth of July that created "Little Forrest," thereby reinforcing the relation between paternity and the futurity of the nation.

26. I owe two notes of thanks here. One is to Eva Cherniavsky, who offered me an understanding of the material investment in whiteness as a relation of inexhaustability to the commodity. The other is to Patricia McKee, who discussed with me the way that whiteness needs to be thought of as a process of simultaneous materialization and dematerialization.

27. Jonathan Scott discusses the differences between Roediger and Allen in his review article, "Inside the White Corral," *Minnesota Review* 47 (fall 1996): 93–103.

28. As Roediger explains, "Complexity arises when we cease to regard racial and ethnic identities as categories into which individuals simply are 'slotted'. . . . James Baldwin's point that Europeans arrived in the US and became white—'by deciding they were white' powerfully directs our attention to the fact that white ethnics . . . by and large chose whiteness, and even struggled to be recognized as white" (*Abolition*, p. 185). See Baldwin, "On Being "White" . . . and Other Lies," *Essence* (April 1984): 90–92.

29. See Lipsitz, "The Possessive Investment in Whiteness: Racialized Social Democracy and the 'White' Problem in American Studies," *American Quarterly* 47, no. 3 (September 1995): 369–387.

30. One of the challenges of thinking about the antiracist subject in the contemporary period is precisely to imagine that subject's political practices within categories of racialization that

confer privileges based on color of skin. The current critical interest in rendering the visible unintelligible as a realist determination of racial belonging and self-definition, as Michael Berube would argue, does not undo the force of the visible as this culture's reigning logic, even if it unearths its faulty epistemology. No matter how many exceptional cases of passing and of non-white whiteness we can cite, it is the desire to make these paradigmatic for the material histories of racialized bodies that must be examined.

31. The quote here is from "What is 'White Trash'?" *Minnesota Review* 47 (fall 1996): 107.

32. "What is the distinctive element of the American experience?" Ignatiev writes. "It is the shock of being torn from a familiar place and hurled into a new environment, compelled to develop a way of life and culture from the materials at hand. And who more embodies that experience, is more the essential product of that experience, than the descendants of the people from Africa who visited these shores together with the first European explorers . . . and whose first settlers were landed here a year before the Mayflower?" (p. 19).

33. "White Savagery and Humiliation, Or A New Racial Consciousness in the Media," in *White Trash: Race and Class in America*, ed. Matt Wray and Annalee Newitz (New York: Routledge, 1997), p. 149. Further citations from Newitz's essay will be cited parenthetically in the text.

34. Matt Wray and Annalee Newitz, eds., *White Trash: Race and Class in America* (New York: Routledge, 1997), p. 5. Further citations from the introduction will appear parenthetically in the text.

35. In drawing attention to the discourse of injury, I do not mean to discount—and I feel like I need to say this in capital letters—the importance of analyzing the many ways that the white permanent and working poor are representationally "trashed" in U.S. popular culture. Nor do I mean to obviate the way that both Wray and Newitz remark in their introduction on the problem of a vulgar multiculturalism that attends to whiteness only as victim. But I do think that the introduction is contradictory enough that these caveats are not constitutively formulated within the project's theorization of the permanent poor; rather, the very risks that the authors note seem to be the foundational effects of their discursive practices.

36. In his contribution to *White Trash*, Timothy J. Lockley focuses on nonslaveholding whites in the antebellum period under a similar set of disturbing assumptions: "whiteness per se was not a ticket to the life of leisure. Living in a society which was based on a system of human bondage, and having little or no part in that particular system, gave non-slaveholding whites a unique social status" ("Partners in Crime," p. 59).

37. Evidence actually indicates the contrary. In a survey of recent recipients of Ford Foundation Minority Fellowship, 80 percent failed to be placed in permanent jobs.

Inderpal Grewal and Caren Kaplan

Warrior Marks: Global Womanism's Neo-Colonial Discourse in a Multicultural Context

Imperialism's image as the establisher of the good society is marked by the espousal of the woman as object of protection from her own kind.[1]

—Gayatri Spivak

In the past ten to fifteen years, the fields of colonial and postcolonial discourses have produced a by-now standard critique of objectification, essentialism, exoticization, and Orientalism as the representational practices of modern Western imperialism. That is, an oppositional power relation between colonizer and colonized has come to be understood as a crucial dynamic at work in the disciplines, institutions, subjects, and practices of modernity. Less understood or less examined in the interdisciplinary cultural studies of colonial and postcolonial discourses are the power relations between the different hybrid subjects produced during centuries of imperialism and modernity. Thus, the center-periphery model, or West/non-West binary, is inadequate to understand contemporary world conditions under globalization: the relations among gendering practices, class formations, sexual identities, racialized subjects, transnational affiliations, and diasporic nationalisms. Constructing monolithic notions of Western and non-Western subjects in binary opposition cannot always account for the complex, hybrid, and often contradictory subject positions that mark the era of postmodernity.

We begin with this premise in order to understand the practices, womanist and feminist, that underlie *Warrior Marks* (1993), a film directed by Pratibha Parmar and produced by Alice Walker. Since its first screenings, responses have ranged from celebration to angry denunciation. It has been hailed, on the one hand, as a film that brings to light the misogynistic practice of female genital mutilation and, on the other hand, it has also been condemned as a colonialist narrative that depicts African women as victims of their own culture, a "postcolonial civilizing mission," as Rogaia Mustafa Abusharaf calls it.[2] Sorting through these divergent responses helps us understand the contemporary transnational formations through which sexuality, race, and gender create new subjects. Under globalization, by which we mean the expansionary economic and cultural processes of advanced capitalism, these subjects participate in the construction of an identity politics that draws upon both Euro-American cultural and global feminisms to articulate an antiracist multiculturalism. Such a multiculturalism, as evidenced by the Walker–Parmar film, remains embedded in the practices of Western modernity. The modernity of this multicultural subject lies in the humanist metaphysics and liberal political formations that comprise its liberatory agenda. In *Warrior Marks*, this modernity produces a global womanism—the belief that the intersection of race and gender creates a homogeneous colonized female body as well as the conditions for the liberation of that body. The Walker–Parmar film assumes that a Euro-American multicultural agenda travels freely across national boundaries. Thus, we need to understand multiculturalism in a transnational perspective in order to come to grips with this relatively under-recognized legacy of colonial discourses at work in contemporary Euro-American feminist and womanist practices.

In *Warrior Marks*, a film made presumably with the very best intentions by two committed feminist activists of color, the articulation of a global version of womanism derived from Euro-American cultural feminism results in a neo-colonial representational practice. U.S. cultural feminism constructed an unproblematic narrative of liberation based on a universalized and essentialist identity as woman. This form of cultural feminism, as it has been practiced in the United States and in Europe from the 1970s to the present, often turns its attention to global sisterhood when faced with the dilemma of transnational feminist politics. This form of global feminism, as Chandra Mohanty and others have pointed out, can result in imperializing and racist forms of "knowing" those constituted as "others."[3] Our task in this essay is to investigate the complex positionality of the subjects constructed through this representational practice. In order to analyze the contemporary reach of what we call multiculturalism's global sisterhood, we will examine the genealogies of these practices in colonial discourses about women.

As Martin Jay has argued, within Western modernity's "scopic regime" the visual plays a primary role in communication and the institutionalization of knowledge.[4] Western ethnographic and documentary film traditions are fully implicated in the empiricist, realist, and positivist ideologies of modernity, ideologies that Walker and Parmar rely upon in their multiculturalist project. While scholars have begun to examine the ways in which multiculturalism has been co-opted and commodified (limiting its oppositional possibilities),[5] we argue that in a transnational framework, U.S. multiculturalists cannot address issues of inequalities and differences if they presume the goal of progressive politics is to construct subjects, feminist or womanist, that are just like themselves.

Multiculturalism's Global Sisterhood: Reading *Warrior Marks*

After several decades of struggle and resistance to ethnocentric and Eurocentric articulations of feminism, multicultural feminism and its variants such as womanism and global womanism have achieved considerable recognition as feminist practices in the United States. Even within the enabling and demystifying paradigms of feminist multiculturalism, a tendency to elide geopolitical considerations and to promote a universalized identity for women of color can also produce points of alliance with colonial discourses. When Euro-American feminist multiculturalism links with colonial discourses that articulate binaries of tradition and progress, for example, or civilized and barbaric, a powerful form of neo-colonialism recurs in activist and progressive representational practices.

The film *Warrior Marks* and its accompanying coffee table print version, *Warrior Marks: Female Genital Mutilation and the Sexual Blinding of Women*, are recent examples of contemporary Euro-American multicultural feminism in its imperializing vein as global womanism.[6] Proposing "benevolent" rescues and principled interventions, *Warrior Marks* advocates a return to the interlocking traditions of missionary projects, modernizing practices, and global sisterhood. Claiming to demystify a practice from faraway lands that appears to have origins deep in a patriarchal past, the *Warrior Marks* texts remystify genital surgeries in Africa, creating conventional subjects of an anthropological gaze already well-known to Western viewers through ethnographic and documentary cinema and their popular and mainstream counterparts.

Ethnography, as Claude Lévi-Strauss defined it, represents "societies *other* than the one in which we live."[7] This displacement from the location where we live to a gaze upon a place where others can be observed forms a foundation for representational practices and discourses under the sign of modernity. The ethnographic impulse, that is, the authority conferred upon the observer by modernity's scopic regime, underlies the birth of cinema itself—the films of Lumière have been referred to as "direct" or "actuality" cinema, terms that can be linked to the rhetorical structure of classic ethography's reliance upon positivist realism.[8] The rise of modern science and its link to discourses of vision and rationality in the West inform the voyeuristic practices of ethnographic cinema in its documentary mode. Western subjects learn to see in a specific set of historically constructed interpretive regimes based upon discourses of unmediated visuality, scientific evidence, objectivity, and the real.[9]

Ethnographic film as an anthropological practice, David MacDougall has argued, has been defined by its intercultural and interpretive focus, in which foreignness, exoticism, travel, and adventure were necessary elements in constructing knowledge about others.[10] Visual anthropologists who produce ethnographic films become cultural brokers in what MacDougall calls "the economic exchange of global images."[11] While this tradition has been subverted and critiqued by anthropologists and filmmakers such as David MacDougall himself, Jean Rouch, Trinh T. Minh-ha, Laleen Jayamanne, and others, ethnographic cinema, as Fatimah Tobing Rony argues, continues a tradition of "pervasive 'racialization' of indigenous peoples."[12] Such a racialization, according to Rony, denies people of color "historical agency and psychological complexity."[13]

Warrior Marks not only relies on the positivist production of empirical knowledge as documentary testimony but recuperates the racialization and gendered othering of non-Western subjects from the ethnographic cinematic tradition. That the cultural producers of this work are two women of color raises important issues about new forms of racialization and power relations between women from First and Third World locations. While we have seen the appropriation and recuperation of positivist visual logics in Third World cultural production (for instance, in nationalist, anticolonial narratives),[14] what is new here is the construction of a global womanist project framed epistemologically by U.S. multiculturalism.

Given the particular intellectual and political trajectories of both Alice Walker and Pratibha Parmar, respectively, certain questions arise in relation to how *Warrior Marks* continues the tradition of ethnographic visual representation. Walker is best known as an award-winning novelist and antiracist activist who has refused the label *feminist* in favor of what she terms *womanist*.[15] Instrumental in moving U.S. cultural feminism into discussions of racial difference, sexual identities, and resistance to white supremacy, Walker is a primary figure in the U.S. women's movement in general and the movements of women of color in particular. Parmar, who began as an antiracist feminist activist in Britain, is an increasingly well-known independent filmmaker whose films have ranged from investigations of racialized sexual identity to profiles of well-known women of color writers and activists. Parmar's interest in coalitions with U.S. women of color and Walker's desire to address a topic with global dimensions has led to a collaboration that presents the tensions that arise in multicultural feminism's imbrication within racialized diasporas.

The collaboration between Walker and Parmar forms a compelling and complicated coalition between a U.S.-based writer and cultural figure who has struggled to make a space for African American women's concerns and a British filmmaker whose family's diaspora includes South Asia and East Africa and who has made a commitment to lesbian feminist and antiracist cultural production. Their process of building an alliance and finding a method of working together is powerfully depicted in the print text of *Warrior Marks*. Consequently, in discussing Walker and Parmar's collaborative work, we need to refer to both the film and the print text. The book *Warrior Marks* records the production of the entire project in both narrative and glossy visuals, giving more context for the project as a whole and adding appendixes that document resources. The print text, then, is interesting in and of itself even as it comments self-reflexively on the production of the film. Framed by maps of West Africa, the book utilizes epistolary devices, organizing sections around letters sent between Walker and Parmar throughout the pre- and post-production periods. In this text, the narration is evenly divided between Walker, the film's producer and narrator, and Parmar, the director. A third section of the book is devoted to interviews, informational tables, networking information, and other appendixes. This section attempts to provide the voices of other women, including African and European activists as well as native informants. In this sense, the print text differs significantly from the film, providing the kind of production information that is edited out of conventional film products. Nevertheless, both texts adhere to a set of ideological and discursive formations that produce specific subjects; in this case, victimized females in rural Africa and their First World saviors.

Because Walker and Parmar's work has helped to shape both multicultural and antiracist feminist practices, the emergence of colonial discourse in their collaborative texts raises important questions for many of us who share their political concerns. Thus, the problem is not that Walker and Parmar are not "poststructuralists" or "postcolonial theorists"—Parmar is the author of a significant contribution to feminist postcolonial theory and Walker is a well respected public intellectual.[16] Our critique does not cast them outside our fields but, rather, seeks to situate our feminist arenas of activism and political struggle within a transnational framework of cultural production that can never be seen to be apart from the politics of representation. As producers of representations, Walker and Parmar can be held accountable for their choices of genre, format, and discursive practices. Since they chose a documentary form for their film, intending to use the techniques of montage, interview, voice-over narration, and travelogue to make a political statement about a set of practices in a distant location, we read the text as feminist cultural critics of the history of modern imperialism. Consequently, we are concerned that such interventions, since they rely on colonial tropes, cannot be effective because they do not provide a sociocultural and historical context in which activism, as the intersection of gender and agency, can become possible.[17]

The project of *Warrior Marks* is circumscribed at the outset by its rhetorical strategy of global womanism. Given the history of discussions of female genital surgeries in Africa in the anthropological literature and the Western cultural feminist discourses of human rights and domestic violence, the multicultural feminist or womanist approach to the topic cannot escape a colonial legacy. In the history of the multitudinous ways in which the female gender is produced in various cultures, female circumcision has been given an overwhelming and problematic attention in the West.[18] The value-laden terminology justifies and rationalizes interventionist narratives and practices. The surgical removal or alteration of women's genitals is referred to by a range of terms, including circumcision, excision, genital mutilation, and clitoridectomy. FGM, the acronym for female genital mutilation, has come to stand for the surgical practice itself in many U.S. feminist/womanist communities. Given that terms are always political and contingent, we are opting to use the phrase *genital surgeries* following

Isabelle Gunning's argument that "mutilation" is ethnocentric and judgmental while "circumcision" is misleadingly benign.[19] The problem of terms marks the social relations that structure the sexual-, gender-, and geo-politics of these discourses. That is, each term is attached to a history of colonialism linked to Enlightenment concepts of individuality and bodily integrity, medicalized notions of cleanliness and health, sexualized notions of the primacy of clitoral orgasm, and cultural organizations of pleasure. Terminologies produce epistemic violence—the silencing and erasure that specialized language enacts in particular situations in reference to particular inequities.[20] Such problems of vocabulary characterize the fraught terrain of cultural commentary in international and cross-cultural contexts.

Alice Walker has been investigating female genital surgeries (although she would insist upon the term FGM) for many years. Her novel, *Possessing the Secret of Joy* (1992), revolves around a circumcised protagonist, picking up one of the narrative threads of *The Color Purple* (1982). *Warrior Marks* uses a documentary format to rally opposition to FGM and enhance the international activist movement for its abolition. In the film, Walker interviews women in Europe and Africa to demonstrate the destructive effects of FGM and to draw a connection between violence against women in general and this practice in particular. The film advocates a global sisterhood composed of diverse women of color living in the United States and Europe intervening in order to "save" the lives of women and girls in Africa and African immigrant communities in the First World.

In the print text, Walker outlines clearly her personal stake in this project when she discusses her understanding of the metaphorical link between various kinds of "patriarchal wounds." Drawing upon her own experience of violence in a family setting, Walker describes a terrible childhood trauma. Her brother aimed his b-b gun straight at her and struck her in the eye. In Walker's recounting of this frightening event, it is clear that her injury was as deeply psychic as it was physical. Her mother and father's distanced response to her pain and fright only compounded her sense of betrayal and danger. Walker makes a direct association between this betrayal and the role that African mothers and grandmothers play in FGM as reproducers of the legitimating ideology and as colluding participants. Her identification with the African victims of FGM is based on her own experience of the vulnerability of young girls in patriarchal families.

This logic of identification is used in the film to link Walker to the African women and children and to link the film spectators to Walker's point of view. Her practice depends upon a notion of interpretation whereby one subject comes to know another or others based on a perceived similarity that precludes any self-consciousness of the contingent and power-laden nature of relations between women. In *Writing Diaspora*, Rey Chow argues that several strands of the word *identification* are at stake in the politics of identifying "authentic" natives: "How do we identify the native? How do we identify with her? How do we construct the native's 'identity'? What processes of identification are involved? We cannot approach this politics without being critical of a particular relation to *images* that is in question."[21] *Warrior Marks* utilizes visual colonial tropes not only to identify the natives but also to enable Walker herself, as narrator, to identify with this native. Doris Sommer has argued that a romanticized identification with cultural Others can be "the ultimate violence" as appropriation and can foreclose the possibility of any political alliance or solidarity across identities.[22] Thus, Walker legitimates her view of African genital surgeries by projecting her own tragedy— her brother's assault and her injured eye—onto the bodies of women whom she perceives to be in peril from patriarchal violence. "I chose to be part of the subject of *Warrior Marks* and not a distant observer because I wanted to directly align myself with genitally mutilated women," Walker explains. "Like them, I knew I had a patriarchal wound."[23]

Without taking away from the horror of attack by a family member, how can an analogy be made between such different practices and events? Each has their own complex articulation within a specific patriarchy and a particular historical context that includes race, nation, gender, class, and other social factors. Walker's experience of violence can be read through the lens of a male dominance that is complexly sanctioned within a nuclear and extended family both shaped and constrained by histories of racism and class among other social forces at work in the American South. Her identification with the "victims" of female genital surgeries does not inform us about the nuanced relations between men and women, between women and women of different classes, ages, nations, ethnicities, and their differential participation in modernity in contemporary Africa. Like so many acts of identification, it enacts its own epistemic violence and erasures.[24]

As a representational strategy, "identification" requires an elision of material difference in favor of a fantasized similarity. In her section of the print text, Parmar describes how working on the project caused her to become increasingly emotionally swept up into Walker's point of view. She reports that once she arrives in Africa, she wakes up screaming from dreams that she is in danger of being infibulated. This aura of terror and helpless victimization pervades the entire film, contradicting some of the footage itself (which shows local women looking healthy and happy), and punctuating the dry, documentary reportage of health workers, doctors, and activists. Throughout the film, a dancer is used to demonstrate the filmmakers' emotional projections of terror onto the symbolic body of the African victims. The visual logic brings viewer and dancer together into a state of fused identification.

Based in part on these kinds of techniques, the film has generated strong and deeply felt support within particular feminist communities in Europe and North America. The relatively widespread advance publicity and distribution of the film and print text can be attributed to Walker's popularity as a novelist and cultural figure as well as to Parmar's growing reputation as an independent filmmaker. For example, *Warrior Marks* has been picked up for distribution by the influential Women Make Movies group, and flagged for special attention beyond their general catalogue in special flyers on the subject of global feminism tied to the 1995 UN Beijing Women's Conference. We attended the screening of the rough cut of the film at the 1993 San Francisco Gay and Lesbian film festival, where a capacity crowd enthusiastically applauded the presentation of a special director's award to Pratibha Parmar. Similarly large crowds greeted with strong emotion the film's opening in several metropolitan locations in the United States. The journalist who covered the Washington, D.C. premiere at Howard University for the activist publication *off our backs* described an auditorium-size audience "openly weeping" and "spontaneously cheering," for instance.[25]

The reception of the film in print has been divided between the global womanists (many of whom identified with the film's construction of universalized racial and sexual communities) and those who critiqued the neo-colonial representational practices of the film (many of them Africanists). The film was reviewed positively in most U.S.-based feminist and lesbian-feminist publications, where the global womanist viewpoint was overwhelmingly valorized.[26] The enthusiastic support for the film, reflected in the reviews, may come from an affirmation of the Parmar–Walker project which, at the moment that it constructs the African woman as silent victim or global womanist/feminist, constitutes Western subjectivities. This imperialist subject is affirmed by the film's recuperation of the civilizing project of colonialism within which the figure of the colonized woman as silent victim played a key role.

Although the most prominent mainstream critique of the film appeared as an op-ed piece by Seble Dawit and Salem Mekuria in the *NY Times*,[27] other critiques have built upon earlier responses to Walker's previously published novel on the topic, *Possessing the Secret of Joy*. These reviews argue that Walker's overgeneralizing of African history and culture leads to errors of fact and the reproduction of long-standing stereotypes.[28] Most recently, a special issue of the *Case Western Reserve Law Review* that focused on female circumcision included detailed critiques of Alice Walker's work.[29] For example, while L. Amede Obiora argues that many Western representations of female circumcision ignore the diversity and complexity of this practice, Micere Githae Mugo focuses on Alice Walker's work as an example of a Western "external messiah syndrome" in which activism becomes an invasive practice imbued with unequal power relations.[30]

The Construction of Knowledge through Gendered Representations in Colonial Contexts

The "civilizing" practices of modern European imperialism have generated specifically gendered forms of colonial discourse within which the figure of the woman plays a key role in subject constitution. Practices that pertain to women's lives such as *suttee*, seclusion, footbinding, veiling, arranged marriages, and female circumcision have come to symbolize the "barbarism" of non-Western cultures.[31] Singling out such practices as moral anathemas, imperialist discourses condemn entire cultures. Feminist scholarship on colonialism has given us profound insights into the ways in which such isolated tropologies work to mystify histories of social relations, particularly interlocking patriarchal forms and the recastings of various hegemonic formations under colonialisms and nationalisms.[32]

More recently, gendered colonial tropologies are visible in the media as debates over the *hijab* (head covering), in attacks on Muslim fundamentalism, sensationalized accounts of sex tourism, and efforts to legislate against female genital surgeries. These representational practices produce images of Third World women as objects or victims who require First World assistance and direction. Within modernity, First World discourses of the Third World as well as nationalist discourses about its female or subaltern subjects continue such representational practices in a variety of historical contexts. When women are raped during a war, for example, their bodies function symbolically as metaphors for "nation," generating patriotic, patriarchal, nationalist responses.[33] Yet, at the same time, local domestic violence and physical abuse do not resonate within geopolitical recuperations of nationalism. For example, the high incidence of rape and domestic violence in the United States is not addressed as an international human rights problem in the mainstream press. Our point is not that any of these tropological instances are in and of themselves morally or politically defensible. Rather, their popular representation constructs a binary opposition between West and non-West that disallows an examination of the links between patriarchies in modernity and postmodernity.

For instance, female genital surgeries clearly need to be examined as a problematic social practice within the reconstruction of patriarchies in the context of decolonization. Yet, in Western contexts there is very little discourse on genital surgeries that does not reproduce social relations inherited from European imperialism.[34] Poor women everywhere, especially in the formerly colonized parts of the world, face limited health care and educational opportunities as well as the denial of economic and political agency due to global inequalities, rearticulations of patriarchies in specific regions, and the legacies of colonization. Western discourse on female genital surgeries does not incorporate these complex factors, but continues to direct a "horrified gaze" toward its colonial and postcolonial subjects.

In order to understand what is at stake in such a horrified gaze, we have to place female genital surgeries in the context of a long representational history in Western cultures. The ascription of such surgeries as a sign of non-Western "barbarism" requires the suppression of the history of this practice in the West, displacing these surgeries onto an ontological other.[35] This kind of displacement occurs in accounts constructed by colonial bureaucrats, missionaries, health workers, educators, anthropologists, and travelers throughout the nineteenth and twentieth centuries.[36] Such accounts form an important textual archive as well as a discursive practice of empire that disciplines colonized bodies in historically specific ways.[37] This process of othering has constructed colonizing subjects as well. Thus the colonial classifications of racial and ethnic types includes notions of whole and fragmented or mutilated bodies. The mutilated body is at once an object of fascination, desire, and repulsion, differentiating between colonizer self and colonized other.[38] European modernity utilizes horror, romance, and adventure genres to gain power and to construct a Western identity of a fixed and stable self.

The modalities of such knowledge are visible in the binary division between modernity and tradition, the identification processes of humanist subject formation, the construction of subjects and objects through "ethnographic authority," the descriptive and stylistic genres of cultural productions of "difference" as "otherness."[39] In this context, "knowing" can mean the violent imposition of one's values, perspectives, and agendas on those seen as mirrors of the self rather than as complex, historical subjects.[40] These identification practices proliferate in both visual and print traditions in Western modernity.

Reproducing Colonial Discourse: Global Womanism's Narrative and Visual Conventions

Feminist scholarship on colonial discourse has been crucial in pointing out the ways in which imperialist social relations produced the female subaltern as a specifically embodied subject situated in the Third World. Yet, the history of Western feminist ideas and practices includes imperializing and racist formations. Contemporary feminist scholarship on women travelers, for example, has been divided between celebrations of adventurous heroines and condemnations of racist "memsahibs." Such a division in representation can obscure the complicated class and ethnic distinctions that structure Western women's travel and immigration as well as the history of both pro- and anti-imperialist activities on the part of Western feminists. Enmeshed in either the romance of individual achievement over the rigors of travel or a nationalist resistance to European or North American traveling cultures, Western feminist representations of travel remain uneven, undertheorized, and deeply troubling. For instance, the presence of African American missionaries in Africa in the nineteenth and twentieth centuries requires more research into and discussion of these kinds of complex positionalities that cannnot be understood fully within the binary of colonizer/colonized.[41]

One of the primary technologies which Walker and Parmar use to convey knowledge is a map of their "travels." It is standard practice in colonial discourse to naturalize the social world through representation. Such maps, used in the broadest metaphorical sense, chart the flows of goods, resources, and peoples in the uneven trajectories of capital. *Warrior Marks*, markedly uninterested in class issues, makes a map of ethnic and racial diaspora that is superimposed upon a map of a unified and universal female body. This complex mapping of modern subjects conflates an African diaspora with a Western cultural feminist construction of woman to argue for a return to the mother country, to the body of the mother, to the source of female identity.[42]

This universalized body—whole, unified, and organic in relation to the circumcised body of the Other—forms the standpoint for the feminist practices visible in *Warrior Marks*. Such a standpoint prevents recognition of the ways in which Western patriarchies are inscribed on women's bodies through various technologies and disciplinary practices—breast augmentation, liposuction, rhinoplasty, tubal ligations, in vitro fertilization, mastectomies, hysterectomies, cosmetic surgeries—within the context of a lack of health care and reproductive freedom for metropolitan women, especially poor women and women of color.[43] Geopolitics and cultural asymmetries must be included in our analyses of the formation of specific sexed and gendered subjects in various locations. The histories and relations between such subjects are important topics of analysis in our struggle to deconstruct global feminist discourses. Western feminism's essentialist notions of bodies and sexuality pervade the globalizing discourse of sisterhood, through imperializing representations. *Warrior Marks* is only one such cultural product in circulation, generating neo-colonialisms in the name of multicultural feminism. One response to *Warrior Marks*, therefore, is to begin a discussion of the ways visual representations, identities, and subjects in modernity collude with the power relations of late capital's colonial ventures.

In the film *Warrior Marks*, the primary tropes of travel that centuries of imperialist economic expansion have engendered are easily identifiable. First and foremost, a designated area—here Africa—must be emptied metaphorically and made culturally blank.[44] Thus, the film depicts an overwhelmingly rural Africa peopled only by natives dominated by cultural tradition. *Warrior Marks* acknowledges a few African doctors and activists who work against the practice of genital surgeries but suggests that their actions are ineffectual and can only be strengthened by help from abroad. Both the film and the book present Walker and Parmar on a heroic mission to an Africa that is the site of unspeakable practices against its "women." Indeed, in its portrayal of Africa as a relatively undifferentiated space of otherness, *Warrior Marks* erases the histories of decolonizations and diverse formations of nation-states, including decades of "development," "modernization" programs, and localized strategies of resistance.

Instead, *Warrior Marks* prefers to deploy images that could easily be culled from the magazine pages or documentary footage of *National Geographic*.[45] The world the film conjures for its female heroines to travel through is one in which tradition is drastically differentiated from modernity. This distinction is drawn as a geographical map where some regions remain "dark," unenlightened, and thus more dangerous for women than others. In the print version, this map is rendered literally, complete with insets and scales in a manner reminiscent of such nineteenth-century travel accounts as Mary Kingsley's *Trav-*

els in West Africa.[46] The book is organized into sections that recount the "journeys" of Walker and Parmar. These journeys are further linked to a particular set of Western feminist conventions through the use of epistolary communications: "Dear Pratibha," the book begins.[47] The film also uses the letters between Walker and Parmar as part of its narrative strategy. But before the literary convention of the epistle fully structures our understanding of the film, we see and hear the most typical of colonial discourse tropes—we hear drumming and we see a muscular leg draped in a multipatterned fabric resembling native garb. We are from the first instant "abroad." More specifically, the drumming signals Africa to non-Africans raised on both Hollywood and standard ethnographic films. That is, we, the viewers, must be assumed to be people who are not living in western Africa—who are not at home there.

Although Walker's early intention was to make a film to educate and raise African consciousness about genital surgeries, she and Parmar soon discover financial and technical constraints—the cost of subtitling a film made in English and the lack of screening or viewing facilities, for example. In the film project, the rhetorical effect of "knowledge" must be produced in the face of a profound lack of information on the part of the filmmakers. African women in diverse locations and of different classes become subsumed under the category "African" as the film's shooting sites in Gambia and Senegal become generalizable to an entire continent and the specific practices of genital surgeries are universalized. Although Parmar and her assistant were able to spend only a week in Gambia researching locations and setting up contacts before Walker arrived and the two-week shoot began, the presentation of information in the text is asserted with great confidence as "fact." Yet, without local guides and with elusive and unreliable contacts, the film crew is literally lost; none of the visitors speaks the relevant languages, no one has spent time in these places before, and no one is knowledgeable about this part of Africa. While Parmar spent part of her childhood in Kenya, her adult life in England has not been focused on African topics or studies. By the grace of her research for her novel, *Possessing the Secret of Joy,* Walker becomes the production's "expert" on female genital surgeries. The relatively short pre-production period, the great distances and language barriers, and their difficulties in linking up with prominent activists such as Awa Thiam mean that such contacts are more haphazard than they are the product of long-term coalitional activity.

The mistrust of some local figures toward the filmmakers may be justified. For in order to create a global subject—woman—as victim of generalized patriarchal oppression, Walker and Parmar have to utilize both antifeminist and Eurocentric discourses in the form of authoritative texts. The "Selected Bibliography and Suggested Reading" that appears at the end of the print version of *Warrior Marks* is interesting in several regards. The key citations fall into categories such as African nationalists (Jomo Kenyatta), Euro-American popular sexologists (Masters and Johnson, Shere Hite, etc.), randomly selected and uncritiqued ethnographies (Marcel Griaule, Jacques Lantier), and African and Euro-American activists on women's health issues who are heavily identified with the fight against FGM. Absent from the bibliography are feminist histories of colonialism and nationalism or decolonization, critiques of ethnographic knowledge in general or the surgeries in particular, and sociopolitical accounts of the lives of women in Africa. While Walker and Parmar acknowledg that contemporary practices of FGM may be attributed in part to colonialism, such an acknowledgment disallows any infiltration or impact on their own thinking or ideological formation as Western subjects in modernity. The burden of an oppressive practice falls on an ahistorical "tradition" in an exoticized culture.

The appearance of a binary opposition between tradition and modernity is a primary paradigm of colonial discourse. As critics and historians including Edward Said, Talal Asad, Johannes Fabian, Gayatri Spivak, and Ella Shohat have pointed out, this binary division creates a logic for Western intervention because it constructs a view of modernity as a corrective to tradition.[48] Modernity becomes a signifier for a range of attributes, including the enlightened West, progress, civilization, democracy, self-determination, and freedom of choice. Tradition becomes the other by which non-Western cultures mark their own empowerment socially, politically, and culturally. It is only by deconstructing this binary opposition through historicization and contextualization that tradition and modernity emerge as constructs of a European worldview that emphasize a teleological and rational course over and above other modes of representing change, difference, and similarity. As two aspects of the same paradigm, then, the oppositional relationship between tradition and modernity masks the power of one term to describe and evaluate cultures that are designated as the "other."

Warrior Marks reinscribes this oppositional relationship that is so central to colonial discourse and Western, metropolitan subject formation. Rural Africa comes to signify "tradition," a destructive environment for women. In the film, the camera utilizes standard ethnographic shots to establish cultural difference. The gaze behind the camera penetrates the social space of the local people, moving in and out of doorways, searching for "secrets." The pivotal scene around which all these issues seem to revolve occurs in Walker's interview with an elderly female circumciser (who has no identity or name except "Circumciser 1" in both print and film texts). This scene summons many of the tropes of colonial discourse as it is interpellated through global feminism, especially the missionary discourse of eradicating ritual practices by outing them, by bringing light onto the subject, as it were.

Following Gayatri Spivak's and Rey Chow's examination of the representation of subaltern subjects in colonial discourse, this scene between Walker and the circumciser illustrates the way resistance and silence—often coded as "secrets"—challenge Western, liberal political formations.[49] In the interview, the elderly woman is portrayed as sinisterly witholding information from the interviewer, Alice Walker.[50] This witholding is presented as being crucial to maintaining tradition. Walker's telling, on the other hand, is seen as the key to liberating the prisoners of traditional culture. The struggle between Walker and the nameless Gambian circumciser is visually and textually presented as a moral victory for Walker's viewpoint. The camera focuses repeatedly on the crude blade the woman holds in her lap, suggesting its deadly and cruel uses. Many reviewers comment on the powerful impact of the struggle between the circumciser and Walker's efforts to force her to reveal her secrets. Indeed, the *San Francisco Chronicle's* reviewer refered to the elderly woman as "wizened" and "ominous" while applauding Walker's speech, here termed "giving the woman a piece of her mind."[51]

In this and other scenes, the film makes no effort to question ethnographic authority (as the films of Trinh Minh-ha or Laleen Jayamanne have attempted for over a decade) or to make dialogical or epistemological innovations.[52] An uncritical use of ethnographic texts builds upon the nineteenth-century literary tradition that Mary Louise Pratt refers to as "manners and customs description," constructing the native as object.[53] Walker and Parmer utilize ethnographic materials as "authoritative" when it suits their end. For example, in the print text at the end of the transcript of Walker's interview with "Circumciser 1," the reader finds a description of an infibulation from a 1978 medical thesis from the University of Bordeaux.[54] Parmar cites A.M.I. Vergiat's *Moeurs et Coutumes des Manjas* (1937) as the source of a ritual song sung by circumcised girls.[55] Many Third World and anti-imperialist feminist filmmakers and writers have struggled against the reproduction of ethnographic colonial discourses in cinematic and cultural practice, critiquing and resisting its representational strategies. The *Warrior Marks* texts reinforce and reproduce colonial discourse through an unproblematized reliance upon and alliance with "authoritative," Eurocentric studies.

In the standard colonial gesture of constructing a native through the operation of difference, the elderly circumciser in *Warrior Marks* is depicted as actively evil and passively deluded by tradition. Walker, the interviewer, on the other hand, throws off the mantle of objective questioner to reveal the enlightened metropolitan subject who "knows" all. In "Can the Subaltern Speak?" Gayatri Spivak calls the position and power of the investigator or interviewer into question in order to examine how the "third-world subject is represented within Western discourse."[56] Rejecting the liberal demand that all subjects constitute themselves through public "speech," Spivak argues that social and political movements cannot break the epistemological stranglehold of imperial culture by resurrecting the "shadows" of subjectivity, the categories that imperialism created. Without deconstruction, the "possibility of collectivity itself is persistently foreclosed through the manipulation of female agency."[57]

Read against the grain, as it were, the print text opens up some questions of knowledge production that could have been pursued in the film itself. For instance, "Pratibha's Journey," Parmar's section of the print text, chronicles, among many things, the contradictions and tensions that emerge in the representational politics of the project. Despite Parmar's increasing identification with

Walker's "vision," she expresses concern during pre-production and the shoot about making sufficient contact with local activists. Awa Thiam, for instance, remains relatively elusive for reasons upon which Parmar can only speculate. Parmar worries that if Thiam will not cooperate by leading the filmmakers to the "right" contacts in Senegal and elsewhere or by endorsing the project, their work will be hampered logistically and their credibility will suffer. Thiam, as it happens, is in the midst of a preelection campaign for the opposition political party in her country and does not seem able to drop everything to meet with Parmar. While Parmar presents this situation as Thiam's obstinate resistance, the text leaves the question open as to whether Thiam is playing the powerful diva/native informant or whether she is just a busy professional who has not been asked far enough ahead of time whether the film schedule would be convenient for her.

In an interview included in the print text, Thiam makes it very clear that she agrees with Walker and Parmar on the symbolic import of female genital surgeries. Since Thiam comes from a local group that practices, as she says, "80 percent female circumcision and sometimes infibulation," she views the situation as urgent and agrees with the filmmakers on the need to organize internationally. However, her analysis of the practice as an indication of women's subordination that is embedded within the power structures of particular societies leads her, after ten years of working in what she calls the "female circle," to "get involved in the sphere of politics," and to "succeed in convincing the decisionmakers, both male and female, and to try to struggle for the abolition of sexual mutilation."[58]

Thiam's move toward participation in electoral politics highlights the suppression of such sociopolitical and economic continuums in *Warrior Marks*. In addition to their fuzzy relationship to both state and nongovernmental structures, Walker and Parmar's texts erase many facets of transnational economic factors, mystifying the division of labor that makes possible, for instance, the funding of a film instead of a refrigerated truck. In the print version of *Warrior Marks*, the authors recount an extraordinary anecdote that describes a meeting between a group of women who run a collective garden and the filmmakers. Asked their feelings about FGM, these women respond by asking the "rich Americans" for a refrigerated truck they need badly to get their produce to outlying areas. The filmmakers, who do not perceive themselves as "rich" by their own cultural standards, joke that they could probably only pay for one tire for such a truck. The request for a truck is not mentioned again. This will to ignore or misrecognize information that does not seem to pertain to their own project marks the imperialist tendencies of this project. The power to set an agenda, to arrive uninvited in a country for a brief period of time, to tell people how they ought to feel and think about their sexuality and their bodies, to assume the right to rescue other people's children, and to use this experience as a yardstick of one's own freedom is standard operating procedure in the textual tracks of imperialism's cultural production. These gestures and moves are a historical legacy—*Warrior Marks* does not take the opportunity to unlearn or even to question this representational heritage and thus cannot do more than repeat its signs. As Chandra Mohanty argues in her critique of Western feminist discourse on female genital surgeries: "Sisterhood cannot be assumed on the basis of gender; it must be forged in concrete historical and political practice and analysis."[59]

Thus, Walker and Parmar make a film that speaks directly, vividly, and authoritatively to demand a change in the way people conduct their lives in particular locations. Their right to make this demand, apparently, comes through their superior ethical positioning—their "knowledge" of right and wrong—that is, they "know better"—as well as through an unquestioned adherence to Western medical science. This positivist ethics is conjoined with an appeal to liberal juridical practices, engendering a powerful set of philosophical, medical, and legal certainties in the effort to "civilize" in the name of a multicultural global womanism.

Multiculturalism's Globalizing Discourses

It is clear from the work of many scholars in recent years that what we call "imperial feminism" emerged during the nineteenth century to create simultaneously new feminist subjects in the West and their objects of rescue in the "periphery"— "sisters" with drastically different material conditions of life. The collusion between some Western feminist practices and colonial discourses has been amply documented in over a decade of emergent critical work. The advent of postcolonial theory constructed by diasporas of scholars who settled in Europe or North America created a new demand for increased attention to the aftermath of colonialism. Furthermore, the politicization of racial minorities through multiculturalism as a social and cultural movement in the United States has gained its voice through the articulation of rights claims against the modern state. These political and cultural movements inform feminist practices in metropolitan locations in a profound and complex manner.

With this complicated social and cultural field in mind, we might see figures such as Walker and Parmar, with quite different historical trajectories, coming together for a project such as *Warrior Marks* through their links with movements that have emerged through anticolonialist efforts. This means that Walker's concern with the aftermath of slavery in the United States and Parmar's participation in antiracist movements in Britain have contributed to a heightened understanding of present-day gender as constructed through colonized patriarchies around the globe. Multiculturalism, then, has been one way to demand the rights of citizens racialized as well as gendered in particular ways. Yet, when multiculturalism remains fixed upon state remedies, reinforcing national agendas and placing less emphasis on socioeconomic formations, the alliance between "women of color" may become strained.

To a certain extent this dilemma is being addressed by solidarity movements that draw upon a range of ideologies of cosmopolitanism and global unity.

Thus, the global and transnational are all interpellated by feminist subjects who also rely upon a discourse of multiculturalism. Yet differences between subjects of less powerful and more powerful states remain to be addressed. This process conflates the racialized subject of the state with the global feminist or womanist who constructs a universal woman as the paradigmatic female subject of global sisterhood. Thus, Walker and Parmar, in solidarity with this global woman, wish to rescue and include her in the privileges of modernity and its emergent sexual subjectivities and embodied practices. What drops out of this gesture is any recognition that this global woman exists only to reaffirm the metropolitan subject of feminism. The multicultural subject, as it is constituted through such a globalized practice of feminism, may be part of an antiracist strategy but its only space of negotiation is a modern nation-state.

In order to create a film that satisfies the demands of Western subjectivity and the ethnographic tradition, all the complex negotiations between the multicultural subject and the imperial state fall away so that what remains are the conventional colonial tropes—the very tradition of representation that leads to a racism that the multiculturalism project seeks to resist. To have made a less "popular" film, Walker and Parmar would have had to include many of the tensions and conflicts that emerge in the print text (even if only in passing), such as the links between an analysis of diverse surgical practices as gendered and racialized modes of subject constitution or the difficulty of forging alliances and gaining the cooperation of women activists in the regions of Africa visited by the film crew.

Warrior Marks is just one prominent instance of the difficulties of globalizing a multicultural feminist agenda. It is important to read the texts that come out of the political movements we are committed to not only in a celebratory manner but with an attention to these dilemmas in representational practice and politics. Our aim is not to destroy or take away important icons and cultural practices that support communities of resistance. Rather, we want to generate debate and discussion about our representational practices and politics. In many ways, the dilemma for twenty-first century multicultural feminists is similar to that faced by late-nineteenth-century national feminists—how to work with, around, and against the state. Asking for rights from the nation-state, representing others through identitarian practices, is an inevitable and necessary process for all social movements in modernity. But in acknowledging that inevitability, we should not abandon critique. These are challenges offered by the extremely difficult task of public policy formation and activist work. Our reading of an activist, multiculturalist feminist/womanist film and its accompanying print text is not, therefore, simply one of opposing aesthetic tastes or political correctness. Given that genital surgeries and refugee asylum claims based on FGM are now a matter of governmental debate in the United States and Europe,[60] it seems timely and necessary to examine the connections between discourses of human rights, racialized nationalisms, and multiculturalism in feminist and womanist frameworks.

NOTES

We would like to thank the many colleagues and friends who shared their own work, suggestions for research, and comments on our work in progress: in particular, Isabelle Gunning, Carolyn Dinshaw, Eric Smoodin, Ella Shohat, Sharon Willis, Jean Walton, Rogaia Mustafa Abusharaf, L. Omede Obiora, Kagendo Marungi, Jacqui Alexander, Donald Moore, Norma Alarcon, Minoo Moallem, Tani Barlow, Lisa Cartwright, Lisa Rofel, Cathy Davidson, Rebecca Jennison, and our students at San Francisco State University and UC-Berkeley (who gave us lots of excellent discussion, feedback, and support).

1. Gayatri Chakravorty Spivak, "Can the Subaltern Speak?" in *Marxism and the Interpretation of Culture*, ed. Cary Nelson and Lawrence Grossberg (Urbana: University of Illinois Press, 1988), p. 299.

2. Rogaia Mustafa Abusharaf, "The Resurrection of the Savage: *Warrior Marks* Revisited," paper delivered at the Pembroke Center for Teaching and Research on Women's seminar on "The Future of Gender," April 2, 1997, p. 2.

3. Chandra Talpade Mohanty, "Cartographies of Struggle: Third World Women and the Politics of Feminism," and "Under Western Eyes: Feminist Scholarship and Colonial Discourses," in *Third World Women and the Politics of Feminism*, ed. Chandra Talpade Mohanty, Ann Russo, and Lourdes Torres (Bloomington: Indiana University Press, 1991), pp. 1–47, 51–80. See also Norma Alarc=n, "The Theoretical Subject(s) of *This Bridge Called My Back* and Anglo-American Feminism," in *Making Face, Making Soul: Haciendo Caras*, ed. Gloria Anzalda (San Francisco: Aunt Lute Books, 1990), pp. 356–369; and "Traddutora, Traditora: A Paradigmatic Figure of Chicana Feminism," in Inderpal Grewal and Caren Kaplan, *Scattered Hegemonies: Postmodernity and Transnational Feminist Practices* (Minneapolis: University of Minnesota Press, 1994), pp. 110–133; and Inderpal Grewal and Caren Kaplan, "Introduction: Transnational Feminist Practices and Questions of Postmodernity," in Grewal and Kaplan, *Scattered Hegemonies*, pp. 1–33.

4. Martin Jay, "Scopic Regimes of Modernity," in *Modernity and Identity*, ed. S. Lash and J. Friedman (Oxford: Blackwell, 1992).

5. See Ella Shohat and Robert Stam, *Unthinking Eurocentrism: Multiculturalism and the Media* (New York: Routledge, 1994); Avery F. Gordon and Christopher Newfield, eds., *Mapping Multiculturalism* (Minneapolis: University of Minnesota Press, 1996); David Theo Goldberg, ed., *Multiculturalism: A Critical Reader* (Oxford: Blackwell, 1994).

6. Here we need to differ from approaches such as Faye V. Harrison's toward Alice Walker's representation of women in a global framework. While Harrison argues that Walker's novel, *In the Temple of My Familiar*, is a "world cultural history from a pluralistic Third World feminist perspective" which "deessentializes gender as well as race and class," we view such projects as recuperating new kinds of global gendered subjects. See Faye V. Harrison, "Anthropology, Fiction, and Unequal Relations of Intellectual Production," in *Women Writing Culture*, ed. Ruth Behar and Deborah A. Gordon (Berkeley: University of California Press, 1995), pp. 233–245.

7. Claude Lévi-Strauss, *Structural Anthropology* (New York: Basic Books, 1963), pp. 16–17.

8. Noel Burch, *Life to Those Shadows* (Berkeley: University of California Press, 1990), p. 16. For discussions of "ethnographic authority" and the history of anthropological cultures of representation, see James Clifford and George Marcus, eds., *Writing Culture* (Berkeley: University of California Press, 1986); and James Clifford, *The Predicament of Culture: Twentieth-Century Ethnography, Literature, and Art* (Cambridge, Mass.: Harvard University Press, 1988).

9. See Denise Albanese, *New Science, New World* (Durham, N.C.: Duke University Press, 1996); John Berger, *Ways of Seeing* (Harmondsworth: Penguin, 1977); Lisa Cartwright, *Screening the Body: Tracing Medicine's Visual Culture* (Minneapolis: Univerity of Minnesota Press, 1995); and Valerie Hartouni, *Cultural Conceptions: On Reproductive Technologies and the Remaking of Life* (Minneapolis: University of Minneapolis Press, 1997).

10. David MacDougall, "Prospects of the Ethnographic Film," in *Movies and Methods*, ed. Bill Nichols (Berkeley: University of California Press, 1976), p. 136.

11. David MacDougall, "Beyond Observation Cinema," in *Principles of Visual Anthropology*, ed. P. Hockings (Paris: Mouton, 1975), p. 118, cited in Kathleen Kuehnast, "Visual Imperialism and the Export of Prejudice: An Exploration of Ethnograhic Film," in *Film as Ethnography*, ed. Peter Ian Crawford and David Turton (Manchester: Manchester University Press, 1992), p. 186.

12. Fatimah Tobing Rony, *The Third Eye: Race, Cinema, and Ethnographic Spectacle* (Durham, N.C.: Duke University Press, 1996), p. 8.

13. Ibid., p. 71.

14. See Parama Roy, *Indian Traffic* (Berkeley: University of California Press, 1998); Nalina Natarajan, "Women, Nation, and Narration in Midnight's Children," in Grewal and Kaplan, *Scattered Hegemonies*, pp. 76–89; Rey Chow, *Primitive Passions: Visuality, Sexuality, Ethnography, and Contemporary Chinese Cinema* (New York: Columbia University Press, 1995); and Shohat and Stam, *Unthinking Eurocentrism: Multiculturalism and the Media.*

15. Alice Walker, *In Search of Our Mother's Gardens* (New York: Harcourt, Brace, Jovanovich, 1983).

16. See Valerie Amos and Pratibha Parmar, "Challenging Imperial Feminism," *Feminist Review* 17 (1984): 3–19.

17. For an extended discussion of the importance of sociocultural context for black women cultural producers, see Gloria Gibson-Hudson, "Aspects of Black Feminist Cultural Ideology in Films by Black Women Independent Artists," in *Multiple Voices in Feminist Film Criticism*, ed. Diane Carson, Linda Dittmar, and Janice R. Welsch (Minneapolis: University of Minnesota Press, 1994), pp. 365–379.

18. For a variety of anthropological, legal, historical, and cultural perspectives on female genital surgeries as a question of "tradition" in an era of human rights activism, see Bettina Shell-Duncan and Ylva Hernlund, eds., *Female 'Circumcision' in Africa: Culture, Controversy, and Change* (Boulder: Lynne Reinner Publishers, 2000).

19. Isabelle Gunning, "Arrogant Perception, World-Travelling and Multicultural Feminism: The Case of Female Genital Surgeries," *Columbia Human Rights Law Review* 23 (1992): 189–248. We have been inspired and encouraged by Gunning's interventions in human rights discourse and by her complex, materially grounded theorization of multicultural feminism.

20. For an extremely useful discussion of the history of Western representations of the clitoris, see Lisa Jean Moore and Adele E. Clarke, "Clitoral Conventions and Transgressions: Graphic Representations in Anatomy Texts, c1900–1991," *Feminist Studies* 21, no. 2 (summer 1995): 255–301.

21. Rey Chow, *Writing Diaspora: Tactics of Intervention in Contemporary Cultural Studies* (Bloomington: Indiana University Press, 1993), pp. 28–29.

22. Doris Sommer, "Resistant Texts and Incompetent Readers," *Poetics Today* 15, no. 4 (winter 1994): 543, cited in Diana Fuss, *Identification Papers* (New York: Routledge, 1995), p. 9.

23. Evelyn C. White, "Alice Walker's Compassionate Crusade," *San Francisco Chronicle,* Monday, November 15, 1993, p. D1.

24. Here we disagree with Diana Fuss and other psychoanalytic feminist theorists who argue for a politicized recognition of the erotic and mobilizing powers of identification as a compensation for lost love-objects. While we acknowledge the rigor of these arguments, examples such as *Warrior Marks* demonstrate the cultural and political limits of such an approach. See Fuss, *Identification Papers.*

25. Amy Hamilton, "Warrior Marks," *off our backs* 23, no. 11 (December 1993): 2.

26. See Diane Minor, "*Warrior Marks*: Joyous Resistance at Walker Film Debut," *National NOW Times* (January 1994): 7; Mari Keiko Gonzalez, "Culture or Torture?" *Bay Area Reporter,* November 18, 1993; White, "Alice Walker's Compassionate Crusade," p. D1; David A. Kaplan, "Is It Torture or Tradition?" *Newsweek* (December 20, 1993): 124.

27. Seble Dawit and Salem Mekuria, "The West Just Doesn't Get It," *New York Times,* Tuesday, December 7, 1993, p. A27. This piece is an exception to the rule. Most *New York Times* op-ed pieces on the topic echo the tone and approach found in A. M. Rosenthal's "Female Genital Torture," *New York Times,* Friday, November 12, 1993, p. A33.

28. Critiques of *Possessing the Secret of Joy* include: Margaret Kent Bass, "Alice's Secret," *CLA Journal* (September 1994): 1–10; Diane C. Menya, "Possessing the Secret of Joy," *Lancet* 341 (February 1993): 423. Critiques of *Warrior Marks* include: Leasa Farrar-Frazer, "An Opportunity Missed: A Review of *Warrior Marks*," *Black Film Review* 8, no. 1 (1994): 41–42; Gay Wilentz, "Healing the Wounds of Time," *Women's Review of Books* 10, no. 5 (February 1993): 15–16; Kagendo Murungi, "Get Away From My Genitals: A Commentary on *Warrior Marks*," *Interstices* 2, no. 1 (spring 1994): 11–15; and Abusharaf, "The Resurrection of the Savage."

29. *Case Western Reserve Law Review* 47, no. 2 (winter 1997). See in particular L. Amede

Obiora, "Bridges and Barricades: Rethinking Polemics and Intransigence in the Campaign Against Female Circumcision," pp. 275–378; Micere Githae Mugo, "Elitist Anti-Circumcision Discourse as Mutilating and Anti-Feminist," pp. 461–479; and Isabelle R. Gunning, "Uneasy Alliances and Solid Sisterhood: A Response to Professor Obiora's 'Bridges and Barricades'," pp. 445–459.

30. Mugo, "Elitist Anti-Circumcision Discourse," 462.

31. The second wave, Western feminist salvo against footbinding as "gynocide" was fired by Andrea Dworkin in her well-known text *Woman Hating* (New York: E. P. Dutton, 1974), pp. 95–117. Although Elizabeth Gould Davis also outlines the history of atrocities committed against women, reserving special scorn for those from non-European or non-Christian cultures in *The First Sex* (New York: Penguin Books, 1971), it is Mary Daly who is best-known for her analysis of patriarchal violence that includes "Indian" *suttee*, "Chinese" footbinding, and "African" genital mutilation. See *Gyn/Ecology: The Metaethics of Radical Feminism* (Boston: Beacon Press, 1978). This approach lent support to and in many ways instigated the contemporary movement to create International Tribunals on Crimes Against Women; see Diane E. H. Russell and Nicole Van de Ven, *Crimes Against Women: Proceedings of the International Tribunal* (East Palo Alto, Calif.: Frog in the Well Press, 1984). Lata Mani has documented both British and South Asian nationalist discourses on *sati* (or *suttee*) in "Contentious Traditions: The Debate on Sati in Colonial India," in *Recasting Women*, ed. KumKum Sangari and Sudesh Vaid (New Delhi: Kali for Women, 1989), pp. 88–126. For a more historically complex approach to footbinding in East Asia, see Alison R. Drucker, "The Influence of Western Women on the Anti-Footbinding Movement, 1840–1911," in *Women in China*, ed. Richard W. Guisso and Stanley Johannesen (Youngstown, N.Y.: Philo Press, 1981).

32. In addition to Gayatri Spivak's groundbreaking work collected in *In Other Worlds* (New York: Methuen, 1987) and *Outside in the Teaching Machine* (New York: Routledge, 1993) as well as in Sarah Harasym, ed., *The Post-Colonial Critic* (New York: Routledge, 1990), see also Cynthia Enloe, *Bananas, Beaches, and Bases* (Berkeley: University of California Press, 1989); Trinh T. Minh-ha, *Woman/Native/Other* (Bloomington: Indiana University Press, 1989); Shohat and Stam, *Unthinking Eurocentrism*; Chow, *Writing Diaspora*; Lisa Lowe, *Critical Terrains* (Ithaca, N.Y.: Cornell University Press, 1991); Françoise Lionnet, *Postcolonial Representations* (Ithaca, N.Y.: Cornell University Press, 1995); Nupur Chaudhuri and Margaret Strobel, *Western Women and Imperialism* (Bloomington: Indiana University Press, 1992); Jenny Sharpe, *Allegories of Empire* (Minneapolis: University of Minnesota Press, 1993); Kumari Jayarwardena, *The White Woman's Other Burden* (New York: Routledge, 1995); Antoinette Burton, *Burden's of History* (Chapel Hill: University of North Carolina Press, 1994); Anne McClintock, *Imperial Leather* (New York: Routledge, 1995); and Helen Callaway, *Gender, Culture, and Empire* (Urbana: University of Illinois Press, 1987)—among others.

33. See Mary Layoun, "The Female Body and 'Transnational' Reproduction; or, Rape by Any Other Name?" in Grewal and Kaplan, *Scattered Hegemonies*, pp. 63–75; and Sharpe, *Allegories of Empire*. See also Susan Jeffords, "Fantastic Conquests: In U.S. Military History, Only Some Rapes Count," *The Village Voice*, July 13, 1993, pp. 22–24, 29.

34. Important exceptions include Vicki Kirby, "On the Cutting Edge: Feminism and Clitoridectomy," *Australian Feminist Studies* 5 (summer 1987): 35–55; Angela Davis, "Women in Egypt: A Personal View," in *Women, Culture, and Politics* (New York: Vintage, 1990), pp. 116–154; Françoise Lionnet, "Feminisms and Universalisms: 'Universal Rights' and the Legal Debate Around the Practice of Female Excision in France," *Inscriptions* 6 (1992): 98–115; and the work of Isabelle Gunning, "Arrogant Perception, World Travelling and Multicultural Feminism."

35. See Terry Kapsalis, *Public Privates: Performing Gynecology from Both Ends of the Speculum* (Durham, N.C.: Duke University Press, 1997); G. J. Barker-Benfield, *The Horrors of the Half-Known Life: Male Attitudes Toward Women and Sexuality in Nineteenth-Century America* (New York: Harper and Row, 1976); Elaine Showalter, *The Female Malady* (New York: Pantheon, 1985), pp. 75–78; John Money, *The Destroying Angel* (Buffalo, N.Y.: Prometheus Books, 1985), pp. 119–120; John Duffy, "Masturbation and Clitoridectomy," *Journal of the American Medical Association* 186, no. 3 (October 19, 1963): 246–249; J. B. Fleming et al., "Clitoridectomy—The Disastrous Downfall of Isaac Baker Brown, F.R.C.S. (1867)," *Journal of Obstretrics and Gynaecology of the British Empire* 67, no. 6 (October 1960): 1017–1034; and

Isaac Baker Brown, *On the Curability of Certain Forms of Insanity, Epilepsy, Catalepsy, and Hysteria in Females* (London: Robert Hardwicke, 1866).

36. Female circumcision or genital surgery in general has been represented in "modern" discussions of anatomy as well as marked as "culturally significant" in ethnographic discourse. For example, P. C. Remondino's *History of Circumcision From the Earliest Times to the Present* (Philadelphia: F. A. Davis, 1900), combines ethnographic "knowledge," folk legend, and medical "facts." Richard Burton supplied ethnographic data on female infibulation and excision in a lost first version of *First Footsteps in East Africa* (1856) that has been recovered by Gordon Waterfield in a 1966 edition. Burton's characterization of this "remarkable method" of maintaining chastity as "barbarous" is continued in the stringently "scientific" discourse of an article by Allen Worsley published in the *Journal of Obstetrics and Gynaecology of the British Empire* in 1938 in which the author refers to female circumcision as "evil." The practice is referred to in soft-core pornography in 1939 in Felix Bryk's *Dark Rapture: The Sex-Life of the African Negro* (New York: Walden, 1939) as well as in academia in an article by the celebrated Ashley Montague in *The American Anthropologist* in 1945. Second wave, Western feminist approaches to the topic follow the parameters and tone established by Fran Hosken in her work since the 1970s (gathered in her 1983 *The Hosken Report: Genital and Sexual Mutilation of Females*). See also Henny Lightfoot-Klein, *Prisoners of Ritual: An Odyssey into Female Genital Circumcision in Africa* (New York: Haworth, 1989); Daly, *Gyn/Ecology*; Robin Morgan and Gloria Steinem, "The International Crime of Genital Mutilation," *Ms* 8, no. 9 (March 1980): 65–69. Third World feminists who have published denunciations of the practice include Awa Thiam, *Speak Out, Black Sisters: Feminism and Oppression in Black Africa* (London: Pluto Press, 1986); Olayinka Koso-Thomas, *The Circumcision of Women: A Strategy for Eradication* (London: Zed Books, 1987); Asma El Dareer, *Woman, Why Do You Weep?* (London: Zed Books, 1982); Efua Dorkenoo and Scilla Elworthy, *Female Genital Mutilation: Proposals for Change* (London: Minority Rights Group International, 1992); Nawal el Saadawi, *The Hidden Face of Eve: Women in the Arab World* (London: Zed Books, 1980). Female circumcision has also been featured in nationalist and decolonization discourses. See Jomo Kenyatta, *Facing Mount Kenya: The Tribal Life of the Kikuyu* (New York: Random House, 1975). For a stellar discussion of the politics of female circumcision discourse in the decolonization struggle in Kenya, see Susan Pedersen, "National Bodies, Unspeakable Acts: The Sexual Politics of Colonial Policy-Making," *Journal of Modern History* 63 (December 1991): 647–680. We identify significant participation in the discourse of sexual surgery in activist writing generated by groups such as the Intersex Society of North America. See, for example, the ISNA's newsletter, *Hermaphrodites With Attitudes*, and their call for an end to "IGM"—intersexed genital mutilation. See also our work-in-progress for a fuller discussion of this complex site of alliance between queer, transgender, and global feminist activism around sexual surgeries.

37. See Ann Laura Stoler's work: "Carnal Knowledge and Imperial Power: Gender, Race, and Morality in Colonial Asia," in *Gender at the Crossroads of Knowledge: Feminist Anthropology in the Postmodern Era*, ed. Micaela di Leonardo (Berkeley: University of California Press, 1991), pp. 51–101; and *Race and the Education of Desire: Foucault's "History of Sexuality" and the Colonial Order of Things* (Durham, N.C.: Duke University Press, 1995).

38. See Ann Balsamo, *Technologies of the Gendered Body* (Durham, N.C.: Duke University Press, 1995); Jennifer Terry and Jacqueline Urla, eds., *Deviant Bodies* (Bloomington: Indiana University Press, 1995); Cartwright, *Screening the Body*; Kathy Davis, *Reshaping the Female Body* (New York: Routledge, 1995); David Bell and Gill Valentine, eds., *Mapping Desire: Geographies of Sexualities* (New York: Routledge, 1995); and Mary Jacobus et al., eds., *Body Politics* (New York: Routledge, 1990).

39. See Edward W. Said, *Orientalism* (New York: Random House, 1978); Clifford and Marcus, *Writing Culture*; and Clifford, *The Predicament of Culture*.

40. See Mary Louise Pratt, *Imperial Eyes: Travel Writing and Transculturation* (London: Routledge, 1992); Shohat and Stam, *Unthinking Eurocentrism*; Inderpal Grewal, *Home and Harem: Nation, Gender, Empire, and the Cultures of Travel* (Durham, N.C.: Duke University Press, 1996); Caren Kaplan, *Questions of Travel: Postmodern Discourses of Displacement* (Durham, N.C.: Duke University Press, 1996); and Caren Kaplan, "'Getting to Know You': Travel, Gender, and the Politics of Representation in *Anna and the King of Siam* and *The King and I*," in *Late Imperial Culture*, ed. Roman de la Campa, E. Ann Kaplan, and Michael Sprinker (London: Verso, 1995), pp. 33–52.

41. See Sylvia M. Jacobs, ed., *Black Americans and the Missionary Movement in Africa* (Westport, Conn.: Greenwood Press, 1982). See also Sylvia M. Jacobs, "Give a Thought to Africa: Black Women Missionaries in Southern Africa," in Chaudhuri and Strobel, *Western Women and Imperialism*, pp. 207–228.

42. This point is more fully discussed in our work-in-progress as part of the discourse of global feminism whereby a unified and unfragmented female body becomes equated with an ideal "lesbian body." In this context, female genital surgery eradicates or alters a zone that is configured in historically specific ways by contemporary Western cultural and lesbian feminist discursive practices.

43. See Davis, *Reshaping the Female Body*; Jennifer Craik, *The Face of Fashion: Cultural Studies in Fashion* (London: Routledge, 1994); Hilary Radner, *Shopping Around: Feminine Culture and the Pursuit of Pleasure* (New York: Routledge, 1995); Shari Benstock and Suzanne Ferriss, eds., *On Fashion* (New Brunswick, N.J.: Rutgers University Press, 1994); Carol A. Stabile, *Feminism and the Technological Fix* (Manchester: Manchester University Press, 1994); Ann Balsamo, "On the Cutting Edge: Cosmetic Surgery and the Technological Production of the Gendered Body," *Camera Obscura* 28 (1992): 207–238; and Cartwright, *Screening the Body*. Walker does mention cosmetic surgeries and pressures on Western women to conform to patriarchal ideal forms in the written text when she is in the planning stages of the project, but this set of crucial ideas drops out of the film (*Warrior Marks*, pp. 9–10).

44. See Pratt, Clifford, Shohat and Stam, and Said. See also Christopher Miller, *Blank Darkness: Africanist Discourse in French* (Chicago: University of Chicago Press, 1985).

45. See Lisa Bloom, *Gender on Ice: American Ideologies of Polar Expeditions* (Minneapolis: University of Minnesota Press, 1993); Catherine A. Lutz and Jane L. Collins, *Reading National Geographic* (Chicago: University of Chicago Press, 1993); William M. O'Barr, "Representations of Others, Part 1: Advertisements in the 1929 *National Geographic* Magazine," in *Culture and the Ad: Exploring Otherness in the World of Advertising* (Boulder: Westview Press, 1994), pp. 45–72; Tamar Y. Rothenberg, "Voyeurs of Imperialism: *The National Geographic Magazine* before World War II," in *Geography and Empire*, ed. Anne Godlewska and Neil Smith (Oxford: Basil Blackwell, 1994), pp. 155–172.

46. Mary H. Kingsley, *Travels in West Africa* (1897) (Boston: Beacon Press, 1988). Kingsley's influence on contemporary "women's travel" literature can be seen in works such as Caroline Alexander's memoir *One Dry Season: In the Footsteps of Mary Kingsley* (New York: Vintage Books, 1991) and in Alison Blunt's critical monograph *Travel, Gender, and Imperialism: Mary Kingsley and West Africa* (New York: Guilford Press, 1994). See also Katherine Frank, *A Voyager Out: The Life of Mary Kingsley* (New York: Ballantine Books, 1986).

47. For a discussion of epistolary conventions in women's writing, see Linda S. Kauffman, *Special Delivery: Epistolary Modes in Modern Fiction* (Chicago: University of Chicago Press, 1992).

48. See Said, Spivak, Shohat, as well as Johannes Fabian, *Time and the Other: How Anthropology Makes Its Object* (New York: Columbia University Press, 1983); and Talal Asad, *Anthropology and the Colonial Encounter* (London: Ithaca Press, 1973).

49. See Spivak, "Can the Subaltern Speak?" pp. 271–313; and Chow, *Writing Diaspora*.

50. Alice Walker and Pratibha Parmar, *Warrior Marks: Female Genital Mutilation and the Sexual Blinding of Women* (New York: Harcourt Brace, 1993), pp. 301–308.

51. White, "Alice Walker's Compassionate Crusade," p. D1.

52. For critiques of ethnographic authority in anthropological and cultural discourses, see Clifford and Marcus, *Writing Culture*; George E. Marcus and Michael M. J. Fischer, *Anthropology as Cultural Critique: An Experimental Moment in the Human Sciences* (Chicago: University of Chicago Press, 1986); and Clifford, *The Predicament of Culture*. See also Laleen Jayamanne, "Do You Think I Am a Woman, Ha! Do You?" *Discourse* 11, no. 2 (spring/summer 1989): 49–62; and Trinh T. Minh-ha, *Framer Framed* (New York: Routledge, 1992).

53. Pratt, *Imperial Eyes*, pp. 58–68.

54. See "Alice Walker and Circumciser 1," pp. 301–309 (including the excerpt from Alan David, *Infibulation en RTpublique de Djibouti*, pp. 308–309).

55. Walker and Parmar, *Warrior Marks*, p. 179.

56. Spivak, "Can the Subaltern Speak?" p. 271.

57. Ibid., p. 282.

58. Walker and Parmar, *Warrior Marks*, p. 284.

59. Mohanty, "Under Western Eyes," p. 58.

60. See Kay Boulware-Miller, "Female Circumcision: Challenges to the Practice as a Human Rights Violation," *Harvard Women's Law Journal* 8 (spring 1985): 155–177; Isabelle R. Gunning, "Modernizing Customary International Law: The Challenge of Human Rights," *Virginia Journal of International Law* 31, no. 2 (winter 1991): 211–247; Georgia Dullea, "Female Circumcision a Topic at U.N. Parley," *New York Times*, Friday, July 18, 1980, p. B4; Marlise Simons, "France Jails Woman for Daughter's Circumcision," *New York Times*, January 11, 1993, p. A8; Tomothy Egan, "An Ancient Ritual and a Mother's Asylum Plea," *New York Times*, Friday, March 4, 1994, p. A25; Clyde H. Farnsworth, "Canada Gives Somali Mother Refugee Status," *New York Times*, Thursday, July 21, 1994; Jill Lawrence, "Women Seek Asylum in West to Avoid Abuses in Homeland," *San Francisco Chronicle*, Monday, March 21, 1994, p. A3; Sophfronia Scott Gregory, "At Risk of Mutilation," *Time* (March 21, 1994): 45–46. For a vigorous discussion of the pitfalls of cultural defense arguments and the rhetoric of human rights in the context of racism, see Sherene Razack, "What is to be Gained by Looking White People in the Eye? Culture, Race, and Gender in Cases of Sexual Violence," *Signs* 19, no. 4 (summer 1994): 894–923.

Talitha Espiritu

Multiculturalism, Dictatorship, and Cinema Vanguards: Philippine and Brazilian Analogies

The years 1964 to 1985 were politically turbulent ones for both the Philippines and Brazil. Not coincidentally, the period engendered what is now considered to be the most creative work in the cinemas of both countries. While repressive political regimes in both countries sought to intrumentalize nationalism in the service of "modernization" and "national security," vanguard filmmakers sought to politicize auteurism in ways that would address those communities whose continued marginalization would pay the price for these lofty "nationalist" goals. Significantly, the two vanguard movements closely identified themselves with popular movements and traditions, provoking deep-seated ambivalences among national elites. These films pointed to the deep social divisions that belied the nationalist agendas of the state—agendas subtended by the persistence of social, political, and economic institutions that guaranteed the backwardness of certain groups, even as official state policies ostensibly pursued the eradication of such unwanted signs of underdevelopment within the nation.

In the Philippines, the dictatorship of Ferdinand Marcos was crucial to the political "coming into consciousness" of the Filipino auteurs during the 1970s. Marcos, who was reelected in 1969 following the bloodiest and most fraudulent elections the country had ever seen, declared martial law in 1972. The dictator's seizure of power was directed against an upsurge of peasant uprisings in the countryside and growing labor unrest in the cities. Indeed, the regime's own nationalist rhetoric co-opted discrepant nationalist discourses variously invoked by emerging social groups: a radical intelligentsia led by left-leaning middle-class students forging an alliance with urban laborers and communist peasant rebels; and a new class of technocrats, drawn from roughly the same middle-class strata as the radical intelligentsia, but who were concerned less with the social injustices suffered by the country's marginalized communities than with the "irrationalities" of the country's political and economic systems. When Marcos declared martial law, he singled out the two primary enemies of the state: the radical Left and the oligarchy—the mestizo minority which controlled 90 percent of the country's wealth as well as the political life of the nation. In the words of the president, martial law was declared to "save the Republic and to reform Philippine society."[1]

Filipino film auteurs had a complicated relationship with the Marcos regime. The state had in fact functioned as the midwife for a national cinema movement, and conscripted the local film industry into a larger project of nation-building. While the press and the broadcast media were harshly repressed, the cinema enjoyed a significant degree of support and was exhorted to aspire toward the creation of a truly national art form. Paradoxically, Filipino auteurs utilized this moment to expose the rampant social unrest of the period. Drawing from the momentum of the radical student movement, these filmmakers worked to connect art cinema and political activism. However, much like the technocrats, the work of these auteurs begged questions of cultural leadership and political direction, and thus, underscored the uneasy relationship between cinema vanguards and the popular audience.

The Philippine case bears striking analogies with contemporaneous national cinema movements in Latin America. Despite the geographic distance from these movements, the political consciousness of the Filipino auteurs was similarly shaped by the shared history of Iberian colonialism, Catholicism, and U.S. imperialism in the region. The case of Cinema Novo in Brazil is particularly illuminating. In Brazil, the negotiation between left-leaning cultural nationalists and the repressive state was likewise underpinned by a process of conservative modernization. Just before the military coup of 1964, Brazil was undergoing a period of economic expansion and industrialization that nonetheless belied a period of political and social crisis. Much like the situation in the Philippines, power was disproportionately concentrated in the hands of a small minority, which was in this case confronted by labor unrest in the industrialized south and a peasant movement in the regionally underdeveloped and economically depressed northeast.

When the military seized power (1964–1985), it co-opted the developmental nationalism of the previous democratic regime, but exploited a repressive national security doctrine in order to revamp the political culture of the nation and to transform the economy. All political dissent was silenced and the radical Left was suppressed. Meanwhile, under the banner of scientific rationality and enlightened leadership, technocrats were enlisted to push the economy into rapid industrialization. The significant upshot of these developments was the much vaunted "Brazilian miracle" during the 1970s. Through policies that encouraged foreign investment and the exploitation of the underdeveloped interior regions of the country, the military dictatorship shepherded Brazil into becoming the tenth largest economy, and the largest industrialized nation in the developing world. However, this "miracle" paradoxically reinforced traditional power structures. The gap between rich and poor intensified even as the economy grew faster than any other in the world.

In both the Philippines and Brazil, vanguard filmmakers sought out the urban slums and the underdeveloped countryside as places where the social contradictions of nationalist development and modernization were most pronounced.

Not incidentally, these were the places where the marginalized majority of both nations was also most represented. Brazil is of particular interest because of the significant size of African-descended populations in these geographic and structural locations. This is particularly striking given the official self-image of the nation as an egalitarian and assimilationist society. While the Philippines does not have an equivalent "black" population, its marginalized majority nonetheless bears the stigma of colonial forms of racial oppression. This colonial baggage is likewise striking, given the prevalent myth that the Philippines is a racially unified nation, one in which the absence of "blacks" automatically guarantees the absence of racial and ethnic conflict. In both countries, myths of assimilation and national unity were seized and jealously guarded by the state in times of social conflict. Consequently, vanguard filmmakers in both countries, in their engagement with the popular could not escape the terms and implications of these powerful myths.

As Ella Shohat and Robert Stam remind us, "issues of multiculturalism, colonialism, and race must be discussed in relation."[2] The experiences of conquest, colonialism, and neo-colonialism link the Philippines and Brazil in at least one significant way. In both countries, this experience has generated similar structures of social inequality and political turbulence that have lent themselves to authoritarianism and clientism. I would argue that the similarities and differences between them make the Philippine and Brazilian cases mutually illuminating and informative. Following this relational methodology, I would like to explore how overt and implicit racial discourses informed the cultural politics of the Filipino and the Cinema Novo vanguards—their messy and contradictory engagement with the state and with the popular national audience.

Colonialism, Race, and Ethnicity: Philippine and Brazilian Analogies

Despite the differences in their official views on race relations within the nation, there remains a striking affinity between the Philippines and Brazil. In both countries, immense wealth coexists with immense poverty, and these power imbalances have racial and ethnic correlates. In the 1970s, a Brazilian economist suggested that Brazil be named "Belindia"—because its modern industrial base resembled that of Belgium, while its backward social structure looked like that of India. At roughly the same time, the Philippines was often described as an "anomaly." Up until the 1950s, the Philippines was one of the wealthiest nations in the Third World, its economy considered to be more impressive than those of the current Asian newly industrialized countries (NICs). Well into the Marcos regime, however, the majority of the population still did not enjoy the minimal standards of food, housing, and employment.[3] In both countries, only a small minority—"whites" in Brazil and a mestizo oligarchy in the Philippines—enjoyed the social benefits of modernization.

To smooth out the glaring problems of social inequality, dictators in both countries had recourse to powerful myths—that of a racially unified nation in the Philippines and that of racial democracy in Brazil. These myths worked to bracket power imbalances within the nation from any consideration of racial difference. The historical record, however, paints a different picture. It is worthwhile to briefly consider how the dynamics of racial difference, identity formation, and social inequality elided by these powerful myths were crucially shaped by the distinct colonial experiences of both countries. As we shall see in a moment, these dynamics would feed into the problematic political positions of the cinema vanguards.

Benedict Anderson points out several factors that make the Philippines a curious country. It stands out among its Southeast Asian neighbors for pioneering a nationalist, anticolonial movement (1896–1898) which was both "too early" (for Asia) and "too late" (for Latin America).[4] He notes also that while the Philippines resembles many Latin American countries in terms of its predominantly Roman Catholic society, Spanish was curiously never established as the lingua franca.[5] He points out that while the powerful presence of the United States in Asia was sustained by the opening of the Cold War, American domination of the Philippines had preceded this international realpolitik by fifty years.[6] But in racial and ethnic terms, what makes the Philippines so unusual for Anderson is the highly visible presence of Chinese mestizos in positions of economic and political power.[7] Coming to economic power under the Spanish colonial regime, Chinese mestizos had consolidated their wealth with political power under the American regime. It is the dominance of this group, Anderson states, that decisively marks off the Philippines from Spanish America and the rest of Southeast Asia.[8]

The presence of Chinese mestizos in positions of power and influence in the Philippines was the protracted result of the nation's colonial experience. Through limited immigration and miscegenation, the Chinese presence in the Philippines grew alongside the growing internationalization of the economy beginning in the 1830s. The category *mestizo* was a colonial term of distinction which implicitly functioned as a naturalized ideal—privileged for its symbolic approximation of "whiteness." As Anderson points out, the word would in due course typically refer not to the offspring of Spaniards and indigenous people, but to the offspring of Chinese and local women.[9]

Beginning in the nineteenth century, Western liberal ideals were grafted onto a colonial society that has since regarded the attainment of social status based on wealth and mestizo descent as supreme values. Racism in the Philippines thus consists not in a Manichean binary between "black" and "white," or "brown" and "white," but in the projection of a naturalized ideal—the mestizo—as an integrationalist norm that all should aspire toward. It is not uncommon, for instance, for mothers to urge their daughters to marry into a fair-skinned family so as to "improve the family stock (*lahi*)," just as it is not uncommon in Brazil for black or mulatto mothers to speak of "improving the race." It is also commonplace to hear dark-skinned Filipinos referred to as "natives" by their own countrymen, as if they were still being regarded from under the colonial gaze. In extreme cases of racial distortion, dark-skinned Filipinos are sometimes referred to as "ethnics" by those who identify with a "white" or mestizo ideal which refuses to be named. So powerful is the normative power of whiteness that "race" appears as something that only applies to nonwhite peoples in other places.

In this regard, the Philippines appears as a distorted mirror image of Brazil. The national imaginary of Brazil is closely bound up with exceptionalist claims regarding its multiracial society. Rather than burying race underneath abstract liberal notions of the nation, Brazilian intellectuals have exhumed the crucial role played by racial mixing—*mestiszagem*—in the historical formation of the nation. Gilberto Freyre, the chief exponent of racial democracy, celebrates the ideology as the key feature of Brazilian exceptionalism: "With respect to race relations, the Brazilian situation is probably the nearest approach to paradise to be found anywhere in the world."[10] Brazil, so the argument goes, is an egalitarian society which "allows" peoples of color to gradually "cleanse" themselves through intermarriage and self-improvement.[11] But as Robert Stam points out, the often romanticized notion of miscegenation was, in historical practice, never divorced from questions of power. In fact, miscegenation functioned as a powerful technique of domination within the colonial context.[12] *Mamelucos*, the mixed Indian/Europeans who conquered the Brazilian territory, were simultaneously the first victims and perpetrators of the ideology of whitening in Brazil. They were "riven in their allegiances between their indigenous ancestors whom they often despised, and the Europeans who despised them."[13]

The political ambivalence that characterized the *mamelucos* of Brazil finds an analogue in the ambivalent relationship between mestizos and *indios* in colonial Philippines. The term *indio*, generated by Columbus's mistaken idea that he had traveled to India, and which had crossed over from the Americas, would serve the same purpose of institutionalizing racism in the Philippines. Imputing biological, cultural, and even spiritual inferiority to the indigenous populations of the colony, the racist hierarchies implied by the term helped justify the political subjection and religious conversion of the indigenous population. Mestizos in the Philippines, like the *mamelucos* in Brazil, were thus similarly burdened by the need to transcend the inescapable stigma of colonial racism.

However, there are significant differences in the colonial formations of both countries, and consequently, differences in the modalities of racism. Brazil was a slaveholding society; the Philippines was not. Brazil's colonial economy was underpinned by a monocultural latifundiary system based on vast land-grant plantations. The importation of African slaves played a significant role in sustaining the plantation economy.[14] Racist ideologies worked to justify slavery. When slavery became incompatible with the competitive dynamics of developing capitalism, Brazilian elites pushed for abolition less out of a concern for the welfare of slaves than out of narrow, class-based interests in a competitive "free" labor market.[15] Policies that encouraged the immigration of white free laborers and the preferential treatment given these immigrants in most jobs pushed ex-slaves, blacks, and mulattos into the margins. The result, as Fontaine points out, is that the competitive class society reinforced the racist views of blacks and mulattos characteristic of the plantation society.[16] Thus, well after abolition in 1888, the same racist ideologies that justified slavery underwrote the political, economic, and social exclusion of those of African descent.[17]

In the Philippines, on the other hand, the one substantial source of rapid wealth for Spain lay not in hacienda-based commercial agriculture, but in commerce with Imperial China. Manila was in fact a thriving port city.[18] The privileging of trade in the colony meant not only a concentration of Spanish populations in Manila, but the lack of any sustained interest in the massive exploitation of the indigenous population as a labor force, much less the importation of slaves.[19] The provinces, then, emerged as that particularly differentiated space in which a "backward" *indio* population was largely confined. Prior to the nineteenth century, *provincianos* seldom experienced direct contact with alien authority.[20] However, the economic empowerment of mestizos during the nineteenth century was to significantly transform the countryside. Mestizos of Chinese descent began systematic investments in land. Overwhelmingly Hispanic in their cultural orientation, these *principalia* elites enjoyed an aristocratic lifestyle that was in stark contrast with the hand-to-mouth existence of the *indio* masses. As the century wore on, the contrasts between these two classes intensified. *Principales* were literate; peasants were not. *Principales* spoke Spanish; peasants spoke in local dialects. And as David Sturtevant points out, this dichotomy had racial dimensions:

> Sheltered faces, soft muscles and long fingernails designated educated leaders or *ilustrados* (the enlightened). Sun-ravaged flesh, wiry bodies and work-worn hands distinguished commoners or *taos*. The fact that a Spanish superlative was reserved for the elite, while a Malay noun was retained for the peasantry underlined the cultural nature of the developing gap. As it widened, the basis for mutual trust and understanding diminished. (translation mine) [21]

For the indio peasants (*taos*), the *ilustrado* mestizos were so unlike themselves as to be almost alien. Marked disparities in living levels were reinforced by the pronounced contrasts between the "foreign" conduct of fair-skinned "superiors" and the "traditional" ways of dark-skinned "inferiors." The fundamental difference in social perspectives led to internal, racially inscribed friction between the classes that would intensify during and after Philippine hostilities with Spain and the United States.[22]

The black and mulatto majority in Brazil and the *indio* majority in the Philippines were thus effectively marginalized by colonial power structures that installed a white/mestizo minority in positions of disproportionate economic and political power. These power imbalances, however, are obscured by paternalistic myths that have shaped the self-images of both nations—racial democracy in

Brazil, racial and national unity in the Philippines. In both countries, the ideology of whitening has operated to smooth over social inequalities. According to this view, the "exceptional" person of color can, through intermarriage and self-improvement, undergo symbolic whitening. Brazil is particularly interesting in that it openly acknowledges, even celebrates, its racially mixed heritage—an outlook that is pointedly absent in the Philippines. However, the same Brazilian elites who have the privilege to invoke this heritage nonetheless succeed in bracketing issues of culture from issues of power. As Stam points out, Brazilian elites may conveniently celebrate the cultural contributions of Afro-Brazilians, but they steadfastly refuse to empower this majority in economic and political terms.[23] In the Philippines, the absence of slavery and the limited nature of immigration worked to intensify the ambivalent relationship between mestizos and indios while simultaneously contributing to the image of the nation as a country of undifferentiated "natives" in which the mestizo is the exception that is also the unstated ideal. In fact, race continues to be experienced and lived in the Philippines as an interiorized sense of colonial subjection.

In both countries, the "backwardness" of the marginalized majority often occasions embarrassment and hostility among national elites anxious to promote an unblemished vision of the modern nation. In particular, the popular images of the mystic and the bandit—symbols of popular resistance to conservative modernization—were anathema to both radicals and technocrats attempting to redefine the nation in its postcolonial moment. In Brazil, the terrible memories of the massacre at Canudos and the extermination of *cangaceiros* during the nineteenth century are deeply embedded in the regional identity of the northeast, a region most often described in terms of economic deprivation and resistance to modernization. In the Philippines, millenarian cult societies like the Colorum and various guerrillas called *tulisans* are associated with the provincial identity of central and southern Luzon, hotbeds of peasant-based armed movements. When Cinema Novo filmmakers like Glauber Rocha and Filipino auteurs like Ishmael Bernal took up these figures in their films, they did so as an explicit provocation of both elite and popular understandings of the nation. By appropriating such symbols of the "national popular," these filmmakers were burdened by the need to represent the persistence of colonial forms of racial oppression while also offering a radical critique of the popular classes whom they hoped to transform.

Modernization, Nationalism, and Cinema Vanguards

In Brazil, the social contradictions of modernization have explicit regional underpinnings. Three-quarters of the white population is concentrated in the south and southeast regions, the most developed parts of the country, compared to almost three-fifths of the nonwhite population, who live in the less developed northeast, north, and central west regions.[24] The massive industrialization that marked the Brazilian "miracle" during the 1970s pushed peoples of color farther into the margins. They would pay for the miracle by accepting government programs that encouraged foreign investment by keeping wages down. In the Philippines, a decade-long experiment in import substitution industrialization (ISI) at the end of World War II propelled the economy to unexpected heights. However, the parasitic plundering of the state by the oligarchy pushed the country into a protracted period of decline. The most advanced capitalist society in Southeast Asia in the 1950s had become the most economically depressed in the 1980s. By the end of the 1950s, 5 percent of the country's income-earners received about half of the nation's wealth. The result: the massive pauperization of the country's marginalized majority.[25]

As the social contradictions wrought by modernization intensified under dictatorship, leftist cultural production paradoxically thrived in both the Philippines and Brazil. In both countries, the cinema became highly politicized as vanguards sought to present critical visions of the nation. For some, the popular symbols of the mystic and the bandit would serve this purpose.

Mystics, Bandits, and Cinema Novo: Glauber Rocha

In his manifesto "An Esthetic of Hunger," Rocha took up the powerful reality of hunger in Brazil to emphasize the political goals of the Cinema Novo movement.[26] Hunger, for Rocha, encapsulated the very urgency behind the political project of Cinema Novo: to present a critical vision of Brazilian society as a crucial first step to promoting social change. And not coincidentally, hunger was also Rocha's powerful symbol for the conditions of Brazilian film culture in general, and filmmaking in particular. "Our originality," Rocha writes, "is our hunger and our greatest misery is that this hunger is felt but not intellectually understood."[27] As Johnson and Stam point out, the impact of Rocha's manifesto was to call for a cinematic style appropriate to the social realities of Brazil. In Rocha's words:

> We know—since we made these sad, ugly films, these screaming, desperate films where reason does not always prevail—that this hunger will not be cured by moderate governmental reforms and that the cloak of technicolor cannot hide, but only aggravates its tumors. Therefore, only a culture of hunger, weakening its own structures can surpass itself qualitatively; the most noble cultural manifestation of hunger is violence.[28]

Rocha's statement obliquely points to the precarious position of the vanguard movement at the cusp of the military dictatorship. As a movement, Cinema Novo had in fact preceded the military regime. The movement itself grew out of a process of cultural renovation that began in the early 1950s.[29] The dominant ideology of that decade, developmentalism (*desenvolvimentisimo*), had captured the national imaginary. Much like the situation in the Philippines, national elites came to the consensus that Brazil's future economic growth hinged on increased industrialization. Thus driven by economic nationalism, the developmentalist ideology was an effective way of defusing social and political conflict. But because the new ideology placed Brazil in a vulnerable position with regard to neo-colonial foreign interests, the radical Left became increasingly antagonistic toward the state. The young male artists at the helm of the Cinema Novo movement were closely attuned to the ongoing national liberation movements in the Third World. They translated the Fanonian discourse of liberatory violence into the Brazilian context, with particular attention to its cinema-specific implications. Concerns about the commercialization of the cinema, the prevalence of the Hollywood aesthetic, and the domination of the local film industry by Hollywood distributors informed their common desire to transform filmmaking into political praxis. Filmmaking, for these young artists, was a way to participate in the struggle against neo-colonialism and class injustice.[30]

It is not surprising then, that filmmakers like Rocha, Rui Guerra, and Nelson Pereira dos Santos had a particular interest in the northeast. Cycles of droughts and a tradition of popular movements bequeathed the northeast with a distinctive culture of hunger and violence. The legacy of Canudos and the *cangaceiros* was crucial to this culture. Canudos was a millenarian settlement founded by religious penitent and mystic Antonio Conselheiro. Preaching an inverted reality in the backlands (*sertao*) in which the poor would inherit the earth, the mystic drew enough followers as to create the second largest city in Bahia. Conselheiro denounced the Republic, and repeatedly called for its destruction. Charged with rebellion, the community was crushed by the military in 1897. The *cangaceiros*, on the other hand, were bandits who wandered the backlands, the most famous of whom was Virgolino Ferreira da Silva, or "Lampiao." He and his followers terrorized the region in the late nineteenth and early twentieth centuries. Like the Canudos community, this band was eventually exterminated through a state-supported campaign to wipe out banditry in the area. For the Brazilian elites, these mystic and bandit figures were symbols of the backwardness of the northeast. But for the rural poor—the *povo*—Conselheiro and Lampiao were profound symbols of popular resistance to the merciless social and economic institutions that had marginalized them. A rich literary tradition, both erudite and popular, has accrued around these figures. Robert Levine points out that beginning in the nineteenth century, elite interpretations of these popular symbols hinged on an emergent *visao do littoral*, "an urban outlook that has deprecated rural life as primitive."[31] A deep embarrassment underpinned this elite outlook. While Brazil was entering into a long period of modernization and industrialization, the vast traditional rural society remained unchanged. The sporadic eruptions of banditry and revolts in the region were painful reminders to the elites in Rio and São Paulo of the "primitive" non-European side of their society. But on the side of popular traditions, *cordel* poems and wandering troubadours or *violeros* celebrated the histories of these popular figures. For the mostly illiterate *povo*, these traditions would help preserve the memories of popular resistance.

Rocha's 1964 film *Deus e Diabo na Terra do Sol* (Black God, White Devil) specifically thematizes and deconstructs the legacy of Canudos and the *cangaceiros*. Rocha's dictum that violence is the most authentic cultural expression of hunger is powerfully manifested in the film on at least three registers. The film literally visualizes the culture of violence in the northeast, particularly in terms of the historical experiences of mystics and bandits. On another level, its narrative and filmic strategies also assume strategies of provocation that tend toward what might be called an ambush of the audience. And on yet another level, the film works by provocatively raiding the cultural repertoires of both elite and popular northeastern traditions; and in radical juxtapositions of "high" and "low" cultural citations, performs violence to both.

The plot structure of the film follows the desperate circumstances of a peasant couple, Manuel and Rosa. They are forced to flee their home in the *sertao* after Manuel confronts, then murders his cattle rancher boss who had been trying to cheat him. The death of Manuel's mother by the hand of one of the landlord's henchmen moves him to join the followers of Sebastiao, a mystic cult figure with strong affinities to Antonio Consilheiro. The cult begins to draw the ire of landowners and the local curate. They hire Antonio das Mortes, the legendary "*cangaceiro* killer" to suppress the movement. In a pivotal moment, das Mortes massacres Sebastiao's followers as Rosa unexpectedly turns the knife on the cult leader. A blind singer then leads the couple to Corisco, the only *cangaceiro* to survive the massacre of Lampiao's gang. Manuel shifts his devotion to the bandit, in the hopes that Sebastiao might be revenged. However, their profound differences regarding the use of violence leads to a confrontation that brings the film to a dramatic standstill. Antonio das Mortes then comes to kill the Corisco, the last *cangaceiro*. The film ends with the couple running through the *sertao* to an uncertain future.

The film self-reflexively foregrounds its own materiality through a series of stylistic moves that threaten to explode the seams of the narrative. Expositionary sequences are offered up in rapid, dizzying edits. Deliberate mismatches between sound and image provoke, and at times, frustrate, audience expectations. Intricate camera work oscillates between self-effacement and hand-held movements that stifle dramatic sequences. In short, it is not an easy text to read, nor is it meant to be a pleasurable one. The complexity of the film is furthermore underpinned by its extremely dense citations of conflicting northeastern traditions, both literary and popular.

In the sequence in which Manuel murders his boss, the film references the stereotype of the backlander—the *sertanejo*—as inherently irrational. Perhaps the most influential literary work to promote this stereotype was Euclydes da Cunha's *Rebellion in the Backlands*.[32] In his masterly reportage of the Canudos incident, da Cunha describes the event as a battle between the forces of civilization and darkness. He describes the backlander mestico as "degenerate . . .lacking the physical energy of his savage ancestors and without the intellectual elevation of his ancestors on the other side."[33] This elitist and in some ways contradictory assessment of the racially mixed *povo* underscores da Cunha's ambivalent views on the rural masses. While he despised their atavism, he was forced to admire their raw courage and rugged individualism. Rocha's film seems to continue this elite tradition.

Sebastiao's world, Monte Santo, is an alter-image of Conselheiro's Canudos. Indeed, the film was shot in the actual locale of the events depicted. The film makes direct references to the legendary mystic's position against the Republic ("The Republic is a curse upon all of us"). But perhaps the most direct reference to Conselheiro's vision is the line that resonates through the film: "And the *sertao* will turn into the sea, and the sea into the *sertao*." Monte Santo, and the couple's complex relationship with Sebastiao, condenses the significance of popular religiosity in the northeast. But in a surprising twist, the film shatters any utopian notions that Sebastiao's vision might inspire. Drawing on historical events not linked to Canudos, the film's purification sequence, in which the mystic sacrifices an infant, renders Sebastio unquestionably mad. That Rosa slays him in the end puts closure on the issue and buries the memory of Canudos along with it.

The *cangaceiro* stage of the film, like the mystic phase before it, draws heavily on popular traditions, particularly cordel literature. The traditional role of the *violero* as the *povo*'s historian and intermediary to the outside world is literalized on screen by the figure of the blind singer who leads the couple to Corisco. We first see the bandit in the midst of executing unnamed enemies, after which we hear him say, "I have kept my promise. I shall not let the poor starve to death." The statement, delivered in hyperbolic acting and dramatic camera framing, seems to parody the rhetoric of the cordel literature which held the *cangaceiros* up as Robin Hood figures. Later, Corisco's long monologue on violence is accentuated by close-up shots of the *cangaceiro*'s symbols of power—the weapons and artillery on his body. These references to the violence of the *cangaceiro*'s way of life is then radically subverted by his poetic, genteel rhetoric, reminiscent of Shakespearean monologues. And like Hamlet, he is rendered impotent by his bouts of self-reflection.

The film's demystification of the figures of the mystic and the bandit hinges on a provocative collision of elite and popular worldviews. On the one hand, the film seems to profess an advocacy for the "popular," and it does so by foregrounding the northeast and taking the *povo*'s culture seriously. But on the other hand, Rocha interprets these figures as anticipatory but flawed images for a future revolutionary consciousness. And thus, the film cannot completely escape the paternalistic terms of the elite point of view. The figure of the *violero*—literalized in the film by the blind singer—serves as an analogue of the film's own intermediary position between these two social worlds. Recalling Rocha's manifesto and its claims regarding violence, the film's political position can perhaps be understood as a simultaneous provocation of elite and mass audiences. The former is forced to look at what it would rather not see. The latter is forced to recognize its "errors," and is spurred on to act.

Cinema Novo filmmakers grappling with the social realities of the northeast could not escape the ideology of racial democracy that animated the elite point of view regarding the backlands. The assumption of a progressive evolution from a racially coded "black" or mestico backwardness to a "white" ideal of modernity overlapped with Cinema Novo's goal of transforming the *povo* into a revolutionary mass. While choosing to downplay race in favor of such categories as class, the movement's early politics nonetheless fell back on a notion of cultural leadership that failed to recognize its whiteness. Stam points out that it was the 1964 military coup that forced Cinema Novo filmmakers to name themselves as white and elite, shattering the illusion of vanguardism.[34] This would lead to a period of self-reflection within the Cinema Novo movement which effected a reconfiguration of its politics.

How would things change under dictatorship? A number of problems haunted the Cinema Novo filmmakers as they made the transition from the reformist, populist politics of the pre-dictatorship period to life under dictatorship. For one, they realized that while the "popular" was often the subject of their films, these films were not popular with the mass audience. As Johnson and Stam point out, the Cinema Novo filmmakers realized that "for a cinema existing within a system which it does not adhere, power means broad public acceptance and financial success."[35] Many Cinema Novo filmmakers would align themselves with Embrafilme, a state-run distributing agency founded in 1969, later empowered to produce films in 1973. This radical move to work with a government organism in a period of military dictatorship would trigger heated debates among the Cinema Novo group regarding the possible political co-optation of the movement by the regime. Filmmaker Carlos Diegues argued that Embrafilme's contributions to Cinema Novo outweighed the risks, since the agency allowed their films to have a broader reach. Embrafilme, for Diegues, allowed for the democratization of Brazilian cinema. Cinema Novo's politics might be oppositional to the *government*, but it behooved the filmmakers to seize state assistance as a *popular right*.[36] Rui Guerra, on the other hand, argued that popular cinema involved much more than merely having a large audience. For Guerra, a popular cinema should be backed up by a *viable political program* with the goal of reaching a potentially revolutionary audience. Cinema Novo should not lose sight of its original political goal: social transformation. How could Cinema Novo expect a state-run agency to fund projects that critiqued the very power structures that the agency represented?[37]

Meanwhile, on the other side of the world, similar polemics and problems were encountered by filmmakers in the Philippines, who also had an interest in the national and the popular. And some, like Rocha would be attracted to the powerful pull of mystics and bandits.

Mystics, Bandits, and Filipino Auteurs: Ishmael Bernal

While Cinema Novo filmmakers were grappling with the demise of the Left, Filipino filmmakers were just beginning to examine the meaning of the national and the popular. Prior to martial law, the local cinema was a popular, profit-driven institution specifically targeted to *probinsyanos,* or the rural classes. The economic imperative that had driven the industry was to operate as a minor alternative to Hollywood. As film historian Bienvenido Lumbera put it:

> Philippine film companies had no choice but to aim their products at a special market consisting mainly of viewers whose low socioeconomic status had impaired their ability to fully comprehend the language and content of Hollywood cinema. Gearing its products to this public was to goad the industry to typify the audience for local films as clog-wearing yokels . . . whose taste was forever lower than that of city folk.[38]

The film industry was thus complicit in the discursive construction of the rural sector—the provinces—as culturally inferior spaces. What is striking is that the racism of the colonial era, which had posited the racial inferiority of the *indio* as the justification for their religious conversion and colonial subjection, had transmuted into cultural paternalism with regard to the *probinsyano*—the "clog-wearing yokels" of the industry's rhetoric. This paternalism had racial correlates as well. In the 1950s, the film industry had created a star system closely modeled after the Hollywood system. Local studios contracted, trained, and promoted local movie personalities on the basis of their physical likenesses to (Caucasian) American actors and actresses.[39] At the same time, the local studios had also patterned their productions after Hollywood genres. As many commentators have noted, Filipino productions were either localized versions of the American Western or melodrama, or adaptations of popular comic books, serialized novels, or radio plays.[40] Thus, the paternalism of the local film industry represented a kind of doubles-peak. While the industry purported to model its film practices after the tastes of a specific constituency, it did so by playing to the assumed cultural inferiority of this group. And far from affirming the popular culture of the rural sector, the films of the local industry perpetuated a racist structure of power: their films served as boundary markers of the group's provincialism, at the same time as these were seen as providing access to a whitened culture always beyond the regional.

The emergence of an art cinema headed by Filipino auteurs was coextensive with the Marcos regime's cultural policies. When Marcos declared martial law, he publicly attributed the growing social unrest in the nation to the structural conditions of an "Old Society" which he was to reform through a program of "national regeneration." Integrating the cinema into a broader program of technocratic modernization, the regime purported to use the media to liberate the rural masses from their backward traditions. But in a double move, the repressive state also sought to socially engineer a sanitized national identity by recovering or recuperating the "native" traditions of a "noble race." For some filmmakers working under the watchful eye of the regime, popular religiosity, social banditry, and the peasant movements they have inspired proved to be particularly useful themes. Filmmakers could safely package these popular themes as "heritage" cinema. Moreover, the focus on rural life would satisfy strict censorship standards that proscribed representations of urban poverty and political ferment. However, on another level, filmmakers committed to political activism found a potential store of revolutionary language in these themes. If they could successfully encode this language in their films, they could surreptitiously mobilize a mass audience.

One filmmaker who used this strategy was Ishmael Bernal. His 1983 film *Himala* (Miracle) transposes a popular tradition of mysticism, in some ways not alien to the millennial movements in Brazil, onto the present-day struggles of a provincial town, Cupang. The film's narrative centers on a curse that has blighted the town. When a peasant woman, Elsa, claims to have seen a vision of the Virgin, the town's fate is opened up to the fulfillment of a prophecy. According to folk tradition, Cupang was cursed when the Virgin, pretending to be a leper, was driven out by the townspeople. It is believed that the curse of drought and hunger will be lifted following a series of signs from heaven. The validity of Elsa's vision then becomes the enigma that the film's narrative is posed to resolve.

As Elsa proceeds to conduct a ministry of healing, her poverty-stricken town begins to taste the benefits of economic amelioration. Blessed water and other religious items are transformed into consumer goods in a thriving new industry, initiating speculations on the viability of exportation as state officials assume a more active presence in the previously static town. Elsa's power, however, remains shaky throughout the film's narrative. The authenticity of her vision and her status as a charismatic leader are rendered tenuous. Actual healings are reported, but these are never completely confirmed. The film also adds a meta-discursive level to this enigma when a filmmaker, Orly, comes to the town to film Elsa and to solve the enigma for himself. The film then spins out two subplots. The prostitute Nimia returns to Cupang from a period of exile, and becomes Elsa's double and inverted figure. Two of the village men, Narding and Pilo, plan to find contractual work overseas,[41] but become bandits instead. They brutally murder a rich Chinese mestizo who was drawn to Elsa's ministry. These two manifestations of discord in the town correlate with the rising chaos and hysteria that Elsa's healing begins to provoke. As more and more people are drawn to Elsa, all in need of liberation, the question of leadership and a plan of action becomes inescapable. This volatile situation climaxes when Elsa and her disciple, Chayong, are raped by strangers from Manila, an incident surreptitiously captured on film by Orly. The rape forces Elsa herself to confront the validity of her vision, and her moment of self-reflection signals the rapid decline of her ministry. After Chayong's suicide and Elsa's fatal inability to save two children from cholera, Elsa is ostracized by the townspeople. But she is later seen vomiting, and rumors quickly spread concerning an immaculate conception. It also rains on the long-arid town. Elsa commands the people to assemble on the hill of the Marian apparition, but in a dramatic reversal, confesses that there is no miracle. She is assassinated, and a riot ensues. The secret of her vision dies along with her. The film ends with one of Elsa's disciples, Sepa, declaring her a saint and martyr. She assumes the now-vacant seat of spiritual leadership.

Himala allows us to think about the national within the language and conceptual framework of popular traditions, in this case, popular religiosity. What is striking in this identification with the popular is its gendering of tradition. Women are represented as atavistic figures, whose bodies must guarantee the authenticity of national traditions. Men, by contrast, are represented as agents of progress. The film refuses to name the nation, and instead, draws from popular traditions to see what a potentially revolutionary experience might mean for the impoverished peasants of Cupang. Unfortunately, as the film dramatically portrays, the people are torn between a sense of fatalism (that everything is foreordained) and a sense of agency. This ambivalence about the meaning of the national is figured in the ambiguous biography of the film's central character, Elsa. While the term *nation* derives from *natio* (to be born), the facts surrounding Elsa's birth remain shrouded in mystery throughout the film's narrative. However, the film makes various suggestions that her birth was of a supernatural order. Repeated references are made of Elsa as a *putok sa buho*, the colloquial term for one of questionable parentage. Her adoptive mother, Aling Saling, herself an old maid, confesses that she found Elsa on the very same hill of the Marian apparitions.

Orly's camera literalizes on screen the film's own process of interrogating the origins of the nation. Elsa's link to the Virgin is encoded as an enigma, a secret that the film itself is careful not to violate. However, the question of Elsa's origins in a supernatural order (and by extension, the nation's origins in some anterior time), is constantly juxtaposed with Elsa's status as a social outcast. She has not been raised by a "normal" family. Located outside its naturalized hierarchies, Elsa is a potentially disruptive force, more so because she is a woman.

Interviewing Elsa, an incredulous Orly asks why she chose to identify with the Virgin. She replies: "Lumipas na ang sa Ama. Ngayon naman ang sa Ina" (The time of the Father has passed. Now it is the Mother's turn). Although the film's narrative structure draws heavily on the millenarian concepts of folk Catholicism, this statement is nonetheless a provocative reworking of its terms. Note that Catholicism privileges Christology and the Christ event. While Elsa is represented as a Christ figure—attracting the lowly classes and healing the sick— she is also represented as a Virgin figure on whose purity the fate of the town rests. Not coincidentally, the reification of Elsa's purity serves as a commentary, not only on the chauvinism implied by nationalism, but also on the overt masculinity of national liberation movements, and for that matter, the masculinity of the cinema vanguards themselves.

Equally interesting is the film's representation of the traditional figures of elite oppression in the countryside. The film explicitly references the system of patron-client relationships emblematic of what Benedict Anderson has termed "cacique democracy" in the Philippines.[42] Within this system, landholding elites of mestizo descent secure their economic positions by maintaining links with the state apparatus or by building political dynasties of their own. In the film, the town's patron-client relationships are curiously feminized and channeled through

Mrs. Alba, the town matriarch for whom both Elsa and Aling Saling work as day laborers. When she hears of Elsa's ministry, Mrs. Alba moves to organize it, appointing other women from the town to serve as administrators. Furthermore, it is Mrs. Alba who instigates the commercialization of Elsa's ministry. In one scene, Mrs. Alba and the town mayor rapaciously discuss the exploitability of Elsa's work among the poor and the sick. The town, she notes, could be modeled after Lourdes. After inquiring about the possibility of exporting Elsa's blessed water, she states that she is currently building a resort to absorb the large numbers of people who have begun to flock to Cupang. The mayor states that he is counting on the town's thriving new industry to finance his reelection.

But Cupang's new prosperity comes at a price. While Elsa's ministry was originally meant to heal people, Cupang itself is besieged by the threat of social contamination as a result of her work. Repeated references are made to "undesirable" elements coming from Manila. One sequence shows throngs of people, bustling to get a glimpse of Elsa. Invisible editing stitches together shots of media representatives, urbanely dressed mestizos and white tourists, mixing freely with the sick and the truly destitute. In a reversal of sorts, it is the latter that appear to be threatened by contamination. On the sound track we hear the plaintive sound of mass prayer, layered over with the sounds of babies wailing and the sick moaning. The mounting hysteria is punctuated by a jump cut to two policemen talking. One of them comments, "Rebolusyon na yata 'to" (It's starting to look like a revolution).

The prospect of a revolution, however, is foreclosed. Again drawing from the language of folk Catholicism, the film defers this revolution because the people have not adequately demonstrated true spiritual renewal. This lack is encoded, in Fanon's terms, as the incomplete political and social consciousness of the people. And it is Elsa's rape that confirms this. Interestingly, we only come to know about the incident from Orly's camera. The disclosure is made on two overlapping frames. The sequence begins with Orly, a proclaimed atheist, confessing to the parish priest that he did something terrible. The film then cuts to the film within the film, and in voice-over, Orly guides us through the incident. We see Elsa and Chayong making their dawn pilgrimage to the hill of the Marian apparitions. A group of stoned "addicts from Manila" ambushes them. Orly's film captures them from a distance, and we have to rely on his commentary to interpret what's on screen. He tells us that Chayong's screams were unnerving, and that she repeatedly begged for Elsa's help—so complete was her faith in the visionary's powers. Orly's film then cuts to Elsa and Chayong, their clothes torn, running through the village. In voice-over, he tells us that Elsa told the matriarchs that they were attacked by the Devil, posing as a wild boar. The elders believed this fantastic story. He confesses to a profound sense of guilt, not only for not helping the women, but also for his desire to use the sensational footage to better his career. The sequence is a crucial, self-reflexive discourse on the part of Bernal. Like Orly, Bernal is potentially exploiting the popular traditions and the actual hardships of the rural classes. The sequence finds resonances in Mrs. Alba's commercialization of Elsa's ministry. The blessed water she plans to export is much like Bernal's film—prepackaged misery for sale to the world. Note the following review of the film from the international trade press:

> It is rich in details of backward village life that should fascinate foreign viewers intrigued with exotic Third World poverty, hunger, oriental funeral services, physical ugliness and handicapped human bodies cinematically framed by the magic of faith healing as its main theme.[43]

The cultural politics of Bernal's film are rife with ambiguities. Bernal and his contemporaries at the Experimental Cinema of the Philippines[44] believed that it was the artist's role to show the social problems of the nation. The ultimate goal was to mobilize a critical mass audience and to effect social change. However, the Filipino auteurs at the ECP were paradoxically dependent on the patronage of the Marcos regime. *Himala* could not help but bear the traces of this patronage in its text. While it used some politically progressive strategies—the foregrounding of popular traditions and the privileging of popular conceptual frameworks to encode and decode the film—it nonetheless undercuts the very logic of these themes and these strategies. It is significant to note that the tradition of popular religious revolt in the Philippines hinged on a conception of the restoration of an originary social order. Bernal's film, while referencing this order, is conflicted between effecting total revolution and securing its own position within the Marcos patronage system. Or to put it another way, the film could only speak about revolutionary goals in ways that would not offend the very regime it aimed to critique. It is a form of doublespeak that paradoxically saves itself by being neither completely authentic (faithful to the original spirit of popular revolt) nor completely sanitized (capitulating to Marcos policy). What is striking about the film's politics is its feminization and racialization of underdevelopment, a crucial factor in the film's analysis of a "failed" revolution. It is significant to note the international trajectory of the film. It was originally produced as an entry to the 1983 Manila International Film Festival. It makes sense then to focus on rural blight and misery—powerfully captured by images of "exotic Third World ugliness"—because this was assumed to be what the First World desired to see. That these images got past the Marcos administration's watchful eye can ultimately be explained by the film's own parroting of the Martial Law rhetoric—its references to social contamination and the need to suppress "undesirable" elements. Note Elsa's final words:

ELSA

Nitong mga nakaraang araw, sa loob lamang ng napakaikling panahon, parang naranasan natin ang pinaghalong langit at impiyerno

These past few days, within such brief amount of time, we've experienced heaven and hell.

Maraming sakit ang gumaling, maramaing tao ang bumuti at nagkaraoon ng panampalataya Pero nakakita rin tayo ng kamatayan, ng epidemya, ng pagpuputa, ng krimen at panloloko.	Many with afflictions were healed, many have found faith. But we have also seen death, disease, whoring and deceit.
Walang himala! Ang himala ay nasa puso ng tao! Nasa puso nating lahat! Tayo ang gumagawa ng himala! Tayo ang gumagawa ng mga sumpa at mga Diyos!	There is no miracle! The miracle is in us! Inside all of us! We make the miracles! We make the curses and the gods!

Recall Rocha's *Black God, White Devil.* That film ends with the statement "the earth does not belong to God or the Devil but to man." Bernal's film ends with a similar conclusion. Having made their respective cinematic interventions, the vanguards imagined that they were empowering the *povo*/people. However, in both films, the ambiguous class position of the leftist intellectual was complicated by their simultaneous affirmation and disavowal of racial difference. Are the *povo*/people really free to make their own curses and miracles? Consider for a moment how this utopian view of the marginalized majority meshes with the rhetoric of the repressive state. In a 1974 speech delivered before the Film Academy of the Philippines, First Lady Imelda Marcos provided the following rationale for state intervention in the film industry:

> I can no longer accept the idea that the Filipino is frivolous, for example, or that the audience for films—the much-derided mass audience—is too ignorant and indifferent to appreciate productions which follow the timeless dictum of all art: the exaltation of the human spirit. *We would like to see films of our native epics, portrayals of our native soul. Dramatizations of our authentic lives as individuals and as a people* . . .At a time when the eyes of the world are upon us, at a time when we are embarked on the task of regeneration through discipline, the challenge begins with our arts and our artists. Let us not, therefore, betray this vision. Let us be worthy of it. (emphasis added)[45]

We have seen how the social contradictions and political ambiguities that riddled authoritarianism provided the context within which Filipino and Brazilian vanguards worked to present a politically progressive and critical vision of the nation. Closely identifying themselves with the popular traditions of marginalized communities, Brazilian and Filipino filmmakers simultaneously sought the "national popular" as a form of social critique *and* political mobilization. A profound sense of ambiguity thus marked both vanguard movements. On the one hand, the two movements worked for a radical film culture that would not only challenge mainstream aesthetics and practices but also perform a revisionary function in the nation's perception of itself and its contradictory formation. Placing young, male left-wing and middle-class cultural producers at critical positions in this historical rewriting, the two movements hinged on powerful assumptions about cultural leadership. Animated by the goal of developing a revolutionary mass consciousness, vanguards from both movements sought social change. But as a cultural elite, the vanguards assumed the responsibility, traditionally bestowed on the bourgeoisie, of representing the aspirations and values of the popular classes. At issue here is the profound tension between cultural leadership and the popular classes whom the vanguards hoped to both represent and transform. While the cultural imperative behind a radical art cinema hinged on a romanticized conception of the artist, the political impetus behind a cinematic activism hinged on the notion of a revolutionary mass. Who were the real agents, and conversely, who were the real targets of social change supposed to be? But what is to my mind most striking about these analogous polemics and problems is the way ethnic and racial identity politics were simultaneously inscribed and effaced by the conservative modernization of the state on the one hand, and vanguard film movements committed to national liberation on the other.

The repressive state and the cinema vanguards seemed to borrow from each other's discourses. Both seemed to oscillate between a recognition of racial difference and a liberal-humanist belief in the perfectibility of the marginalized majority. It is this double movement that makes the cultural intervention of the Filipino auteurs, much like their Cinema Novo counterparts, simultaneously provocative and incomplete.

NOTES

1. Ferdinand Marcos, *Notes on the New Society of the Philippines* (Manila: Marcos Foundation, Inc., 1973), p. 71.

2. Ella Shohat and Robert Stam, *Unthinking Eurocentrism: Multiculturalism and the Media* (London: Routledge, 1996), p. 48.

3. Gerald Sussmann, "The Transnationalization of Philippine Telecommunications: Postcolonial Continuities," in *Transnational Communications: Wiring the Third World*, ed. Gerald Sussman and John Lent (London: Sage, 1991), p. 125.

4. Benedict Anderson, *The Spectre of Comparisons: Nationalism, Southeast Asia, and the World* (London: Verso, 1998), p. 6.

5. Ibid., p. 195.

6. Ibid., p. 6.

7. Ibid., p. 193.

8. Ibid.

9. Ibid.

10. To which critics add, "yes, for white people." See Gilberto Freyre, *New World in the Tropics: The Culture of Modern Brazil* (New York: Alfred Knopf, 1959), p. 9; quoted in Pierre-Michel Fontaine, "Research in the Political Economy of Afro-Latin America," *Latin America Research Review* 15, no. 2 (1980): 111–242.

11. Robert Stam, *Tropical Multiculturalism* (Durham, N.C.: Duke University Press, 1997), p. 32.

12. Ibid., p. 4.

13. Ibid., p. 5.

14. Octavio Ianni, "Research on Race Relations in Brazil," in *Race and Class in Latin America*, ed. Magnus Morner (New York: Columbia University Press, 1970); cited in Pierre-Michel Fontaine, "Research in the Political Economy of Afro-Latin America," p. 117.

15. Florestan Fernandes, *A Revolucao Burguesa no Brasil* (Rio de Janeiro: Zahar, 1975), cited in Pierre-Michel Fontaine, "Research in the Political Economy of Afro-Latin America," p. 124.

16. Pierre-Michel Fontaine, "Research in the Political Economy of Afro-Latin America," p.

125; Paulo De Carvalho-Neto, "Folklore of the Black Struggle in Latin America," *Latin American Perspectives* 5, no. 2 (spring 1978): 53–88.

17. Stam, *Tropical Multiculturalism*, p. 29.

18. Manila was the entrepôt of the "galleon trade," through which Chinese silks and porcelains were exchanged for Mexican silver, to be resold at huge profits in Europe. See Alfred W. McCoy and Ed C. de Jesus, eds., *Philippine Social History: Global Trade and Local Transformations* (Quezon City: Ateneo de Manila Press, 1982).

19. Anderson, *The Spectre of Comparisons*, p. 194.

20. David Sturtevant, *Popular Uprisings in the Philippines 1840–1940* (Ithaca: Cornell University Press, 1976), p. 35.

21. Ibid., p. 39.

22. Ibid., p. 41.

23. Stam, *Tropical Multiculturalism*, p. 48.

24. Carlos Hasenbalg and Nelson do Valle Silva, "Notes on Racial and Political Inequality in Brazil," in Hanchard, *Racial Politics in Contemporary Brazil*, p. 155.

25. The literature on patrimonial politics and the plundering of the Philippine state is vast. A seminal work is Benedict Anderson, "Cacique Democracy in the Philippines," *New Left Review* 169 (May/June 1988); reprinted in *Spectre of Comparisons*, pp. 192–226.

26. Glauber Rocha, "An Esthetic of Hunger," tr. Randal Johnson and Burnes Hollyman, in *Brazilian Cinema*, ed. Randal Johnson and Robert Stam (New York: Columbia University Press, 1995), pp. 68–71.

27. Ibid., p. 70.

28. Ibid.

29. Johnson and Stam, eds. *Brazilian Cinema*, p. 30.

30. Stam, *Tropical Multiculturalism*, p. 179.

31. Robert M. Levine, *Vale of Tears: Revisiting the Canudos Massacre in Northeastern Brazil, 1893–1897* (Berkeley: University of California Press, 1992), p. 2.

32. Euclydes da Cunha, *Rebellion in the Backlands* (Chicago: University of Chicago Press, 1945).

33. Ibid., pp. 78, 85.

34. Stam, *Tropical Multiculturalism*, p. 234.

35. Johnson and Stam, *Brazilian Cinema*, p. 37.

36. Carlos Diegues, "A Democratic Cinema," in Johnson and Stam, *Brazilian Cinema*, pp. 99–101.

37. Rui Guerra, "Popular Cinema and the State," in: Ibid., pp. 101–103.

38. Bienvenido Lumbera, "Problems in Philippine Film History," in *Readings in Philippine Cinema*, ed. Rafael Ma. Guerrero (Manila: Experimental Cinema of the Philippines, 1983), p. 69.

39. Nicanor Tiongson, "The Filipino Film Industry," *East-West Film Journal* 6, no. 2 (1992), p. 28.

40. John Lent, *The Asian Film Industry* (Austin: University of Texas Press, 1990), p. 157; Clodualdo del Mundo, "Philippine Cinema: An Historical Overview," *Asian Cinema* (spring/summer, 1999): 33–34.

41. At the time of the film's release, one prevalent trend in the economy was the growing exportation of labor to the Middle East. These overseas workers now contribute a significant share to the country's GNP.

42. Benedict Anderson, "Cacique Democracy in the Philippines," in *Spectre of Comparisons*, pp. 192–226.

43. "Himala" (Review) in *Variety* (January 26, 1983): 16, 18.

44. The Experimental Cinema of the Philippines (ECP) was a comprehensive support institution for filmmakers that was established by the Marcos administration in 1982. Ironically, it was the administration's active patronage that helped build the careers of Filipino auteurs, who, like Bernal, had leftist politics. Notable examples include Lino Brocka and Mike De Leon.

45. Imelda Marcos, "Film as Art," Filipino Academy of Movie Arts and Sciences Awards. Manila Hilton, Manila, April 21, 1974, speech reprinted in *The Compassionate Society and Other Selected Speeches* (Manila: National Media Production Center, 1976), pp. 58–59.

Jennifer González

The Appended Subject: Race and Identity as Digital Assemblage

To append is to attach or fix something onto something else. The Latin root *pendere* means *to hang*—to hang something (an arm, a leg, a text) onto something else. In an uncanny way, an appendage is always considered integral to the object to which it is also an addition. The simultaneous necessity and marginality of the appendage also characterizes many of those material practices, objects, and signs that are said to construct forms of social and cultural identification. Signs grafted onto the human subject—such as clothing or names, projections of others based upon historical circumstances, location, language—enunciate both defining elements of that subject and part of an external, changing narrative into which that subject is drawn, voluntarily or involuntarily, as a participant. The "appended subject" has several connotations here—that of a subject that is comprised of appendages, of parts put together, of supplementary materials, or that of a subject or person who is defined by a relation of supplementarity, added to some other principal body—as the colonized subject might be perceived by an imperial nation as an appendage to a centralized state. Finally, the appended subject describes an object constituted of electronic elements serving as a psychic or bodily appendage, an artificial subjectivity that is attached to a supposed original or unitary being, an online persona understood as somehow appended to a real person who resides elsewhere, in front of a keyboard. In each case a body is constructed or assembled in order to stand in for, or become an extension of, a subject in an artificial but nevertheless inhabited world.

The concept of an appended subject is used in this essay to account for contemporary artists' representations of utopian spaces on the World Wide Web and the visible models of embodied subjects produced therein. This relatively new domain for the phantasmatic projection of subjectivity (new in comparison to other media, such as film, television, advertising, and forms of cultural spectacle that produce patterns of identification) has also been championed as an innovative space for the reinscription or redefinition of social relations, as well as the reconceptualization of the traditional markers of race and ethnicity, sexuality and gender. There are currently thousands of online spaces that allow users to experiment with identity in an artificial world. The original form of such sites—MUDs or MOOs—are collaborative writing projects in which people describe or define a physical presence, contribute to a textual architecture, and converse with other online participants. Media theorists and communications scholars have provided the most sophisticated and extensive readings of this social collective practice. Much has already been written about the agony and ecstasy of gender swapping, virtual sex, passing, and politics on these sites.[1] As computer monitors and Internet interfaces have increased in their capacity to display visual information over the past decade, online sites with image and sound components have become popular. In these "habitats" or "palaces" a textual description of the user is superseded or supplemented by a visual icon—usually called an avatar.

Even a superficial glance at online sites that distribute or sell avatars is instructive, revealing a common set of identificatory fantasies created by individual whim as well as popular demand. Simple grids of images (scanned photographs, drawings, cartoons) are arranged thematically (as movie stars or "avamarks," soft-porn models or "avatarts," muscular men or "avahunks," troublemakers or "avapunks," cats, dogs, Native Americans, blondes, brunettes, happy faces, Hula dancers, space aliens, medieval knights, and corporate logos) apparently following an internal logic of demand but tacitly referencing a social typology in which such categories mark out a hierarchy of social relations and stereotypes. The availability of these images for sale makes literal a public circulation of ego ideals while simultaneously naturalizing the marketplace as the privileged domain—beyond family, church, or state—of contemporary identity construction and consumption.

The enactment of racial identity online takes a variety of forms. In some cases users will self-identify (as white, black, Latino) in chats that solicit discussion on the topic of race. In other cases, race or ethnicity will be a defining feature of a web site to which users send photographs of themselves, such as sites that function as support groups for mixed-race couples. My focus here, however, is on the phantasmatic representation of race or ethnicity and in particular on models of hybrid racial identity that take the form of avatars or other visual assemblages of human bodies. Insofar as racial and ethnic identity are conceived in many cases to be limited to visible signs such as skin color, eye color, or bone structure, they are also conceived as decorative features to be attached or detached at will in the so-called artificial or virtual context of cyberspace. Such play with racial identity nevertheless can and does have concrete consequences as real as those occurring in other cultural domains of social exchange, such as literature, film, or music. Because "passing" (or pretending to be what one is not) in cyberspace has become a norm rather than an exception, the representation of race in this space is complicated by the fact that much of the activity online is about becoming the fantasy of a racial other.

Homi Bhabha's 1986 essay "The Other Question" has been useful to my own work for its elaboration of the link between racial stereotyping and the struc-

tural disavowal that characterizes fetishism. Stereotypes are created by colonizing cultures, Bhabha asserts, in order to mask real cultural difference. In order to
disavow this difference, as well as the complex subjectivity of the colonized population, the stereotype presents itself as a fetish—in the form of literature, images,
speech—by which the possible threat of the other's difference is transformed into
a safe fantasy for the colonizer. Thus "the recognition and disavowal of difference
is always disturbed by the question of its representation or construction."[2]
Bhabha's analysis succeeds in drawing out the relations of power that underlie the
colonialist enterprise and that become manifest in social and material practices.
Something on the same order of analysis is required, I believe, to address the fantasy utopias or dystopias of the Web that reproduce stereotypes (particularly of
race and gender) at an impressive pace.

My brief analysis here is motivated largely by a curiosity concerning representations of human bodies online. How do such visual representations extend
or challenge current conceptions of racial and cultural identity and relations of
power? In what ways is human identity equated with the notion of a bodily assemblage? What are the possible ramifications of such an equation for conceptions of
cultural hybridity on the one hand, or a revived eugenics on the other?

Two provocative sites will serve as a point of discussion, although there
are many others appearing daily. UNDINA, by the Russian artist Kostya Mitenev,
and Bodies© INCorporated, by U.S.-based artist Victoria Vesna, appear inspired,
at least in part, by the contemporary phenomenon of avatar production. Both web
sites deviate somewhat from the norm, putting an unusual spin on the production
of "appended subjects," particularly as those subjects are conceived as assembled
from disparate iconic elements. Each site offers the user the opportunity to construct or "submit" visual images of a body or of body parts, and to examine other
bodies that have been put on display. These two sites were chosen for comparison
because the human body is their primary focus and race or ethnicity as elements
of identity are conspicuous by their presence or absence in each case. Both sites
use the space of the computer screen to depict bodies in pieces, either as photographic images or as three-dimensional renditions of corporeal fragments (arms,
legs, heads, torsos) that can be selected from a menu or reassembled. I am particularly interested in the ramifications of such artistic projects for thinking about
the interpellation of individuals as embodied subjects and the political, ethical,
and aesthetic notions of choice that they imply.

Identity as Bodily Assemblage: Parts and Proximate Relations

The title of Kostya Mitenev's web site, UNDINA, is an acronym for United Digital
Nations. UNDINA may also be a reference to the Tchaikovsky opera by the same
name, which was quickly written in 1869 and never performed. Tchaikovsky

destroyed the score, of which a few fragments are preserved. Linked to a collective web page for a group of Russian artists and scholars who identify themselves as Digital Body and who participate in exhibitions held in the Bionet Gallery, as well as to the home page for the city of St. Petersburg, the site has an international, cosmopolitan, and diplomatic feel. At the same time, UNDINA is clearly positioned as a work of contemporary art, sited within its own electronic gallery and addressing an audience of other artists and designers. Indeed, the line between so-called high art and the visual culture that pervades the World Wide Web has long been institutionally crossed insofar as museums of art (ICA London, the Guggenheim Museum, the Museum of Modern Art, and so on) regularly display online art projects; institutions of art education in industrialized nations offer computer graphics as a central component of their curricula; and art critics produce many online and offline publications that address exclusively online art practice. At the same time, the work is not unlike other sites that are presented for entertainment, commerce, or information. The space is electronic, the vernacular is based on standards of hardware and software, and the audience is unpredictable. To study works of art in this context thus invites comparison to a broader field of visual culture (i.e., avatar production) as well as to parallels in other fine art practices and performances.

On the opening page of Kostya Mitenev's UNDINA appears the familiar figure of Leonardo Da Vinci's fifteenth-century Vitruvian Man, with arms and legs outstretched, floating in geometric perfection (see Figure 1). An ironic gesture on the part of Mitenev, the Vitruvian Man situates this work within and against a tradition of figurative normativity. Leonardo's geometry becomes a sign of the standard against which the artist develops a model of contemporary human form and being, while at the same time the body of man is read as the central axis in a futurology of body archetypes. Mitenev accuses this standard (here renamed Xyman) of having dominated European cultural representations of the body "for half a millennium."[3] Part of the goal of the UNDINA web site, according to the artist, is to decenter this traditional form with a set of collectively constructed new future bodies.

Comprised of three separate domains, the UNDINA site includes a virtual gallery space that can be navigated with VRML technology, a planetary system populated by cultural archetypes, and, the central focus of the work, what might be called a future-body table of new physical types. This last consists of a screen space divided into a grid of nine squares, depicting the head, torso, and legs of three vertical figures (see Figure 2). Body or body-part images that have been submitted by users or by the artist are joined or stacked together to form a monstrous or fantastical mixing of sex, age, and race into a single body. The artist comments, "In the project of UNDINA the intrigue of the collective modeling of the body of the future is maintained." The plan is to make "a wide range catalog of visual delirium of future images of the body and to create a model or space of international foresight of artistic images of future bodies." In the process, Mitenev suggests that "you can choose your own model of a body, alternatively you can create it your-

Figure 1. UNDINA, 2002

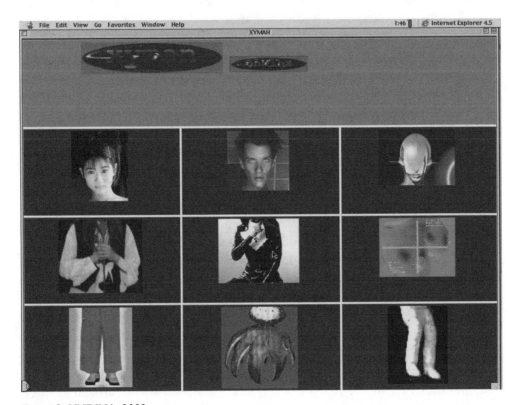

Figure 2. UNDINA, 2002

self with your computer. The bodies are timeless and anonymous, that frees the self in the space of the meta-world," adding, "Artists of non-European traditions of conceptualizing and visualizing of the body are specially invited."[4] Mitenev's project appears progressive in so far as it aims to undermine narrow conceptions of human beings; to shift European standards of body normativity from center to margin; to offer a United Digital Nations of diverse international membership as a model for future cultural contact, perhaps even a "global" village. But UND-INA's effort to escape the culture of the stereotype oddly reinscribes its narrow confines. The result is more akin to what might be a fantasy in the form of a surrealist exquisite corpse game.

The bodies in Mitenev's body grid are "timeless," or perhaps more precisely heterochronic, insofar as they are comprised of both historical and contemporary images that are constantly flashing on and off the screen, the mix-and-match elements recurring or transforming into new configurations. In the row of heads, for example, one might see a portrait by Archimboldo or Rosetti, a 1940s photograph of a beautiful black woman's face, or the head of a white male fashion model; at torso level there might appear the bare breasts of a pornography model, a scantily clad dark-skinned woman or a white man in a suit and tie; and for legs a pair of combat boots, a photograph of female—or on the rare instance, male—genitalia and bare legs, or the tender feet of an infant. These and many other images flash continually on and off in this imaginary game of human exhibition and hybridization. Fantasies of undressing and connecting with cultural "others" are expressed in a painfully awkward montage resulting in a strange dysplasia.

Leaving behind this screen of automated flesh, the user can visit the planetary realm of UNDINA populated by selected archetypal figures of the artist's futurology. Rather than dissecting these bodies into a set of interchangeable parts, Mitenev situates them in familiar categories. With a simple click of the mouse one travels to, for example, the planet of the gods, the aliens, the heroes, the mythological heroes, the wonderland heroes, the cult images, the fantastical images, or the monsters. Here, future bodies are not so much hybrids as characters within an archetypal literary taxonomy. There seems to be only a small step between Mitenev's work and the cultural stereotypes provided by other avatar sites. For example, aliens are blue space creatures; heroes are white men with blond hair; killers wear African headdresses; and cult images include nude women of color.

Mitenev's work, perhaps unconsciously, perpetuates damaging racial and sexual stereotypes—in itself nothing new in art or visual culture; yet, UNDINA's presentation is more insidious because of its utopian and inclusive rhetoric. Indeed, I would probably not address this work if it were not for its supposed attempt to picture a progressive model of future subjectivity. In this context, the most interesting aspect of the site is the series of images that comprise the automatic body table, those future bodies exemplified in a nonunitary, hybrid form. This ambitious attempt to reproduce a model of cultural mixing through an intersection of photographic images appears in an equally insidious way in *Time* magazine, in an article entitled "The New Face of America" (1993). Donna Haraway has commented, "*Time* magazine's matrix of morphed racial mixtures induces amnesia about what it costs, and what might be possible when flesh-and-blood people confront the racialized structure of desire and/or reproduction collectively and individually."[5] Evelynn M. Hammonds comments that

> Morphing, with its facile device of shape-changing, interchangeability, equivalency, and feigned horizontality in superficial ways elides its similarity with older hierarchical theories of human variation. . . . With the *Time* cover we wind up not with a true composite, but a preferred or filtered composite of mixed figures with no discussion of the assumptions or implications underlying the choices.[6]

What both UNDINA and *Time* magazine offer in the form of a visual representation is a dissection of a fantasy subject along the gross criteria of bodily appendages or genotype, with little or no consideration of other cultural factors such as language, economic class, or political practice. It is similar to the process that Margaret Morse sees operating in the morphing of human faces in Michael Jackson's *Black or White* music video: "Ideologically, the work of achieving harmony among different people disappears along with the space in between them."[7] The artist's desire to produce timeless and anonymous bodies creates precisely the kind of historical elision that erases any complex notion of cultural identity. Here a hybrid identity is presumed to reside in or on the visible markers of the body, the flesh. In a sense, Mitenev beautifully illustrates the projective power of stereotyping. Here *subjectivity* is distilled from the assembled components (appendages) of the *body*.

This reading of the body as a coded form—a visible map—of the subject is as familiar as the idea of the psychoanalytic symptom, as basic to visual culture as the process of photographic mimesis that followed painting in a long line of efforts to capture the subject through a record or imprint of the body. But it is not this history that is of greatest importance here. Mitenev's work has less in common with the history of portraiture than with the experiments enacted in the name of modernity, the split and divided corporeality of twentieth-century visual collage, photomontage, and assemblage that attempts to map an unstable subjectivity with the collection or appropriation of disparate images and objects. I have already suggested a parallel with the parlor game the surrealists called exquisite corpse Here the collaborative production of a composite image of the body is played out electronically. In addition, an oblique reference to Hannah Höch's Dadaist photomontage can be found in Mitenev's use of an African headdress that bears a remarkable resemblance to *Denkmal II: Eitelkeit* (Monument II: Vanity) from the series *Aus einem ethnographischen Museum* (From an Ethnographic Museum) of 1926.

Insofar as Kostya Mitenev's project relies upon, or at least gestures toward, these artistic precedents, it is tempting to read UNDINA as simply an electronic extension of a familiar avant-garde art practice. The site might also be read as a progressive recognition of the *fact* of cultural hybridity, a recognition that humans are all produced through genetic and linguistic mixes. Yet, as I note above, the mix in Mitenev's universe depends upon cultural stereotypes for its model of the future. I have written elsewhere that the very concept of hybridity is haunted by its assumption of original purity.[8] UNDINA, finally, does little to subvert the racial or cultural hierarchies that underlie its playful, monstrous hybrids.

Mary Shelley's *Frankenstein* was an exploration of psychological and moral transformation, but it is best remembered in popular culture as the story of the reanimation of dead flesh, the production of a monstrosity out of parts of human bodies. The monstrous, as Barbara Maria Stafford reminds us, derives etymologically from the Latin *monstrare*, "to show," from *monere*, "to warn," and has come to mean the unnatural mixing of elements that do not belong together—a mixing of elements most often read as a tragic accident.[9] While Frankenstein's monster was no accident, Shelley's novel implies that the monstrous is nevertheless a product of tragedy. It is as if the various parts of the beast, acting in disunion or disharmony, create his inability to cohere as a subject.

The step from the tragic monster to the tragic mulatto or mestizo was a short one in the nineteenth century. The hybrid subject was never considered immune from the vicissitudes or the repercussions of unnatural union. The mixed-race body was somehow always in pieces, unable to become accurately assembled into a properly functioning subject or citizen—hence the laws banning miscegenation that were on the books in some parts of the United States until 1968. More than thirty years later, this once forbidden phenotype has become an unlikely, if popular, ideal. What is the appeal this subject position (still presented as monstrous) at the beginning of the twenty-first century?

In the context of post-Soviet Russia, it may be a radical act to suggest or visually represent racial and cultural hybridity. This gesture may have some impact on contemporary political activism. At the same time, UNDINA does little to undo the essentializing tendency common in many well-intentioned efforts to populate the World Wide Web with a variety of human types. Instead, the body fragment is used as a fetish to make cultural difference palatable, as an element of desire, of consumption. The synecdochic quality of the fetish, its status as a part object that allows pleasure, appears in UNDINA's formal, visual dissection and literal truncation of corporeal signs. Even the body as a whole, represented in parts, reproduces a fetishistic structure of disavowal, an occlusion of both the original subject and of the *historical relations between concrete bodies*, of enforced racial mixing, of colonialism. Yet, Mitenev's future bodies are presented as part of a new archetypal architecture of diplomacy. If the artist wishes the audience to play out the metaphor of a United Digital Nations, then what kind of diplomacy, dialogue, or action can take place in this context? Is the lack of a fixed subject position, a shifting set of bodily apparati, enough to constitute or provoke, as the artist seems to hope, a new international consciousness? In short, what set of relations is being offered to the audience as the model of future global interchange?

Despite its claims to offer collaborative construction, UNDINA perpetuates a uni-directional, uncritical reiteration of precisely the hegemony it seeks to critique, and it does so using racial mixing as its model.

In a different way, shifting from an imagined global community to a corporate one, artist Victoria Vesna also takes up the visual metaphor of the body-in-pieces to configure a new elemental species. Bodies© INCorporated is an art project based at the University of California at Santa Barbara, created by Victoria Vesna and a team of collaborators including Robert Nideffer, Nathanial Freitas, Kenneth Fields, Jason Schleifer, and others (see Figure 3). The site is designed to allow users to "build out bodies in 3-D space, graphically visualizing what were previously bodies generated as text-only."[10] Bodies© INC clearly situates its origins within the world of avatar manufacturers, yet it also foregrounds the manner in which bodies are conceived as part of a corporate or institutional structure in contemporary capitalist culture. It hovers in its own liminal space, a pun on the term *incorporated* that becomes a simultaneous critique of corporate culture and a capitulation to its terms of enunciation. For example, as with many other web sites, visitors to the site must agree to recognize and abide by various copyright restrictions, legal disclaimers, and limits of liability—including liability for *disappointment* in the outcome of the body one constructs. This witty, self-conscious irony runs throughout the text of the site, drawing upon the rhetoric of

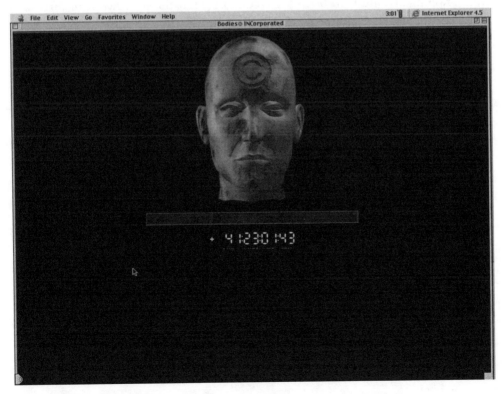

Figure 3. Bodies© Inc., 2002

advertising as well as making subtle and often satirical gestures toward the politics of identity and, in this case, the very notion of satisfaction guarantees or the lack thereof in the complex construction of a bodily identity. For here, as in Mitenev's world, the construction of a body is expressly linked to the construction of identity. The opening page of the site welcomes the new visitor, who is informed that the site "functions as an institution through which your body gets shaped in the process of identity construction that occurs in, and mutually implicates, both the symbolic and material realms."[11] The important relation between the material and the symbolic for Vesna is that between the shaping of the body and the construction of identity (the former being the apparent process by which the latter is achieved). While this equation echoes the assumptions of eugenics, it also can be read, alternatively, as a progressive assertion that identities are always inseparable from corporeal encounters and the symbolic inscription of bodily signs. The corporate rhetoric continues in the assertion that the body created "becomes the personal property" of the person who assembled it. The notion of the body as property also has its own historical connotations, not only in the traditional examples of prostitution and slavery, but also in a contemporary moment when body parts, organs, and vital tissue are bought and sold on a black market.[12] Body parts are also for sale in Bodies© INC, and the more shares the user accrues, the more parts he or she can buy.

Bodies© INC aptly reconstructs the bureaucracy that inspired its inception, drawing attention to bodies threaded through the paperwork of birth and death certificates, census forms, and medical records, and simultaneously emphasizing the necessity and ludicrous limits of creating selfhood through the apparatus of checked boxes and a narrow range of multiple choices. Birth and death are reduced to nothing but the mechanical act of filling out a form—accompanied by the frustration of waiting indefinitely to see the body-object one has created to appear as a visual model in 3-D graphics. The process of constructing a body for Bodies© INC sensitizes the user to the categories of identity and identification already standardized in the culture at large.

The administrative forms are simple black and white, divided into various subsections beginning with a "personal validation" in the form of a name, e-mail address, and password. One must next choose a name for the body to be constructed, then a sex assignment (choices include: female, male, hermaphrodite, other), then a sexual preference (choices include: heterosexual, homosexual, bisexual, transsexual, asexual, other), then an age group (any number with three digits or fewer), then body parts. One arrives at the construction of the body after already declaring its attributes. Continuing with the reductive model maintained throughout, the body is conceived as an object composed of six essential components: a head, torso, left arm, right arm, left leg, and right leg. No logic is given for this decomposition, although it is likely that the design is dependent upon a number of technical constraints as well as conceptual focus. Each body part can be masculine, feminine, infantile, or nonexistent. One could produce a body without a head, for example. Each part can be sized either small, medium, or large, and is finally surfaced by one of twelve textures: black rubber, blue plastic, bronze, clay, concrete, lava, pumice, water, chocolate, glass, or wood (see Figure 4). Vesna contends that the bodies are "constructed from textures, in order to shift the tendency to perceive the project from a strictly sexualized one (as frequently indicated by people's orders and comments) to a more psychological one (where matters of the mind are actively contemplated and encouraged). Before long, each of the textures is given detailed symbolic meaning."[13]

Bodies© INC thus establishes its own community of bodies with symbolic meaning intimately tied to a surface texture. Given the kinds of images available on the Web, this gesture is probably groundbreaking, although it remains to be seen how successful it is in desexualizing the body, as the normative adult body in Bodies© INC are tall, slim, and decidedly reflect Euro-American ideals. Indeed, to construct a fat body or to produce an unusual or monstrous body in this context requires more shares and expertise. Textures are also a convenient solution to the problem of skin color(s). Yet, the progressive potential of a rejection of racial typology falls into its own essentialism when character traits are equated with physical attributes, and limited to a prescribed system of behaviors. Black rubber

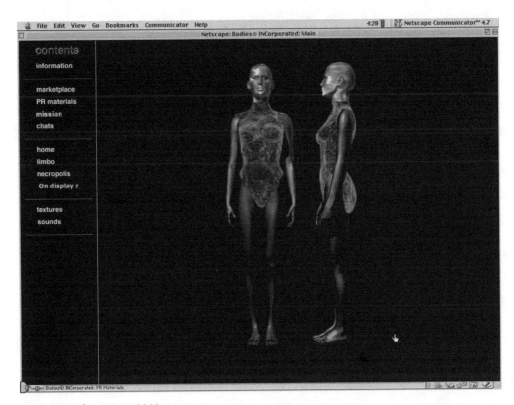

Figure 4. Bodies© Inc., 2002

is hot and dry, sublimates at a relatively low temperature, and is a fashion and style element; bronze is hot and cold, hard and wet, very reactive when heated with most substances and is a corporate leader element; clay is cold, dry, and melancholy, it works on subliminal levels to bring out the feminine and is an organizational element; concrete is cold and wet, a powerful desiccating agent that reacts strongly with water and is a business element; lava is hot and dry, conceived as light trapped in matter or perpetual fire and represents a team leader sense; chocolate is sweet and moist, an integrative force that interweaves and balances and is a marketing element, and so on. What emerges from this list is a set of corporate types that are simultaneously humorous and disturbingly familiar. They combine traits that are already linked in the popular preconscious of the culture at large (the melancholy female, the reactive corporate leader) in the form of archetypes or stereotypes. Hybrid figures may also be composed of different elements, perhaps even a schizophrenic set of surfaces that may implicate the body in a set of conflicting power relations. More ironic and sophisticated than those produced in UNDINA, these body textures are still problematic for those who may already be identified as "black" or "bronze."

In addition to a visual body, the user is able to choose from one of twelve sounds that will provide an otherwise mute figure with a kind of vocal presence: breath, geiger, history, nuclear, sine, or voice, for example. The sound components are clearly conceived as conceptual signs that function evocatively rather than mimetically. Finally, the user can mark whether the newly designed body functions as an alter ego, a significant other, a desired sexual partner, or "other," and may add special handling instructions or body descriptions and general comments.

Unlike Mitenev's UNDINA, Vesna's Bodies© INC has extensive written documentation on the web site that creates a metadiscourse for the user. An essay by Christopher Newfield defines Bodies© INC as a specific kind of corporate structure that

> establishes a virtual corporation as an "active community" of participants who choose their own bodily form. The primary activity is the creation of a body in exchange for which the creator is given a share of stock. Corporation B thus exists to express each member's desire about his or her physical shape. Production serves self-creation. Firm membership formally ratifies expression. These expressions have none of the usual limits: men become women; black becomes white and white becomes brown; flesh turns to clay, plastic, air; clay, plastic, air are attached on one body. Bodies need be neither whole nor have parts that fit.[14]

Indeed, this work clearly produces what I have called an appended subject whose limbs and flesh are accessorized, linked to personality traits, and used as values of exchange. The miscegenation of this world is one of hot and cold, wet and dry, mind over matter. But the underlying notion of easily transformed gender and skin color—"men become women; black becomes white and white becomes brown"—more accurately denotes the fantasies inherent in the project.

To her credit Vesna writes, "There is a need for alternate worlds to be built with more complex renditions of identity and community building and not simply replicating the existing physical structures or hierarchies."[15] She also comments that Bodies© INC is conceived "with the intention of shifting the discourse of the body from the usual idea of flesh and identity. Every member's body represented is the locus of the contradictions of functioning in the hi-tech environment while being in the Meta-Body, the Entity in the business of service."[16] Vesna here maps the internal logic of her own work, criticizing and at the same time reproducing a corporate ontology. Unfortunately, the users of the site do not seem to share her self-conscious take on the function of bodily representations. Lucy Hernandez, quoted in the discussion section of Bodies© INC, writes in May 1997, "I am very pleased to have found your site. I am looking for avatars that can be used in any VRML world. Can my new body leave this site and visit other places? How can I get my new body code? Thanks for making 'real' people. I'm tired of being a bird!" What happens to these real people when they are no longer needed? Like the leftover packaging of mass-produced commodities, the bodies created in Bodies© INC are sent to the wasteland of Necropolis after their creators chose a method for their death. Never really gone, they haunt the floating world in cold rows of gray geometric blocks. Other bodies circulate and purchase parts at the "Marketplace" (where a *Star Trek* Vulcan head might currently be on sale), or exercise their exhibitionism in "Showplace" return "Home" or loiter in "Limbo." Each domain is a separate VRML world within Bodies© INC that can be navigated with the proper software.

Sardonic, slick, and beautiful, Bodies© INC offers a critical response to a corporate structure and hierarchy. Its irony is also part of its complicity. And for this group of artists, complicity seems to be the primary mode by which any kind of cultural transformation and critique will take place. Christopher Newfield writes

> There's no more important change right now than culture recapturing technology—recapturing technology not to reject it but to make culture its partner again as we invent our future, our society, our redemptions. An excellent place to begin is the [corporate] B-form's recolonization of business power for the artist's mode of continuous invention business now says it seeks. You will know the recolonization is working when you say, paraphrasing Louis Massiah, "it makes revolution irresistible."[17]

This unlikely mix of neo-Marxist and marketing rhetoric suggests a new critical form for art production. Bodies© INC's financial sponsors include, among others, Viewpoint Data Labs, Netscape, alias/Wavefront, Silicon Graphics, Meta-Tools, and Siggraph. It remains to be seen whether a "recolonization" of business power is the most effective method for its critique. Bodies© INC succeeds at least in foregrounding relations among bodies, bureaucracy, and power in a culture based on consumption.

The Global Ideological Apparatus and Getting a Head

The bodies under construction in UNDINA and Bodies© INC populate a built environment of supposedly global proportions. The Internet, when seen as an infinite realm of marketing and promotion, primarily interpellates subjects as consuming bodies, or as subjects in need of appending. Victoria Vesna writes, "One thing is certain—the avatar business is booming. Major companies are investing in creation of online communities and placing their bets on this becoming a 'virtual entertainment ground.'"[18] She cites Rich Abel, president and CEO of Worlds INC, who declares, "Consider this: a virtual trade show that never closes, complete with booths, displays, product demonstrations, and shows. Or a showroom with operating products on display. Or a virtual visit to a theater, a hotel, or cruise ship. There is no more powerful way to market and promote. What kind of world would you like us to build for you?"[19]

In writing about the World Wide Web, scholar Joseba Gabilando turns to Louis Althusser's concept of ideological state apparatuses—conceived as those laws and social institutions that produce concrete individuals *as subjects* through nonrepressive means (church, family, advertising)—in order to elaborate the concept of an ideological global apparatus. Gabilando comments that just as individuals are interpellated as national subjects by the state, cyberspace interpellates individuals as global subjects, hence "cyborg" subjects. But what is the nature of this subjectivity? For Gabilando the interface of cyberspace (as in much of the rest of the world) interpellates the subject primarily as a consumer—not as a citizen, a voter, or a worker. But this new kind of subject position, which at first seems free of cultural specificity, is in fact contingent upon the very differences it appears to overcome. As Gabilando comments,

> Postcolonial subject positions are necessary in order to create the outsidedeness that cyberspace and consumer culture need to constitute themselves as the new hegemonic inner spaces of postmodernism. . . . In a time when multinational capitalism can simulate multiculturalism nevertheless race, gender, ethnicity and sexuality still function as forms of discrimination and opression.[20]

Indeed, it is often argued that the problems of racial discrimination are miraculously overcome in the process of the creation of new subjects and new bodies online. In a tone similar to that taken by Christopher Newfield, Bruce Damer in his recent book *Avatars!* writes, "One of the best features about life in digital space is that your skin color, race, sex, size, religion or age does not matter; neither . . . [do] academic degrees you have."[21] This naive yet pervasive notion that subjects who are online are able to leave behind the very social categories that define them in the "real world" misunderstands the complexity of human subjects, who inevitably enact and perform their new identities through the sign systems they already inhabit and through which they are already interpellated. It would be equally naive to suggest that subjects are somehow not also powerfully *shaped by* the images and activities that take place for them online. Indeed, the distinction between real and artificial is not in the least useful when attempting to address the kind of subjects that are created in the "interfacial" moment of body/avatar construction. Althusser's claim that ideology interpellates subjects by mimesis or mirroring is replaced in Gabilando's account with interpellation by subject position. "The postmodern Ideological Apparatuses do not interpellate individuals through a process of mimetic reflection in which individuals identify themselves as subjects but rather as through a process of interfacing in which individuals identify their subject positions. The individual is interpellated only as the subject who takes part in a specific interfacing."[22]

Since the "'global condition" does not exist as such (we do not *function* globally but only locally, always defined through an interface with a machine that *seems* to be spatially infinite) the subject becomes conceived as a subject *position* within a matrix of other signs of exchange or location within cyberspace: an e-mail address, a URL, a credit card number. Yet Gabilando also ignores the possibility that, with online visual representations of bodies (not to mention the complexity of textual exchange), there continues to be a mimetic element to the interface and to ideology. I am interested in this slippage between the idea of interpellation through *mimesis* and by location or *position*. For it seems that these are both at stake in online virtual worlds and in the kind of play with bodily assemblage inherent in UNDINA and Bodies© INC. The user is called upon to identify with bodies visually presented, to find a reflection of subjectivity there, as well as to retain a position outside of this body, a kind of transcendent position that guarantees the meaning of this electronic appendage.

In a section entitled "Gender-bending, Race-shifting, and Generally Not Being Yourself," Bruce Damer continues: "Part of the most thrilling and enticing aspect of the virtual experience is to live the fantasy of being another person."[23] That there is power in such fantasy is undeniable. Psychoanalysis offers the most nuanced vocabulary for understanding the relations between identification and desire, and in particular the states of mind through which the subject assembles the fragmented material and linguistic elements that comprise an identity. While I do not attempt to offer a psychoanalytic or symptomatic reading here, I will note that the fantasy of being an Other person, represented in a visual form, is a scenario familiar to those scholars who find in the Lacanian mirror stage a model for the formation of subjectivity and the production of ego ideals. The process of bodily construction, of being an Other, in the context of UNDINA or Bodies© INC or some of the other avatar construction sites, has the function of a secondary revision, a reversal of narrative, a double reconstruction. Rather than an infantile body-in-pieces searching for a unifying device in an external, mimetic reflection, the supposedly unified subject (at the keyboard) seeks to reconstruct subjectivity through a new fragmentation and reconstitution of body parts. Once again, the body becomes the site where identity is reshaped. All the elements of cultural difference or of individual character are reduced to visual signs that stand for flesh. In his essay entitled "Chance Encounters" Victor Burgin cites Sandor Ferenczi's observations concerning the function of the body as an apparatus for understanding the world:

> Thus arise those intimate connections, which remain throughout life, between the human body and the objective world that we call *symbolic*. On the one hand the child in this stage sees in the world nothing but images of his corporeality, on the other he learns to represent by means of his body the whole multifariousness of the outer world.[24]

If such forms of representation in childhood shape the symbolic construction of the world in adulthood, then reconstruction of the body as an adulthood rite is hardly an insignificant event in the course of subject formation. True, in the case of UNDINA and Bodies© INC the end result is still a fantasy of coherence, but a coherence borrowed from a variety of sources. Moreover, the threat of difference (cultural, sexual) is, once again, overcome, not only as a fetish in the form of a stereotype, but now in the projection of one's own subjectivity into or onto that very difference. Race is understood not to "matter" precisely because the conditions of power that produce racism are not perceived, in this online domain, as under any kind of threat from the material realm cyberspace supposedly escapes. Bodies are conceived as products of bureaucracy, and hence largely as property. The idea of not being oneself is intimately tied to the conditions of leisure and the activity of consumption. The "outside" of the system—the multicultural or postcolonial domain that Gabilando identifies as the boundary to a privileged cyberspace—is brought inside, literally for the sake of appearances. Only under conditions of historical amnesia and with a blindness to those cultural contexts where bodies are already dismembered through political torture, and those in which racial identities are fraught with a history of violent, forced miscegenation, can one imagine such fantasies operating freely. Yet, of course, they do operate in the neo-colonial rhetoric of a global interface.

Randy Farmer, one of the creators of the early virtual world *Habitat*, writes,

> In *Habitat* the primary way to change your appearance is by changing your head. You can buy new styles of head from a vending machine in the local "Head Shop," or you might win a unique head in a contest sponsored by the service administrator. . . . [Eventually] there is nothing left to buy except the special one-of-a-kind prize heads. As a result, these rare heads trade for hundreds of times the price of the others. Without a doubt, the dominant symbol

of wealth and stature in the Habitats is a large collection of unique heads, proudly on display in your virtual living room.[25]

The consumption of identity is here made explicit in the form of a competitive trophy exhibition. The more identities one displays, the more status one accrues. An individual user becomes identified with multiple subject positions through collecting and disguise. Given the interdependent histories of colonialism and collecting (especially for museums of anthropology), it is worth asking *who* is collecting *whom* online, and whose bodies are on display.

Transcendental Subjects Embodied

Embedded in fantasies of collecting body specimens and creating hybrid subjects is a matrix of desire that seeks to absorb or orchestrate cultural differences. The racial, ethnic, or gender hybrid is usually read as a break with the traditional Enlightenment concept of the unified individual. Joseph Nechvatal writes that in Bodies© INC "the digit-body is a motif—a trope—of the entirety of the self, and in its numericalization of the body is the site of and metaphor for the disintegration of the modern notion of the self."[26] By offering an image of a body in pieces and made up of pieces, the Bodies© INC site, Nechvatal suggests, rejects the transcendental, universal, timeless self of modern European philosophy.[27] Instead, a postmodern subject is expressly evoked, a subject able to be represented by discontinuous elements, entirely present in electronic form. The model of a miscegenated subject that is not reducible to fixed categories such as male/female, black/white, natural/artificial thus acquires the utopian status of an imaginary figure of possible future identifications. At the same time, however, a narrow conception of hybridity threatens to reproduce a new "transcendental" subject that floats through cyberspace free from historical conditions or social constraints while nevertheless perpetuating a familiar social hierarchy. Because it is refreshing and exciting to see an effort on the part of artists and theorists to move beyond essentializing notions of subjectivity, and because there is a progressive element in efforts to map cultural hybridity, it is all the more imperative that such important efforts be examined for the ways in which they unwittingly perpetuate the very stereotypes they may be attempting to subvert.

Problems arise primarily when cultural identity or self-representation is equated with a configuration of body parts. Each appendage becomes the sign of a different race, ethnicity, natural element, or characteristic. The assumption that this electronic body might somehow inhabit a privileged space because of this multiplicity—a universal translator with interchangeable parts—reprises an equally romantic notion of the mulatto or mestizo as someone able to inhabit more than one cultural paradigm as a result of phenotype. By reducing cultural hybridity to genetic hybridity it becomes possible to ignore how hybridity is also, as Homi Bhabha writes, "inscribed as a historical narrative of alterity that explores forms of social antagonism and contradiction that are not yet properly represented, political identities in the process of being formed, cultural enunciations in the act of hybridity, in the process of translating and transvaluing cultural differences."[28] Other scholars have also emphasized the importance of dissociating the conception of a complex, transcultural politics, with a simple conception of ethnic or racial types. Chela Sandoval suggests that a "cyborg consciousness" avoids the forms of control that plague the reified or immobile subject by taking steps such as deconstruction, appropriation, and differential movement to disrupt the hold of a hegemonic culture over individual subjects. For Sandoval this model of an oppositional or differential position, akin to "U.S. third world feminism" and "*mestizaje,*" is produced through a series of concrete *practices* that can never be reduced to a type of *body*. Instead, the nonessentialized subject for her becomes identifiable through a map of possible *action*.[29]

For Bodies© INC it is the construction of a body that performs the process of identity formation. The different appendages and their accompanying bureaucratic data are what constitute the character of the subject depicted. In UNDINA the process is even more simple, as it relies on a simple grid of interchangeable parts, without even the pretense of action or choice. By representing a shifting locus for a distributed subject—radical in the sense that it is perhaps shifting and changing, living, dying and nonessentialized—the appended subject in the form of an online body also defines a relation to a so-called global interface as primarily one of consumption, not opposition.

Nestor Garcia-Canclini has written,

> For my part, I think that the fragmentary and scattered view of the experimentalists or postmodernists appears with a double meaning. It can be an opening, an occasion for again feeling uncertainties, when it maintains the critical preoccupation with social process, with artistic languages and with the relations that these weave with society. On the other hand, if this is lost, the postmodern fragmentation is converted into an artistic imitation of the simulacra of atomization that a market—in fact monopolistic and centralized—plays with dispersed consumers.[30]

As works of art, UNDINA and Bodies© INC fall somewhere between these two models of postmodernism. If the transcendental subject of an enlightenment reason was a unified, predictable subject that could only be imagined because of a homogeneous cultural context, and if the postmodern subject emerged from a recognition of, among other things, a complex heterogeneous cultural context, then these two artworks enact the *return* of a transcendental subject as an *endlessly appendable subject*. What the creation of this appended subject presupposes is the possibility of a new cosmopolitanism constituting all the necessary requirements for a global citizen who speaks multiple languages, inhabits multiple cultures, wears whatever skin color or body part desired, elaborates a language of romantic union with technology or nature, and moves easily between positions of identification with movie stars, action heroes, and other ethnicities or races. It is precisely through an experimentation with cultural and racial fusion and fragmentation, combined with a lack of attention to social process, a lack of attention to history, and a strange atomization of visual elements that a new transcendental, universal, and, above all, consuming subject is offered as the model of future cybercitizenship.

Political or ethical choice is reduced to the consumption and incorporation of new appendages to the body. When these appendages are "racialized," a new form of colonization takes place on the level of symbolic exchange. UNDINA and Bodies© INC offer one view into this global ideological apparatus and serve as a reminder that human bodies continue to be the material and visible form through which human subjectivities are defined and contested today, despite the now popular belief in cyberspace as the ultimate realm of disembodiment.

NOTES

1. See the writings of Allucquère Rosanne Stone, Julian Dibbell, Steven Jones, Anne Balsamo, Margaret Morse, Mark Dery, Ken Hillis, and others.
2. Bhabha, "The Other Question," p. 169.
3. Written e-mail comments to the author, January 1998.
4. Ibid.
5. Haraway, "Monkey Puzzle," p. 42.
6. Hammonds, "New Technologies of Race," pp. 109, 118.
7. Morse, *Virtualities: Television, Media Art and Cyberculture*, p. 96.
8. González, "Envisioning Cyborg Bodies."
9. Stafford, *Body Criticism*, p. 264.
10. Victoria Vesna, Bodies© INCorporated.
11. Ibid.
12. See Beadie, "Body-Parts Black Market on Rise, Film Says."
13. Victoria Vesna, Bodies© INCorporated.
14. Christopher Newfield, Bodies© INCorporated.
15. Victoria Vesna, Bodies© INCorporated.
16. Ibid.
17. Christopher Newfield, Bodies© INCorporated.
18. Victoria Vesna, Bodies© INCorporated.
19. Rich Abel, Worlds INC., 1996, cited in Vesna, ibid.
20. Gabilando, "Postcolonial Cyborgs," pp. 424, 429.
21. Damer, *Avatars!* p. 136.
22. Gabilando, "Postcolonial Cyborgs," p. 428.
23. Ibid., p. 132.
24. Sandor Ferenczi cited in Burgin, *In/Different Spaces*, pp. 97–98.
25. Farmer, *Habitat Citizenry*.
26. Joseph Nechvatal, Bodies© INCorporated.
27. Nechvatal writes, quoting Robert C. Solomon, "'The self in question is no ordinary self, no individual personality, not even one of the many heroic or mock-heroic personalities of the early nineteenth century. The self that became the star performer in modern European philosophy is the transcendental self, or transcendental ego, whose nature and ambitions were unprecedentedly arrogant, presumptuously cosmic, and consequently mysterious. The transcendental self was the self—timeless, universal, and in each one of us around the globe and throughout his-

tory' (Solomon, *Continental Philosophy since 1750*, p. 4). The body in Bodies© INCorporated then is a negative space denoting the bodies former presence."

28. Bhabha, *The Location of Culture*, p. 252.

29. See Sandoval, "New Sciences."

30. Garcia-Canclini, *Hybrid Cultures*, p. 280.

REFERENCES

Bodies© INCorporated: http://www.bodiesinc.ucla.edu/UNDINA: http://www.dux.ru/virtual/digbody/undina/!undina.htm

Balsamo, Anne. *Technologies of the Gendered Body: Reading Cyborg Women.* Durham, N.C.: Duke University Press, 1996.

Beadie, Anthony. "Body-Parts Black Market on Rise, Film Says." *Arizona Republic,* November 12, 1993.

Bhabha, Homi. "The Other Question: Difference, Discrimination and the Discourse of Colonialism." In *Literature, Politics and Theory,* ed. F. Barker et al. New York: Methuen, 1986.

———. *The Location of Culture.* London and New York: Routledge, 1994.

Burgin, Victor. *In/Different Spaces.* Berkeley: University of California Press, 1996.

Damer, Bruce. *Avatars!* Berkeley, Calif.: Peachpit Press, 1998.

Dery, Mark. *Escape Velocity.* New York: Grove Press, 1996.

Dibbell, Julian. *My Tiny Life: Crime and Passion in a Virtual World.* London: Fourth Estate, 1999.

Farmer, F. Randall. *Habitat Citizenry,* http://www.communities.com/people/crock/habitat.html, 1993.

Gabilando, Joseba. "Postcolonial Cyborgs." In *The Cyborg Handbook,* ed. Chris H. Gray. New York: Routledge, 1995.

Garcia-Canclini, Nestor. *Hybrid Cultures.* Minneapolis: University of Minnesota Press, 1995.

González, Jennifer. "Envisioning Cyborg Bodies: Notes from Current Research." In *The Cyborg Handbook,* ed. Chris H. Gray. New York: Routledge, 1995.

Hammonds, Evelynn M. "New Technologies of Race." In *Processed Lives: Gender and Technology in Everyday Life,* ed. Jennifer Terry and Melodie Calvert. New York: Routledge, 1997.

Haraway, Donna. "Monkey Puzzle." *World Art* 1 (1996): 42.

Jones, Steven. *CyberSociety 2.0: Revisiting Computer-Mediated Communication and Community.* Thousand Oaks, Calif.: Sage, 1998.

Morse, Margaret. *Virtualities: Television, Media Art and Cyberculture.* Bloomington: Indiana University Press, 1998.

Nechvatal, Joseph. Genealogy, Bodies© INCorporated, http://svsvwarts.ucsb.edu/bodiesinc. 1997.

Newfield, Christopher. Essay, Bodies© INCorporated, http://www.arrts.ucsb.edu/bodies.ucsb.edu/bodiesinc, 1997.

Sandoval, Chela. "New Sciences: Cyborg Feminism and the Methodology of the Oppressed." In *The Cyborg Handbook,* ed. Chris H. Gray. New York: Routledge, 1995.

Solomon, Robert C. *Continental Philosophy since 1750: The Rise and Fall of the Self.* Oxford: Oxford University Press, 1988.

Stafford, Barbara Maria. *Body Criticism: Imagining the Unseen in Enlightenment Art and Medicine.* Cambridge, Mass.: MIT Press, 1991.

Stone, Allucquère Rosanne. *The War of Desire and Technology at the Close of the Mechanical Age.* Cambridge, Mass.: MIT Press, 1995.

Vesna, Victoria. Genealogy, Bodies© INCorporated, http://wsvw.arts.ucsb.edu/bodiesinc, 1997.

Contributors

PETER BLOOM is assistant professor of English (film studies) at Indiana University–Purdue University at Indianapolis. His work has addressed contemporary Francophone cinema, African art, cinema and aesthetics, the cinema of International Scientific Industrial Management, and French colonial cinema. In addition to numerous articles published in French and English, he is currently revising a book manuscript entitled *Colonial Suture: The Cinema of French Hygienic Reform*.

JULIANNE BURTON-CARVAJAL of the University of California, Santa Cruz, has published five books on Latin American film, the most recent a life history of the pioneering Mexican film director *Matilde Soto Landeta: Hija de la Revolución* (Mexico City: Imcine and Conaculta, 2002).

EDWARD D. CASTILLO is an associate professor in the Department of Native American Studies at Sonoma State University.

MANTHIA DIAWARA is professor of Africana studies and comparative literature at New York University. His publications include *In Search of Africa* (1998); *African Cinema: Politics and Culture* (1992); and *Black American Cinema: Aesthetics and Spectatorship* (1993).

TALITHA ESPIRITU is completing her doctorate in the Department of Cinema Studies, Tisch School of the Arts/New York University.

FAYE GINSBURG is director of the Center for Media, Culture, and History and the David Kriser Professor of Anthropology at New York University. Her various research projects—from her award-winning studies of abortion activists to a decade of work on indigenous media—are linked by a strong interest in social movements, cultural activism, and the place of media in contemporary cultural worlds. A documentary filmmaker, award-winning author, and editor of three books and numerous articles, she has been a recipient of numerous honors, including MacArthur and Guggenheim Fellowships for her research and work in support of indigenous mediamakers. She has two new books forthcoming: *Mediating Culture* and a collection *Media Worlds: Anthropology on New Terrain*, (California, 2002) edited with Lila Abu-Lughod and Brian Larkin. She is also curating a film exhibition for 2003 at the Museum of Modern Art entitled *First Nations/First Features*.

JENNIFER GONZÁLEZ is assistant professor of art history at the University of California, Santa Cruz. Her scholarly essays and reviews have appeared in *Frieze, World Art,*

Diacritics, Visual Anthropology Review, Inscriptions, Art Journal, and *Aztlan.* She has also contributed chapters to books such as *The Cyborg Handbook* (Routledge, 1995), *Prosthetic Territories* (Westview, 1995), *The Encyclopedia of Aesthetics* (Oxford, 1998), *With Other Eyes: Looking at Race and Gender in Visual Culture* (Minnesota, 1999), and *Race in Cyberspace* (Routledge, 2000).

INDERPAL GREWAL is director of the Women's Studies Program at University of California, Irvine. She is the author of *Home and Harem: Nation, Gender, Empire and Cultures of Travel* (Duke, 1996) and a forthcoming book, *Transnational America: Gender, Race and South Asian Diasporas* (Duke, 2002). She has co-edited and co-authored a number of publications with Caren Kaplan, including *Scattered Hegemonies: Postmodernity and Transnational Feminist Practices* (Minnesota, 1994) and *An Introduction to Women's Studies: Gender in a Transnational World* (McGraw Hill, 2001).

CAREN KAPLAN is associate professor and chair of the Department of Women's Studies at the University of California at Berkeley. She is the author of *Questions of Travel: Postmodern Discourses of Displacement* (Duke, 1996) and the co-editor with Inderpal Grewal of *Scattered Hegemonies: Postmodernity and Transnational Feminist Practices* (Minnesota, 1994) and *Introduction to Women's Studies: Gender in a Transnational World* (McGraw-Hill, 2001) as well as *Between Woman and Nation: Nationalisms, Transnational Feminisms, and the State* (Duke, 1999) with Norma Alarcón and Minoo Moallem.

BRIAN LARKIN is assistant professor of anthropology at Barnard College, Columbia University. He is currently finishing a book on media and the urban experience in northern Nigeria.

ANA M. LÓPEZ is an associate professor of communication at Tulane University. She has published widely on Latin American film and media and is currently writing a book on Latin American film genres.

BINITA MEHTA is completing her dissertation on the representation of India in French theater at the City University of New York. Articles related to her area of study appear in *Francographies* (1995) and the *Dictionary of Literary Biographys.*

HAMID NAFICY is professor of film and media studies and chair of the Department of Art and Art History, Rice University, Houston. He has published extensively about theories of exile and displacement; exilic and diasporic cultures, films, and media; and Iranian, Middle Eastern, and Third World cinemas. His English-language books are *An Accented Cinema: Exilic and Diasporic Filmmaking; Home, Exile, Homeland: Film, Media, and the Politics of Place; The Making of Exile Cultures: Iranian Television in Los Angeles; Otherness and the Media: The Ethnography of the Imagined and the Imaged* (co-edited); and *Iran Media Index.* He has also published extensively in Persian, including a two-volume book on the documentary cinema, *Film-e Mostanad.* His forthcoming book is *Cinema and National Identity: A Social History of the Iranian Cinema.* His works have been cited and reprinted extensively and they have been translated into many languages, including French, German, Italian, and Persian.

ELLA SHOHAT is professor of cultural studies at the Departments of Art & Public Policy, Middle Eastern Studies, and Comparative Literature, New York University. She has lectured and published extensively on the intersection of post/colonialism, multiculturalism, and gender, both nationally and internationally. Her award-winning work includes the books *Israeli Cinema: East/West and the Politics of Representation, Unthinking Eurocentrism* (co-authored with R. Stam), *Dangerous Liaisons: Gen-*

der, Nation and Postcolonial Perspectives, and *Talking Visions: Multicultural Feminism in a Transnational Age.* She has also curated a number of cultural events and has served on the editorial boards of several journals, including *Social Text, Critique, Jouvert,* and *Public Culture.* Her writings have been translated into French, Spanish, Portuguese, Arabic, Hebrew, German, and Turkish.

ROBERT STAM is University Professor at New York University. He is the author of over ten books on cinema and cultural studies, including *Subversive Pleasures: Bakhtin, Cultural Criticism and Film; Reflexivity in Film and Literature; Tropical Multiculturalism: A Comparative History of Race in Brazilian Cinema and Culture; Film Theory: An Introduction,* and *Unthinking Eurocentrism: Multiculturalism and the Media* (with Ella Shohat). Three books on the subject of literature and cinema are forthcoming from Blackwell Press. His writings have been translated into French, Spanish, Portuguese, Hebrew, German, Korean, Chinese, Japanese, and Swedish.

ROBYN WIEGMAN is Margaret Taylor Smith Director of Women's Studies at Duke University. She has published *American Anatomies: Theorizing Race and Gender* (Duke, 1995) and five edited collections: *The Futures of American Studies* (Duke, 2002), *Women's Studies On Its Own* (Duke, 2002), *Who Can Speak? Authority and Critical Identity* (Illinois, 1995), *Feminism Beside Itself* (Routledge, 1995), and *AIDS and the National Body: Writings by Thomas Yingling* (Duke, 1997). She is currently completing a manuscript on feminist knowledge formations and the university called "Object Lessons: Feminism and the Knowledge Politics of Identity."

Index